ELIZABETH: BEHIND PALACE DOORS

ELIZABETH
BEHIND PALACE
DOORS

Nicholas Davies

MAINSTREAM
PUBLISHING PROJECTS

First published in Great Britain in 2000 by
MAINSTREAM PUBLISHING PROJECTS
Edinburgh

ISBN 1 84018 401 9

This edition 2000

A catalogue record for this book is available from
the British Library

All photographs in this book have been
reproduced by kind permission of PA News

Typeset in Bembo
Printed and bound in Great Britain by
Cox and Wyman Ltd

CONTENTS

1. WINDS OF CHANGE

Elizabeth walked into her drawing room at Buckingham Palace having just returned from one of her official engagements. She placed her handbag on the side table, took off her dark blue full-length coat and matching hat and passed them to her dresser who had walked into the room behind her. Then she sat on the sofa, a look of fatigue, almost resignation, on her face.

'Would you like tea, Ma'am?' a maid asked, knowing only too well that the queen would find a cup of refreshing tea most welcome.

'Yes, thank you,' came the automatic reply.

But there was no smile on Elizabeth's face as there had been for most of that cold, wet February day in 1999 when she had been carrying out yet another of her official royal duties, opening yet another new building she knew not where, and cared little. Throughout this royal engagement, Elizabeth, who was fast approaching her seventy-third birthday, had felt tired and somewhat weary, and she was thankful to be back in the comfort of her surroundings, to rest alone with only a cup of tea for company.

This was no sudden change of heart. During the past few weeks and months Elizabeth had come to realise that she was feeling the pressure of her royal duties – not any physical exhaustion, for she knew she was still fit and well for a woman of her years; but more a dawning realisation that she might have to continue carrying out these same duties for another twenty years – and the thought gave her a feeling of hopelessness, almost despair.

She knew that within the hour her stalwart Principal Private Secretary, Sir Robert Fellowes, would appear and ask yet another series of questions to which she knew she would have to supply an answer, though the last thing she needed at this moment was to talk through her schedule for the coming days and weeks. She would miss

Sir Robert, the man who had steadfastly advised her for 20 years, for he was due to retire within a matter of days. From somewhere deep inside her heavy heart, however, Elizabeth knew she would somehow find the strength and patience to answer him as she had done on countless occasions.

Elizabeth confided these worries to Lady Susan Hussey, the woman who has become her close friend and confidante over the past two decades or more, but who officially holds the title of Lady-in-Waiting. Elizabeth also has a couple of other female confidantes outside Buckingham Palace whom she sees on a regular basis. During the past twelve months or so, some of these friends have noted that Elizabeth has become more introspective and looked more weary, on occasions even worn, by the never-ending job which, until recently, she was fully prepared and very happy to continue till her dying day. But now, for the first time since she ascended the throne in 1952, doubts are arising.

Since the untimely death of Diana, Princess of Wales, the young woman who caused her such heartache and many sleepless nights, Elizabeth has found herself examining her own life, a life in which the pattern never varies, the job never changes and the routine has become monotonous. After nearly 50 years on the throne, Elizabeth has found her enthusiasm waning and she no longer finds much joy or satisfaction in her role as monarch. She finds herself contemplating the future with trepidation and not a little unease.

Elizabeth has come to recognise that during the past few years her approach to her lifelong task has changed; the role of monarch to which she had every intention of continuing to her last breath has undeniably been transformed through the decades and so, too, has Elizabeth's attitude. She misses those faithful retainers in whom she had implicit faith; those men and women whose families before them had often been in royal service and who cherished working for the royal family. To Elizabeth in particular, senior figures like her Private Secretary Lord Adeane, the Keeper of the Privy Purse Lord Cowdray, Sir Philip Moore, a diplomat and confidant – all of whom are now deceased – and even Sir Robert Fellowes, had been companions and friends, not just civil servants. These people were all steeped in the traditions of royalty primarily because, in many cases, their parents or other close relatives had been employed in the upper echelons of the royal household.

Elizabeth now feels almost friendless in the palace. She feels as though she is surrounded and advised by career men and women who want to spend a few years working in the palace to enhance their *curriculum vitae*. She no longer feels she can totally trust these new recruits to the palace and she certainly has no wish to form close friendships with them or even sit down for an informal lunch or supper with them. In many ways the queen almost feels like a stranger in her own home and has not taken to the new streamlined regime which during the past twenty years has transformed the way in which Buckingham Palace operates. Many of the old traditions have disappeared and the relationships between the different levels of the royal household have become less distinct. Nearly everyone who works inside the palace now, for example, eats each day in a staff dining hall, so unlike yesteryear when there were three dining rooms signifying the rigid social strata within the palace.

Already, the queen has sounded out her close friends, mainly old family friends she has known most of her life, asking their opinion as to whether she should ever contemplate abdicating in favour of Charles. All of these conversations have taken place in private, in one-to-one conversations, overheard by no one and treated in the strictest confidence. Usually, the queen will ask the person with whom she wants to discuss the matter, to go with her for a drive. Then they leave the car and the chauffeur behind and walk on together to a secluded spot where no one can possibly overhear their conversation.

Throughout the past twelve months, Elizabeth has wondered now and then if she should carry on, and whether the day will eventually come when she awakes and discovers that she no longer has the will to continue. Usually, on such occasions, she has confessed to simply shaking off such dire feelings and manages to get on with the job in hand, despite the fact that such thoughts are now more frequent than ever. Nevertheless, Elizabeth has come to accept that she may not continue as sovereign until her death, although that day of abdication has not yet arrived for various reasons, principally those involving her own family and her dogged determination to see through the task her beloved father bequeathed her.

In November 1999 Philip raised speculation that the Queen might consider abdication in an interview he gave to *Saga* magazine. Reflecting that it is better to retire 'while you're still capable than wait till people say you're so doddery', Prince Philip did not rule out the same sentiment being applied to the monarch. In the interview he talked at length on the onset of old age and the need for people to retire.

When it was suggested that he was in a rather different position, Philip replied, 'Why?' The interviewer replied, 'Well, the fact is that the Queen is not going to abdicate.' To that, Philip retorted, 'Who said that?'

The interviewer replied, 'Well, it has always been my understanding that the Queen would never abdicate.'

Philip replied, 'Well, you've said it.'

Philip's comments and questions created great media interest and caused a considerable stir particularly in the upper echelons of power inside Buckingham Palace. The Queen's officials have always been most emphatic that there is no question of the Queen abdicating. The very word is regarded as blasphemy in some quarters, and Prince Charles issued a furious personal denial in 1998 when it was suggested that he favoured the idea of abdication by the Queen.

Philip's remarks, which some at Westminster believed could well have been his way of testing the political waters on such a sensitive issue, received scant attention from official sources at the Palace. A spokesman commented, 'It would be to misconstrue the Prince's comments to say that he's giving any indication of the likelihood of the Queen abdicating. The position is clear. The Queen will not abdicate.' Nonetheless, it was the first time that someone so close to Elizabeth had ever publicly raised the issue.

Over the past few years the queen has undertaken more duties than ever before and this she agreed to do in an effort to restore the good name of the House of Windsor. No matter how popular Diana became and how much she dominated the headlines and television coverage, every single opinion poll showed that the queen was still popular and the British people praised her for doing a good job as monarch. Because of those polls, and because of the fact that many people turned their back on Prince Charles, blaming him for the collapse of his marriage, Elizabeth decided that it was her duty to step into the breach, and increased her already heavy workload.

Elizabeth knows that she cannot contemplate stepping down while her mother, the Queen Mother – who will celebrate her hundredth birthday in August 2000 – is still alive. To do so would seem almost a betrayal of the heritage her father, King George VI, passed on to his beloved Lilibet. And not for one moment would Elizabeth want her mother to believe that she would even consider the possibility of abdicating, especially being in such good rude health. Elizabeth knows full well that there is every possibility, perhaps even likelihood, that she too could live to be a hundred and look forward to another twenty-eight years or so on the throne. It would also mean, of course, that Charles would be an old age pensioner, aged nearly eighty, if and when he finally ascended to the throne. On the other hand, Elizabeth may be tempted to celebrate her golden jubilee in 2002, and then abdicate in favour of Prince Charles.

At present, however, Charles is one of those reasons why she cannot contemplate stepping down just yet. Throughout her life Elizabeth has always held firm to the dedication she made to her father, that she would strive to ensure that the House of Windsor continued and flourished throughout her reign. She fears that while the memory of Diana, Princess of Wales is still firmly held in the nation's psyche, the esteem in which the House of Windsor is held might be seriously jeopardised. She would never contemplate such a risk.

She also fears that Prince Charles, whom she believes has discovered in Camilla Parker Bowles the woman with whom he wants to share his life, may not yet be welcomed by the British public as their king. Elizabeth believes more time is needed until politicians, the Church of England and the general public come to accept Camilla as Prince Charles's confidante, close friend and partner, if not his wife. Elizabeth believes that the day Camilla is accepted by the great majority of the nation, is the day she will consider abdicating.

Together Charles and Camilla now act as many a fond, middle-aged married couple enjoying quiet dinners at home together, listening to classical music and reading. During the week Camilla will usually drive over from her house nearby and they will dine together, sometimes enjoying an *apéritif*, at other times sharing a bottle of wine. She will stay the night, they'll breakfast together and she will leave at 10.15 sharp, when Charles starts his working day. She then drives back to Ray Mill House near Chippenham, a fifteen-minute drive from Highgrove, to a typical country house with an Aga, dogs, horsey clothes and genial muddle.

In company, both Camilla and Charles call each other 'darling' and there is little or no formality at dinner as there is at Balmoral. To Charles, Camilla has been, and still is, the most important person in his life. In the same way that she came to his rescue following the assassination of Mountbatten, so during years of battling with Diana and her tantrums, Camilla was in the background giving constant support and only giving advice when Charles invited it. During those years of emotional tension and constant guilt, Charles would turn to Camilla when all seemed lost. Now, at last, he is relaxed, no longer terrified that Diana will launch some devastating pre-emptive strike against him.

Camilla has become the mother Charles never had; the support he always craved but never found. She is, above all, understanding of Charles, his situation, his destiny, his probable future and his prodigious responsibilities, something which Diana never seemed to accept.

Charles adores Camilla because in many respects she is the opposite of his own mother. Camilla hates formality and protocol; cares little about clothes and fashion; smokes and swears like a trooper and, like Charles, roars with laughter at lavatorial jokes. But she is a country woman to her riding boots, which Charles loves.

There is another important point. Camilla has no desire whatsoever to be queen. Indeed, Camilla wants nothing less. 'Perish the thought' is the phrase she uses whenever anyone has the temerity to raise the matter. She is very happy in the role she has chosen, and so is Charles. He, in fact, finds the whole set-up as near perfect as possible but he knows that one day there may come a time when he has to make a decision. But not necessarily so.

Despite reports that Elizabeth totally disapproves of Camilla, that is not the queen's personal opinion. Camilla was always accepted as part of the royal 'in' crowd, one of the few people Elizabeth would automatically kiss whenever they met at a function or dinner party. But Elizabeth strongly disapproves of Camilla's involvement with Charles simply because he is the heir to the throne and should, indeed must, set an example whatever his own personal feelings. Elizabeth now makes sure that she never comes into contact with Camilla, fearing the message it might give to the nation, that she approves of the relationship. The reality is that Camilla lives the life Elizabeth would have loved with horses and dogs, little responsibility and time to enjoy the country life. The problem as Elizabeth sees it is that, unlike Diana, Camilla would prove an unpopular queen, constantly being compared unfavourably to Diana, and that would be bad news for the House of Windsor.

Since the trauma of Diana's death, Elizabeth has noted that Charles has become a more confident, out-going man. He felt genuine sorrow but no guilt for Diana's death – in vain had he pleaded with her to keep her Scotland Yard bodyguards. And now, during the past two years, Charles has won back the respect of the nation, though not yet the affection. His intelligence has at last been rewarded. Gone are the days when Charles was considered a crank because he talked to the flowers and vegetables. Now he has the support of most of the population in his war against GM – genetically modified – foods and his firm belief in organic farming.

In the summer of 1999 Charles went so far as to challenge the Labour Government and respected scientists about the safety, ethics and efficacy of genetically modified crops, asking ten key questions. His intervention delivered a body blow to the Government's attempts to reassure people that GM crops are safe. He even suggested that the assertion that GM technology will be important to feed the world when its population doubles in the next century sounded 'suspiciously like emotional blackmail'. For making the challenge and joining the argument so forcefully he won both praise and gratitude.

The nation's growing acceptance and respect for Prince Charles are matters Elizabeth now turns to more frequently as she ponders her destiny and a future with a routine she already finds tedious. Whenever Elizabeth indulges in such thoughts and talks about it with one of her close friends, she invariably brings up a subject of extraordinary importance to her – duty. Throughout her life Elizabeth has put duty above all else, including her husband, her children and her grandchildren. Today, those duties of reading and signing government papers, making speeches, handing out honours, travelling the country, meeting dignitaries, entertaining Heads of State, touring other countries, opening hospitals and schools and waving and smiling to multitudes of crowds, are no longer a fulfilling pleasure and have become nothing but that, a duty. Nevertheless she carries on because of her overwhelming belief that duty comes above all else and that she should show by her example that duty is still a vital and important part of public life. She recognises that such an axiom may be *passé* in today's world but she still clings to the principle.

In public, Elizabeth smiles more often than ever before, especially for the cameras, yet now there is a tinge of sadness about her. As Ben Pimlott, Professor of Politics and Contemporary History at Birkbeck College, University of London, wrote in his biography *The Queen* in 1996, 'In her reserve . . . she remained self-sufficient, and did not lose her grip . . . The stilted addresses, gracious handshakes, dutiful pleasantries, acknowledging waves belonged to her nature.'

Still, 'abdication' is a word Elizabeth grew up to hold in great disrepute, the very act of abdication being anathema to her as it is to the Queen Mother. Every member of the extended royal family is left in no doubt that the abdication of the throne by King Edward VIII in 1936 had brought severe discredit to the monarchy and should never, but never, be contemplated. It may be difficult for today's generation to understand the profound shock, disbelief and consternation that the abdication wrought throughout the nation when Edward abdicated in order to marry a divorced American, Mrs Wallis Simpson. And it is even more difficult for people to comprehend the deep sense of shame and guilt the royal family felt at that time when many believed that the abdication would herald the end of the monarchy. The Queen Mother never forgave her brother-in-law for the action she considered to be nothing short of treachery, and she instilled in her elder daughter Elizabeth the belief that abdication should never be considered, whatever the reason.

Despite all that the royal family experienced way back in 1936, abdication has undoubtedly entered the queen's vocabulary. But when the time comes, as Elizabeth believes it will, her abdication will not be seen as traumatic or sensational but simply a passing on of the duties of the monarch to her son as should be the case in every hereditary monarchy. She simply wants to ensure that when she finally comes to make that decision there will be no national trauma, no soul-searching and no examination of the worth of either Prince Charles or Britain's constitutional monarchy.

Elizabeth has confessed to some intimates that abdication could become more alluring to her as the years roll by. During the past two decades in particular she has suffered a number of rebuffs, criticisms and reforms which she did not warrant, as well as displays of envy and ingratitude from government ministers, some quarters of the press and even members of the general public. Some have suggested that only her exceptional sense of duty and her promise to her father have deterred her from throwing in the towel and retiring to end her days surrounded by a few faithful retainers and her dogs in solitary splendour in her favourite home, Balmoral.

Elizabeth's long reign has been marked by the erosion of most of the royal prerogatives, though the monarchy does still retain the three rights enunciated by Walter Bagehot: to be consulted, to encourage and to warn. Although they remain, however, their effectiveness depends on the willingness of the queen's Prime Ministers to co-operate and there have been very few occasions, if any, during the queen's reign when she has deterred a government from their preferred course of action.

It seems to Elizabeth that the survival of Britain's constitutional monarchy no longer lies in the sovereign's political skills but rather in their relinquishment. No longer does even the Conservative Party invite the queen to nominate the next Prime Minister, as it did in 1963 when a sick Harold Macmillan persuaded Elizabeth to nominate Lord Home rather than 'Rab' Butler to succeed him. The Tories have followed Labour's lead and now elect their own leader whose name is then submitted to Her Majesty for formal endorsement. As a consequence, of course, the monarch's judgement can never again be disputed when formally inviting a new Prime Minister to form a government.

But what has upset, indeed infuriated, the queen during the past few years has been the steady erosion of many of the privileges of the sovereign, the Head of State, a situation which she believes has been designed to deliberately reduce the status of the monarchy. Today, Elizabeth believes the Head of State is little more than another citizen of the realm. Elizabeth felt bitterly hurt when she realised that the British people, to whom she had dedicated her life, had no wish to contribute towards the cost of restoring Windsor Castle, the most historic building in Britain, after the great fire of 1992. Some believe that realisation became a watershed in the queen's relationship with her people. The love and trust Elizabeth believed existed between the sovereign and her people had been nothing but a figment of the imagination, a falsehood, simply lip-homage and cant, a deceit now rudely and brutally exposed.

This affront was followed by other decisions taken by successive British governments which, as far as Elizabeth was concerned, was done so that the Prime Minister could be seen by the nation to be a people's First Minister, siding with the mass of the population rather than courting the approval of the reigning monarch. She was not unduly upset when the government decided to do away with the Queen's Flight, the collection of aircraft used by the sovereign, but in fact used far more frequently by senior government ministers. She simply believed this was yet another example forced on her to take away her privileges as Head of State. When the Queen's Flight was in operation she knew the pilots and the cabin crew and they knew her. They knew her likes and dislikes and they felt privileged to be part of the Queen's Flight. No more. Now the squadron which flies the queen and other senior members of the royal family, has no dedicated crew at all. The queen might fly half a dozen times without seeing the same crew twice. She dislikes that. Now that she has reached the ripe age of seventy-two she wants friendly faces around her, people with whom she has a rapport, not total strangers who have no idea of her predilections.

But the decision to scrap the Royal Yacht *Britannia* and not replace it, a decision which she believed portrayed all the elements of spite, was a source of pain and upset for Elizabeth. She knew there were no good commercial or social reasons to scrap the Royal Yacht and refuse to replace it with another, similar, floating advertisement for Great Britain. She knew that replacing *Britannia* would have cost less than £100 million, a pittance in terms of Treasury expenditure, but a magnificent backdrop for Britain's exporters, tourist industry, national pride and prestige. But she believes there were those in Government who believed *Britannia* smacked too much of royal privilege at a time when the nation was not in favour of such privileges.

And the cutbacks continued with the Royal Train, which the queen, Prince Philip and Prince Charles found so useful when travelling to different parts of the country on official visits. It was considered too costly to keep solely for use by the royal family. So now the Royal Train can be hired by any company that wishes to do so – at a price – and, as a result, the queen, Philip, Charles and other members permitted to use the train are served and cared for by strangers, which saddens the queen and, on occasion, enrages her.

For years Elizabeth grudgingly accepted the battle over the Privy Purse though she was embarrassed by the constant sniping by some MPs and sections of the press. She disliked the constant public scrutiny of the Privy Purse, when newspapers would delve into every minute piece of expenditure to highlight what they believed were unnecessary privileges and inconsistencies to be gloated over and exposed. Some of the tabloid press would portray the queen and the royal family as hugely wealthy people living in the lap of luxury and demanding even more while the poor and impoverished struggled to survive in squalor and degradation. To end this huge and unfair embarrassment it was finally decided that the Civil List should be debated only once every eleven years to remove the unseemly wrangle over the royal finances. In 2000 the Civil List will be renegotiated once again and it is likely that the allowance increase will be kept to the rate of inflation *minus* eight per cent. As a result, Britain's monarchy will cost the taxpayer below the amount received by the Swedish Court and only £1 million or £2 million more than other royal families despite the fact that Britain's economy is far bigger.

One of Elizabeth's most cherished responsibilities is her position as Head of the Commonwealth which she has coveted and held in high esteem since 1947 when, as Princess Elizabeth, she said in a speech, 'My whole life, whether it be long or short, will be devoted to the service of our great imperial family to which we all belong.' That promise, frequently updated in Christmas broadcasts and Commonwealth Day speeches, has remained as stubbornly binding today as when she made that speech. As queen, Elizabeth has visited every Commonwealth capital, known every Commonwealth leader and remained adamant that no matter what the views of British prime ministers throughout her reign, no British government has the right to impose its views of the Commonwealth upon her. Throughout her reign, Elizabeth believes, and rightly so, that she has been an active force in the Commonwealth more than any single person. As a result, Elizabeth feels entitled to the belief that while she inherited the title of Queen of England, her Headship of the Commonwealth is something she has striven for, and, indeed, earned.

In April 1999, however, New Labour produced a report *Making the Commonwealth Matter* which acknowledged that the queen should remain its honorary leader for the time being but suggested that a non-British political figure should be appointed alongside her to speak for the international stage. 'The queen is popular in the Commonwealth, but her role as Head of State is an appointed not hereditary position and, when her reign ends, Commonwealth countries should think carefully about how to replace her,' said the report. They further proposed that the administrative headquarters of the Commonwealth should be moved out of London, locating the secretariat in New Delhi or Cape Town perhaps, to underline that the organisation is prepared to break with the imperial heritage from which it emerged.

The idea infuriated Elizabeth. Once again, she feared a new governmental onslaught on her status and position, this time on the one, highly responsible task in her life that she held most dear. Elizabeth had held firmly to the belief that her unique position, as lifelong head of the Commonwealth, has enabled her to be a force for good in the institution, standing above the chicanery and perfidious ambition of politicians. She believes New Labour's plans for such a shake-up would overturn the achievements of the last fifty years, and for what? Within that time span a club of white dominions was transformed into a dynamic multi-racial association with a commitment to human rights as shown by action against South Africa in 1961 and Nigeria in 1995. Above all, the modern Commonwealth is today, more than ever, an association of peoples headed by someone above politics. By constitutional conjuring, the declaration replaced the institution of the Crown with the respected person of the monarch, 'the symbol of the free association of its independent member nations'. According to conversations the queen has held on this matter, she believes the suggestion of a non-British political figure being appointed alongside her for the remainder of her reign is simply another method of eroding the monarch's power and responsibilities.

It is for all these reasons that Elizabeth has become emotionally tired of late, that she genuinely believes that one day she will tell Prince Charles and the Prime Minister of her decision to step down in favour of her son. That day has not yet arrived but unless Elizabeth acquires a new zest for the job, there is every probability that one day she will make that all-important decision and retire gracefully to live out her days in the secluded peace and quiet of Balmoral.

2. LILIBET

Elizabeth's arrival into the world on a cold, rainy April night in 1926 turned out to be complicated, for her's was a breech birth. Her mother, the Duchess of York, had been in labour for more than twenty-four hours because the doctors had persisted in trying to bring about a normal birth. But, in the early hours of the morning, they performed a Caesarean operation and Princess Elizabeth was born.

Apart from the doctors and nurses, a secretary from the Home Office also witnessed the delivery to ensure that the baby really did exist. This rather quaint English royal custom grew out of the so-called 'warming-pan' plot, when it was alleged in 1688 that a substitute baby had been placed in the bed of James II's wife. Though untrue, a senior government official has attended every royal birth since that date to make sure the baby is really 'of royal birth'.

More than a matter of pride and joy to her parents, baby Elizabeth was particularly special because her mother, the Duchess of York, had previously suffered a miscarriage and they had feared she might not be able to have children. Later that day Elizabeth's father, the Duke of York, known as 'Bertie', the future King George VI, wrote to his parents: 'You don't know what a tremendous joy it is to Elizabeth and me to have our little girl. We always wanted a child to make our happiness complete, and now that it has at last happened, it seems so wonderful and strange . . . '

Elizabeth was in fact only third in line to the throne because the reigning monarch, King George V, who had reigned since 1910, was her grandfather. King George's eldest son, Edward, whom the family always called David, was then Prince of Wales and heir apparent. There was no reason to believe at that time in 1936 that baby Elizabeth would one day become Queen of England.

Many people believe Queen Victoria introduced the traditions and ideals of today's royal family and, to a certain extent, that is the case. However, Mary of Teck, King George V's wife, was primarily responsible for transforming the British monarchy from the dull, dowdy image of Victoria to the values of duty, morality and family life so beloved of the emerging middle-class at that time. Not an English woman but a German princess, Mary of Teck also made sure the nation understood that as monarch, King George embodied extra-human qualities of king – priest, father of his people and the sacred and anointed heir of the British nation and the far-flung British Empire.

Queen Victoria recognised that Mary of Teck was remarkable for her intelligence, her ambition and, above all, her passion for the monarchy. Queen Victoria badgered her eldest grandson, the weak, dissolute, idle Duke of Clarence, second in line to the throne, to marry Mary. They became engaged but shortly afterwards Clarence died of a mysterious illness. Victoria had become so intent on Mary of Teck joining the family that she urged and pushed her second grandson George, the next in line, to court and marry her. Not wishing to disappoint or displease his mother, George did so a year later.

Following Queen Victoria's death in 1901, her son became King Edward VII, and George and Mary, the Prince and Princess of Wales. It wasn't only Queen Victoria who was enamoured of Princess Mary. So was Edward VII. He ordered that Mary, his daughter-in-law, should be sent all the official red boxes containing the government papers so that she would thoroughly understand the workings of government when she became queen. It was, of course, a remarkable, even revolutionary idea to involve his daughter-in-law, and a German, so closely in the secret affairs of the monarchy and the government in an era when women were considered second-class citizens.

Some historians go so far as to attribute the survival of the British monarchy to Queen Mary who was a most resolute woman. She was determined that the monarchy in Britain would not only survive but thrive, unlike the monarchies of the rest of Europe which in the early part of this century were either swept away or changed to modern Scandanavian-style affairs. On his death bed in 1910, Edward VII feared his son George would be the last King of England, but Mary had other ideas.

Queen Mary, Elizabeth's grandmother, ruled the royal family and in particular her husband, George V, with firmness and determination.

King George would much rather have stayed at Sandringham, his country home in Norfolk, living the life of a country squire rather than carry out the duties of monarchy. George V had some fine qualities but he was an uneducated, ignorant, boorish man uninterested in things of the mind. He had enjoyed his life in the Royal Navy – one reason he was called the 'Sailor King' – and was also a first-class shot, a good yachtsman and, somewhat surprisingly, a keen stamp collector. It seems that George was at his happiest during the hours he spent cleaning and polishing his guns and poring over his stamp collection. He also had a reputation as a martinet with a fierce temper and a sadistic tongue. And yet he also seemed to have a deep love and respect for his wife.

Queen Mary seemed to have an uncanny understanding of the British people and she embodied the formidable ideals of middle-class British womanhood of that era: thrift, service, self-control and unshakable devotion to the home. Queen Mary persuaded the mass of the people that the royal family was 'just like us' but, at the same time, made her husband something of a paragon with whom the people could identify.

Her view of the monarch contrasted sharply with the court of her husband's predecessor, Edward VII, who led a life of self-indulgence surrounded by party-goers, gamblers, womanisers and drunks. He also had a string of lovers, paramours and even loose women. Mary changed all that. She and her husband George would dine frugally together in Buckingham Palace each night, usually alone, and would be in bed promptly by 11.15 p.m. with lights out. They hardly ever entertained privately. Yet despite this frugal lifestyle, she insisted that every evening they dress formally for dinner even when dining alone: she would appear resplendent in a majestic full-length ball gown with a tiara, and the king would be dressed in white tie and tails and wearing the Order of the Garter!

Queen Mary took it upon herself to maintain the prestige and influence of the monarchy by example and service to the nation. And to illustrate the crown's new attitude to the nation's morals she began at the pinnacle of Britain's society, the palace itself. As if to cast out the adulterers and womanisers who surrounded the previous king, Queen Mary decreed that all divorcees, whether the wronged party or not, should never be permitted to appear at court; on no occasion would they be introduced to the king or herself, nor would they be permitted to join royal shooting or hunting parties and must never be granted entrance to the royal enclosure at Royal Ascot! Queen Mary's values and principles would be religiously followed by Queen

Elizabeth and, in the early days of her reign, by her daughter Elizabeth.

Poor, hen-pecked George, never very bright, also had to toe the new royal line of duty and dedication. It was fortunate for him that during his years in the Royal Navy he had come to understand the meaning of the word 'duty'. Mary advised, cajoled and persuaded her husband to follow her advice and he did so willingly despite the fact that he could be the most irritable of men.

Mary was also determined to show the power and the glory of the British monarchy, which in those early days of her reign was the wealthiest and most powerful nation in the world: the Royal Navy had command of the seas across the world, the British Army was apparently invincible and the British Empire at its peak. Mary wanted the whole world to realise it and pay homage. One of her more extraordinary ideas turned into the most magnificent show of king-ship ever organised by the British crown outside the country. The demonstration of obsequious obedience to the British crown was organised in India and King George, along with Queen Mary, stood on a dais, dressed in their full, heavy, coronation robes and crowns as well as bearing their imperial regalia. The Indian princes, in full view of their massed armies of immaculate Indian troops, paid homage to them while be-jewelled elephants knelt before their Emperor. It was a bizarre but brilliant illustration of Britain's power.

Back home, Mary insisted the monarchy should also be seen as splendid, wealthy and powerful. When the king and queen went to Balmoral for their August holiday, seventeen locomotives were placed along the royal route just in case the royal engine should break down. At royal picnics, liveried footmen would serve the food and wine and Buckingham Palace was staffed by 100 upper and 400 lower servants. (The palace provided the upper servants with a four-course meal with wine and liqueurs every day.)

But it was World War I which secured the survival of the monarchy in Britain while finishing off the monarchies of Germany, Austria and Russia. Much of the credit for the survival of the English royals must be given to Queen Mary; it was her finest hour.

Mary insisted that the royal family share the burdens of the Great War with their subjects. She declared that the court would abandon alcohol 'for the duration of hostilities' and when this became known the people understood and appreciated that the royal family was not living in luxury while the common folk did without. Though little more than a gesture, it touched a nerve and drew the people and the monarchy closer together. To show her dedication, Queen Mary spent the war touring hospitals, tending the wounded soldiers herself, even helping out in the wards. And she seemed indefatigable. Mary persuaded other female members of the royal family to follow her example. One of them finally took the courage to complain to her, saying, 'I'm exhausted and I hate hospitals.' Queen Mary snapped back, 'You are a member of the British royal family. We are never tired and we all love hospitals.'

Queen Mary made sure her sons were at the war front, sharing the appalling conditions like every other mother's son. Her eldest son, the dashing Prince of Wales, was in the muddy, water-logged trenches; her second son, Prince Albert, commanded a gun-turret at Jutland; and King George himself made frequent visits to his troops in the trenches. During one visit he was thrown from his horse and badly injured. All these patriotic acts won great respect for the royal family and closed the gap between them and the nation.

And yet, despite such signal success in rebuilding and remodelling the monarchy, forging close links with all sections of society, Queen Mary left behind a disaster – the effects of which have continued to plague the royal family to the present day. The relations with her own children, her five sons and daughter, proved an unmitigated failure.

It was, in effect, the relationship between Edward, Prince of Wales, and his parents that led to his rejecting everything his parents stood for, and finally rejecting the throne itself, bringing about the greatest crisis the House of Windsor had ever faced. Edward's abdication in 1936 has haunted the royal family ever since and even today Elizabeth judges the success or failure of the monarchy by that yardstick. As the failures and disasters of three of her children's marriages have cast deepening shadows over the crown, Elizabeth has clung to one, single consolation – that the crisis confronting the House of Windsor in the 1990s is nothing compared to those dark days of the abdication. Some at the time even believed that the abdication heralded the end of the monarchy in Britain.

It is extraordinary that so many senior members of the House of Windsor should have proved to be such pathetic, if not deplorable, parents, incapable of bringing up their own children, even after they themselves had experienced such hardships at the hands of their own mothers and fathers.

Unfortunately for the House of Windsor, Queen Mary's understanding of the British people did not extend to that of her offspring whom she treated as though she was their hard-hearted teacher rather than their mother. And King George V, brought up in the harsh discipline of the Royal Navy, believed that to spare the rod was to spoil the child. He treated the slightest childish misdemeanour as rebellion to be dealt with sternly and severely.

In such circumstances it is usual for the mother to come to the defence of her offspring, but not Queen Mary. She took her husband's side because he was the king and could do no wrong. Unfortunately for her children, Queen Mary was no natural mother and some contemporaries remarked that she didn't have a maternal instinct in her body despite having borne six children. Shortly after birth, each child was handed over to the royal nanny – Mary wanted as little to do with them as possible.

All became casualties in one way or another. Albert, called 'Bertie' by the family, who became the Duke of York and later George VI, was a stammering, nervous wreck of a young man; George, Duke of Kent, was addicted to cocaine and a practising homosexual; Henry, Duke of Gloucester, became a drunkard and an alcoholic; and the eldest, David, Prince of Wales and heir to the throne, rejected everything his parents held most dear, including the monarchy. (King George decided to use that name when he succeeded to the throne following the abdication of his brother Edward VIII. His first name was actually Albert, named after Queen Victoria's husband, but he didn't wish to be called King Albert.)

Poor Bertie had been a miserable, sickly child. Queen Mary could not seem to care less about him, going away for days on end and only seeing him once or twice a week. She did not even notice that his nanny, neurotic and unfit for her job, was failing to feed him properly. He spent his early years screaming for food. Shy, retiring and nervous, Bertie suffered from an appalling stammer which was put down to constant bullying by his father. Queen Mary considered his legs were too bandy so she ordered that braces be put on both of them for two years to straighten them. They caused Bertie enormous discomfort and pain. Because of his appalling diet, and lack of food, Bertie also suffered from indigestion which made him nauseous. It was only after many years that doctors diagnosed a duodenal ulcer. Nevertheless, Bertie displayed remarkable courage. He served in both the Royal Navy and the Royal Air Force and despite being knock-kneed, he won the RAF Tennis Doubles at Wimbledon in 1920.

Queen Mary and King George's treatment of their youngest son, Prince John, was a sad and disgraceful blot on the royal family. Poor John developed epilepsy when he was about seven, due, according to some biographers, to the treatment meted out to him by his strict parents. As a result, he was removed from the family, locked away in a small house on the Sandringham Estate in Norfolk and cared for by a single nurse.

One night at dinner Queen Mary simply announced to the family, 'John is unwell and has gone away to be cared for. It is very unlikely that we will ever see him again.'

He was, in fact, never seen again by his brothers or sister, nor, to their everlasting shame, by his parents. He died in 1919 unloved, unnoticed and unmourned. He was only fourteen.

Queen Mary and King George had been surprised and happy that Lady Elizabeth Bowes-Lyon, the youngest daughter of the 14th Earl of Strathmore, had eventually agreed to marry their son Bertie after twice refusing his offer of marriage. Elizabeth Bowes-Lyon was one of the prettiest debutantes of the decade and a great attraction to all the young aristocrats. She wasn't at all sure she wanted to become enmeshed in the royal family with its strict formalities and unyielding protocol. Young Bertie was then a shy, tense young man, lacking in confidence who found it difficult holding conversations because of his appalling stammer. On better acquaintance, however, Bertie showed a sense of humour and kindness, a sensitivity so absent from his father. Lady Elizabeth, on the other hand, was sweet, engaging, sensible and strong-willed. She had formidable charm but she also had a will of her own which no one could successfully challenge. In retrospect, this strength and sweetness were exactly what Bertie needed to counteract his own rather weak, ineffectual character. It did not matter to Queen Mary that Lady Elizabeth was not of royal blood, that she was technically a commoner, though from a wealthy, Scottish landowning family.

At that time, in 1923, King George and Mary never thought for a moment that Bertie would ever be king; they were simply keen to find a good, sensible, strong-willed young woman to take care of their second eldest son.

Considering Mary's domineering relationships with her own children, it was quite remarkable that she should have sought such a close involvement with her first granddaughter, the baby Lilibet. From the beginning, Queen Mary took the little princess under her wing as though she had a premonition that one day she would be queen. When entertaining guests at tea-time, a ritual Queen Mary always observed, she would send a car for baby Elizabeth who would be brought to Buckingham Palace. The future queen would be shown off to the guests as they sat and ate their cucumber sandwiches and fattening cakes. She was absorbed by her granddaughter, describing her in letters as 'a white fluff of thistledown', a baby with 'the sweetest air of complete serenity'.

Fifteen months after Lilibet was born, Queen Mary of Teck

persuaded her husband that the Yorks should undertake an official royal visit to Australia and New Zealand, a trip by sea, of course, that would take them away from Lilibet for four months. While overseas, baby Elizabeth was brought to live at Buckingham Palace and Queen Mary would see her at least three times every day, something she had never done with her own children. Elizabeth could do no wrong and her grandparents pandered to her every wish.

At twelve months of age, Lilibet would sit on a rug throwing packs of cards around the room or grab balls of wool and unravel them as she ran around the room and down the corridors. She would find boxes of matches, spill them everywhere and then, on occasion, light them. She would rip the arms and legs off her dolls and teddy bears and throw them round the room, but one set of toys she cherished above all – her painted lead soldiers, which she would put on parade and pretend to inspect – like a future monarch.

Mary and King George were always arranging photographs of the little Elizabeth and one was particularly striking, of grandmother and grandchild sitting correctly, neither looking at the camera; Queen Mary wearing a long, flowing dress with a multiple rope of pearls and Lilibet, sitting on a table, looking almost doll-like with a small row of coral beads. Both look aloof, regal. It was Queen Mary's favourite photograph.

Gruff, crotchety King George also thought butter wouldn't melt in his granddaughter's mouth. George would not permit his own children to even talk to him unless he addressed them first. In contrast Elizabeth would sit on his knee, pull his beard and call him all sorts of names – such as 'Big Ears' – and he thought her wonderful.

When the twelve-month-old princess made her first appearance on the famous Buckingham Palace balcony, Queen Mary, not her parents, proudly held her for the crowds to cheer. And in a letter to Queen Mary, Elizabeth's mother wrote, 'It almost frightens me that the people should love Elizabeth so much. I suppose that it is a good thing, and I hope she will be worthy of it, poor little darling.'

The nickname 'Lilibet' took on because, as a child, the present queen could not pronounce her own name and, for some members of the family, it has stayed with her throughout her life. Queen Mary would invite Elizabeth's mother and father to visit Buckingham Palace and Windsor Castle as frequently as possible in order that she could watch, and supervise, the child's progress. As a royal child, Lilibet, at the ages of four and five, would return the salute of the guardsmen on duty by madly waving both her arms at them, causing great laughter. She seemed natural and carefree in comparison to the stiff and formal behaviour that King George and Queen Mary demanded of everyone else, including their own children, who attended court.

For most of her young life, Elizabeth lived at 145, Piccadilly, opposite The Green Park, only a few hundred yards from Buckingham Palace. Her nanny was Mrs Clara Knight, forever called Allah, a childish form of Clara (nothing to do with the Moslem religion). Allah was the royal nanny *par excellence*, and was rewarded for her work and devotion to the family by being given the honorary title of 'Mrs', though she never married. She was never photographed out of uniform and would usually be seen in her navy-blue belted coat and navy felt hat pushing a royal pram in one of the royal parks.

In August 1930, a few months after she had turned four, Lilibet's sister Princess Margaret Rose arrived, a child that would test Elizabeth's patience as well as that of her parents, over the ensuing years.

Bertie, the Duke of York, with memories of his awful childhood still in his mind, was determined that his children should enjoy a lyrical youth and look upon their childhood years as 'a golden age'. His wife Elizabeth, Duchess of York, had fortunately experienced a wonderful childhood and wanted her daughters to have the same happy experience. And so it was to be. Elizabeth was fortunate, growing up in a close-knit, affectionate family.

Queen Mary had ruined her eldest child, David, by spoiling him rotten simply because he was the Prince of Wales. But as his life became more indulgent, displaying many of the characteristics of his desolute grandfather, Queen Mary drew closer to the Yorks, especially after Lilibet was born. As a result she changed her allegiance and began spoiling the Yorks. She decided that Bertie and Elizabeth had become the quintessential royal family, a living example of the monarchy which embodied all the radiant domestic virtues (despite the antics of the heir to the throne). For David was proving irresponsible and a gadfly, having love affairs with older, and usually married, women, gambling, partying and clubbing with his young racy friends and living the sort of life condemned as sinful by his mother Queen Mary.

In 1930, Mary decided on the publication of a full-length biography of Elizabeth, then just three: *The Story of Princess Elizabeth* appeared with the 'sanction of her parents' and was written by Anne Ring, formerly attached to HRH the Duchess of York's Household. It was an immediate bestseller. The slim volume offered such paragraphs as: 'From the moment of her birth not only has our little

Princess been wrapped about with the tender love of parents and devoted grandparents, of cousins and uncles and friends, but she has been the admiring object of affection from thousands in the country and beyond the seas who have never seen her.'

A description of bedtime read: 'When Princess Elizabeth's nurse descending to the morning room or the drawing room, says in quiet tones, "I think it is bedtime now, Elizabeth,"there are no poutings or protests, just a few joyous skips and impromptu dance steps, a few last minute laughs at Mummy's delicious bedtime jokes, and then Princess Elizabeth's hand slips into her nurse's hand, and the two go off gaily together across the deep chestnut pile of the hall carpet to the accommodating lift, which in two seconds has whisked them off to the familiar dear domain, which is theirs to hold and to share.'

Other books appeared, with the full approval of the royal family, emphasising the 'joyous, delightful, radiant' family of the Duke and Duchess of York. It seemed that in the 1930s Princess Elizabeth – described as 'the most celebrated and best loved child in the world' had become Britain's answer to America's child star, Shirley Temple.

But Lilibet began to take on the airs and graces that little girls, even princesses, should not have, and Queen Mary realised she was creating a little monster. One morning the Lord Chamberlain met Lilibet in a palace corridor and said cheerily, 'Good morning, little lady.' Lilibet retorted: 'I'm not a little lady, I'm Princess Elizabeth.'

Later that morning Queen Mary knocked on the Chamberlain's door and, with Lilibet in tow, announced, 'This is Princess Elizabeth, who hopes one day to be a lady.'

On another occasion, her mother took her young daughter along when entertaining a society lady to tea, and Lilibet soon became bored. She left her seat and rang the bell for a footman. When he arrived Elizabeth said rudely, 'Kindly ring for a taxi, our guest is leaving.' Needless to say, Elizabeth was immediately sent to her room without her tea.

Toys were discouraged for Lilibet despite the fact that hundreds arrived each year at the house from total strangers, enraptured by the little princess. Instead she learned to read and write from a young age, though dolls and teddy bears were permitted. Rather surprisingly, she was given a dustpan and brush when just three and loved to help the maids clean her nursery. Tidiness and cleanliness were traits Elizabeth never lost and she came to believe the old adage that cleanliness was next to godliness. At four she was given her first pony as a Christmas present, and she also received the necessary brushes and grooming kit which she kept lined up outside her nursery door. Though so young,

Lilibet was taught that a pony had to be cared for and she would groom her little horse before every ride.

Mary decided to glamorise and publicise the Yorks still further, this time using the modern medium of film, so that the British nation could see and rejoice in their royal family and follow their example. The film, shot in the1930s, depicted Bertie, slim and serious, and neatly dressed; his adoring wife, Elizabeth, smiling sweetly; and two little princesses perfectly behaved and immaculately dressed in party frocks playing together.

It was extraordinary the way in which Queen Mary decided, and the Yorks readily agreed, that they and their daughters should be exposed to the media in a way and a manner that had never been seen before and that would be absolutely unthinkable today. Privileged royal watchers from selected newspapers were invited to Buckingham Palace and Windsor Castle to see the two princesses at play or at their school lessons; others came to watch the Yorks' own Christmas pantomime at Windsor, starring of course Elizabeth and Margaret.

Even more extraordinary, ladies-in-waiting and other servants were encouraged to earn pin money by writing about the princesses' lives in the popular papers and women's magazines – all so very different from today's coverage of the royal family when press officers are employed to provide as little information as possible about the royals.

While still a child, Lilibet began her lifelong love affair with animals. Lilibet had been given a cairn puppy for her third birthday and adored it, but she would later become enthralled with corgis, starting with her mother's two, Carol and Crackers. Lilibet would become strongly attracted to both dogs and ponies, spending hours grooming and playing with them. To a great extent they took the place of childhood friends, who were few and far between while she was growing up.

Generally, Lilibet lived a solitary and lonely childhood though she always had Nanny Allah and, of course, her irritating younger sister to play with, but nevertheless she appears to have been a happy child. Remarkably few restrictions were put on the girls, which was most unusual at a time when most of the aristocracy still believed that children should be seen and not heard. They could roam through the entire house and were encouraged to jump into their parents' bed in the early mornings. They were even permitted night-time pillow fights before settling down and listening to Nanny Allah or their mother read a bedtime story.

Margaret McDonald, 'Bobo' to the princesses, came to work for the Yorks as a nursery maid shortly after Margaret arrived. From caring for four-year-old Lilibet, Bobo was to spend her entire life with Elizabeth. Bobo remained a close personal friend until she died in September 1993 at the age of 89, one of the most important influences on Elizabeth's life. Bobo lived in a small suite of rooms at Buckingham Palace until the end and still chatted to Elizabeth once or twice a day. For their first ten years together they shared a bedroom until it was decided that Lilibet, then fourteen, was old enough to sleep alone. Bobo was to become Elizabeth II's official personal maid and dresser but the relationship was much closer than that. Lilibet confided in Bobo totally and the loyal Scots woman was to know every secret of the future queen. The grown-up Elizabeth was to say of her: 'I talk over everything with Bobo; she is so sensible and down to earth, and I would trust her with my life.'

In 1932, with Elizabeth just six, the Yorks moved from their home in the centre of London to the seclusion of the Royal Lodge in Windsor Great Park. For four years the family revelled in the country-like atmosphere of Windsor Park, where Lilibet was given a small garden plot to grow her own vegetables and flowers. It was in the park that she learned to ride, her pony stabled nearby.

As she emerged out of the cocoon of her early childhood Lilibet became a stickler for detail, tidiness and punctuality. She seemed too self-disciplined, too correct, too orderly for a girl of just seven years of age. She would put away her toys neatly, fold her own clothes immaculately, pack up her books according to size and even arrange her sweets in colours and sizes. She learned to dress herself at the age of four, doing up all her buttons, but she showed no flair for clothes, happily wearing whatever her nanny put out.

At the age of seven another new arrival entered Elizabeth's life who was also to have a profound influence. Miss Marion Crawford, the famous Crawfie, was employed by the Yorks as the girls' governess. She would be responsible for their entire education. It seemed from the very beginning that their father did not have much ambition for his children's learning. The only instruction he gave Crawfie was, 'For goodness sake, teach the girls to write a decent hand, that's all I ask you.' And she did. Both Elizabeth and Margaret have good, strong handwriting.

There was never any suggestion that Elizabeth or Margaret attend an ordinary school, not even a select private one. Neither the Duke nor Duchess, nor especially Queen Mary, believed that royal children should go to an ordinary school with other pupils. The Duchess had attended a London day school for a while and hated every moment and she had no intention of inflicting such penance on her own children; a governess was considered far preferable. As a result, Elizabeth's entire education was a quiet, solitary and lonely under-taking, controlled and organised by the sensible Crawfie.

In 1950 Crawfie published a book entitled *The Little Princesses* which became Book of the Month in the United States. The book detailed the lives of Elizabeth and Margaret in the 1930s. One paragraph showed their isolation: 'Other children always had an enormous fascination, like mystic beings from a distant world, and the little girls used to smile shyly at those they liked the look of. They would so have loved to speak to them and make friends, but this was never encouraged. I have often thought it a pity. The Dutch and Belgian royal children walked about the streets in their countries as a matter of course.'

In her book, Crawfie also revealed the pugilistic side of Elizabeth's nature, describing the ten-year-old Lilibet as having a nifty left hook which, when roused, she used on her sister. Crawfie described Margaret as a good close fighter who was known to bite on occasions. She added, 'But Elizabeth was the one with the temper.'

Lilibet and Margaret hardly ever escaped from the confines of their home. They were once taken, as a special treat, for a ride on a subway train but someone unfortunately recognised the two girls, who were in the hands of Crawfie and one detective. A royal car had to be called to help rescue them from the crowds that had gathered to gaze at them. Occasionally, the girls rode *incognito* on the top of London buses but after a few months these trips were also stopped for fear they might be recognised and become the centre of attention.

The girls were taken to one pantomime a year around Christmas and were permitted to attend the annual Horse Show at London's Olympia. Most of the time they had to rely on their own devices, organising their own games at home. Often these games would revolve around playing at running around the house with one of the girls pretending to be the horse while the other held the reins.

During the 1930s the royal family reached a pinnacle of popularity which greatly surprised King George V. In May 1935 a celebration was held to mark his twenty-five years on the throne and the people cheered wherever he went. Coming at the end of the great depression with millions unemployed and abject poverty everywhere, the Silver Jubilee celebrations proved a wonderful tonic. There were bonfires and parties in the streets and parks. Indeed, it was recorded that park attendants had to call for extra trolleys to cart away the thousands of used condoms!

Only twelve months later the monarchy and the nation were

enveloped in the dramatic trauma of Edward's abdication. In 1936, Lilibet was just ten and hardly aware of the unfolding drama which was to have such an effect on the rest of her life. Lilibet did meet the American divorcee, Wallis Simpson, once, when King Edward, who had succeeded to the throne on the death of King George, came to visit the Yorks. She shook hands with the Duke's paramour whom Queen Mary called 'that scarlet woman', and commented later about her American accent which, of course, was strange to her.

For her part, the twice-married divorcee Mrs. Simpson did remember Elizabeth and Margaret, commenting later, 'Those girls are unbelievable, wonderfully blonde, brightly scrubbed and beautifully mannered.'

For some time before King George V died, Queen Mary had been anxious about Edward, the Prince of Wales, succeeding to the throne. Both the ailing George and Queen Mary were appalled with the behaviour of Edward and Mrs Simpson. Edward escorted her everywhere in London; Wallis, usually over-dressed, bejewelled, would turn up on the arm of the heir to the throne at parties, balls and even the Royal Opera House. Her appearances were treated as sensational and, to many in the 1930s, scandalous.

Following the sudden death of George V, Queen Mary feared for the monarchy itself. She simply did not trust her eldest son to do the right thing. She was horrified at his gambling, drinking and womanising. Edward continued to shock his mother by escorting Mrs Simpson around London although society knew she was a married woman who was still living with her second husband.

Queen Mary told Edward of her fears and suggested that he should put aside his interest in Mrs Simpson 'for the sake of the nation'. Mary pointed out in no uncertain terms that as King he was no longer simply responsible for himself but for the entire nation, and must therefore end his self-indulgence like a true monarch. In blunt language Mary told her son that Britain did not need a twice-divorced woman as queen.

The family took great care not to discuss Mrs Simpson or the threat to the monarchy in front of the children. However, Elizabeth was a naturally bright and inquisitive child and she sensed something was afoot. She asked her nanny, her governess and her mother: 'What's wrong with Uncle David?' And frequently she would then ask, 'Is Uncle David in trouble?'

Elizabeth's natural curiosity wasn't answered directly. In that respect she was in the same position as the vast majority of the British people who had no idea whatsoever that there was the slightest possibility

Edward might abdicate. No British newspapers printed a word of the unfolding drama until it had actually occurred.

In October 1936 Mrs Simpson brought successful divorce proceedings against her husband Ernest. He would be the second husband she had divorced. In six months, after the *decree nisi* had been made absolute, she would be free to marry a third time. The satirical magazine *Punch* put the issue into perspective, showing Prime Minister Stanley Baldwin urging King Edward to give up Mrs Simpson, saying, 'All the peoples of your Empire, Sir, sympathise with you most deeply; but they all know – as you yourself must – that the Throne is greater than the man.'

Indeed, the Prime Minister did plead with King Edward on many occasions to drop Mrs Simpson, explaining that the cabinet, the government, dominion governments, the church and public opinion would not accept a twice-divorced woman as queen. But Edward would not listen; if he could not marry the woman he loved then he would abdicate the throne.

It was on a Thursday afternoon, 10 December 1936, that Elizabeth, aged ten, heard crowds outside her home in Piccadilly calling her father's name and cheering. She went downstairs and asked a footman what all the commotion was about. The servant told her that her father was now king and that meant that one day she would be queen. She raced back upstairs and told her sister Margaret, then six, the exciting news.

'Does that mean that you will have to be the next queen?' asked Margaret.

'Yes, some day,' replied Lilibet.

'Poor you,' said Margaret.

It seems Elizabeth took in her stride the realisation that one day she would be queen. Despite all the comings and goings at the house that day, she was more interested in going for a swim.

Downstairs, however, poor Bertie was not at all happy with the turn of events. He had never believed his elder brother would actually abdicate. The news put him in a state of shock for several days and he had to retire to bed. His wife, now Queen Elizabeth, had just begun to recover from a bad bout of flu. Her response was typical: 'We must take what is coming to us, and make the best of it.' She had never wanted to be too closely enmeshed in the affairs of the royal family. Now she was going to be queen and the thought filled her with trepidation.

In truth, Edward had been forced to abdicate by the will of parliament after the Tory Prime Minister Stanley Baldwin told him bluntly that Mrs Simpson would be totally unacceptable to the parliaments of Britain and the Empire as royal consort. Baldwin asked him openly during one of their discussions: 'Do you really think the people would accept a Queen Wally?' Edward looked at Baldwin for a while without making a comment. He then nodded his head, saying: 'You're right.'

The abdication caused the most extraordinary soul-searching in England but it also had its effect in the United States, for many Americans saw in Mrs Wallis Simpson a true woman of the people. Some took the refusal of the British government to sanction Edward VIII's love for the woman he wanted to marry as an insult to the United States. After all, it was argued, the wife of the Duke of York, who was to succeed his brother on the throne, was also a commoner. They asked, 'What is the difference between a king marrying a commoner from America and a king marrying a commoner from Scotland?' The correct reply, of course, was that Mrs Simpson had been divorced, twice, and Elizabeth had not. And, of course, Queen Mary, by far the strongest royal character at the time, was passionately against divorce.

There were also those in the United States, particularly among the young, who believed that King Edward VIII should have refused to abdicate, should have insisted on marrying Mrs Simpson, should have challenged the government, should have appealed to the British people over the heads of parliament and married 'the woman I love'. Winston Churchill also urged such action.

Shortly after Edward's abdication, when it was obvious Elizabeth would eventually become queen, her grandmother, Queen Mary, took command of her education. She was amazed to find that the two princesses appeared to be learning nothing more than the three Rs – reading, writing and arithmetic. At that time Elizabeth, then 11 years old, and Margaret, six, spent only one and a half hours a day doing school work, from 9.30 to 11.00 each morning, followed by an hour's play and lunch. Then another hour's rest was followed by singing, music, drawing and dancing. When weather permitted the girls were taken outside for an hour's walk – all as part of their education!

The total education of Britain's future queen consisted of just seven and a half hours of academic work a week. Mary immediately decreed that her granddaughter would study history, so that she would learn about Britain's past glories; geography, with emphasis on the scope and extent of her beloved British Empire; poetry, to perfect memory; and Bible-reading for her understanding of religious history. She also arranged for Sir Henry Marten, vice-provost of Eton,

Britain's foremost school, to instruct Lilibet in English constitutional history.

Surprisingly, Queen Mary did not order further intellectual stimulation or extra academic work, which was clearly needed for the development of the two princesses. Mary and Elizabeth's parents were apparently concerned that their daughters might become 'blue stockings' (studious young women). As a result, Princess Elizabeth succeeded to the throne fifteen years later virtually uneducated in all but the most rudimentary and basic disciplines.

With the full approval of Queen Mary, those courtiers in command at Buckingham Palace decided that revealing the new king in the fullest possible royal splendour would be the best way to overcome the crisis that the abdication had caused the monarchy. Establishing the sacred image would persuade the nation to accept George VI as king and obscure the fact that he was not the rightful heir to the throne. And so the frail George was subjected to the most rigorous and magnificent coronation Britain had ever witnessed.

The coronation had a profound effect on Lilibet, who was then eleven years old. The divine service, the sacred image of the sovereign and the actual crowning were all explained to her in great detail. She already understood that one day she too would be crowned queen and would take on the responsibilities of the crown. Queen Mary decided the two princesses would take part in the coronation and they watched the entire three-hour-long service. Elizabeth took everything most seriously, never smiling throughout. Margaret spent much of the time looking about her, too young to understand what was happening. Elizabeth gasped as the hundreds of assembled peers in their glorious robes shouted loudly 'God Save the King' at the moment the crown was placed on her father's head by the Archbishop of Canterbury. That fabled sense of a monarch's sacred and divine right to rule stayed with Elizabeth well into her adult life and caused ructions in her marriage.

Supported in rehearsals by both Queen Mary and his wife Elizabeth, King George's coronation in May 1937 was a triumphant success, but he needed the moral support of Queen Mary at the actual ceremony, breaking a centuries-old tradition that no dowager queen was present at a crowning. On newsreels and film the world witnessed the amazing spectacle of the coronation and was left in no doubt that, with all its dignity, splendour and sacred rights, the English throne was as strong as ever.

King George and his consort Queen Elizabeth were determined to produce a male heir to succeed to the throne but it was not to be.

And Lilibet told her nanny she prayed to God to send her a little brother who could one day be king. The family would never again mention Uncle David or the abdication to Elizabeth until she became queen at the age of twenty-six.

But Uncle David's banishment upset Elizabeth because she had found him a likeable man, always laughing and joking with her. The Duke and Duchess of Windsor, the titles awarded them after the abdication, were banished for ever, forbidden from returning to Britain, exiled to live wherever they wished outside Britain. They were given an annual stipend, though the amount was never revealed, allowing them to live in comfort, but not splendour, until they died. The royal family's treatment of the Duke of Windsor has been seen by generations as cruel and unnecessary but the House of Windsor is ruthless. Uncle David had put his own personal happiness before duty and he had to take the consequences for the rest of his life. All was explained to Elizabeth at a later date, but she had learned a most salutary lesson.

George VI feared his severe stammer would make him incapable of carrying out his role as monarch when he realised he would be expected to continue the tradition, begun by his father, of broadcasting to the nation and the empire at Christmas time. His wife hired the Australian speech therapist Lionel Logue and after months of therapy, his stammer did improve enough so that on Christmas Day 1937 he managed to make his speech. But the nation, which had been informed in advance of his speech impediment, shared the king's ordeal as he struggled with many of the words. His obvious courage and discomfort added to his popularity, for the people warmed to the monarch, a man who had personal problems just as they did.

Meanwhile, Queen Mary's campaign to popularise the monarchy by selling Lilibet to the nation, continued inexorably. Now her name was given to bone china, hospitals and even chocolates; her wax effigy, sitting on a pony, now stood in Madame Tussaud's, her portrait was in the Royal Academy and her picture appeared on the cover of *Time* magazine.

Convinced that Lilibet would one day be crowned monarch, Queen Mary again intervened, checking to see whether her granddaughter's education was up to scratch. Once again she found her education wanting but still did nothing to encourage proper formation. Instead, she decided to educate the two princesses herself. She personally conducted the girls on cultural tours of London, taking them to the Tower of London, the Royal Mint, the Bank of

England and further afield to Kew Gardens, Hampton Court and Greenwich Palace. Queen Mary would march ahead of the children talking with whoever was in charge while the girls would have to hurry on behind, exhausted at the end of two-hour visits. Margaret later swore she would never allow her children to see more than three pictures at a time while visiting art galleries, so they would plead for 'just one more' rather than long to go home.

Elizabeth's more formal education remained in the hands of Miss Crawford, the prim spinster and former primary school teacher from Scotland. Then in her thirties, she had never taught anyone over the age of eleven. And yet Crawfie remained Elizabeth's only teacher from the age of nine until she was eighteen. Then her education ceased altogether. She spent much of her time enjoying long walks in the park, taking dancing lessons in Buckingham Palace, reading schoolgirl books and resting for long periods each afternoon. Elizabeth never spent more than two hours a day – ten hours a week – actually learning. It was as if she was living in the nineteenth rather than the twentieth century.

But the most important influence on the young Elizabeth was her father, who impressed her with his sense of duty, his industry and conscientiousness. Elizabeth noted how methodical her father was in dealing with all official matters, even opening and reading all his own mail. And he loved routine for, to the king, routine was akin to duty. The king influenced his daughter by example rather than by command. She saw her father working extremely hard at a job he never wanted; saw him struggle with his speech impediment and attend to all his duties with grit and determination. Elizabeth would take note of all these things and follow his example when she became queen.

But Elizabeth wasn't all work. The royal sisters brought some much-needed life to Buckingham Palace, which had never known the boisterous noise of two young girls running, laughing and enjoying the long corridors and huge rooms of the palace. Servants and courtiers welcomed their arrival and their irreverence for the place, which many thought more like a mausoleum than a palace.

The king and queen loved to spend as much time as possible with their daughters. Weekends were mostly spent at Windsor Royal Lodge where they all enjoyed do-it-yourself entertainment like charades, card games, parlour games, sing-alongs and walks together in Windsor Great Park. All of these were simple pleasures, which were not designed to help expand the mind of either of the young girls.

This idyllic family life came to a shattering halt as Europe became engulfed in war, a war in which Buckingham Palace would be bombed and set ablaze by Luftwaffe raids over London. The day in September 1939 when Britain declared war on Germany, Lilibet and Margaret were at a Girl Guide camp in Scotland. They were both members of the Brownies and the Girl Guides but never took part in any activities or attended any parties where boys were present. Even at the age of fourteen Princess Elizabeth still only attended all-girl birthday parties.

Throughout the war the sisters spent most of their time at Windsor Castle, thirty miles west of London. It had been suggested they should be sent to the safety of Scotland or to Canada, particularly as Elizabeth was now heir to the throne. But the king and queen refused. They had no intention of leaving the nation to face Nazi Germany without their family also being in the firing line and in any case, they wanted to keep their family together as all other British families did during those years of war. The girls spent most of the week living in the Brunswick Tower, a strongly built part of Windsor Castle, while their parents stayed throughout the week in the heart of London at Buckingham Palace.

The Second World War came to the royal family as much as anyone else in Britain. Most nights during those first three years the family heard the wail of air-raid sirens and the drone of enemy bombers overhead. More than 300 high-explosive bombs would have fallen around Windsor Castle before the war ended, as well as incendiaries and buzz bombs.

When the sirens sounded the girls were woken by Bobo and Allah, who shared their bedrooms throughout the war, and dressed in 'siren suits' – warm, one-piece suits, with a hood. (Children had to wear them whenever the sirens sounded.) Quickly, they made their way down darkened stairs to the basement where the rest of the staff also took refuge. They took with them little suitcases containing their favourite dolls, a book and the diaries their mother gave them at Christmas each year. They slept in a two-tier bunk which had been installed and the girls would sometimes spend the entire night in the tiny basement waiting for the all-clear to sound. Life in Windsor Castle wasn't much fun. In each corridor only one naked light bulb illuminated the darkness, and all the paintings, the silver, the antique furniture, the wall hangings and the rugs had been carefully stored beneath the castle.

Throughout the war, King George and his wife had no intention of leaving Britain, believing it tantamount to deserting their people. They hoped, by their example, to instil the same grit and determination in the nation as Prime Minister Winston Churchill did in his wartime speeches. With her parents, Elizabeth often listened to those stirring radio broadcasts.

In 1940 Churchill made one of his most memorable speeches when he pledged: 'We shall defend our island, whatever the cost may be; we shall fight on the beaches, we shall fight on the landing grounds, we shall fight in the fields and in the streets, we shall fight in the hills; we shall never surrender.'

It was following that speech that King George and his wife let it be known they had decided to take up arms in case the day came when they needed to defend themselves. Each week they practised with rifles, 'tommy' guns and revolvers in specially erected ranges in Buckingham Palace and Windsor Castle. On occasion Elizabeth and Margaret were allowed to watch their parents and handle the revolvers, but they never learned to shoot. That was to come later.

On Churchill's orders, a secret hideout was built, as a fully equipped bomb shelter at Madresfield, Worcestershire, 120 miles north-west of London, which would become the royal headquarters if ever German forces were to land in Britain. At Windsor Castle, baggage for an immediate departure was kept packed throughout the war. The crown jewels, wrapped in newspaper and tied with string, were hidden in vaults below ground along with other valuables, ready at any time to be taken to a ship at Liverpool. Along with the princesses, the valuables would sail for Canada.

Elizabeth was thirteen at the outbreak of war and nineteen when Japan finally surrendered. She had been just thirteen when she first met Prince Philip, and spent most of the war years thinking about the young man on whom she had had an instant teenage crush. Yet for her sixteenth birthday, Princess Elizabeth, now a young woman, was given a child-like tea party with jelly, ice cream and paper hats. And the few people who attended, including her parents, Bobo, Allah and Crawfie sang 'Happy birthday, Lilibet' as though she was still a little girl.

The following day Elizabeth enrolled in the wartime youth service scheme, a national organisation set up to permit young people over sixteen to 'do their bit' to help the war effort. From the outbreak of war Elizabeth had pleaded with her parents to let her help out in any way possible. Now she was given the chance to prove to the nation, who read of the item in the papers or saw the newsreel film at the local cinema, that the teenage princess was helping in the war effort. As a result, Elizabeth was accepted by the entire nation as 'one of us', prepared to help in the war effort just like every other British family to defeat Hitler. And when Buckingham Palace suffered direct hits during a bombing raid in 1941, King George and his wife let it be known they had no intention of quitting London. That decision won them much praise and admiration.

The war brought one piece of good fortune for Elizabeth's education with the arrival in London of Mme Antoinette de Bellaigue, a vivacious Belgian lady who had escaped from Belgium with her family just ten days before the German invasion. It was decided she should teach the princesses French and she remained their tutor from 1942 to 1946. She also suggested the princesses learn German which they did, but only to schoolgirl level.

Only once during the war did Elizabeth face any real danger. She had gone off on a Girl-Guide hike in Windsor Park in 1944 when a flying-bomb, sometimes called a 'doodle bug' or 'buzz bomb' was heard flying overhead. An army officer in command of the hike ordered the girls to run flat out into a slit trench and the bomb exploded nearby with a shattering roar. From that moment on an armoured car followed the princesses whenever they went on walks.

Elizabeth became increasingly frustrated and annoyed that she was not being allowed to carry out more adult duties to help the war effort as other sixteen- and seventeen-year-old girls were being encouraged to do. She refused to accept that she couldn't just because she was the heir to the throne and in potential danger. She wanted to become a nurse so that she could tend the wounded and help in hospitals. But her parents would not permit it. After much argument she was eventually allowed to join the Sea Rangers, a group activity for teenage girls interested in seafaring. But it didn't satisfy Elizabeth's craving to carry out more responsible and worthwhile duties.

Finally in 1945, at the age of 18, Lilibet became a soldier of sorts. Thrilled to be allowed to dress in khaki, Elizabeth told Bobo, 'Now I'm like a real soldier.' She was given number 230873, as Second Subaltern Elizabeth Alexandra Mary Windsor of the Auxiliary Transport Service (ATS) No. 1. Mechanical Transport Training Centre. Her army records show she was eighteen, five feet three inches tall, with blue eyes and brown hair.

For those last few months of war, Elizabeth was treated like any other young woman in the army transport service. She drove a three-ton truck, changed spark plugs, adjusted brakes, greased axles and changed tyres. At last she felt part of the war effort and revelled in her new-found adventure. But even during those months she led a privileged, closeted existence, and was never subjected to the rough life of the other ATS girls in the transport training centre. Instead of living in barracks she travelled each day by chauffeur-driven car from Windsor Castle to the training centre. She was back home by 4 p.m. each day and ate in the Officers' Mess. At nineteen she was still living a quiet, mainly cloistered life, cut off from the real world as she had been throughout her childhood and teenage years, hardly ever meeting boys of her own age and mixing with few girls.

Occasionally, rather stiff, formal lunches would be held at Windsor Castle when boys from Eton were invited to attend. Elizabeth acted as hostess, sitting at the centre of the table, and opposite her sat Margaret, already earning herself a reputation as an *enfant terrible*. Even in her early teens there was something essentially mischievous about Margaret which could never be said about her more staid elder sister. Crawfie also talked of occasional madrigal classes, treasure hunts and games of sardines but these were only played with other girls.

In fact, her only real experience of the opposite sex was during occasional parties at Buckingham Palace or Windsor when Elizabeth played host to visiting airmen from other nations, among them Americans, New Zealanders, Australians and Canadians. The parties took place in the afternoon, however, lasted thirty minutes and tea was the only drink served! It wasn't surprising that at the end of the war her father King George wrote of his daughters in his diary on VE-Day: 'Poor darlings, they have never had any fun yet.'

Victory in Europe, celebrated on 8 May 1945, was a day Elizabeth never forgot. At 19, she had never tasted such a feeling of freedom as she did that night. After much pleading, King George permitted them to leave the palace and join in the merrymaking. Chaperoned only by their beloved Crawfie and escorted by a few junior army officers, the princesses mixed with the crowd, unrecognised by the tens of thousands who had joined in the wild celebrations. They ran through the streets of London, danced in Piccadilly Circus and mingled with the thousands who had walked from Trafalgar Square to the palace where they joined in the wild cheering, singing and chanting. Crawfie recalled that Elizabeth and Margaret shouted as loudly as everyone else that night: 'We want the king! We want the queen!'

With the war over, Elizabeth hoped she would spend much more time with her beloved Philip. They had first met just before the outbreak of war in 1939 when she was barely 13. She had been with her parents at the Royal Naval College, Dartmouth, when Philip, then 18, was chosen to escort her and Margaret around the school. Immediately attracted by his athletic good looks, blonde hair, sporty appearance and big smile, Elizabeth had never forgotten the young man whom she called 'My Viking Prince'. For six years she thought continually of the exciting young naval officer she had only seen a few times during those six years of war. She had written him letters, not love letters but friendly ones, giving him news of life in London and of her family.

Occasionally, of course, they did see each other. At Christmas in 1943, Philip, on leave in England, was invited to attend the royal family's annual pantomime at Windsor Castle. Elizabeth, then sixteen, played the lead role in Aladdin, and Margaret played Roxana. Elizabeth tried to persuade the 22-year-old Philip to join in the pantomime but, to her disappointment, he refused. Other royals in the cast included the Duke of Kent and Princess Alexandra. Elizabeth was visibly animated as Philip clapped and cheered from his seat in the front row. During the pantomime Elizabeth leapt from a laundry basket dressed as a young Chinese boy, tap-danced and sang solos and duets and cracked jokes, some of which were quite risqué! Philip laughed in loud appreciation.

As the war drew to a close, Elizabeth, in her excitement and anxiety, was like many other young women waiting back home for their men to return from the war; she desperately hoped that the man she had thought about for so many years would return to her. She repeatedly asked Bobo, the one person she felt she could confide in, 'Do you think Philip will come back to me? Will he have forgotten me?'

She also asked Bobo all those impossible questions that many girls fret about as teenagers: about love and romance, boys and girls and, of course, marriage.

Elizabeth had already decided she wanted to marry Philip but her father had no idea at that stage that his beloved Lilibet was thinking seriously about marriage at all. He had other ideas. King George wanted her to enjoy her young life for a few more years. In his eyes Lilibet was far too young to even contemplate a serious relationship with anyone, let alone think of marriage. In early 1944, however, King George II of Greece wrote to Elizabeth's father urging him 'to take most seriously' the possibility of a marriage between his cousin Philip and the heir presumptive Elizabeth. King George didn't even mention the letter to his beloved daughter.

King George often spoke to Elizabeth about their family, always referring to 'the four of us', meaning himself, his wife, Elizabeth and Margaret. He never included anyone else and never spoke of a future which included any husbands. It seemed he wanted to preserve his family, cocoon-like, away from the real world and keep his daughters to himself. Understandably, George was annoyed when King George of Greece raised the question again when visiting Buckingham Palace in 1945. He announced to the surprised English King George, 'It seems Lilibet is in love with Philip and I know that he adores her.' Elizabeth's father scowled and replied, 'Philip had better not think any more about it at present; they are both too young.'

He took a closer interest in Lilibet, hoping to turn her mind away from thoughts of love and marriage. He suggested she should concentrate on her riding lessons and other field sports. He taught her to fish, to stalk deer and to shoot, deer as well as birds. But that wasn't the only reason for wanting to turn her thoughts away from the opposite sex.

Elizabeth, now twenty, was a good-looking young woman who carried herself well. She had a good figure and shapely legs, the muscles toned by riding. Her hair, light brown and curly, was just above shoulder length. She had a lovely complexion and a ready smile. Queen Mary's lady-in-waiting Lady Airlie commented at the time, 'The carriage of her head is unequalled and she has about her that indescribable something which Queen Victoria had, regality.'

King George felt that during the war years – her teenage years – he had neglected his favourite daughter due to the enormous pressure that war had inevitably created. To some extent it made this sympathetic man feel guilty that he had neglected 'his' Lilibet, and he wanted her to enjoy life now that the restrictions of war were lifted. King George hoped that Lilibet would become the son he had always wanted. He was devoted to her in every sense: he wanted her to have the very best in life, to remain single until her mid-twenties, to be his close companion, to go on walks, to stalk, fish, shoot, to spend as much time together as possible. But it was a forlorn hope. King George did not realise it but Lilibet had grown up and she had already made her choice.

Elizabeth had always been an endearing, loving and obedient daughter, and she went along with her father's wishes. After the war, King George found the time to go to Scotland with her and they would spend hours together but, understandably, the young woman yearned for the bright lights of London, now springing to life after the dark days of war. More importantly to Elizabeth living in London would bring her closer to Philip, the man she wanted to see as much as possible. But being the dutiful and patient daughter she was, she resolved to keep her real thoughts from her father, waiting for the day she would be able to declare her love.

Both Elizabeth and her father were unaware that Lord Louis Mountbatten, working behind the scenes and using whatever friends and relations were necessary, was as determined as Elizabeth that a betrothal between the two families should take place. A great-grandson of Queen Victoria, Mountbatten was Prince Philip's uncle and he was to have a long and deep involvement with the House of Windsor, particularly with Elizabeth and later Prince Charles.

King George realised the time had come for his daughter to start understanding and taking part in the affairs of state. He decreed that she should attend occasional official functions, like launching ships and opening exhibitions, as well as formal lunches and dinners which were often rather stuffy, boring affairs. It was after attending a number of these that Elizabeth realised how poor her general education had been, how little she knew of the outside world, of general knowledge, of politics, and she felt embarrassed when people, people she thought important, talked of matters she did not understand and knew little about. She told Bobo, 'Sometimes I don't understand what people are talking about at table. And I'm absolutely terrified of sitting next to strangers in case they talk about things I have never heard of.'

She appeared equally terrified at the prospect of attending the debutante dances which began again at the end of the war. King George and his wife encouraged their return so that Elizabeth, now 20, and Margaret, 16, could meet young people, have some fun and perhaps meet suitable young men that they might one day marry. But Elizabeth had little or no interest in these dances. She was shy and reticent, found it difficult to handle small talk and, though considered pretty and attractive, would tend to hold back and stay in the background, making it difficult for young men to dance with her, let alone get to know her except in the most superficial fashion.

King George kept a discreet but sharp eye on his daughters. After a dance at Windsor Castle when Margaret was eighteen he checked to see if his daughters were in bed. Finding Margaret's empty, he went downstairs to discover her lying on a sofa with very few clothes on, locked in a passionate embrace with a young Guards officer. The King ordered his daughter to bed and the officer to leave immediately after asking his name and rank. Forty-eight hours later the young man was posted overseas.

At the age of 18, Elizabeth seemed both older than her years, and at the same time, younger and immature. She had little, if any, experience with boys or young men, and had probably never been kissed. She was most certainly a virgin and would act rather coldly whenever young men tried to talk to her. She was seen as a happy, wholesome young woman of some spirit, but rather serious, perhaps lacking in warmth and spontaneity. She was certainly without conceit, however. To some in the palace, Princess Elizabeth seemed almost a saint. And yet she could be stubborn, even imperious and would sometimes give people a look that sent shivers down their backs. And as well as inheriting her doting father's strength of character, she had also inherited his temper.

Through the summer of 1945, Elizabeth, then 19, saw more of Philip who was five years older. The more time they spent together, the more Elizabeth was determined that one day they would marry. And, despite the wishes of her father, she was in a hurry to make the relationship official and become engaged. It was in 1946 that the young couple found a secret rendezvous – secret, that is, from her father. Occasionally they would meet up at weekends at Coppins, Kent, forty miles south-east of London where the Duke and Duchess of Kent lived. They understood that there was a teenage romance going on and thought they should encourage it. Elizabeth took them into her confidence, telling them, 'Daddy doesn't want me to see too much of Philip or anyone so please don't tell him.' And they didn't.

It is not surprising that Elizabeth fell for the dashing Philip. Most of the men she knew were middle-aged, and she considered most of them stuffy and boring. In addition, they nearly all worked at Buckingham Palace. The young men she did meet were always so very correct and respectful in the presence of the king's daughter that she never got to know any of them at all well.

To the young Lilibet, Philip was not only a war hero but an invigorating, self-confident athletic young man who laughed a lot, enjoyed life, was never boring, and who brought a sense of excitement into her life, something she had never felt before. It was no wonder she fell for his boyish charms and stunning good looks.

During the autumn of 1945 Elizabeth's teenage dream of love became a reality. The couple spent hours together whenever Philip was on home leave from his ship, which was not very often as it was stationed in the Far East. They walked in the grounds, talked, dined together, listened to all kinds of music and, more importantly, simply spent time alone. They had spent very little time together since first meeting in 1939 and they hardly knew each other. Lilibet had had a schoolgirl crush on the young handsome naval officer. Now she knew she was in love.

Behind the scenes, Philip was being encouraged by his uncle Louis Mountbatten. Whenever they met, Mountbatten would ask his nephew about the romance: how much time they spent together, what they said to each other, what they did together and whether Elizabeth talked of a future together. After Philip reported to

Mountbatten in July 1946 that Elizabeth had declared her love, Mountbatten encouraged Philip to ask her to marry him. It may seem extraordinary that someone with Philip's character needed prompting but he was well aware that the young Princess Elizabeth was the greatest 'matrimonial catch' in the western world, not only among the whole of European royalty. He was also aware that he was a penniless young naval officer without a home or a proper family.

On 11 August 1946, during the royal family's summer holiday at Balmoral in Scotland, Philip, then twenty-five, asked Elizabeth to be his bride. They were walking together in the grounds on a beautiful sunny day when he proposed. Later, Elizabeth told Bobo, 'It was wonderful, magical. I just threw my arms round his neck and kissed him as he held me to him, my feet off the ground.' Elizabeth knew her father did not want her to become engaged or get married at such a young age and she told Philip. But she did accept, without first obtaining parental approval. Such an act was utterly out of character for Elizabeth, the dutiful, obedient and loving daughter. She had always been determined to marry her 'Viking Prince' and not even her parents would stop her from doing so. It certainly showed Elizabeth had a most determined streak to her character. She would need it.

To some critics, Philip's wooing and winning of Princess Elizabeth, with the assistance of Uncle Dickie, would be seen as cold and calculating. Mountbatten's secret ambition had always been to link his family with the House of Windsor. Elizabeth's attraction to his nephew Philip was the opportunity he had waited for and he had done all in his power to bring about his ambition. That view was encouraged by Philip himself who, when asked about his marriage to Elizabeth, told biographer Basil Boothroyd, 'I suppose one thing led to another. I suppose I began to think about it seriously oh, let me think now, when I got back in '46 and went to Balmoral. It was probably then that we, that it became, you know, that we began to think about it seriously, and even talk about it . . . ' Not exactly the words of a young man desperately in love with the girl he wanted to marry and spend the rest of his life with.

The night after he proposed, Philip phoned his uncle and told him of the secret engagement. A delighted Mountbatten had known, of course, that King George VI was against the marriage of his daughter, not just because Philip was a member of the Greek royal family, without an immediate family, a fortune or a home, but because, Mountbatten believed, King George's love for and devotion to his daughter had become too obsessive, even unhealthy.

Mountbatten immediately phoned his other nephew, King George II, who had just been returned to the Greek throne after a successful plebiscite. He suggested George leak the news that Prince Philip and Elizabeth of England had become engaged. It was, of course, true, though still highly secret and absolutely unofficial. Mountbatten knew that a betrothal of the future heir to the English crown had to receive permission not just from King George VI and Queen Elizabeth, but the British government. Mountbatten was desperate to secure the hand of Elizabeth for Philip before any other contender could be found. And George II believed, and prayed, that an engagement between Philip and Elizabeth would not only bring the power, authority and prestige of the Royal House of Windsor to support his position on the Greek throne but, more importantly, would seal Britain's obligation to back Greece against the insurgent communists who sought to overthrow the Greek royal family.

On 7 September 1946, the *New York Times* reported King George II's rumour, saying that Londoners had been thrilled by a report that Princess Elizabeth, who would one day rule over them, was to become engaged to her second cousin, Prince Philip of Greece, but that their expectations of marriage had been ended by a denial from the royal household. In private, Elizabeth's father was furious.

King George VI first called his wife and inquired as to whether she knew about the rumour, which she did not. Then he ordered his daughter to come to Buckingham Palace and he asked her face to face whether the rumour was true. Dutifully, Elizabeth explained to her father that Philip had unofficially asked her to marry him, and that she had accepted. George was angry but said nothing. However, he did tell her that Philip had ignored all the rules of protocol and had been extremely rude by not asking him first. In her father's view, Philip had behaved disgracefully.

King George told Elizabeth that he could not give his permission or his blessing because the Prime Minister and his government had to be first forewarned of the possibility and their permission obtained. George was a very angry man, angry with Philip, Louis Mountbatten and, as he put it, 'all those bloody Greeks'.

The king had been alerted some months earlier by Prime Minister Clement Attlee that the Greek royal family wanted Philip to marry Elizabeth to help their cause. King George VI wanted nothing whatsoever to do with such an arrangement; the future happiness of his beloved Elizabeth was far more important to him than the internal or external politics of Greece. But King George saw it as a legitimate reason to put off Elizabeth's intended engagement which, he hoped, might provide a breathing space for his daughter to come to her senses and change her mind. But as many a father has discovered, there was little he could do. Lilibet was in love.

In an effort to postpone the day, King George refused to allow the engagement to be announced until all the formalities had been sorted out. Elizabeth could not and did not want to understand the problems; she only knew she wanted to spend romantic evenings with the man she was determined to marry, whatever the obstacles put in her way.

Her mother tried to persuade Elizabeth to wait, explaining that it had taken two long years after Elizabeth's father had asked her to marry him before she made the decision. Her mother explained that she wanted to be sure he was the right man, and by waiting she had become convinced their marriage would be happy. The young Lady Elizabeth Bowes-Lyon's marriage to the Duke of York was remarkably successful. He adored her. He claimed he could not have lived without her and many testified that she gave him the backbone to become a much-loved and respected wartime king. She has been a widow for nearly fifty years now and has made a magnificent success of her role as Queen Mother, loved by the entire nation. But behind the smile and the twinkling eyes, and under the floating pastel dresses, is a woman of considerable strength. As her staff would comment, 'She's as tough as old boots but we all love her dearly.'

In 1945 the Churchill Government planned a royal trip to South Africa to thank that nation for its help and support throughout the war. The invitation came as a godsend to King George for here was another reason to postpone his daughter's engagement. He informed Elizabeth that the whole family had to visit South Africa and that the trip would last three months. Elizabeth asked her father if it was really necessary that she should go, but he was adamant. As he explained, it was the family's duty and duty must come first. Elizabeth had to endure another long, forced separation from Philip, travelling by ship to South Africa, spending weeks touring with her family. She desperately missed Philip and wondered what sort of life her husband-to-be was leading back in London. Occasionally, she spoke to him by phone but her father did not encourage her to do so. Despite pining for Philip, however, she went about her duty, smiling, looking happy and carrying out her royal duty with self-assurance and much dignity.

She would not have been happy to read that a poll in the down-market *Sunday Pictorial* tabloid showed that 40 per cent of its readers opposed a possible marriage between Elizabeth and Philip, demanding that if she went ahead she should immediately renounce the throne. The reason: they did not want Princess Elizabeth or the royal family involved in any way with the Greek royals, whom they did not consider good enough for the heir to the English throne.

King George returned to London seventeen pounds lighter and in poor health. Along with conflicts in Palestine and rebellions in India, the worry over his daughter's future had taken a severe toll. At a Guildhall banquet shortly after his return, the king could hardly finish a sentence. He displayed a rasping cough, his voice often inaudible.

But Elizabeth had turned 21 and the king knew that he could not stand in the way of his daughter's wishes much longer. Prince Philip had relinquished all his Greek titles and agreed to join the Church of England, renouncing the Greek Orthodox Church in which he had been baptised. And King George finally received formal permission from the British and Commonwealth governments for the heir to the throne to become betrothed. With a heavy heart he finally gave his permission.

In private King George gave his permission to Elizabeth, holding her face in his hands and kissing her on both cheeks. But there were tears in his eyes, though Elizabeth believed he was tearful with joy. Unable to afford an engagement ring, Philip appealed to his mother Princess Alice, now living in Greece as a nun. She sent him the diamonds from her favourite tiara so they could be made into a ring. By July 1947, Elizabeth and Philip had been secretly engaged for nearly a year and the newspapers were full of the real-life fairy story of the princess and her handsome prince. That myth would continue for decades.

King George, unhappy and anxious for his beloved Lilibet, knew the sort of man-about-town Philip had become during the past two years. He feared he might continue his hedonistic life and, in so doing, break his daughter's heart. Nor did he feel confident that Philip would ever accept the discipline of royal life. Wary and suspicious of his future son-in-law, King George did not create Philip a Prince, or Prince Consort, on marrying his daughter. Prince Consort was the title used by Victoria's husband Prince Albert, and customary in all the royal families of Europe. It was suggested by Mountbatten and other courtiers but King George would not hear of it. Indeed, Philip was not to receive the title of Prince for almost a decade though the king used 'Prince Philip' as a courtesy title. He was never to be Prince Consort, however.

Despite marrying the heir to the English throne, Prince Philip and his best man, David Milford Haven, were determined that Philip should have a traditional stag party. Philip went one better and had two, both on the same night. The first was a five-course dinner, held in the Park Suite at the Dorchester in Park Lane, Mayfair, a stone's throw away from Buckingham Palace with a small select band of just twelve men, all from the Royal Navy. Along with Mike Parker, Milford Haven and Commander George Norfolk, who had been Philip's captain on HMS *Whelp*, Louis Mountbatten also attended.

The press discovered the stag dinner and asked to be allowed to take pictures. Philip and Louis Mountbatten agreed and the photographers trooped in for the last picture of the bachelor Prince. After taking the photographs Philip asked whether, in return, he and Mike Parker could take pictures of the photographers. They agreed and handed over their cameras. With the cameras in their possession they pulled out the flash bulbs and smashed them on the floor so the photographers could take no more pictures that night. 'Now it's our turn to have the last laugh,' Philip said triumphantly as he ushered the unhappy group of press photographers and reporters out of the door. Philip's indiscreet and aggressive behaviour towards the press that night would later be seen as a serious mistake on his behalf, for, at a stroke, he had alienated the vast majority of Britain's newspaper industry.

After dinner, Philip wanted to thank the chef in person, so Parker and Milford Haven put Philip on a tea trolley and rushed him at speed down the long corridors to the kitchens where an astonished French chef, Jean Baptiste Virlogeux, received Philip's thanks in fluent French.

Philip's second stag party began just after midnight when he, Parker, Milford Haven and two others went to the Belfry Club off Belgrave Square where they drank balloons of brandy and smoked Havana cigars for three more hours. They sang bawdy naval songs, told their favourite *risqué* jokes and could hardly walk out of the club when they finally decided they had drunk enough.

Milford Haven recalled, 'Philip and I were staying at Kensington Palace and the next day had to go and see a very senior bishop who was to take us through the wedding ceremony. After breakfast I remember we both had stiff gin and tonics to stabilise us; we were in such a state.'

Elizabeth's wedding was no grand affair, as far as royal weddings go, because Britain was still suffering the harsh effects of the war. Rationing still ruled everyone's lives, including the royal family, and King George was anxious that the nation should not think his family any different. Due to a shortage of timber for housing, no spectator stands were erected along the route from Buckingham Palace to Westminster Abbey and only a few decorations and flags were flying because of King George's deference to the austerity caused by the war. And Labour Prime Minister Clement Attlee went further, refusing to permit the day to be declared a public holiday. As he put it, 'We cannot permit the luxury of a public holiday while potatoes are still rationed.'

Clothes rationing meant that Elizabeth had to be careful with her wedding dress though she was granted a hundred extra coupons for her trousseau and 23 extra coupons for each of her eight bridesmaids. Her white satin gown shimmered with garlands of stars embroidered in crystals and ten thousand costume pearls had been painstakingly sewn on to the dress to form garlands of York roses and ears of corn. The train was twenty-five feet long.

The day, however, reflected the nation's mood rather than Elizabeth's youthful happiness. The morning of 22 November 1947 was damp, cold and grey, and chill mist hung about the streets of London. Elizabeth, quiet and nervous, didn't speak a word as her wedding dress was being fitted by the dress designer, Norman Hartnell, and his assistants, and her own maids who took just over an hour to dress her. And she didn't speak while her hair was being dressed and the tiara fitted. But she did react when no one could find her bouquet of white orchids, appealing to everyone to search everywhere for the missing flowers. Maids, servants, pages literally ran through palace apartments searching for the missing flowers. With only minutes to go, a maid discovered the bouquet in the porter's lodge icebox, put there to keep the orchids cool and fresh until the last minute.

And there were further dramas. Her 'sunray' tiara, a gift from Queen Mary, that she wore to hold back her headdress, snapped in half as it was being put on. Elizabeth panicked. But the down-to-earth Queen Mary, who was in the room at the time, rescued the situation. 'Don't worry my dear,' she said, 'there's time and more than one tiara in this palace.' She called for another. Then it was discovered that Elizabeth's double-pearl necklace, given as a present by her parents, had mysteriously disappeared until someone realised that it had been put on public display with all the other 1,500 wedding gifts at St James's Palace, 300 yards down the Mall. John Colville, Elizabeth's able private secretary, was dispatched to collect it but, with all the security surrounding the palace that day, he only just made it back to the palace in time.

Nevertheless, despite the hitches, Elizabeth left for the abbey on schedule. She rode with her father in the Irish State Coach, her veil off her face, a royal custom to allow the people to see the royal bride. Along the route, thousands who had spent the night heavily wrapped against the chill night gathered to cheer and wave, but there were not the wild celebrations that had greeted VE-Day two years earlier. Many women in the crowd shouted 'God bless you! God bless you!' as the royal coach trundled past. Elizabeth hardly smiled. She looked tentative, even nervous, as her father waved regally to the crowd and held her hand.

In the marriage ceremony Elizabeth insisted on including the word 'obey' though she was always to out-rank her husband from the moment they became husband and wife. Elizabeth believed her promise to obey would help Philip understand that she intended to be a good and dutiful wife. In turn, Philip promised the non-smoking Elizabeth that on their wedding day he would give up smoking cigarettes forever, which he did, though it took considerable will-power – he had become a chain-smoker during the war.

Philip, standing tall and erect in his naval uniform, placed the gold ring, fashioned from the same Welsh nugget from which Elizabeth's mother's ring had also been made for her wedding in 1923, on his bride's finger.

Back at the palace the 150 guests sat down to the wedding breakfast but the meal was interrupted by a crescendo of noise from the 150,000 people who had broken through police barriers and rushed towards the palace. They kept chanting, 'We want the bride, we want the bride', until Elizabeth and Philip went out on to the balcony and waved to the crowds. Two hours later, after non-stop demands to see the bride once more, Elizabeth and Philip again went on to the balcony.

For King George, Lilibet's wedding was not a time for rejoicing and happiness, for his heart was heavy at losing her. Afterwards, he wrote to her, 'I was so proud of you and thrilled at having you so close to me on our long walk in Westminster Abbey, but when I handed your hand to the Archbishop I felt that I had lost something very precious. You were so calm and composed during the service and said your words with such conviction, that I knew it was all right.' He signed it, 'Your ever loving and devoted Papa.'

To many who attended, the royal wedding has never been forgotten. One of the bridesmaids, Lady Elizabeth Longman, 23 at the time, remembers: 'The wedding was the first ray of sunshine during that austere period after the war when there was still rationing. The lovely bridesmaids' dresses with the pearl-trimmed satin bows on the skirts made me feel life was on the up and up again. And I still treasure the lovely silver powder compact Philip gave to all the bridesmaids. But it's so precious I never use it.'

After the ceremony, Elizabeth finally relaxed and pictures show her looking radiantly happy. She was not to know, of course, but her strikingly handsome husband was to bring her many tears and much unhappiness. Neither of them could have foreseen that one of their bridesmaids, the pretty, vivacious, 11-year-old Princess Alexandra, Elizabeth's first cousin, would play such a remarkable part in their lives.

Elizabeth and Philip spent their honeymoon at Broadlands, the lovely country home in southern England which belonged to Uncle Dickie Mountbatten, the man who had plotted, planned and worked for eight years to bring the couple together. Elizabeth could not have found a more peaceful and beautiful house, set in 350 acres of stunning country. But it was not to be. The press that would plague much of their married life discovered their hideaway and were at the gates.

3. YOUNG PHILIP

The man who would live a life of absolute privilege, indulged by wealth and surrounded by pomp, servants, maids and courtiers, was born on 10 June 1921 on the dining-room table of a rented summer villa on the Mediterranean island of Corfu. An after-thought baby, Philip was the son of Prince and Princess Andrew of Greece, and the youngest of five children. The only boy, his nearest sister Sophie was seven and his mother, Princess Andrew, had turned 36 at the time of his birth.

The imposing Regency-style villa that served as his birth place boasted balconies and terraces, but no gas, electricity, inside lavatory, running hot water or heating of any sort. There was a bathroom of sorts but water had to be carried to the bath. Only the kitchen possessed a cold water connection. The lavatories could be found at the bottom of the garden. Though architecturally elegant throughout, the villa was not in good decorative order. The reason was simple. When Philip was born, his parents, though officially royal, were all but poverty-stricken. They even had problems paying the rent on their villa which they were obliged to pay three months in advance.

Philip was one of those numerous royal descendants of Queen Victoria and her consort Albert, who produced nine children. Today, Victoria and Albert's descendants number nearly seven hundred.

Philip's grandfather was the King of Greece, but he was in fact Danish. Born in 1845, he was the second son of King Christian IX and Queen Louise of Denmark. In 1863 the Greeks, searching for a monarch for their throne, approached young Prince William of Denmark and invited him to be their king. Following years of Turkish rule, only non-Greeks were eligible.

Prince William, then an 18-year-old lieutenant in the Danish navy, did not want to live in such a faraway, backward place whose language he could not speak or understand. His father, however, was adamant and ordered him to take the throne, going so far as to threaten his son with imprisonment if he did not obey. Reluctantly, William was crowned King George of the Hellenes but he soon fell in love with Greece and its people and became a passionate Greek. Four years later he married Olga, the granddaughter of Tsar Nicholas I of Russia, and together they raised seven children. Andrew, Prince Philip's father, was the second youngest and born in 1882.

While Prince Philip clung to many old-fashioned ideas, his grandfather seemed remarkably modern, holding three-hour-long sessions on Monday mornings in his palace where any citizen could come to air his or her grievances. His wife Olga, the queen, devoted herself to charities and good works, modernising hospitals and jails and pushing through penal reform.

And yet, despite his efforts to improve the lot of the Greek nation, King George was never universally popular and, after surviving several assassination attempts, he was eventually shot dead after the end of the First World War.

Philip's father, Andrew, joined the Greek army at the age of 14. His day would begin at 6 a.m. with a cold bath and would be followed by intensive physical training and education in every facet of war. Five years later, aged 19, he was commissioned into the cavalry.

In 1903, Andrew married Princess Alice of Battenberg, a great granddaughter of Queen Victoria whom he had met at the coronation of Britain's King Edward VII in 1901. He had fallen passionately in love with the fair-haired young Alice, then 17, and described at the time as 'the prettiest princess in the whole of Europe'. Alice's younger brother, Louis, 15 years younger, would become Earl Mountbatten of Burma and a major influence on Philip, Queen Elizabeth II and the entire British royal family.

Philip's mother was described as beautiful, indomitable and strong-willed. She was also deaf but managed to learn to lip-read. Remarkably, by the age of 20 Alice could lip-read in four different languages. Prince Philip's father and mother returned to Greece, set up home and raised a family, but his father spent much of the time away, enjoying the army life he loved. To start off their married life they had received some money from royal relatives who had collected a small fortune for them to live off. But it was not to last long.

Philip's father was something of a dandy. He sported a monocle and cut a dashing figure in his cavalry officer's uniform, and, like his son, he enjoyed jokes and making people laugh. He had no income other than the paltry pay of an army officer which meant that after the wedding gifts had been spent there was very little money on which the family could survive. Though they were always poor, and often lived in real poverty, Prince Andrew insisted on keeping a valet even when there was virtually no money to feed and clothe their five children.

The politics of Europe at that time forced Prince Andrew to leave the army because of his royal connections. When his experience and military acumen were needed, Prince Andrew was brought back into action, and in 1920 he was invited to return and promoted to the rank of Major-General. He later took command of an Army Corps. He described the officers and troops under him as 'riff-raff', 'undisciplined' and 'ill-trained'. He also had little regard for the Commander-in-Chief, whose orders he disobeyed, believing him to be incompetent. He even argued openly with the Army Supreme Command when admonished for his arrogant behaviour. To many, it seems Andrew's arrogance was passed on to his son, Philip.

But disaster and near-death were at hand. In 1922, Andrew commanded the 5th Army Corps of the ill-equipped Greek army, then deep in Turkish territory. The Greeks were attacked by the famous Turkish General, Kemal Ataturk, and forced out of Asia Minor, parts of which Greece had occupied for 2,500 years. Tens of thousands were killed and a million Greek refugees fled before the advancing Turks. Andrew's brother, the king, was overthrown by a military junta and exiled while politicians and senior officers judged responsible for the defeat were imprisoned and put on trial. At the first of the trials the six accused were found guilty and the following morning executed by firing squad.

Philip's father learned that if he resigned his commission he would be allowed to retire to Corfu and live there with his family. Philip was just one year old. But a month later the junta arrested Andrew, brought him to Athens and tried him in the Chamber of Deputies by a jury of junior officers. The jury had decided before the trial took place that Andrew should be found guilty and shot. Accordingly he was found guilty of disobeying orders and abandoning his position in the face of the enemy. He was sentenced to death.

Philip's strong-willed mother was determined she would save her husband's life. She travelled to Athens and appealed to the junta but to no avail. Then she sent letters and telegrams to the Pope and the most powerful crowned heads of Europe – nearly all relatives – pleading with them to intervene and save her husband's life.

Prince Andrew was brought before the Greek dictator Pangalos and asked, 'How many children do you have?'

'Five', Prince Andrew replied.

Pangalos smiled and commented in a quiet voice, 'Poor little orphans.'

In desperation, Alice telegraphed her 21-year-old brother, Louis Mountbatten, and urged him to appeal directly to Britain's King George V. The chances of help from Britain were slim because Greece, and the Greek royal family, had been pro-German during the First World War and, understandably, feelings were still running high in the early 1920s. But Louis Mountbatten not only secured an interview with King George V, but persuaded him to come to the rescue of his distant relative Prince Andrew and his young family. George V called his Foreign Secretary Lord Curzon and ordered him to do all in his power to rescue Prince Andrew, going so far as ordering him to send a gunboat to Athens in case it might be needed.

Commander Gerald Talbot, a member of the little-known British secret service, had served as Naval Attaché in Athens. With false papers and an assumed name Commander Talbot travelled from Geneva, where he was then stationed, to Athens. He arrived in the Greek capital and arranged a meeting with the Dictator Pangalos, a man he had known earlier in his diplomatic career. In no uncertain terms Pangalos was informed that if Andrew was not released unharmed, the British Government, at that time the most powerful force in Europe, would view the new Greek government as its enemy.

Pangalos refused and accused Britain of interfering in the internal affairs of Greece. Prince Andrew had been found guilty, he said, and justice must take its course. Andrew would face the firing squad the following morning. Pangalos informed Andrew's younger brother, Prince Christopher, who had rushed from Paris to Athens in an effort to save his brother's life, that he would not be allowed to see him. Pangalos reported, however, that Andrew was waiting philosophically for death.

As Commander Talbot was making his final, dramatic appeal to Pangalos, an aide rushed into the room and stammered, 'Sir, there is a British warship in the bay.'

HMS *Calypso* had arrived, the Royal Navy ship was at action stations, its mighty guns raised, and trained on the government offices. Pangalos was furious, swearing and shouting at Commander Talbot. But within the hour, the British Commander had extracted a promise from Pangalos and the other revolutionary leaders that Andrew would not be shot.

The following day, Andrew was brought before the court again. The judge ordered him to be stripped of his military rank and all royal titles and banished from Greece for life. His honour had been dealt a mortal blow but he had escaped with his life. That night, Pangalos himself, along with Commander Talbot, drove Prince Andrew by car to the waiting HMS *Calypso* where Princess Alice was waiting to welcome her husband aboard.

Word was sent to Mon Repos on Corfu and the entire royal family – nearly all of them women, save for 10-month-old Philip – were told they had only a few hours to pack and leave the island. Princess Sophie, Philip's older sister who was eight at the time, recalled later, 'It was a terrible business. Absolute chaos. My sisters had to get everything ready. I remember everyone rushing around, packing what they could. Except for Philip it was all women with Greek ladies-in-waiting, a French governess and an English nanny. All we took with us were a few suitcases with our personal belongings; the rest we left behind.'

The entire family trekked down to the port, with Philip carried in a wooden fruit box. They clambered into a small boat and chugged out to HMS *Calypso* which had steamed into Corfu harbour.

Princess Sophie went on: 'The sea was very rough and nearly all of us were sick. The officers had moved out of their cabins and into hammocks so that the royal exiles could enjoy some creature comforts. We didn't realise what a tragedy it was. The officers put on a concert to entertain us all. It was all very exciting.'

Later that day HMS *Calypso* sailed into Brindisi harbour and the family and their entourage caught a train to Paris in the early hours of the next morning. After their dramatic escape from Corfu in the summer of 1922, Prince Andrew and his family settled in France, where they took a house in the grounds of a larger mansion owned by Andrew's brother, George, who had married Princess Marie Bonaparte, a rich heiress. A descendant of Napoleon Bonaparte, she was also the granddaughter of the man who had founded the famous casino of Monte Carlo.

As with other poor relations of royal families in exile, Philip led a fun-filled life in Paris. He met and mixed with many relatives and, as the youngest of the family, he was spoiled by his mother and his four older sisters. Except for his father, everyone else in the household was female. His father taught him to paint and care for animals and, from an early age, Philip had a remarkable way with those creatures. His sister Sophie remembers, 'He really loved animals and they loved him.'

To make ends meet, Philip's mother opened a shop in the Faubourg St Honoré called 'Hellas' which sold Greek products, from embroidery to honey. Despite her inability to hear she remained a strong character all her life, and Sophie recalled the redoubtable Louis Mountbatten being 'terrified' of her.

Life eventually became too much for poor Princess Alice. Her husband spent much of his time with other Greek exiles in Paris plotting their return to power. At the same time, the dashing, charming Andrew, still in his early forties and with a military bearing, found himself most popular with the fashionable ladies of post-war France. It seems, once again, that Philip was to inherit the same roving eye his father certainly enjoyed. It was no wonder that Alice was under stress as her errant husband began spending more time away from home and, she suspected, much of that time in the company of other women.

She also had to contend with the good fortune of her peers. Many exiled royals enjoyed substantial wealth and were happy to flaunt it. Alice, meanwhile, had to struggle, dressing her daughters in hand-me-downs from some of those rich relations who had taken pity on her. The family relied on two stout English women to look after the children and keep the household together while Alice tended her shop. Nanny Roose cared for Philip while the housekeeper Mrs Blower, another intrepid, capable Englishwoman, took charge of the cooking and the housework. To save money they fed the children on nourishing rice and cooked tapioca puddings. As a consequence of living in an impecunious household, Philip was taught from childhood to be prudent with his money and, to his credit, despite the wealth into which he has married, Philip never lost that deeply instilled lesson.

The female-dominated household found that the more time Philip's father spent away from his family, the naughtier and cheekier his son became. Nanny Roose reported that Philip was a cheerful little boy who liked his own way but frequently misbehaved. He also demonstrated ferocious energy. His cousin Alexandra remembers holidays at the seaside: 'Philip would wander off and return later without explanation with torn clothes, cuts and bruises. He seemed to adore climbing trees, the taller the better.'

Alexandra recalls one hilarious incident at home when Philip, then nine, released the pigs from their sties and drove them on to the lawn where the adults were sitting enjoying an elegant tea party. The stampeding pigs, with Philip beating them with a stick to drive them forward, caused havoc with the ladies, scattering them and upsetting most of the tables. Before they could catch and punish the naughty Philip, he had run from the scene.

As Philip grew older he became more aggressive, extrovert and bossy. He would flaunt the fact that he was a Prince, but he was never snooty. His English nanny and housekeeper instilled in him the English way of life, English manners and, of course, the English language. It made life much easier for him when he went to school in England, when he joined the Royal Navy and, more importantly, when the time came for him to marry the future Queen of England. In truth, Philip was a child with no country and no feeling of tradition or destiny, all of which he seems to have learned from his nanny and the housekeeper who had watched over him until he was ten years old.

Philip became very friendly with Hélène Foufounis, four years his senior and the youngest daughter of the wealthy Greek family who also lived in exile in Paris. Hélène and Philip became close as children and they were to become a great deal closer in later life. Hélène would later talk of their life together: 'At first I was jealous of him because everyone, especially my mother, loved him, with his blonde hair and angelic smile. At first we disliked each other, but later became friends and spent lots of time together, frequently staying at each other's homes when we were growing up. Our nannies were strict with us, spanking us frequently. We were not even allowed to talk at table unless spoken to, which wasn't very often.'

Nanny Roose spent much of her time trying to control young Philip, and remembered chasing the naked boy along corridors when he escaped from his baths; persuading him to come down from high trees; bathing him after he splashed through muddy farmyards; and trying to stop his favourite holiday sport – dashing fully clothed into the sea.

Philip's mother was also at her wits' end over her four daughters, two of whom were now in their twenties with no marriages in sight. Alice would have hoped and expected her good-looking daughters, of royal blood, to find husbands. But as the 1920s wore on, the daughters of Europe's old royal families became less wealthy and less of a catch. As life grew harder, Alice seemed close to collapse.

In 1931 Princess Alice, with very little emotional or financial support from her husband, suffered a breakdown. Exiled royals paid for her trips to various sanatoria in Switzerland which ordered complete rest and relaxation. But there was some good news for the family. Within eight months, between December 1930 and August 1931, all four daughters were married, and all four married members of the German aristocracy. The family home at St Cloud was closed and the few members of staff dismissed.

Meanwhile, Alice's husband Prince Andrew had fallen in love with a most attractive and, significantly, wealthy widow, Madame Andrée de la Bigne, a former actress. She owned a small yacht, the *Davida*, which she moored in the sunshine of various Mediterranean ports, usually in southern France. She became Prince Andrew's lover and constant companion and they would spend the summer months happily sailing their boat and the winter living in her villa in the south of France. Any hope of returning to Greece faded and Andrew, with a growing fondness for fine French wines, was happy to forget the worries of his life and his family; he drifted into early retirement, happily relaxing in the sunshine with his mistress.

During her years in various European sanatoria, Alice 'discovered' religion and, for the rest of her life, wore a nun's black habit. Eventually, she returned to her beloved Greece to found her own religious order, the Christian Sisterhood of Martha and Mary. Thus contented, she devoted herself to good works forgetting her husband and her family of five children.

Prince Andrew and Princess Alice never sought a formal separation or divorce and hardly ever bothered to contact each other. In those days royalty did not ever contemplate divorce; it was simply never an option to be considered, unlike the young royals of today.

While Philip's mother suffered a breakdown and continued to live in a sanatorium, his father virtually abandoned Philip, then ten years old. Philip was sent off to Cheam, a centuries-old English preparatory school for the rich, selected because other relatives of Prince Andrew's family had been educated there. His father didn't even pay for the boy's education. A less than average student, Philip nevertheless excelled at cricket and other sports. He did win one prize – for French – probably due to his having spent the first ten years of his life in Paris.

During the holidays Philip sometimes stayed at the home of his uncle George, Marquess of Milford Haven, at Lynden Manor, Holyport, a pretty village not far from Windsor. Uncle George became for a time Philip's unofficial surrogate father. He had married Nadejda, always called Nada, a great-granddaughter of the famous Russian poet Alexander Pushkin, a dark, attractive, sexually alluring woman in her thirties and a practising lesbian. She had fallen in love only a few years before with her own sister-in-law, the wealthy Edwina, Louis Mountbatten's wife. In the early 1930s she also fell in love with Gloria Vanderbilt, Sen. Philip spent much of his time at Lynden Manor, a great Victorian folly, with Nada and Gloria Vanderbilt and sometimes with Edwina, an odd sexual environment for a young, pubescent boy.

As Philip's surrogate father, Uncle George paid for his nephew's school fees and attended prize-giving days. And it was Uncle George who first talked to the young Philip about a career in the Royal Navy.

Uncle George owned one of the most extraordinary and comprehensive pornographic book collections in Europe. The library also contained albums of photographs of various people and groups of people having sexual intercourse in every possible position. There were also books on sado-masochism, bondage, whipping, thumb-screws and racks. He also collected odd advertisements for dildoes, vibrators and condoms. George would apparently sometimes play out his violent sexual fantasies with the lovely Nada.

In 1934, Gloria Vanderbilt became involved in a sensational court case over possession of one of the world's wealthiest children, her own daughter and namesake. Mrs Vanderbilt's former maid had accused her and Nada of being lesbians, testifying that she had seen them kissing passionately in her bedroom in Cannes, a charge which Nada emphatically denied. Nada refused to go to the United States to give evidence and, as a result, Gloria Vanderbilt successfully defended the accusation.

As a teenager Philip looked like the quintessential blue-eyed, blond, athletic teutonic boy. He spent most of his school holidays overseas with his sisters in their German castles and learned to speak German fluently. Occasionally, though not very often, his father would visit him during those holidays in Germany.

At 13, Philip attended Gordonstoun, the Scottish school where he would later send his own three sons. He met the founder of Gordonstoun, Kurt Hahn, an eccentric German Jew, while staying with his sister at Salem, in Germany. Philip was to say later: 'Even then Hahn was an almost legendary character. Small boys do not normally have much time to be impressed by other boys' masters, but there was an air about Hahn which commanded instant wariness and respect. Apart from that, his famous mannerisms – the stooping gait, the ball of handkerchief in his mouth, the large-brimmed hat and the flashing quizzical eye – all helped to signal the presence of an exceptional being.'

Originally, Philip was to be raised in Germany, live at Salem with his sister and attend Hahn's school there. But, shortly after Philip had begun at Salem, Hahn was forced to flee Germany fearing he would be murdered by the Nazis. Not before Philip had caught Hahn's irreverence and contempt towards the Nazis, however. The Nazi salute amused Philip greatly because in England, whenever a boy wanted to leave the classroom to go to the lavatory, he would raise his right arm and seek permission to leave the room. To Philip, the sight of thousands of soldiers giving the Nazi salute *en masse*, raising their arm asking to go to the lavatory, struck him as hilarious as well as stupid. And he never forgot it.

In 1990, Philip wrote of Hahn, 'None of that family at Salem was at all enthusiastic about the Nazis so it was thought best that I should move out!!' (The double exclamation marks are his.) Hahn found refuge in Scotland and there reopened his school in a house named Gordonstoun near the cold waters of the Moray Firth. When the school opened in 1934 Philip was one of its first pupils.

Hahn's philosophy of education was a mixture of the teachings of Plato, the Boy Scout movement and the traditions of the English public-school system. Hahn was convinced that it was the education provided by the British public-school system that had ensured England's victory over Germany in the First World War. Despite its eccentricities, Gordonstoun flourished and Philip thoroughly enjoyed his years there.

Jim Orr, later to become Prince Philip's private secretary, was head boy at the school when Philip arrived. He remembers, 'Philip was very friendly, with a sense of fun and known for his white, white hair.'

Both at Cheam and Gordonstoun Philip was a boy with no surname. He was called plain Philip and on formal occasions 'Philip of Greece', but he never boasted about his royal connections, preferring to keep his background a mystery. Many of the Gordonstoun boys had little idea of Philip's royal background and saw him as more of an orphan, since his parents never visited the school.

Besides Uncle George, Philip had another surrogate father, his sister Theodora's husband, Berthold of Baden. Despite being his brother-in-law, Berthold was many years his senior and taught Philip to fly fish and drive a car when he was a teenager. 'He was a major influence on my character,' Philip would comment later.

Uncle George, Philip's principal guardian, contracted cancer in 1937 and died a year later. It must have been a shattering blow to Philip, who had just turned 16. Rootless once more, his family dispersed, his parents living separate lives in different parts of Europe, and with no home to call his own, the young man had now lost not only his real father who had abandoned him, but also the man whom he had respected as his surrogate father.

When Philip left Gordonstoun, Hahn wrote of him, 'His best is outstanding; his second best is not good enough. Prince Philip will make his mark in any profession where he will have to prove himself in a full trial of strength.' That challenge was fast approaching.

With war looming it was inevitable that Philip should join one of the armed services. His grandfathers had served at sea, his father was a career army officer and both his father's and his mother's brothers had gone into the navy. Philip loved flying and wanted to join the Royal Air Force but his uncle Louis Mountbatten persuaded him to find a place in the Royal Navy.

Following the death of Uncle George, Mountbatten began to play a much larger role in Philip's life and invited his nephew to stay at his home. So well did they get on that Mountbatten invited Philip to consider himself at home in Broadlands. Mountbatten seemed to want to 'adopt' Philip – to be the son he always wished for but never had. (Mountbatten and Edwina had two daughters: Patricia, born in 1924, and Pamela, born in 1929.)

At 18, Philip joined the Royal Naval College at Dartmouth where potential young officers were trained and, helped by his experience of Gordonstoun life, he enjoyed naval life immensely. He liked the discipline, the formality and the camaraderie of the officers' mess which he found similar to Gordonstoun. In the Royal Navy proper, Philip felt secure for the first time in his young life.

On June 22 1939, ten days after his eighteenth birthday, Prince Philip met HRH Princess Elizabeth, then a shy girl of 13, for the first time. Her father, King George VI, who had succeeded to the throne three years earlier, was aboard the royal Yacht with his daughters Elizabeth and Margaret on their visit to the Royal Naval College, Dartmouth. Captain Lord Louis Mountbatten, Philip's uncle, was in attendance as the king's aide-de-camp. The most ambitious of men, Louis Mountbatten wanted success not only for himself, but also for his new-found surrogate son, Philip.

Mountbatten arranged that among all the young men at the Naval College that day, Philip – a tall dandy-haired, strikingly good-looking young man – would be selected to show the young princesses around Dartmouth.

Elizabeth and Margaret's governess 'Crawfie' wrote in her royal memoirs that Elizabeth said at the time of that first meeting, 'How good he is!' When Philip jumped over the tennis net, she exclaimed, 'How high he can jump!' In fact the young couple did not play tennis, because Elizabeth had never been taught to play properly, but they did enjoy a game of croquet in which Margaret, aged nine, joined in. Crawfie was not so sure of the young show off. She wrote, 'He was good-looking though rather offhand in his manner and rather bumptious. I thought he showed off a good deal, but the little girls were much impressed.'

When the *Victoria and Albert* sailed from Dartmouth that evening all the cadets took to rowing boats and sailing dinghies to wave goodbye. Prince Philip took a single row boat. One by one the other boats fell away leaving just one, manned alone by Philip striking out far into the sea behind the royal yacht. Standing at the stern, Elizabeth, with a pair of large naval binoculars, watched as Philip rowed on. He was ordered to return but, Nelson-like, he ignored the order. Then he too, with a wave, turned his little boat around as young Elizabeth continued her vigil until he was out of sight.

From that day Elizabeth never forgot the handsome Philip. She may have been a very young, immature 13 year old; yet a chord was struck at that first meeting which survived not only a devastating war but long, long periods of separation. According to Sir John Wheeler-Bennett, who wrote the official biography of King George VI, 'This was the man with whom Princess Elizabeth had been in love from their first meeting.' The biography was read and approved by Elizabeth when she was queen and she did not change a single word of that sentence.

Britain declared war against Hitler on 3 September 1939. Philip, at 18, went on active duty, serving on Royal Navy ships. But he was kept out of harm's way because Greece was still neutral and it would not have been diplomatic to have a Greek prince killed in action. Philip was posted as a midshipman to a battleship, based in Colombo, Ceylon (now Sri Lanka), but he wanted to see action. He wrote to his Uncle Louis Mountbatten who at that time was a Captain in the Royal Navy. In return, Mountbatten wrote to Vice-Admiral Harold Tom Baillie-Grohman requesting that he take his nephew and, when Italy attacked Greece, Philip was posted to the admiral's battleship, HMS *Ramilles*, in the Mediterranean. The admiral recalls, 'One day I spoke to the young Philip and told him that as a foreign subject he would not be able to rise above the rank of acting sub-lieutenant unless he became a naturalised British subject. Philip replied that he wanted a career in the Royal Navy. He then went on to say that his uncle had ideas for his future, saying that he thought he could marry Princess Elizabeth. I was totally taken aback and asked if he was fond of her. Philip replied "Oh yes, very fond, I write to her every week."'

In the spring of 1940, Midshipman Prince Philip was transferred to HMS *Kent* and then HMS *Shropshire* before Italy invaded Greece in October 1940 and Philip was free to join the war proper. Within months, the Admiralty, with further nudging from Mountbatten, transferred Philip to HMS *Valiant*, one of the Royal Navy's most modern battleships, then on patrol in the eastern Mediterranean.

Philip first saw action in January 1941 when *Valiant* bombarded Bardia on the Libyan coast. A few days later *Valiant* was the target of German dive-bombers and Philip wrote about the attack in his logbook with youthful excitement. In March, a few weeks later during the Mediterranean Battle of Cape Matapan, Philip was put in charge of the light used to pick up and illuminate the Italian enemy ships during night-time battles. He concentrated so intently on his job that he took no notice of the warning of shots being fired from the Italian fleet. He wrote in his log, 'The result was that the binoculars were rammed back into my eyes and the flash almost blinded me . . . Luckily the searchlight was not affected so that when I was able to see something again the light was still on target.' The Italian fleet, comprising a battleship, eight cruisers and fourteen destroyers, was routed by the British and, for his gallantry, Midshipman Philip was 'mentioned in dispatches'. His senior officers on board considered the award 'well merited'.

When Philip had first joined HMS *Valiant* his fellow officers suspected that because Prince Philip of Greece was royal and Greek – he was in fact sixth in line to the Greek throne – he would prove to be a rather effete, highly favoured officer. However, they were impressed that he employed no airs and graces, and surprised to discover his keenness and efficiency. With his conspicuous gallantry at Matapan, Philip had won his spurs.

A few months later, Uncle Dickie had taken command of HMS *Kelly*, a new Javelin-class destroyer with six 4.7 inch guns and two quintuple torpedo tubes, when German Junkers dive-bombers blew the ship out of the water. Tim Heald in his biography of Prince Philip recalls the story: 'As a bedraggled Mountbatten, still covered in oil, came ashore only 24 hours after *Kelly* was sunk in the Battle of Crete, almost the first thing he saw was the cheery, grinning face of his nephew Philip.'

According to Mountbatten, Prince Philip roared with laughter at his blackened uncle. 'You look like a nigger minstrel!' he said, which was typical of the racist remarks he would sometimes make throughout his life.

Philip was promoted to sub-lieutenant in 1942 and later that year to first lieutenant when sent to HMS *Lauderdale*, a Hunt-class destroyer. On that ship he first met Mike Parker, a first lieutenant in the Australian navy. Parker, just a year older than Philip, would become one of Philip's closest friends over the next 20 years. An orphan, Mike Parker would serve as Philip's equerry and private secretary. The fact that neither had any family brought them closer together. Soon after they met, Philip was posted to another destroyer, HMS *Wallace*, escorting the Canadian landings in Sicily in 1943. When that vessel was harboured in Valetta, Malta, for an extensive refit, Philip joined another destroyer engaged on convoy duty up and down the east coast of Britain, searching for the dreaded 'E-boats', the fast 40-knot speedboats armed with twin torpedo tubes that wreaked heavy damage on British merchant ships.

In 1944 Philip left the European theatre for the Pacific to fight against the Japanese. Mike Parker now served on a sister ship and the two were in the Pacific in September 1945 on their respective ships when they escorted the USS *Missouri* into Tokyo Bay when Japan finally surrendered.

Whenever they were together, Mike Parker and Prince Philip got on famously and shared many of the same interests, thoughts and attitudes towards women. Ever since the war Philip has played down any suggestion that he had had any sexual experiences or any love affairs during those war years. However, it would have been extraordinary indeed if Philip had not enjoyed any sexual activity whatsoever from the age of 19 until he married 8 years later. Mike Parker hinted as much when he commented sometime after the war, 'There were always armfuls of girls.'

Mike Parker and Philip often took leave together and spent time ashore in North Africa and in various Australian cities. During the Second World War the world's ports were notorious for drunkenness, brothels and prostitutes. And there were also numerous highly respectable young women who also loved to be seen with sailors whom they realised were at sea most of the time fighting the enemy.

'Of course we had fun in North Africa,' Mike Parker recalled, 'but never anything outrageous. We'd drink together and then we'd go and have a bloody good meal. People have always asked, "Did you go to the local brothels and screw everything in sight?" We'd reply, "No! It never came into the picture. There was so much else to do."' But many suspect that the faithful Mike Parker might have been telling a little white lie, happy to protect the reputation of the friend who became the consort to Queen Elizabeth of England.

But in Alexandria in Egypt, Philip and Mike Parker certainly visited nightclubs which were, in effect, brothels. They would consume copious amounts of Stella beer, watch the belly dancers and drink with the girls who would come to their tables, sit on their knees, encouraging the young officers to buy high-priced alcohol and then offer themselves for the hour or the night. Other fellow officers saw Philip and Mike attending these clubs, surrounded by young prostitutes and dancers. The two young lieutenants also visited clubs which involved wild sex shows, including the most lewd acts involving young women and donkeys. The naked girls carried out all the known and varied sex acts but it was the animals which everyone remembered.

Philip came into his own during visits to Melbourne and Sydney. Mike Parker was Australian and he introduced Philip to society ladies and their daughters who were most impressed to meet a prince of royal blood.

Alexandra of Yugoslavia, Prince Philip's cousin, wrote a biography of him in which she said, 'Philip hit feminine hearts, first in Melbourne and then in Sydney, with terrific impact.' Those who knew Philip back then recall that the girls were 'lining up' to be introduced to the handsome prince. One hostess, a middle-aged Sydney woman involved in charity work put it bluntly: 'The girls were queuing up to bed him. He was gorgeous, and royal.'

When asked if Philip did in fact bed any girls, she replied, 'What! Of course he did; he was a real ladies' man. He loved his time in Australia. He had a whale of a time.'

On occasion, Philip would swap identities with Mike Parker when they both sported full beards. Philip loved to play that trick on girls because he wished to know whether the girls wanted him for himself or simply because he was a royal prince. The gamble paid off because as Mike Parker he found he also scored with the girls he had sought out. That was why he persuaded Mike Parker to repeat the charade on a number of other occasions; he felt it was a boost to his ego.

Of course, Philip also had to conduct himself correctly on other occasions when his ship sailed into port. As a royal prince he was expected to attend official cocktail parties and dinners, especially if the British ambassador was in the vicinity. He tried to escape such duties because he much preferred to spend shore leave with his fellow officers enjoying all the pleasures of life. But Philip also knew that it was at such parties that he would usually meet some of the loveliest and most eligible young ladies who were looking for escorts if not potential husbands. And a royal prince, even an unknown Greek without a throne, was considered a catch for many of the young women, particularly with Philip's good looks and sense of fun.

According to brother officers who served with him at the time, Philip had numerous affairs during the war, both in Britain and overseas. On most occasions Philip remained remarkably discreet but when he had had a little too much to drink he would become more open about his conquests. As one fellow officer put it, 'Philip always loved to be the centre of attention, loved to be surrounded by pretty girls and loved to be able to take his pick. He could sometimes be arrogant in his approach to girls, adopting a take-it-or-leave-it attitude to which some took offence. But he was hardly ever without a female companion and most were girlfriends in the fullest sense of the word. He certainly loved the girls and they were certainly attracted to him.'

Occasionally Philip would visit Elizabeth while on leave in England. He would sometimes be asked to lunch at Buckingham Palace and if ever he was in England at Christmas time, he would be invited for Christmas dinner at Windsor Castle along with other ex-royals living in Britain at that time.

But throughout his life, Philip has always been remarkably reticent about his affair with Elizabeth. Talking to his official biographer Basil Boothroyd in 1970, Philip said, 'I went to the theatre with members of the royal family once during the war, or something like that. And, at other times during the war, if I was here [in England] I'd call in and have a meal. I once or twice spent Christmas at Windsor, because I'd nowhere particular to go. I thought not all that much about it, I think. We used to correspond occasionally. You see it's difficult to visualise. I suppose if I'd just been a casual acquaintance it would all have been frightfully significant. But if you're related – I mean I knew half the people here, they were my relations – it isn't so extraordinary to be on a kind of family relationship terms. You don't necessarily have to think about marriage.'

However, Philip did not reveal the whole truth to Boothroyd about his relationship with the teenage Elizabeth. They used to meet occasionally at Coppins, the country home of the Duchess of Kent, when they would walk together in the grounds and take tea alone together. They would also stay for lunch or dinner and it was during those meetings that Lilibet fell in love with her handsome prince. Those secret meetings cemented her love for the gallant naval lieutenant. And many biographers believe that was why Elizabeth never tried to find any other eligible man to marry. She had made up her mind that she wanted to marry Philip, and she was determined to do so, despite considerable opposition from many people, including her own parents.

Philip later told Boothroyd, 'I did not think about marriage until 1946 when I was invited to stay at Balmoral. I suppose one thing led to another. It was sort of fixed up. That's really what happened.'

Philip, naturally reticent about showing his feelings in public, appeared to be the perfect husband for the young teenage girl who would one day be Queen of England. Pictures taken before and after their engagement show a formality between the two which makes their relationship seem strained, if not forced. None of the pictures show a young couple madly in love with each other; there was nothing in their body language suggesting love or even affection between them. In every photograph and film clip Philip seemed to be on his best behaviour, determined to show respect for Elizabeth, as though he should act with the utmost decorum because his fiancée would one day become queen.

But the man who persevered, who worked hard behind the scenes to cement the relationship, was the irrepressible Lord Louis Mountbatten. He saw in Philip the once-in-a-lifetime opportunity to stamp the Mountbatten name on the oldest and most prestigious monarchy in the world, the British throne. Mountbatten went out of his way to ensure that the young, impressionable teenaged Lilibet saw Philip whenever possible throughout the war years. He would speak to her about Philip whenever they met, which was quite frequently in the latter days of the war, since Britain's war-time Prime Minister Winston Churchill took the ambitious Mountbatten under his wing and promoted him to positions of considerable power and influence.

Mountbatten would tell Lilibet where Philip was serving, what he was doing, how the war was going for him. And he would provide snippets of information so that Elizabeth's interest and attraction to Philip would be sustained despite the months of forced separation. Elizabeth evidently understood that she had to be patient but she would read the newspapers, listen to the wireless and listen to commentators urging wives and girlfriends to wait patiently for their loved ones fighting the Nazi threat. Elizabeth also followed the example of tens of thousands of other women: the future Queen of England would spend hours in the evening knitting socks for the young man in her life.

Elizabeth had been educated and trained by her mother and tutors to devote her life to duty above all else: duty to the nation, to the British people and to the vast British empire on which, at that time, the sun never set. And Elizabeth believed in her heart that waiting for her prince was part of that duty.

Throughout the war she kept a black and white photograph of Philip beside her bed in Windsor Castle, showing Philip's face with a full, sandy-coloured beard. Her sister Margaret recalled that every night Lilibet would kiss the photograph before going to sleep. She also recalled that her sister diligently wrote to Philip every week, confessing that before going to sleep each night she would kiss his photograph.

From the little Philip has said about his courtship of Elizabeth, it does appear that their relationship was remarkably formal on his part. It was Elizabeth, excited by the relationship, who dreamed of love and who wanted to be loved by her sailor prince. For his part, Philip showed great restraint, more a formality of courtship rather than a passion, so very different from all his other love affairs.

The courtship of Elizabeth by Philip seemed more like a game of chess, with the grandmaster Mountbatten in control of half the board, advising Philip how to conduct himself. For the marriage Uncle Dickie wanted to secure for Philip was of vital importance, such was his determination to cement the Mountbatten family to the House of Windsor. He advised Philip to treat Elizabeth with respect, to never take advantage of her in any way; to remember that he was five years older and to treat her like a flower that needed to be nurtured.

Mountbatten also made Philip realise that Elizabeth was precious, not just to her family but to the nation. He also told him that if, by chance, they were to marry then he must understand that his position as her husband would be one of privilege which he must never forget, for he would be the consort of the queen, the most important person in the kingdom. Philip took the advice but his actions during much of their marriage show he took scant notice of it.

Margaret has revealed that she would sometimes see Philip and Lilibet walking together in the grounds of homes where they had met when Philip was 'courting' her; that she would see them walking side-by-side talking and occasionally holding hands, but that she never saw them kiss or cuddle or embrace passionately. She said that whenever the two of them were together on a sofa, both appeared rather distant towards each other, Philip not daring to appear too pushy or over-eager. They always appeared reticent, even awkward, as though fearing that any passion might break the spell of correctness between them.

As a midshipman, Philip was required to fill in every day the admiralty form S.519, a record in his own language of anything important or interesting that had occurred that day. Whenever one of Philip's ships docked in a port around the world, whether it was South Africa, Egypt, Cyprus, Gibraltar, India, Ceylon (now Sri Lanka), Australia or the Far East, Philip would record many, although not all, shore leaves with an exclamation mark. According to one of Philip's brother officers, that was Philip's sign to remind himself of a romantic liaison in that port.

Philip wrote after leaving Durban in HMS *Kent*, 'The fact that many hearts were left behind in Durban is not surprising.' But on that occasion there was no exclamation mark.

Whenever Philip had shore leave in London, Uncle Dickie would try to ensure that he saw Elizabeth, whether just for tea or a meal. There were, however, many other young socialites, as well as ambitious mothers, who were most keen that this good-looking young prince, Philip of Greece, should meet their daughters and other young debutantes. He was inundated with invitations to dinners, to house parties and weekend gatherings. No one in London society circles knew at that time that Philip was in fact courting Elizabeth, nor did anyone have the slightest idea that the teenage princess had any thoughts as to whom she might one day marry.

It was not until 1943 when Lilibet had turned 17 that Philip let it be known that he was indeed courting the heir to the throne. She was, of course, still seen as far too young to fall in love and her father George VI was not at all happy when the queen told him that Elizabeth was infatuated with Philip. King George had no wish to lose his daughter, especially at such a young age. But Queen Elizabeth saw how love-struck her daughter had become with Philip and she persuaded her husband to allow the romance to continue and 'let love take its course'.

For a while during 1943, Philip's ship HMS *Wallace* went into dock for a refit and Philip stayed in the attic of Uncle Dickie's house in Chester Street, Belgravia, less than a mile from Buckingham Palace. For most of that time Mountbatten continued in command of operations in south-east Asia while the extremely wealthy Lady Mountbatten worked devotedly with the Red Cross. It meant that the young Philip had the house to himself.

That Christmas, the governess 'Crawfie' had the opportunity of really studying Philip when he came to the palace. She wrote: 'He was greatly changed. It was a grave and charming young man who sat there, with nothing of the rather bumptious boy I had first known about him now. He looked more than ever, I thought, like a Viking, weather-beaten and strained, and his manners left nothing to be desired.'

Crawfie added, 'Lilibet acted better than she had ever done before. She was animated; there was a sparkle about her.'

From that Christmas on Philip began to correspond openly with Elizabeth and it was common knowledge to those aboard his new ship, HMS *Whelp*, a ship of the 27th destroyer fleet, then engaged against the Japanese in the Pacific, that Philip's girlfriend was in fact

Princess Elizabeth. Understandably, it won him both admiration and respect.

Back in London those close to King George and his wife, including those who worked in Buckingham Palace as well as the other royal palaces, heard the rumour that Princess Elizabeth, now 18, had fallen in love and that her intended husband was Prince Philip. Few people, particularly members of the aristocracy and the Establishment, could imagine for one moment that the heir to the British throne would be permitted to marry a Greek prince! It was of no concern to them that he was so good-looking or that he was a prince of royal blood. And they ignored the fact he had descended from Queen Victoria. He just wasn't English or British.

Louis Mountbatten had always realised that Philip's genealogical background could prove an impediment to his marrying Elizabeth. He understood that following such a devastating war the British people might not be too keen on the young, innocent Princess Elizabeth marrying someone of foreign blood. Some aristocrats, even distant members of the royal family, like Queen Elizabeth's brother David Bowes-Lyon, described Philip as simply 'un-British'; others described him unfairly as 'a ghastly foreign fellow'. But they had the hugely ambitious and highly intelligent Mountbatten to contend with. He would not let the matter rest, and Philip commented, 'There was much to-ing and fro-ing about my adoption of a surname and just as much argument about the house name', referring of course to the royal House of Windsor, or whatever other name Philip would take if he should marry Elizabeth.

The quick-tempered Philip saw no reason as to why he should not be eligible, as Prince Philip of Greece, to marry the British Princess Elizabeth. He was related to Queen Victoria in just the same way as Elizabeth was descended from her. He had been proud to be called Philip, Prince of Greece, despite the fact he had only lived there for the first year of his life. He liked the title because his father had been a member of the Greek royal family, though, of course, not in any way Greek himself. He let it be known that if the authorities decreed he could no longer keep his title then he wanted to be named officially 'Lieutenant Philip'. But that would not do. The grey men of the palace decreed that he had to have a proper surname.

Amazingly, in the circumstances, Home Secretary Chuter Ede suggested that Philip should take his mother's German family name which was officially Schleswig-Holstein-Sonderburg-Glucksburg. The last thing any self-respecting Englishman, particularly any members of the aristocracy, or anyone who had just fought in a war against Germany, wanted at that time was for Princess Elizabeth to marry a 'Bloody Bosch'!

And there were further problems. All four of Philip's sisters had married into the German aristocracy and two of their husbands had actually fought against the British crown as officers in Hitler's forces. That was enough for many people, especially the average Englishman, to bar Philip forever from even dating Elizabeth, let alone asking for her hand in marriage. Some believed that he should be banished from Britain and only a small minority thought he should be permitted to marry into the royal House of Windsor.

It was Uncle Dickie who suggested that Philip take his surname, Mountbatten. It sounded British and Philip had no objection, especially as Uncle Dickie had done so much of the work behind the scenes to bring about his nephew's marriage to the British crown.

Those weeks and months following the end of the war were a difficult time for Philip. He had no family and no home to call his own and he would spend his life living either at his Uncle Dickie's London home or in the Kensington Palace apartment of his friend Milford Haven. And there was another problem for the young Philip to contend with. He had very little money and only survived on the paltry pay of a Royal Naval Lieutenant.

John Dean, Mountbatten's butler, or Mrs Cable the cook, spent much of their time caring for and feeding young Philip who would arrive looking for a bed for the night or the weekend. Mrs Cable recalled, 'Philip would ring the door bell and I would find him standing on the front door step, sometimes with a suitcase, asking if it was possible to stay the night. I would always ask him if he needed a meal and he would protest that he didn't, but he was only being polite. I would get him something to eat and John Dean would take his clothes and wash and iron them so he would be presentable the following day. He hardly had any civvy clothes at all, just his naval ones. What I do remember is that he was always polite and considerate and he always carried with him a photo of the princess in a battered leather frame which he placed by the side of his bed in the attic.'

Many people, especially those who had fought and survived the war, needed to enjoy themselves and Philip did too. And yet he felt out on a limb, not knowing which way to turn. His home was in effect the Royal Navy and he clung to the hope that he would be permitted to continue his naval career when other officers were being demobbed by the thousand.

Prince Philip had learned a lot during the war. He had grown up fast, as most young men had during that long war, and now he was a mature 25 year old. He had enjoyed the companionship of brother officers and a number of young women, sharing some of the women's beds as well. Philip, who had accepted the hardship of service life, wasn't sure whether he could endure the discipline of a life married to the heir to the throne. Philip loved parties and being the centre of attention, and he loved women too. He knew he was successful with women, that he could attract women whenever he wanted to, despite the fact he had no money and no home; his good looks and sense of humour had always won through. During those months following the war he was the centre of attraction at the society nightclubs he and his fellow officers frequented. But he was discreet and, unlike many of his companions, he never drank too much nor was he ever seen misbehaving with any girl in public. He would spend weekends away from London attending house parties where he was often admired as the object of attention by many of the young ladies present. An officer who went out on the town with Philip recalled: 'Philip was always a ladies' man and he loved their attention. He always had girlfriends but he was most discreet. Occasionally he would wink when leaving a party to escort a girl back home. We had no idea, of course, if anything ever happened, but we had our suspicions. He was a lad, all right, though he never discussed sex. He kept his love life to himself. When it was officially announced he was to marry Princess Elizabeth some of us were taken by surprise, for he had always played the handsome bachelor role so well. For him to settle down with one woman seemed impossible.'

The more Philip enjoyed his bachelor life the more uncertain he felt about spending the rest of his life with Elizabeth. He believed the king objected to his daughter marrying at such a young age and marrying *him*. Though Philip did not know why, he presumed it was because of his Greek and German background.

Elizabeth told Philip of the lengths to which her father would go to persuade her to change her mind, hoping that she would fall in love with someone else. She assured Philip she wanted no one else. King George organised dances, balls and dinners at Windsor, Sandringham and at Balmoral in Scotland, to which young aristocrats were invited so that Lilibet might perhaps take a liking to one of the young men. They, in turn, were expected to dance with her and get to know her. Many of the young men enjoyed the evenings but most of them became enamoured with the lovely, budding Margaret, then 16. She was prettier, more vivacious and flirtatious than her more serious elder sister. The king made sure that Philip was not invited to those evenings. Naturally, such a snub irked Philip and made him feel inferior and self-conscious whenever he met the king. It also put doubts in his mind as to whether he should indeed continue pursuing Elizabeth.

King George went so far as to order the Special Branch to look into Philip's background, to prepare a detailed dossier on his views, politics, allegiance and sincerity. They examined his financial stability, his bank account and every detail of his naval career and war record. As a result, the king's most senior courtiers, as well as members of the aristocracy, persuaded him that Philip should not be permitted to marry his daughter because it would mean that the domineering, conniving Mountbatten would become the power behind the throne. Jealous of his meteoric rise to power and his growing influence in political circles, they all knew that Mountbatten had complete control over Philip.

King George conducted long talks with Winston Churchill about Philip and Mountbatten. Fortunately for Philip, Churchill held Dickie Mountbatten in high esteem. He viewed Mountbatten as a man of action and determination, not unlike himself, and these two characteristics he admired greatly. Indeed Churchill, who finally persuaded the king that Philip would be a valuable addition to the House of Windsor, pointed out that Mountbatten and his nephew had been loyal, obedient exemplary officers throughout the war with distinguished war records. Philip had displayed obedience and courage in the face of the enemy, just the sort of qualities required of the future queen's consort.

Queen Mary, Princess Elizabeth's grandmother on her father's side, believed Philip would make an admirable match and she informed her son of her views. As a German princess herself, who had married George V, she saw no reason whatsoever why a young man, called Philip of Greece, and in fact a member of the Danish royal family, should not marry into the House of Windsor. She noted, 'Three consorts of the same Danish royal family have married into the English royal family, supplying wives for James I and Edward VII, and a husband for Queen Anne: why not a fourth?' At a stroke she had removed the single most powerful argument against Elizabeth's intention to marry Philip.

Queen Mary had met Philip quite regularly and confided to her lady-in-waiting Lady Airlie that she found him to be intelligent, polite, handsome and eminently suitable for her granddaughter. She believed that King George had somehow persuaded his wife to find another, more suitable husband for their daughter. Numerous older, matchmaking women were entrusted with the task. No suitable young men could be found. A number of eminently suitable young aristocrats had died in the war and those considered suitable consorts who were introduced to Princess Elizabeth did not have the slightest attraction for her. No matter how hard her parents tried they were unable to shake her determination and her love for the handsome Philip.

In the summer of 1946 Philip proposed, in secret, to Princess Elizabeth, after taking Mountbatten's advice. Philip knew he should first have asked the king for his permission to marry but he did not do so because he wanted to make sure Elizabeth did really want to marry him before formally asking the king. Elizabeth recalled, 'He proposed to me by some well-loved loch, the white clouds overhead and the curlews crying.' The dream she had nurtured for seven years had finally come true.

Two days later Philip formally asked the king for Elizabeth's hand but the king could not, on his own, give permission. In any case, King George was still uncertain that Philip was the man for his daughter though he was beginning to realise the difficulty of finding someone more suitable. The king explained that the government and various Commonwealth governments had to give their approval to the marriage.

King George decided to put his daughter's intended husband to the test to see if he would fit into the family. Philip was invited to spend a month at Balmoral in the autumn of 1946. He had a terrible time and the experiment ended in disaster. Philip hated the idea of wearing a kilt. He felt it made him 'look like a sissy'. One day, as a joke, Philip curtsyed when King George came in for lunch. George was not amused. He said nothing to Philip but gave him, instead, a withering look. He felt Philip had insulted Scotland and the traditional Scottish dress.

Philip loathed everything about Balmoral. He hated the fact that he had to make do without running water in his room and complained about his noisy bedroom on the ground floor. He could not bear the formal behaviour and felt he was on parade day and night. Philip knew, of course, that he was being observed, something he considered insulting to his family. The two men just didn't get on. Everything Philip did grated on the nerves of the impeccable King George. He criticised Philip's dress sense and noted his scuffed shoes, his ill-fitting dinner jacket (borrowed from Uncle Dickie), the clothes he wore for shooting – grey flannels instead of traditional knickerbockers.

King George was also of the opinion that young Philip did not show enough deference, speaking out of turn at table and showing off in front of Elizabeth and Margaret. Philip simply rubbed up Elizabeth's father the wrong way. In turn, Philip rebelled. He became outrageous, too cheerful and overtly boisterous while the king wanted someone more like himself, someone who behaved correctly, like the archetypal rigid, Victorian officer who remained silent until spoken to. At the end of the month King George was convinced that his daughter had made an awful mistake.

Appalled at Philip's behaviour and attitude, King George asked for a special report on Philip's lifestyle. It did not make very happy reading for a prospective father-in-law who did not want 'to sacrifice' his daughter to marriage. The secret report revealed that Philip lived a carefree life with little or no discipline. His language was peppered with profanity and swear words. Philip lived most of the time in Kensington Palace with his cousin David Milford Haven and they had turned the palace into a shambles. Their rooms were described as a 'disgrace, with clothes, shoes and dirty linen strewn everywhere'. They smoked all day, lounging about the palace or speeding around London in a small, black MG sports car Philip had acquired. At night they went out on the town. It was during this period that Philip was considered by many to be arrogant and unpleasant, showing off with regard to his royal connections while seeking the attention of adoring young debutantes who were only too happy to throw themselves at him.

He was so very, very different from the girl he was to marry. Elizabeth was calm, gentle, sweet, attentive and dutiful to her parents. But she never saw the 'real' Prince Philip, the bachelor who spent most nights partying or clubbing and wining, dining, dancing and flirting with numerous young women. Elizabeth spent her evenings at home in the palace with her parents.

Philip's chauvinistic behaviour was recorded in some detail and George was understandably unhappy and disappointed when Elizabeth told the father who adored her that she had said 'yes' to Philip, adding she hoped it would be possible for them to marry as soon as possible.

King George believed it was his duty to dissuade his daughter, to save her, as he saw it, from marrying such an arrogant man, though granting he was 'damned' handsome. In the autumn of 1946, King George informed his daughter that she first had an important duty to perform, to accompany the family the following year on a ten-week trip to thank the people of South Africa for sending soldiers to the mother country during the war. Secretly, King George hoped the trip might persuade Elizabeth to change her mind.

As the royal family set sail to South Africa on board HMS *Vanguard* in January 1947, King George gave strict instructions that Philip was not allowed to board the ship to say farewell to Elizabeth, nor even be permitted to wave farewell from the dockside. It was the same when the family returned ten weeks later. The king had ordered that no one should know of the real relationship between Philip and Elizabeth.

Philip spent those ten weeks enjoying a bachelor life in London, throwing dinner parties at Mountbatten's London home and frequenting nightclubs. On her return, the young couple began to see more of each other and Philip escorted her to the theatre, to dinners and to the more respectable nightclubs. The press began to report that Elizabeth and Philip now acted like any other young couple in love. The newspapers were full of pictures of them together and the royal watchers wrote of an impending engagement.

For Philip, the announcement of a formal engagement would, in one respect, cause him severe embarrassment. He was unofficially engaged to be married to one of the world's wealthiest heiresses and yet he himself didn't possess more than a few pounds. When their engagement was finally announced in the *Court Circular* in July 1947, Philip, the king's future son-in-law, had precisely £6.10s in the bank and his sole income was a naval lieutenant's pay of £11 a week. He had no home and no family. Nearly destitute, his entire belongings could fit into a pair of suitcases. His entire wardrobe consisted of three naval uniforms, one lounge suit, a blazer and a pair of grey trousers, an evening dress and a shooting jacket, plus some underwear. The only socks he owned were all darned!

Officially, the royal announcement read: 'It is with the greatest pleasure that the king and queen announce the betrothal of their dearly beloved daughter the Princess Elizabeth to Prince Philip RN, son of the late Prince Andrew of Greece and Princess Andrew, to which union the king has gladly given his consent.'

The king had given his consent but with considerable reluctance. Philip celebrated by joining his friends for a night on the town and became outrageously drunk. Now it did not matter that he had no earthly possessions or prospects. He would never have to worry again. He was going to be rich and powerful for his entire life. And he was only twenty-five.

4. BRIDE, MOTHER AND QUEEN

Elizabeth and Philip spent their wedding night – 22 November 1947 – in a magnificent four-poster Tudor bed with an ivory satin padded bedhead, heavy damask covers and pink sheets. The room had been decorated with Salvador Dali gouaches. Edwina Mountbatten, Uncle Dickie's wife, had loaned them her luxurious suite which included separate dressing rooms and a lavish bathroom at Broadlands, the country home she had inherited. It was not until the following morning, however, that they saw the wonderful picturesque view from their bedroom window, across the Test River valley and the forests beyond.

After attending the wedding, Mountbatten and Edwina returned to India where Dickie Mountbatten had been appointed governor-general, and left the young couple to enjoy their honeymoon alone in the beautiful Palladian-style mansion. Looking after their every need was the ever-faithful Bobo and Philip's valet, the chatty John Dean. Also on hand were Frank Randall, the butler, and Charles Smith, Mountbatten's valet.

The couple spent early December walking and riding and lounging around a roaring log fire in the Broadlands sitting room. And Elizabeth had taken her favourite corgi, Susan, with her, for company. Nothing was spared for the royal honeymooners. They feasted on pheasant, lamb, beef and veal and freshwater fish from the Test, washed down with excellent French wines. They drank champagne cocktails before dinner and Elizabeth insisted that each night they dine by candlelight. Their honeymoon at Broadlands was the only time they were to share a bed on a permanent basis throughout their entire married life. As soon as they returned to London they were given separate bedrooms at Buckingham Palace and forever more Elizabeth and Philip have, except on the rare occasion, slept in separate rooms.

Unfortunately the press and the public discovered the place the couple had chosen for their honeymoon and would not leave them alone. Until then, Elizabeth's relationship with the press had been idyllic. Journalists had respected her privacy and she would happily give time for photographs to be taken. The Fleet Street newspaper editors decided the nation wanted more of the fairytale wedding. After years of war, death and destruction they wanted to provide the king's subjects with something that would bring a little sunshine into their lives.

Whenever the couple left Broadlands, reporters and photographers pursued them in cars and even followed them on horseback. Because it was winter and the leaves had fallen, photographers would climb trees to get a better view, even training binoculars and their 'long-tom' lenses on the couple's bedroom.

When the couple attended morning service at Romsey Abbey, more than one thousand people beseiged the church, arriving with ladders, chairs and step-ladders in order to catch a glimpse of the honeymooners through the church windows. Even headstones on the graves were pulled from the ground so they could be stacked up to give people a better view. Unused to such treatment by the press and an army of well-wishers, Philip felt besieged in what was meant to be a quiet, idyllic country honeymoon far from the madding crowd. After one week Philip had had enough and the couple cancelled the last week of their planned honeymoon, returning to Buckingham Palace. Later they spent another week at Balmoral, hidden from the prying eyes of an adoring public and the lenses of Fleet Street.

Understandably, Philip was furious. Fleet Street had nearly ruined their honeymoon. It was the start of his life-long tempestuous relationship with the press, particularly photographers. During the honeymoon he showed an anger and frustration which was to erupt many, many times over the following decades. On several occasions, Philip, his eyes blazing, screamed at the press to go away, and when that didn't work he lost control: 'Leave us alone!' he yelled.

King George had decreed that Elizabeth and Philip should be given Clarence House as their London home, but when they went to inspect it they were in for a shock. Clarence House, in the Mall, where the Queen Mother has lived since her husband died in 1952, had been left derelict for decades. The rooms were still lit by gaslight, the interior walls were covered in mildew, ceilings had fallen down, bomb damage to the roof and top floor had gone unrepaired and there was no central heating or running hot water.

To make matters worse, Philip found it difficult – after his wartime adventures in foreign lands – to settle down to a mundane married life. In order to be near his young bride, he had been given a desk job at the Admiralty which he hated. He would walk to and from work each day, even in the snow and rain, from their temporary home in Buckingham Palace, through St James's Park to his office. Dressed in his mackintosh and trilby hat, Philip would travel the mile on foot, unnoticed and unrecognised by the general public. He showed little happiness and no *joie de vivre* for a young man in love. Much of the time he seemed petulant and short tempered with those he worked with at the Admiralty and he was no fun at home either.

In public it seemed Philip had difficulty coping with his new royal life and he resented having to take second place behind Elizabeth. On a visit to Paris in May 1948, when Elizabeth was three months pregnant, Philip appeared to be moody, unpleasant and even rude to people while his wife, despite the effects of morning sickness, smiled and put a brave face on everything. But even she looked angrily at him when Philip yelled at a photographer he had found hiding under a table during an official dinner engagement.

Back in London Philip continued to show signs of frustration, discontent and even regret. In public he would hardly ever smile and seemed to be stern, even sullen, as he accompanied Elizabeth during her official engagements. In private he always wanted his own way, rewriting speeches, trying to cut through red tape, demanding that he be consulted in matters which really were of no concern to him, only his wife, the heir to the throne. He found it difficult to cope, especially when he discovered that things he had ordered to be done were not carried out because higher authorities had countermanded his orders.

The man who in the past had asserted his masculine pride so forcefully now hated living in the palace, where he had to conform to all the rules, the rigid formality, the protocol and had to accept being waited on hand and foot. He was also prevented from having much time alone with Elizabeth during the day.

Though only 21, Elizabeth showed the resilience and obedience to duty that became a mark of her entire life, attending functions, dinners, luncheons and official ceremonies even when six months pregnant. Philip became so fed up and intolerant of life at the palace that he took a staff course at Greenwich Royal Naval College so that he could live with the other officers rather than at the palace, with all its petty restrictions.

Philip showed no signs of settling down and, in desperation, he turned to his old friend Michael Parker. They would go out for a drink together in the evenings, to the London nightclubs that were doing a roaring trade in post-war Britain. It was only with Michael that Philip seemed to relax, and he poured out his frustration to his fellow naval officer and comrade in revelry. Parker knew how to deal with Philip, how to make him laugh as they talked of their times together in the war, their drinking bouts and the various women they had both loved and left.

Philip discovered that as Duke of Edinburgh and husband to Princess Elizabeth he was entitled to an equerry and he was determined that Mike Parker should be that man. An equerry would be Philip's factotum, his secretary, friend and adviser, paid for by the Crown. During those final few months of Elizabeth's pregnancy, Philip spent more and more time with the engaging, fun-loving Mike Parker, further cementing the strong bond between them.

Throughout 12 November 1948, Elizabeth's nursemaid, Bobo, spent most of the day comforting her and sitting by her bed holding her hand throughout the early stages of labour. Philip popped in to see how Elizabeth was progressing but spent much of the day with Mike Parker.

At 9.14 p.m., just two hours after going into labour, Elizabeth gave birth to a 7lb 6oz rosy, plump, healthy and bawling little boy. King George VI and Queen Elizabeth were informed minutes after the birth, the king cheering as he walked into the makeshift hospital ward in the Buhl Suite at the palace. Philip, who had been playing squash and swimming with Mike Parker, arrived with his hair still wet. Parker brought a bottle of champagne and a huge bouquet of Elizabeth's favourite flowers – camellias, lilies, carnations and roses. He gave them to Philip who handed them over to Elizabeth. A forty-one gun salute was fired in Hyde Park, the bells of St Paul's and Westminster rang out for three hours and bonfires were lit across the country.

Both Elizabeth and Philip had decided beforehand that if the baby should be a boy he would be named Charles Philip Arthur George. It had been 300 years since a King Charles had last sat on the English throne and the name did not bring memories of past glories: King Charles I had been executed in 1649 after losing England's Civil War against the parliamentarians and King Charles II was renowned for a reign of licentious behaviour and merriment following the dour years of Cromwell's military rule. But Charles was Elizabeth's favourite name.

For a few weeks Elizabeth insisted on breast-feeding Charles but it wasn't long before his nurse, Helen Lightbody, took complete charge of him. It seems extraordinary today, yet, within three months of his birth, Elizabeth had begun her strict routine of only seeing Charles twice a day, for an hour after breakfast in the morning and for a further 30 minutes each evening around 6 p.m. Otherwise, Charles never saw his parents. Helen Lightbody and nurse maids were given absolute responsibility for bringing up the future heir to the throne. It wasn't that Elizabeth didn't love her baby boy, although many will argue that such short daily meetings with him could not have produced any worthwhile bonding between them. It was simply the way in which members of the royal family believed babies should be treated by their parents; left to someone else to nurse, educate and train. That had been royal tradition since Queen Victoria's days and Elizabeth and Philip saw no reason to alter the routine. It shows how little Elizabeth had been exposed to everyday life, for after the Second World War the accepted view was that bonding between mothers and their babies was of the utmost importance to the development of the child.

Only months after Charles's birth, Elizabeth travelled throughout Britain, visiting her future subjects while undertaking royal ceremonies and exposing her unhappy and truculent husband to the public gaze. Philip would ignore people or speak to them gruffly, hardly ever smiling or waving to the crowds who had turned out to welcome the young couple. In public, Philip continued to behave in an off-hand way rather than as the loving husband of a royal princess whom he was meant to assist and help as she went about her duty. So fed up did Philip become that he decided to seek re-enlistment in the Royal Navy to escape his role as consort to Elizabeth.

Informed of the couple's formal relationship, King George was understandably outraged at the reports he received. Suffering from constant insomnia and dreadful pains in his legs caused by arteriosclerosis, King George believed Philip should behave more warmly to his beloved daughter. She had taken over many of her father's royal duties and yet Philip seemed to give her insufficient support, earning for himself a reputation for tetchiness and truculence. The fear King George had always harboured about Philip's arrogant personality was proving correct, that he was a penniless young man with little to offer but good looks who now strutted around as if the world owed him everything. He complained bitterly to his wife about Philip's behaviour but she tried to allay his fears, saying that Elizabeth still seemed happy and that was all that mattered.

Elizabeth pleaded with Philip not to go back to sea. But he

insisted. Then she pleaded with him that if he did insist on rejoining the navy then he should stay in home waters so that he could be near her and baby Charles. Elizabeth also told him that because her father had become so ill she needed to be near him. Philip, however, would have none of it. By ignoring Elizabeth's pleas, as she daily watched her father slowly dying in considerable pain, many wondered how much love Philip really had for Elizabeth.

He demanded that he not only be allowed to return to the navy but that he be permitted to serve overseas. Much to Elizabeth's sadness and distress he resumed his duties in Malta on 17 November 1949, joining the destroyer HMS *Chequers* as First Lieutenant and second-in-command. But Philip was not put to sea immediately so Elizabeth, with her father's blessing, flew out to the Mediterranean and spent six glorious weeks with her husband staying at the Governor's house. She tried to understand her husband's view and forgave his selfish behaviour. Alone with her bronzed Viking prince and enjoying Malta's sunshine and carefree friendliness, Elizabeth felt as though she was on a second honeymoon.

Never more happy and relaxed, she became 'a naval wife', having her hair done at the local hairdresser, swimming and sunbathing, and dancing with Philip by moonlight. Elizabeth, then 23, loved the practical jokes Philip, then 28, played on her, like chasing her down corridors wearing a huge pair of false teeth or putting a dummy snake in her powder box. She became so intoxicated with happiness that when news came through that Charles, now one year old, was ill with tonsillitis, neither she nor Philip returned to London. Nor did she return home to be with her son at Christmas. She flew back to London in early January when Philip's ship put to sea. It was not surprising that she found herself pregnant again.

Philip had been posted to the Middle East and was happy to be back at sea; but he began complaining to senior officers that, given he was husband of Princess Elizabeth, he now found it difficult taking orders from other officers, despite the fact they were his seniors. He made it clear that he was desperate for command so he pestered his Uncle Dickie to secure for him the captaincy of his own ship. Uncle Dickie, then Flag-Officer commanding the 1st Cruiser Squadron in the Mediterranean, told his nephew he would 'see what he could do' but urged him to be patient. Mountbatten also introduced his nephew to one of the great joys of his life – polo, a game on which Mountbatten was an authority and, when younger, a very good player. Philip fell in love with the sport and was to play for nearly twenty years.

Finally, on 15 August 1950, Philip heard that he had achieved his life-long ambition and been given command of his own frigate, HMS *Magpie*. The day he was gazetted a Lieutenant-Commander was the day, as luck would have it, that his daughter Anne Elizabeth Alice Louise was born.

In command of his own ship at last, Philip was in his element. Determined to be the best ship's captain in the entire fleet, he worked his ship's crew to breaking point, demanding greater discipline and harder work, determined to prove himself no matter the cost. In the annual regatta his ship won six of the ten boat events and Philip himself was seen stripped to the waist, rowing stroke, as he led one of the whalers to victory. It was the life he loved. Here he was at home.

Once Elizabeth had finished breast-feeding Anne, she flew out to Malta again to spend more time in the sun with her beloved Philip. The Admiralty decided that HMS *Magpie* should become a floating embassy and they made official visits to a number of Mediterranean countries including Greece, where Elizabeth met some of Philip's relations. The *Magpie* became known in the navy as Philip's private yacht. For two wonderful years Philip was on cloud nine enjoying the naval life he loved, revelling in command of his own ship, playing polo whenever on shore leave and enjoying occasional visits from Elizabeth.

Back at Buckingham Palace, there was growing concern for the king's health and it was believed Elizabeth might soon have to take over as Regent. The senior palace advisers decided Elizabeth would have to assume yet more of her ailing father's duties and, more importantly for Philip, that he would have to accept indefinite leave from the navy and accompany his wife during her official assignments. Philip was given no choice whatsoever in the matter. He was told he was expected to return to his wife's side and that he had no alternative. It was his duty.

Back home, Philip once again became impatient with staff at the palace – moody and unpleasant. In public he would try to smile and be pleasant on most official occasions but back home at Clarence House and at the palace he was rude and offensive to the staff, who tried to keep out of his way.

In January 1952 Elizabeth and Philip set off for a royal tour of Australia and New Zealand. It was decided they would stop over in Kenya for a few days to see the wedding present given them by the people of Kenya, the Sagana Royal Lodge, a lovely hunting lodge at Nyeri. On their second night Elizabeth was still asleep when Philip heard tapping at the window shortly after dawn, and went to investigate. It was Mike Parker, 'I'm afraid I have the most terrible news', he said, 'The king is dead.'

'My God,' said Philip. 'Are you sure?'

'Yes, it's been confirmed,' Parker replied.

Philip closed the window and went to wake Elizabeth with the news. She was devastated, at first refusing to believe that her beloved father had died, and desperately upset that she had not been at his side at the end. She burst out crying. Bobo, who was polishing Elizabeth's shoes in the next room, heard her. She immediately went into Elizabeth's bedroom and held her close, comforting the grief-stricken young woman to whom she had been a second mother for most of her life.

Mike Parker recalls, 'The next day I saw Philip and it seemed the weight of the world had suddenly descended on his shoulders. I never felt so sorry for anyone in my life. He looked awful.'

In reality, it was the moment Philip had dreaded, for now he wasn't just married to the heir to the throne, but to the queen, the sovereign, the monarch and that meant he would have to take his place, walking two paces behind her for the rest of his days. The dreams he had of returning to sea and to a long career in the Royal Navy had disappeared forever.

As the British Overseas Airways Corporation four-engine Argonaut landed at London airport the following day, Elizabeth saw the line of black limousines waiting and commented, 'Oh, they've sent those black hearses.' She was using the childhood description she and Princess Margaret had always given the royal cars. But this time the limousines not only meant the death of her beloved father but also the end of her own youth.

For Philip, too, that homecoming would end the fun-loving relationship he had enjoyed with Elizabeth and shatter forever the chances of their enjoying a life together. The role that Philip would play for the rest of his life became clear before they had even left the plane. As he went to escort Elizabeth down the aircraft steps he was told by Sir Alan Lascelles, the late king's private secretary, that he could not do so. Her Majesty had to descend the steps alone and he could follow a little way behind.

As Elizabeth descended the aircraft's steps she saw her government ministers dressed in black, looking most sombre, for the occasion demanded it, standing with bared heads on the freezing wind-swept tarmac. They had come to welcome home their new monarch. Winston Churchill was the first to greet her. The occasion affected him more than anyone. He could not control the tears that welled in his eyes and coursed down his cheeks as he bowed to the twenty-six-year-old queen. For Churchill realised the massive responsibilities that lay before her, knew that she was ill-equipped to cope, and that the death of her father meant an end to any prospect of a normal, happy married life for the young woman who walked so lightly down the aircraft steps towards him.

The realisation that Elizabeth had become queen did not fully take effect until the following day when she was escorted to St James's Palace, next door to Clarence House, to meet her Privy Council. Snow fell outside the tall windows as Elizabeth, dressed in black, entered the chamber to join the 192 councillors arrayed in dark suits before her, headed by Winston Churchill. In a young, clear, high-pitched, child-like voice, Elizabeth read out the declaration of her accession and spoke of the heavy duty laid upon her so early in life.

Indeed she was not allowed to forget it. And much of the blame for the effect on Elizabeth must be laid at the door of Churchill himself, along with her father's dear friend and adviser Sir Walter Monckton and Sir Alan ('Tommy') Lascelles. Uncle Dickie Mountbatten must also take some of the blame for he knew Lilibet, as he always called her, better than all the others, and yet he too would spend hours with the young woman lecturing her unnecessarily. The ambitious Mountbatten was to become even more closely involved with Elizabeth and her family as he sought to unite the two families ever closer.

During the first months of her reign all four men spent hours at a time drilling into Elizabeth the gravity of her responsibilities, the burden of her duties. They talked of the all-important mantle that had fallen upon her and the mammoth task that lay ahead in steering the ship of state with the same firm hand and resolute determination that had been shown by her ancestors, her father King George, her grandfather George V and her great-great-grandmother Queen Victoria. And those were the actual words and phrases her advisers used to illustrate to the poor, young Elizabeth the reality of her future life. It was no wonder she felt so ill-prepared for the job ahead.

Understandably for a young woman who had led such a cloistered life, Elizabeth knew very little about the politics of the nation and nothing about party politics. She had, of course, grown up believing that Winston Churchill, Britain's war-time Prime Minister, had saved the nation from Hitler and his mighty German military machine. She revered him as many other young people did at that time. And it was left to Churchill to explain to her some of the intricacies of British party politics. He would spend hours with her, drilling her for weeks, explaining what was happening, and what had to be done.

Undoubtedly, Elizabeth had much to learn from the 78-year-old Churchill who wanted to be her teacher and professor, her guide and mentor, educating her in the ways of the world. He appeared paternal towards his young pupil and enjoyed their hours together. Inexperienced, naïve and grossly ill-educated for the task before her, Elizabeth came to rely, even depend, on the great man for support and advice. As one of Churchill's contemporaries put it, 'He believed he was teaching her how to be queen; he had this sense of history and of destiny and he wanted to be the man who had educated her into the job. And, to a great extent, he did.'

Sir Walter Monckton, later elevated to the peerage as Viscount Monckton of Brenchley in Kent, was the English lawyer who became attorney-general to Edward, Prince of Wales in 1932. He had been friendly with Edward since they were at Oxford together. It was Monckton who acted as go-between during the abdication crisis of 1936, negotiating on Edward's behalf with Prime Minister Stanley Baldwin, and it was Monckton who wrote the king's abdication statement. He even attended the later marriage of the Duke and Duchess of Windsor and after the king's exile he continued to advise him. His brilliant mind, integrity and coolness under pressure earned him the respect of King George VI and he became his closest unofficial adviser throughout his 16-year reign. Never a week would go by without Monckton coming to the palace for a glass of whisky and a chat with King George.

Monckton had become so important to King George that even after his own divorce and re-marriage in 1947, which at that time would have banned him from ever setting foot in the palace again, he was still welcomed as a valued and trusted friend and adviser.

After Monckton's divorce, George VI told him, 'Of course you understand that it may not be possible from now on for you to enter the palace by the front gates, due to the social consequences of your divorce, but I want you to understand that the back door is open to you twenty-four hours a day and I hope you will make frequent use of it.' That was, of course, a remarkable invitation from George VI given the strictures placed on all divorced people at that time, for the rules of the disciplined Queen Mary were then observed to the letter.

Understandably, then, Elizabeth also turned to Sir Walter, who at that point was 61, and she sought advice from him on many matters. She felt she could trust him, simply because her father had put so much faith in his advice and would see his friend two or three times a week to discuss all manner of subjects, not solely the affairs of state.

It was heavy stuff and, in retrospect, many believe those four old men, all in their sixties and seventies, were too heavy-handed in the way they 'educated' the young Elizabeth during those months, giving her little chance to settle into her awesome new life.

Churchill was particularly worried that Elizabeth had been poorly educated for her new role as monarch, and constitutional lawyers were brought in to explain and educate in every aspect of the monarchy and the sovereign's duties. Elizabeth felt as though she was on a crash course which she would have to learn at this first and only attempt, for there would be no second chance. She felt under great pressure, over-awed by her new role, but she was desperate to learn and determined to succeed.

Other elderly men were also advising her, including the then Archbishop of Canterbury, Geoffrey Fisher, a former headmaster who at sixty-five was the man who crowned young Elizabeth queen in Westminster Abbey in June 1953. As Archbishop of Canterbury, Geoffrey Fisher became the monarch's most important clergyman. He was always on hand offering advice. There were no young people at all at hand to advise Elizabeth, nor did anyone think it necessary or right for anyone approaching her age to help in the process of advising and educating so young a queen. As a result, Elizabeth saw her new role as monarch as a most serious and burdensome one which she took extremely seriously. Not surprisingly, she changed almost overnight.

Before her father's death, Elizabeth was seen as a happy, sometimes extrovert young woman, and those who met her at dinner parties or balls with Philip noted how much she seemed to love him. People who attended weekly polo matches at Windsor Great Park, where she enjoyed watching Philip play, noticed a dramatic change from one season to the next. As princess she was always there, walking around the pony lines, patting the ponies, feeding them lumps of sugar, smiling at everyone, chatting with friends and taking a great interest in the matches, particularly when Philip played. The following season the smiling, fun-loving side of Elizabeth had disappeared and she wore the look of a grave, even solemn person, straight-faced, unsmiling, almost humourless. It seemed her entire character had changed within a matter of months. Photographs taken during those two years show a marked change in her attitude and appearance.

In her everyday work at the palace, she was not helped by the presence of her austere, rather bloodless, bespectacled Principal Private Secretary – her most important adviser – Sir Alan Lascelles.

He was tight-lipped, impeccable and precise, but exactly the wrong person to be advising an inexperienced young woman who sought warmth and understanding, and perhaps even a little humour in her hour of need.

Months later Elizabeth seemed to have adopted the mantle of monarchy, almost like a shroud, not helped by the fact that the court was still in mourning and she was always pictured in black. From that time on Elizabeth came to be seen by the public as a rather glum, unfriendly person, a sovereign who had turned sour, even. The burden of monarchy had also changed her character. Soon after the accession she told a friend, 'Extraordinary thing, I no longer feel anxious or worried. I don't know what it is, but I have lost all my timidity. Somehow becoming the sovereign and having to receive the Prime Minister, for instance, has made me feel more self-assured and uninhibited.' That was hardly the case at all, of course, but now she was playing a role.

The change in Elizabeth obviously affected Philip too. To be fair, he did try to help his wife in any way possible but it was very difficult for this macho man to assume an inferior role, even for his sovereign. He adopted an all-important criterion: he would do whatever he could to save the time and energy of his wife.

For example, Philip tried to persuade members of the palace household to come to him with matters they would normally bring to a husband rather than a wife but he had enormous difficulty persuading anyone to talk to him when there was an opportunity of speaking to the queen herself. In an interview with his official biographer, Basil Boothroyd, Philip said: 'Because she's the sovereign everyone turns to her. If you have a king and a queen, there are certain things people automatically go to the queen about. But if the queen is also the queen they go to her about everything. She's asked to do much more than she would normally do. Many of the household, of course, have to report to her and the fact they report to her is important to them, and it's frightfully difficult to persuade them not to go to the queen, but to come to me.'

Two events made Philip realise that he would never be accepted by the haughty, iconoclastic English aristocracy or the British Establishment who feared a back-door takeover of the English crown by the German Battenbergs. In truth, Philip was just a pawn in the master game that had been plotted since the beginning by his ambitious Uncle Dickie.

Uncle Dickie held the official title of Louis of Battenberg, Earl Mountbatten of Burma, whose father was also called Louis, a full-blooded member of the German Battenberg family. Philip's mother Alice was also a Battenberg. She was also the daughter of Louis of Battenberg and Uncle Dickie's brother.

The moment Elizabeth ascended to the throne Uncle Dickie called for champagne and drank a toast, shouting, 'The House of Mountbatten now reigns!' The plot he had hatched more than a decade before, when he had seen the way the 13-year-old Elizabeth had looked at his young nephew, had come to fruition and one of his life's greatest ambitions had been achieved. Of course, according to all the traditions of genealogy he was correct, for Elizabeth had married a Mountbatten. But Dickie Mountbatten's triumph would prove to be short-lived.

Uncle Dickie now advised Philip that he must send a carefully worded plea to the government for the title Mountbatten-Windsor to be used in place of Windsor in official references to the royal family. Indeed, it was Louis Mountbatten who wrote the letter and gave it to Philip to sign. The letter was sent to his old friend the Prime Minister Winston Churchill, the man who had backed Mountbatten throughout the war and had organised his rapid promotion to the very heights of military glory as Supreme Commander of Allied Forces in the Far East and later Viceroy of India. Churchill and Mountbatten had been a formidable duo throughout the war and Mountbatten now hoped Churchill would support him.

Queen Mary, herself a German, heard that Mountbatten was boasting of his great success in planting a Battenberg, under the pseudonym of Mountbatten, on the throne of England, a most remarkable feat considering Britain had fought two world wars against Germany within the space of forty years. But Mary, a staunch monarchist and a confirmed Englishwoman, could not stand Dickie Mountbatten, whom she constantly referred to as 'an ambitious upstart'. Queen Mary had been informed that Mountbatten claimed at dinners at Broadlands that a Mountbatten now reigned in Britain and she was beside herself with fury, realising of course that 'the upstart' was indeed correct. So she wrote an urgent note to Churchill informing him of the news and asking that he ensure a name change would not be tolerated.

Perhaps more than any other single person, Churchill had been responsible for the defeat of Nazi Germany. He became apoplectic at Queen Mary's news which arrived 24 hours before the official letter from Prince Philip. When he was handed the letter from Philip, Churchill exploded with rage and called an immediate Cabinet meeting to take place within the hour.

At the end of the cabinet meeting the Lord Chancellor, the Lord Privy Seal and the Home Secretary wrote a letter that was immediately sent by hand to the queen and Prince Philip. The letter unequivocally informed them that by a unanimous decision of cabinet the name Mountbatten would not be used by the royal family and the official name would continue to be 'The Royal House of Windsor'.

Ironically, it was on Elizabeth's 26th birthday – 20 April – that she signed the authorising Order in Council, which, with the stroke of a pen, ended once and for all Dickie Mountbatten's ambition. On hearing the news that the name of Mountbatten would never be used, Philip shouted in fury at Elizabeth, 'I'm just a bloody amoeba! That's all!'

Dickie Mountbatten called on Lilibet, as he always called her until the day he died, and asked her quietly why it was that she could not order her government to change the name. Mountbatten's faithful secretary for 12 years was in the room at the time. He recalled: Elizabeth explained to him:

'I tried everything, Uncle Dickie, but they wouldn't let me. They told me I couldn't change it. They told me it was nothing to do with me.'

Mountbatten asked, 'What do you mean they? Who are you referring to? Who are they?'

Elizabeth just looked at him for a moment, perplexed, her brow furrowed, and replied, 'I don't know. I don't know who they are. But they are the people who tell me what I can and cannot do. I'm always told that "they" say and do this or that but I don't know who they are. I've no idea. I never know who they are. I'm afraid there's nothing I can do.'

It was certainly true back then in 1952 and, to a certain degree, it is still true today, nearly fifty years later. Elizabeth has been advised by 'they' throughout her entire reign and she still does not know who the mysterious 'they' are. In fact, 'they' are sometimes the government, perhaps the bureaucrats, the civil servants, sometimes ministers. It is sometimes committees, of which of course there are hundreds, which are filled with mostly faceless men who advise and pass on their recommendations and decisions to the palace. Elizabeth may be the crown on top of the vast edifice that is the government, bureaucracy, armed services, the church and British society, but she really has little or no control or indeed, influence, over the great majority of decisions and recommendations that are all made in her name.

To those who believe Queen Elizabeth has the ultimate power in

Britain it is a salutary lesson, and to Elizabeth it was a lesson she learned very early on in her reign and has never been able to forget or, more importantly, change. Despite her palaces and castles, her wealth and position, Elizabeth's life has far, far more restrictions than any one of her subjects.

To Dickie Mountbatten the decision was a bitter blow. He had faced much opposition in his life because he was seen as an opportunist, but this time Mountbatten knew he could no longer pursue his life's goal. Still, he had to take care of his angry and dispirited nephew, Philip. He invited him to Broadlands where they discussed the situation. Philip told Mountbatten that he felt this decision was another effort to keep him from the pinnacle of power and influence. It bridled him that in public he always had to call his wife 'Ma'am', like everyone else, and bow whenever she entered a public room. Both Mountbatten and Philip felt they had been cheated.

Elizabeth understood Philip's anger but she also realised that she could not oppose the wishes of Queen Mary, her own mother, Churchill and the entire government. Of course she had no wish to upset her advisers or her family, even if it did mean rebuffing the man she loved. Elizabeth discussed the matter with her advisers, Sir Alan Lascelles and Sir Walter Monckton. She wanted to do something for Philip and asked them to investigate the possibilities. After lengthy talks with constitutional lawyers it was decided Philip could be given a more senior position than consort. Before the State Opening of her very first parliament in September 1952, the queen issued a declaration stating she was 'graciously pleased to declare and ordain that HRH the Duke of Edinburgh should henceforth have, hold and enjoy the Place, Pre-eminence and Precedence next to Her Majesty'.

Elizabeth felt overjoyed that she had been able to do something for her husband. Though only a gesture, it was typical of Elizabeth then. She wanted to please and pacify her husband to make him feel important, and not her appendage. And, in a bid to give Philip something of importance to do, Elizabeth decreed that he should head the council planning her coronation.

Philip, however, remained unsatisfied. The restless, energetic, angry young man could not contain himself and set about trying to revolutionise Buckingham Palace. He condemned the place as being Victorian and out of touch with reality; he castigated the senior courtiers for being place-men, promoted to office for reasons other than suitability. He determined to bring the palace up to date by constantly reminding members of the household and the royal servants, 'This is the bloody twentieth century, not the nineteenth.'

He began inspections, as though in command of a ship, trying to instil Royal Naval discipline into the palace staff. He would stride through the corridors finding fault everywhere. He would suddenly storm into servants' quarters, into the kitchens, the scullery, and other areas where he should not have ventured. He would frequently swear at cleaners, footmen, cooks and maids whenever he found a speck of dust, a dirty window or a mark on the floor or wall.

He would stop anyone he met and ask, 'Why is this done like that? Why don't you do this in another way? Why don't you use your initiative? Why don't you use your bloody brains?' Particularly when incensed by members of the household, Philip would often swear at the old retainers and threaten them, 'Buck up your ideas or you'll be out on your bloody neck.' No one, not even the sovereign, had ever spoken to any members of the royal household, no matter how lowly their position, in such a fashion.

Rumblings below stairs drifted upwards as the 400 royal workers took exception to Philip's unwarranted and insulting criticism of their jobs, their competence and their traditions. Finally, workers' representatives told senior members of the household that Prince Philip was going too far and Sir Alan Lascelles was asked to advise him as to where his responsibilities started and where they stopped – that is, to mind his own business.

As a result, a frustrated yet unbowed Philip decided to lead his own life and forget about his plan to modernise the palace and the ancient regime which he despised and ridiculed in private, and sometimes even in public. He retreated into his naval officer's shell, refusing to let flunkies carry his bags or open doors for him, yelling and swearing at them whenever they offered to help him, 'Don't you think I'm bloody well capable of carrying my own case?'

He would insist on driving himself, refuse to allow the servant who operated the ancient palace elevator to ride in it with him, dismissed the projectionist from threading and showing movies he watched, but insisted instead on doing the job himself. He even arranged to have a small kitchenette built in his rooms, equipped with the basic necessities – an oven, gas rings, a refrigerator, a small larder – so he could cook his own meals or make a cup of tea or coffee without having to go through the rigmarole of phoning and asking for something to be sent up from the kitchens which, he complained, took hours and always arrived cold.

He could sometimes be seen heaving furniture around, not only in his private rooms but also in the queen's rooms and other apartments of state simply because he was fed up with the way everything was always placed in precisely the same position. And he went further. Infuriated that he was not permitted to return to active service in the Royal Navy, he went to the extraordinary lengths of having his suite of rooms at the palace converted to look like a replica of a ship's cabin. Carpenters used beautiful African mahogany, given to him as a present on one of his overseas trips. The cabin was constructed to his exact orders, with every piece of furniture, shelving, wardrobes and lighting, designed to make him feel he was back in the Navy on board ship.

He installed a direct telephone system for himself in the palace so he could talk to anyone, including Elizabeth, directly rather than going through the main switchboard. Previously he would telephone the operator and ask to be put through to a particular party, only to find himself ringing back five or ten minutes later demanding to know why his call had not been placed. He would become increasingly angry, believing that senior household members had begun to conspire against him, refusing to let him become involved in any official matters, keeping him away from the affairs of state, from the monarchy, even from his wife, as much as they possibly could. He has, for example, never been permitted to examine the red dispatch boxes that the queen is sent several times a day, containing all government papers and the affairs of state.

In a way, of course, Philip was right. No one in government, including Churchill or any of his senior ministers, no senior civil servants, no one at the palace or any of the Establishment figures, wanted the forceful, arrogant Philip taking over the reins of power from the young wife who was so obviously in love with him and, some feared, under his spell. They knew full well the ambitions of Mountbatten and feared, understandably, that Philip might follow in his uncle's footsteps. The decision was taken to freeze him out of any position of power so that he would have no real influence on the constitution, the monarchy or over his wife.

It was the perfect example of how the British system works; no decision is actually taken, no one causes any fuss at all. There is simply a consensus of opinion that someone, even someone as important as the sovereign's husband, has no right to wield power, or influence the crown, so events unravel to ensure that he is kept away from any decision-making process. And that is what happened to Philip. Even today, at well over seventy years of age, he is unable to come to terms with the fact that he has never been accepted by the Establishment, even after nearly fifty years of marriage to the queen.

During those first few months of Elizabeth's reign, Philip's behaviour grew worse. At official ceremonies and royal functions Philip's voice would often be heard saying in a loud whisper, 'This is a bloody waste of time.' Another of his favourite remarks at that time was, 'Let's get the hell out of here.'

Such comments were obviously extremely embarrassing to Elizabeth and on more than one occasion she would give him a hard, cutting look, effectively telling him to keep quiet and be patient. It was appalling behaviour on Philip's part, especially since Elizabeth had been queen only a matter of months and was desperately trying to find her feet and act according to protocol. The last thing Elizabeth needed was for her husband to behave in such a manner. Unfortunately for Elizabeth, Philip's behaviour did not improve for several years.

Philip talked over his problems with two people, Uncle Dickie and Mike Parker. They could be of little real help. Uncle Dickie explained the system and the situation, shrugged his shoulders and told him to be patient. Mike Parker took him out for drinks and they talked scathingly about the system and the people who ran it. So Philip decided that he would, to all intents and purposes, forget his role as a royal prince, abandon any pretence that he could have any role as consort to the queen and decided instead to concentrate his life and his future on simply being about the palace, a man with a wife to protect and a family to take care of. Ironically, the man who loved to command and who yearned for power and authority, was destined to have none.

Mike Parker would provide some light relief by telling him to look on the bright side. Wasn't he married to the Queen of England, the wealthiest woman in the entire world? Wasn't he being paid, in 1953, the equivalent of £15,000 a year? Didn't he have his own secretary, his own equerry, a valet, a chauffeur and a few Rolls-Royces in which he could drive around? Couldn't he play polo every weekend, ride, shoot and fish at will, and have the run of three or four palaces? As Mike Parker frequently reminded him, 'Not bad for an impecunious naval lieutenant.'

Meanwhile there was more news for Philip that upset and annoyed him greatly. The coronation council that he headed gave permission for his three sisters to attend the grand affair but they refused to allow any of his brothers-in-law to accompany them. Philip's sisters had all married wealthy, aristocratic Germans and one of his brothers-in-law had fought throughout the war against Britain. Before the war, as a teenager, Philip had been very friendly with two of them and had frequently been a guest at their homes in Germany. Now that he was married to the woman who was to be crowned queen he was not even allowed to invite them to the coronation as private citizens. The council remained adamant and Philip could do nothing to reverse their decision and it was evident to him that he had been given a job as head of the council but with no power whatsoever.

Philip protested personally to Elizabeth, begging her to intervene, pointing out that refusing to invite his own brothers-in-law was an appalling insult to him, to his sisters, to his family and indeed to their own marriage, for the decision suggested that his family were not good enough to be invited to the coronation of his wife. Elizabeth took up the matter with her advisers and Sir Winston Churchill but they insisted that no member of the German aristocracy, some of whom had supported Hitler, could be invited to London for the queen's coronation. Elizabeth could do nothing. In an effort to appease Philip, however, she did arrange for him a wonderful surprise, promoting him to Admiral of the Fleet in January 1953. The promotion from Lieutenant to Admiral of the Fleet was an extraordinary leap by any standards, but though he wore the uniform of an admiral and was treated and respected as one, the rank was only honorary.

Despite the fact that he loved wearing the uniform and holding the rank of Admiral in the Royal Navy he was frustrated once more that he had not earned the rank as he would have wished, as his Uncle Dickie had done, working his way up through the officer corps until he had deserved the promotion. To his credit, that was the way Philip would have wished to have been appointed Admiral, not simply being given the honorary title because he was married to the queen.

Meanwhile, Elizabeth had begun to enjoy her new-found royal power. Already basking in the glory of her forthcoming coronation and her divine accession to the throne, she decreed that the occasion was to be the most splendid in British history, despite the fact that the nation was still struggling from the crippling war. She ordered all ceremonial chairs to be re-upholstered; magnificent chandeliers taken apart crystal by crystal, cleaned and refitted; mirrors re-polished; all tables French-polished; furniture re-gilded and all the livery to be examined and re-worked. The cost amounted to a staggering £7 million which at 1999 values equalled about £75 million!

As coronation day approached Elizabeth became more involved with the spiritual and religious side of the ceremony. In her first Christmas broadcast to the nation in December 1952, six months before the crowning, Elizabeth told her subjects, 'Pray for me on my coronation day. Pray that God may give me the wisdom and strength to carry out the solemn promises I shall be making.'

The Rt Reverend Michael Mann, Dean of Windsor and domestic chaplain to the queen for 13 years until 1988 commented, 'The queen looked upon her coronation in much the same way as I looked upon my ordination as a priest, or my consecration as a bishop. It is something that is indelible, that is hers, and she feels that she was called to it by God. To give it up would be an abdication of her responsibilities.'

Elizabeth had been on the throne 16 months by 2 June 1953, the day the crown was ceremonially placed on her head and she was proclaimed queen. She was still only 27 years of age, in love with her handsome husband, the mother of two children and the person the nation hoped would bring about a new Elizabethan Age, with its romantic buccaneering spirit personified by the adventures of Drake and Raleigh. The nation was looking in hope for omens that Britain's glorious history of the sixteenth century would be repeated in the late twentieth. One newspaper headline read: 'The Signs Are Bright for a Great Revival'.

The great moments of the coronation ceremony in Westminster Abbey provided the young, impressionable Elizabeth with even more proof that her life must be dedicated to the British people and those of the Commonwealth around the world, and she readily sacrificed herself to that duty. Churchill described her as 'a gleaming champion'. Backed by her advisers and the Churchill government, all were determined nothing would be spared to make her coronation a spectacle never to be forgotten. Her coronation was the first ever to be televised and though not many people in Britain owned or rented a TV at that time, thousands were rented for the day by village halls, organisations and public houses so that the nation could see the spectacle on the black and white screens. In the United States, the networks fought their first all-out battle for supremacy over who would first show Queen Elizabeth II being crowned.

Westminster Abbey was closed for months before the great event so that 7,000 tiered seats could be accommodated for those who had a right to attend; buildings along the route from Buckingham Palace to Westminster were freshly cleaned and painted, stands erected and supports for flags and decorations put in place. Her wedding may have been a rather subdued affair but Elizabeth was determined her coronation would be majestic. Of course, Elizabeth herself had to rehearse for the great day. For some weeks she walked up and down the ivory and gold ballroom in the palace, trailing behind her 60 feet of bed sheets that had been sewn together, for that was the length of her official coronation train. So worried was she about the size and weight of the crown on her head, that Elizabeth took to wearing it at her desk now and then. Sometimes the rehearsals ended in laughter when Philip, bored with the repetition, fooled around. Occasionally, a half-irate, half-amused Elizabeth would reprimand him, 'Stop being silly and do as you are told.' And Philip, with a laugh, duly obeyed.

The Earl Marshal, in charge of proceedings, had problems with the bishops who had to march in step as they walked down the abbey. Sometimes, head in hands, he would say in an exasperated voice, 'If you bishops don't learn to march in step, we will be here all night. Now come on, concentrate, pretend you're in the army, left, right, left, right.' Finally, a sergeant-major from the Brigade of Guards was brought in to drill the aged bishops until they marched in step.

Elizabeth ordered the pile of the new red carpet to be cut down because the weight of the train made it difficult for her to walk gracefully. She also feared some of the older aristocrats, resplendent in their long robes, would be unable to walk at all unless the pile was cut down. In rehearsal, Elizabeth realised the orb and sceptre were too heavy for her to hold for any length of time and the Lord of the Manor of Worksop was brought in to stand near Elizabeth throughout the ceremony to support her right arm if it should tire under the weight.

Churchill feared the three-hour coronation service would be too arduous for Elizabeth and kept suggesting parts should be cut back or missed out but Elizabeth would hear none of it – 'If my father did it at his coronation,' she would reply, 'then I will at mine.' And she would chide Churchill, telling him, 'Don't you realise? I'm as strong as a horse.'

Bobo gave Elizabeth news of the bad weather when she woke her at 7 a.m. on coronation day. It was cold and drizzling, and the 40,000 people who had lined the route throughout the night were shivering and wet through. But they braved the bad weather to ensure they kept the best positions to witness the royal spectacle.

The Lord Mayor of London led the coronation procession, typifying commerce and the nation's wealth; then followed the ambassadors and representatives of foreign countries who had come to pay homage to the new sovereign. Thirdly came parliamentary leaders, led by Churchill and accompanied by the prime ministers of the Dominions, the Empire and the Commonwealth. Finally came all members of the royal family culminating in the queen herself riding in the golden Great State Coach, drawn by eight Windsor greys.

Surrounding the State Coach were the sovereign's Escort of the Royal Horse Guards, whose duty and privilege it is, by tradition, to guard the monarch personally.

As Elizabeth made her way up the aisle of Westminster Abbey, with eight pages carrying her long train, the choir of Westminster School greeted her with the cry, 'Vivat, Regina Elizabeth, vivat, vivat, vivat!' After kneeling to pray in silence for a few minutes, Elizabeth sat in a chair of state while being formally presented to the people. Around her stood six ladies-in-waiting dressed in virginal white satin, their heads garlanded.

In a loud voice, the Archbishop of Canterbury addressed the huge congregation and presented Elizabeth as their queen, turning to the four sides and repeating his call. All shouted in unison, 'God save Queen Elizabeth.' After the final response, trumpets echoed around the abbey.

Though few could actually hear her words, Elizabeth made the coronation oath in a clear voice. It was the most solemn point of the ceremony. She promised to rule her peoples according to the laws and customs of their separate countries; promised to maintain the Laws of God, the Protestant Religion and the Church of England. Finally, kneeling at the altar steps and with her right hand on the Holy Bible, she sealed her solemn oath. 'The things which I have here before promised, I will perform and keep. So help me God.' She kissed the Bible and signed the oath as permanent witness of what she had just undertaken. And then came the anointing of Elizabeth, the most important gift the sovereign receives at the coronation, for it is by this act that the sovereign is given God's authority to rule. It is perceived as being of mystical significance, the same as an anointment in Old Testament times.

The golden ampulla, a two-handled flask in the form of an eagle, for sacred use only, was taken from the altar along with a golden spoon; four Knights of the Garter held a rich canopy of cloth of gold over Elizabeth's head; a bishop poured oil into the spoon and the Archbishop of Canterbury anointed Elizabeth, tracing a cross on the palm of each hand and on the crown of her head. A hushed silence greeted his words: 'Be thy head anointed with holy oils, as kings, priests and prophets were anointed: and as Solomon was anointed by Zadok the priest and Nathan the prophet, so be you anointed, blessed and consecrated queen over the Peoples whom the Lord your God hath given you to rule and govern. In the name of the Father, and of the Son, and of the Holy Ghost. Amen.'

Finally the moment of coronation. Elizabeth walked through to a side chapel to be robed in private. First, a long full garment of white linen and lace, which reached her feet; next, the Supertunica, a long, close-fitting belted garment of Cloth of Gold. Elizabeth was ready for crowning.

The regalia handed to her is of religious significance. The golden spurs she touched are the emblems of chivalry, of a code of behaviour in which justice is done and the poor protected. The five State Swords define the role of the sovereign, though only two are used in the ceremony. Elizabeth should have placed the Great Sword of State on the altar, signifying the submission of her temporal power to God's spiritual authority, but because of its great weight she exchanged it for a Jewelled Sword. These swords are given to her 'to be used as a minister of God'.

Three other swords, the Curtana, which has a broken blade to denote mercy, the Sword of Spiritual Justice and the Sword of Temporal Justice, were laid on the altar. A crimson and ermine royal robe was placed around her shoulders, and more regalia handed to her. The Archbishop handed over the golden, bejewelled orb, with the words, 'When you see this orb thus set under the Cross, remember that the whole world is subject to the power and empire of Christ the Redeemer.' Then the sovereign's ring was handed over as 'an ensign of kingly dignity and of defence of the faith'.

The Archbishop of Canterbury placed a glove on her hand before presenting the sceptre with the cross in her right hand, and the sceptre with the dove in her left, signifying she would rule with justice and mercy. Visibly endowed with all the symbolic powers of authority, the confirmation of actual sovereignty finally arrived with the placing on her head of the Imperial State Crown with its 3,093 jewels, the supreme sign of the magnificence and majesty of earthly power.

To many, the service evoked admiration and awe. The world saw Elizabeth, small, slight, young and unworldly, dwarfed in her magnificent, overweight monarch's robes, a huge 60-foot long train, and with a large, heavy, solid gold crown on her head, surrounded by peers of the realm resplendent in their robes. All paid homage to someone who a couple of years earlier was just a young woman in love with hardly a care in the world. It was a moving vision, but many felt that Elizabeth was being asked to shoulder too many responsibilities for someone so immature and innocent.* [See page 106]

As she stood in her robes, holding the regalia, the abbey erupted in a crescendo of noise, the 7,000 present shouting, 'God save the queen' as loudly as they could. Trumpets blared and the guns on Tower Hill fired a 42-gun salute. That was the signal to everyone in London that Elizabeth had taken her place in the succession of English sovereigns.

When the noise finally died down the Archbishop handed her a Holy Bible with the words, 'The most valuable thing that this world affords'.

Escorted to the throne, Elizabeth sat wearing the huge crown and holding the two sceptres while Princes of the Blood, Peers of the Realm and Bishops of the Church stood before her and swore allegiance.

Prince Philip's homage to his wife was proclaimed in a hushed silence as he said, 'I, Philip, Duke of Edinburgh, do become your liegeman of life and limb and of earthly worship; and faith and truth I will bear unto you, to live and die, against all manner of folks.' It was a proclamation that few men would want to make to their wives and, unfortunately, it helped increase further the physical and emotional divide between Elizabeth and her husband after just five years of marriage.

Her journey back to Buckingham Palace was even more triumphal, though the rain never let up for a moment. The procession was led by a selection of Her Majesty's forces from all over the world, the entire route guarded, shoulder to shoulder, by British servicemen. Tens of thousands of people cheered and waved every inch of the way as she sat in the Great State Coach, wearing her crown and carrying her orb and sceptre so all could witness her majesty. Elizabeth arrived back at the palace anointed, crowned, acclaimed to reign and very, very tired. All she wanted was a cup of tea.

In jubilant mood, Elizabeth walked around chatting to everyone, not wanting to take off her crown and robes. She would say later, 'I am so happy that everyone has so enjoyed the day with all the street parties, the pageantry and everything, but it was different for me. To me it was a solemn religious act of dedication. Do they realise that?'

Dermot Morrah, of the *Arundel Herald Extraordinary*, wrote, 'Certainly the sense of spiritual exaltation that radiated from her during the service was almost tangible to those of us who stood near her in the Abbey.' And poet and writer Robert Graves commented after an audience with the queen, 'The holy oil has taken for that girl. It worked for her all right.'

Even at the time of the coronation there were those who feared Elizabeth would sacrifice herself too generously. A writer for the *Manchester Guardian* commented, 'The inarticulate hopes of the multitude are centred on her person, but what should one expect of this girl? One feels that she must on no account be "victimised".

There will be a temptation for all of us to place too heavy a burden on her for our own purposes, but no human being should be used in this way.'

The world was at her feet, and the nation was praying for another long and momentous Elizabethan reign. Yet, it was all to go so terribly wrong.

The press caught one unrehearsed moment which attracted great media attention – Princess Margaret was seen innocently flicking a speck of fluff from the uniform of Group-Captain Peter Townsend as they stood together after the ceremony. The following day, news of the speck of fluff and Princess Margaret's flirtation with the handsome war hero was headline news in the United States. The matter was not even mentioned in the British press however, for the palace at that time had the most remarkable control over the media, something unthinkable today. The episode was repeated in the European newspapers, yet still nothing appeared in Britain until two weeks later when *The People* repeated the rumours of a romantic interest between Margaret and Townsend. The first scandal of Elizabeth's reign was about to erupt.

But there was a more serious, more personal side to Elizabeth's coronation. She began to believe that her role as sovereign had to take precedence over every other aspect of her existence including that of being a mother to her two children and a wife to her husband. Elizabeth began to believe in the divine right of kings, the political doctrine that monarchy is divinely ordained, that hereditary right is indefeasible, that kings are accountable to God alone for their actions. At her coronation she had been anointed sovereign by the Archbishop of Canterbury in Westminster Abbey before the sight of God; in effect she had married the monarchy. In those first few months and years Elizabeth viewed the burden of monarchy with desperate seriousness.

As a result, Elizabeth banned Philip from her bed as she believed in her heart that she had done her duty to God and to the British nation by providing two heirs to the throne and that her life should now be dedicated, totally and completely, to her role as sovereign. Elizabeth had been brought up to believe in the Victorian attitude to sex, that the prime reason was to procreate, to produce heirs. That she had done. In her mind Elizabeth simply sacrificed herself to her duty as sovereign, a divine right that had to take precedence over everything else in her life. Her royal duties did not include or necessitate any further sexual activity with her husband. To Elizabeth, that did not mean she did not love or cherish Philip, nor did it mean that he was not head of their nuclear family. It did mean, however, that all her energies, all her strength had to be reserved for her role as monarch to ensure she was able to fulfil her duty to the crown, the Commonwealth and the British people.

So over-powering had been the burden of advice from so many people that Elizabeth had been unable to cope rationally with the dramatic change in her life from princess to queen. The energetic Philip was non-plussed, confused and puzzled by Elizabeth's change of heart and the argument she put forward to him for banning him from the matrimonial bed and withdrawing conjugal rights.

Understandably, Philip tried to discuss and argue the point with her but she would simply reply that her life had changed since becoming queen and she now had a duty to God and to the nation, not just to her husband. Unable to make any headway at all, Philip turned to Uncle Dickie for advice, telling him of Elizabeth's surprising and unreasonable decision. Mountbatten cautioned against any dramatic action, suggesting that Philip should be patient and hope that in the weeks and months ahead, Elizabeth would see the error of her ways and resume their sex life. Philip was not so sure. He also discussed the matter with Mike Parker who believed that given time, Elizabeth would come to her senses. He advised Philip to ignore Elizabeth's present attitude, drop any discussions about the matter and carry on his life as though nothing between them had changed.

The 1950s proved difficult years for Elizabeth who had major problems coming to terms with her life as a wife and mother and her commitments to her duty as the queen, despite the hours of tutoring from her father. Elder statesmen and advisers tried to complete the education which was cut short on the death of King George. They realised soon after she flew back from Kenya that she was ill-prepared for the task ahead. They tried to provide all possible support but often Elizabeth went to her bed alone, worried sick about the huge responsibilities she felt incapable of bearing. She talked over all her problems with her devoted Bobo but the latter could offer no solutions, only solace and understanding.

Elizabeth was confused. Should she dedicate her life to the monarchy, devoting herself to the British people like a nun devoting her life to God? Or should she concentrate on creating the right atmosphere in which to raise a happy family? Yet she could never forget the promises she had made to her father; to serve the people and protect the monarchy and, as a dutiful daughter, she chose the former and has never looked back. Her coronation in Westminster Abbey only confirmed her in the choice she had made. In effect,

Elizabeth 'married' the monarchy at her coronation and her whole life has been dedicated to sustaining that 'marriage'. As a result, Elizabeth became a remarkably lonely woman.

Philip understood his wife's turmoil but didn't believe he could help her. He decided to let Elizabeth and her advisers and courtiers thrash out the problems of the crown and the monarchy while he looked after the family, carried out his royal duties and concentrated on his own life. It was in fact Uncle Dickie, not Prince Philip, who persuaded Elizabeth she should consider having another child in the late 1950s when she talked to him of finding it difficult balancing her family life with that of monarchy. She had told Mountbatten of her 'sex ban' which he believed was not a good idea but he didn't push her into changing her attitude. On visits to Broadlands they talked of her having more children. Eventually, Elizabeth was to bear a further two children, Andrew, born in 1960, and Edward four years later. Apparently Edward was not planned, but Elizabeth was only too happy when she found herself pregnant again.

By denying Philip conjugal rights, Elizabeth provided the reason he needed to behave like a man-about-town who could lead an independent life. Of course he would have to be discreet and act as husband to the queen, but that discretion did not mean that he could not enjoy himself.

Following his marriage, Philip soon discovered that women were even more interested in him, perhaps because his wife had become the most important woman in the land. But Philip, arrogant about his physique and his sexual prowess, believed women liked him for his own attributes, unrelated to his position as the queen's husband. For company, Philip had his stalwart friend, Mike Parker. Like inseparable twins, they seemed to have the same ideas about everything, from competing hard against everyone – and against each other – in every sphere of their lives, including swimming, squash and table tennis to competing even in their ability to charm women. They had both loved the Navy, the camaraderie, the discipline, the officers' mess and the adventure. They had thoroughly enjoyed the competitive spirit the navy offered and had thrown themselves into service life with wholehearted enthusiasm. Indeed, they understood the Royal Navy had made men of them. Together through the war they had lived life to the full and now they would enjoy life in post-war London.

*In the early 1950s, CBS and NBC were battling for supremacy. NBC, the pioneer, had lost the lead to CBS in radio. NBC's lead in television entertainment was being threatened. ABC, then the runt of the litter, was not involved. They decided to transmit Canadian TV's film, scheduled for later that day. The race to screen the coronation would be won or lost transporting the film across the Atlantic. Full broadcasting facilities were prepared by both networks in Boston's Logan International Airport. It was arranged that a Royal Air Force Canberra would fly from London with the BBC telecast and hand over two films to NBC and CBS. Both networks hired private P-51 Mustangs, the American-made World War II fighters, to meet the RAF Canberra and take the film to Boston for broadcast. Determined to win, NBC invested in a secret weapon, hiring a Canberra jet bomber being delivered to the Venezuelan air force. It would be code-named Operation Astro. They arranged for the ferry company to fly via Goose Bay, Labrador. On the morning of the coronation, CBS heard of NBC's secret, that their film was already on its way to Boston on its secret Canberra. They were stunned to hear NBC would screen the coronation at 1 p.m., three hours earlier than scheduled.

Over the Atlantic, the Canberra developed a fuel leak and had to return to Britain. NBC's weapon was no longer secret and they too had to rely on what had been officially arranged. CBS's Mustang took off from Goose Bay 13 minutes ahead of NBC's. In addition, NBC's Mustang developed ice problems and arrived at 4.37 p.m., 20 minutes behind CBS. There was jubilation in the CBS hangar at Boston, gloom throughout NBC.

Then, Charles H. ('Bud') Barry, Jr, NBC's vice president, had a brainwave. He phoned ABC and agreed to pay all ABC's costs to share their Canadian TV film. NBC went on air precisely 13 minutes ahead of CBS. Jubilant NBC took a full-page advertisement in next morning's *New York Times* to celebrate the victory.

Years later the truth emerged. The NBC Canberra turned back in mid-Atlantic not because of a mechanical failure. The two pilots, Royal Air Force reserve officers, were ordered to return by the British Air Ministry. Why?

A senior NBC executive had informed BBC friends of Operation Astro. The BBC bosses decided they did not want any American network to broadcast the coronation before the Canadians, members of the Commonwealth, had seen their queen, their Head of State, crowned. They phoned the Air Ministry and explained the situation.

5. EARLY PROBLEMS

To the British people, Queen Elizabeth II has been an exemplary monarch, a beacon of steadfastness in a fast-changing world, someone who has won their admiration and esteem by carrying out her duties with distinction. Everyone looks to her as a kind of national conscience, setting a moral example. And yet the more Elizabeth is exposed to scrutiny, the more one discovers a different woman, one whose world has been filled with sadness and tragedy and whose life has not been without some blemish.

For 40 years Elizabeth has perpetuated the same dedication to her people – not just in Britain but throughout the Commonwealth – with which she began her reign. Following her coronation in 1952, she decided to undertake a grand 50,000-mile world tour so that her peoples could see their new sovereign. Accompanied by Prince Philip, she flew out to Canada in November 1953 en route to Bermuda and Jamaica. They took a 16,000-ton liner, the *Gothic*, and sailed through the Panama Canal to Fiji and Tonga before steaming on to New Zealand and Australia. Everywhere they went the welcome was tumultuous. On the way back home they landed at the Cocos Islands, Ceylon (Sri Lanka) and Aden before visiting Uganda. Then they flew to Tobruk in North Africa to be reunited with Prince Charles, five, and Anne, three, who had sailed out on HMS *Britannia*. On the voyage back home the family called in at Malta, which brought back happy memories for Elizabeth, and Gibraltar, before returning to London and a tumultuous welcome for the first British monarch to circumnavigate the world.

Throughout that long five-month tour, Elizabeth had been anxious about her sister Margaret, then 23, whom she knew was in love with a divorcé, Group-Captain Peter Townsend, the handsome former Second World War fighter ace, war hero, equerry to King George VI, friend to the family and adviser to the late king. Elizabeth and Margaret had always been close. They had shared a happy, carefree childhood until it became obvious when Elizabeth was ten years old that she would one day become queen. Elizabeth was always a responsible, well-behaved daughter; Margaret, more naughty, mischevious, sometimes wilful.

In the autumn of 1952, Margaret personally told her sister that she was in love with Townsend. Elizabeth, who had also been fond of Townsend, was torn between happiness for her sister and dismay at the problems such a marriage would cause. Elizabeth realised that as Head of the Church of England she could not condone her own sister breaking the church's law against divorce by giving consent to her sister's marriage to a divorced man. Elizabeth understood that Margaret loved Townsend and wanted her sister to find happiness with a man she truly loved. That is why the romance with Townsend caused Elizabeth such heartache and sadness. Elizabeth realised that for all his virtues, Peter Townsend could never be considered as a potential husband for a member of the royal family, no matter what his virtues.

The drama of the ill-fated love affair between the divorced Townsend and the young Princess Margaret divided the nation, the government, the House of Commons, the Church and the royal family. The war had changed so many people's views towards divorce and remarriage. The church, monarchy and the Establishment were desperately trying to stem the tide of divorces while growing numbers of ordinary people were beginning to accept the fact that divorce was an option that couples should consider when they found themselves leading miserable lives in an unhappy marriage.

Peter Townsend was, however, an extraordinary young man. In one of his books about the royals, Douglas Keay described Peter Townsend as, 'a mixture of Trevor Howard in *Brief Encounter* and Leslie Howard in *Gone With the Wind*, which meant that with women at least, he could hardly go wrong.' King George could not have given him more praise, saying that Townsend was the kind of son he would have liked to have had. He promoted him to be his favourite equerry giving him a personal honour, Commander of the Victorian Order. It is ironic that Peter Townsend became Deputy Master of the Household, as did Elizabeth's great friend and confidant Patrick Plunkett a few years later.

But his job as an equerry, with its long hours and lengthy travel, meant Townsend hardly ever saw his wife. Eight years after 'joining' the royal family and ten months after King George VI's death,

Townsend was granted a divorce on the grounds of misconduct by his wife. In those days the court always drew a clear distinction between those considered 'innocent' in a divorce case, and those considered 'guilty'. Townsend was adjudged innocent and thus was not required to resign his post inside the palace. Indeed, shortly afterwards the Queen Mother promoted him to Comptroller, the most responsible job in her household and, as a result, he moved into her home, Clarence House, where 23-year-old Princess Margaret also lived.

Margaret was considered a beautiful young woman and from the age of 18, if not before, had a host of admirers and eligible young men pursuing her. She partied, danced, attended weekend house parties in the country; she smoked, drank and enjoyed her life to the full, and was accepted as a very modern young woman. Newspapers were full of the pretty, indeed, striking, Princess out on the town.

King George and his wife Elizabeth were keen for their daughter to marry a British aristocrat, especially as Elizabeth had married 'a foreigner'. At one time or another Margaret was escorted by a number of young aristocrats, among them the Marquess of Blandford, the son of the wealthy Duke of Marlborough, the Earl of Dalkeith, son of the Duke of Buccleuch, and William 'Billy' Wallace, the grandson of the famous architect Sir Edward Lutyens. But Margaret wasn't really interested in any of them.

In 1948, Margaret, just 18, fell in love with Danny Kaye's crazy humour after meeting him backstage when he appeared for the first time at the London Palladium. Fascinated by his sense of fun, his handsome face and lithe figure, she then fell in love with the man. To Margaret, it didn't matter that he was 35, nearly twice her age. At first King George was amused by his daughter's interest in Danny Kaye, but he became alarmed when informed that Margaret was becoming seriously involved with the entertainer. Danny Kaye was not only married, but his wife, the gifted lyricist Sylvia Fine, lived with him in London. Kaye returned with his wife to the United States and Margaret continued her life of partying. All the time, of course, Margaret was seeing more of Townsend who, as the king's equerry, spent many hours a day with the royal family.

In 1951, Townsend, who was 15 years older than Margaret, wrote: 'She was a girl of unusual, intense beauty, confined as it was in her short, slender figure and centred around her large purple-blue eyes, generous, sensitive lips and a complexion as smooth as a peach. She was capable, in her face and in her whole being, of an astonishing power of expression. It could change in an instant from a saintly, almost melancholic, composure, to hilarious, uncontrollable joy. She was generous, volatile by nature. She was a comedienne at heart, playing the piano with ease and verve, singing in her rich, supple voice the latest hits, imitating the famous stars. She was coquettish, sophisticated. But what ultimately made Princess Margaret so attractive and lovable was that behind the dazzling façade, the apparent self-assurance, you could find, if you looked for it, a rare softness and sincerity.'

That was the young woman with whom he fell in love. She had met and flirted with a number of young men, aristocrats and commoners, but she had never fallen in love with any of them. But sometime in 1952 Margaret and Townsend became lovers, eight years after they had first met and only a few months after the death of her father in February 1952.

When Margaret told her sister about her lover, Townsend went to see 'Tommy' Lascelles, the queen's private secretary, to inform him of the affair. Lascelles, then 66, was a paragon of the Establishment. On hearing the news, Lascelles blurted out, 'You are either mad or bad.' For whatever reason, Tommy Lascelles, determined the marriage should not proceed, decided to pit his formidable authority against it. Lascelles behaved in a hypocritical fashion for which Margaret has never forgiven him. 'I shall curse him to the grave,' she said.

When her relationship with Townsend finally ended Margaret never spoke another word to Lascelles. Many considered Lascelles' behaviour disreputable and it is surprising that Elizabeth did nothing to intervene. Lascelles believed that another abdication-type scandal would seriously damage the monarchy and, with his old-world values, he understood that his job existed to preserve the monarchy, above all else, even if that included refusing to allow the queen's sister to marry the man she loved.

At first, Churchill whole-heartedly supported the marriage, saying 'What a delightful match. A lovely young royal lady married to a gallant young airman, returned safe from the perils and horrors of war!'

However, palace advisers and his wife, Clemmie, finally persuaded Churchill to oppose the marriage, for fear of damage to the crown. He called a cabinet meeting which unanimously decided the Prime Minister must advise the queen against such a royal marriage. Margaret of course was bound by the Royal Marriages Act of 1772 which means that any members of the royal family in line of succession to the throne have to secure the sovereign's authority if they wish to marry before the age of 25. Margaret was convinced, since both Charles and Princess Anne were in line before her, that Elizabeth would give her permission.

Elizabeth faced a heartrending predicament. She knew how she had wanted, and eventually won Philip despite opposition from her father. She understood, as only a young woman can, the craving her sister obviously felt for Townsend. Elizabeth desperately wanted to hug Margaret and say, 'Yes, yes, yes, I am thrilled for you; I hope you will both be very happy.' But she couldn't. She talked to the Queen Mother who broke down in tears, weeping uncontrollably, that her own daughter should have fallen in love with a divorced commoner, exactly the same way as King Edward had become enamoured of Mrs Simpson, a divorced commoner. In anguish, Elizabeth and her mother wept together.

Elizabeth indeed showed remarkable strength of character. She told Churchill, Lascelles and the Archbishop of Canterbury that she would ask the couple to wait a year. She called them together and gave them the news. Margaret threw her arms around her sister, hugging her. 'Thank you, thank you Lilibet,' she said, tears in her eyes. Townsend and Margaret went away believing they would be able to marry 'in a year or so'.

But there were other forces at work. Lascelles, the royal household, Churchill, the cabinet, Church leaders and many members of the House of Lords were determined not to permit the marriage. However, the majority of the British people supported Margaret and her wish to marry a commoner. Michael Foot, the MP and future leader of the Labour party wrote a stinging leader in the left-wing magazine *Tribune,* which he edited: 'This intolerable piece of interference with a girl's private life is all part of the absurd myth about the royal family which has been so sedulously built up by interested parties in recent years. The laws of England say that a man, whether he has divorced his wife or been divorced himself, is fully entitled to marry again . . . If those laws are good they are good enough for the royal family.'

Once again the nation was divided over the royal family and the love of a commoner.

As agreed, Townsend went abroad, exiled to Brussels as Air Attaché to the British Embassy, where the press never left him alone. Against advice from Lascelles, Elizabeth gave the couple permission to write and telephone each other. Before Townsend left London, Lascelles had told them, 'A marriage is not impossible.' But he was deliberately deceiving them. On her twenty-fifth birthday Margaret waited to greet the man she still loved and wanted to marry. Now, according to the law, all she had to do was give notice to the Privy Council and she would be free to marry.

The new Prime Minister Sir Anthony Eden, himself a divorced man, came to see Margaret at Balmoral and told her that some MPs, including the great Tory, Lord Salisbury, had threatened to resign if Margaret married Townsend. In an emotional meeting, in which Margaret cried tears of rage and astonishment, Eden said that if she did marry him then she could not remain in line of succession and would be barred from receiving any salary from the government for carrying out royal duties. She knew that Townsend would have to retire from the Royal Air Force on some paltry pension, which meant they would have virtually nothing to live on.

Elizabeth told Margaret when they met, 'You can still marry him but it will cause the most awful rumpus. They will do everything in their power to stop you.' And Elizabeth, revealing the superficiality and transparency of her power, added, 'You know there is nothing I can do. You know that I want you to be happy but they are very determined to stop you marrying him. They will do anything to prevent the marriage.' Elizabeth was referring to the Establishment figures, government ministers, senior civil servants, even members of her own royal household.

Amid a tumult of journalists and photographers, Townsend arrived back in London in October 1955 and the couple were reunited in Clarence House. That night they left London and drove to a beautiful 50-roomed Georgian mansion, Allanby Park, in Berkshire, forty miles north-west of London, their first weekend together under the same roof for 18 months. As the world's press camped outside, Margaret and Townsend spent three days and three nights together. They were determined to marry, no matter what forces were ranged against them.

The cabinet was informed the wedding would take place and Margaret believed she would be permitted to marry the man she loved once she was over 25, when she would no longer need the sovereign's permission to wed. The Establishment played its final hand and they held a trump card. Tommy Lascelles asked her to come and see him. He told her, 'One fact seems to have been overlooked. If you insist on marrying Group-Captain Townsend you will have to go into exile, and live abroad, in the same fashion as your Uncle David was permitted to marry only on the condition that he abdicate and live abroad.'

Margaret was stunned. David's situation had been so very different, for he was the king. She knew that the Establishment had prevented him from returning to the land of his birth. In that instant of rage at the Establishment, Margaret found courage in anger, screaming at

Lascelles, 'I'm not the sovereign,' she raged. 'There is no chance that I will ever become queen. How can you compare my position with that of Uncle David? How can you?' And she stormed out to see her sister.

She appealed to Elizabeth but there was nothing she could do. Elizabeth kept shaking her head, telling Margaret of the power of the Establishment, the government, the senior members of the royal household, Church leaders, all of whom were implacably against the marriage. Margaret went to see the Archbishop of Canterbury to seek his support but he offered her no hope.

In October 1955, the *London Times*, at that time very definitely the voice of the Establishment and the Church, thundered, 'The queen and her family are a symbol for her subjects throughout the Commonwealth, and the vast majority of these people will not recognise this marriage.'

Townsend wrote later, 'We were both exhausted, mentally, emotionally, physically. We felt mute and numbed at the centre of this maelstrom.' That night Townsend arrived at Clarence House with a piece of paper which he gave Margaret to read. It said: 'I have been aware that, subject to my renouncing my rights of succession, it might have been possible for me to contract a civil marriage. But, mindful of the Church's teaching that Christian marriage is indissoluble, and conscious of my duty to the Commonwealth, I have resolved to put these considerations before any others. I have reached this decision entirely alone, and in doing so I have been strengthened by the unfailing support and devotion of Group-Captain Townsend. I am deeply grateful for the concern of all those who have constantly prayed for my happiness.'

Together they made the decision that in fact they could not marry but they nevertheless decided to spend one last weekend together at a friend's house in the Sussex countryside. Twenty-four hours later, when the world believed an announcement of their forthcoming marriage was to be made, came the stunning statement from Princess Margaret.

It began, 'I have been aware that . . . '

Elizabeth felt guilt, shame and sorrow; guilt that she had not been more forceful; shame that she was not capable, even as queen and Head of State, of being able to persuade the Establishment; and deep sorrow for her sister. She had learned a lesson she would never forget.

Many biographers have suggested that Philip fully supported Elizabeth throughout the scandal and the crisis. That is not true.

Philip had never been Townsend's friend though they had been acquaintances for many years and had spent many ferocious, competitive hours on squash and badminton courts. Philip had always rather envied Townsend's brilliant and courageous war record, his friendship with King George VI and the Queen Mother and his popularity with the entire family. Townsend was a most likeable man, Philip was not.

Townsend, an elegant, introspective man of genteel manners found Philip brash, brusque and over zealous. On one occasion, during a private dinner with Elizabeth, he turned to Margaret and told her in no uncertain terms, 'Stop being so bloody stupid and stop this marriage nonsense.'

Margaret blushed and looked angrily at Philip. Elizabeth said nothing, intimidated by her husband's ferocious attitude to her sister. Philip considered his wife's sister to be vain and frivolous. It is not surprising that Margaret has never forgiven Philip for taking sides against her and, as a result, the two have never been close. And Philip's hard-hearted attitude towards Margaret made it more difficult for Elizabeth to cope with Margaret's distress which had caused her so much personal agony.

A major problem which Elizabeth inherited concerned the family's relationship towards the Duke and Duchess of Windsor, who had been exiled from Britain's shores in 1936 after Edward VIII's decision to marry the American divorcée, Wallis Simpson. Elizabeth was only 11 years of age when her uncle abdicated and her father succeeded to the throne. She hadn't seen either of them since. Naturally, she picked up the bitterness that divided the family, especially from her mother, who never forgave her brother-in-law for forcing her husband into the role of king, something for which he had never prepared and never wanted.

In character, interests and appearance, young Elizabeth, 30 years younger than the Duchess of Windsor, could hardly have been further apart. And yet Elizabeth, far more than her mother, showed the Duchess compassion and, later, forgiveness. Elizabeth tried throughout her reign to heal the breach between her mother and the Duke and Duchess but to no avail. The Queen Mother would not hear of it under any circumstances. She has indeed never forgiven them, not even in the couple's death.

Elizabeth was prepared to grant the Duke's greatest wish – that the title of HRH, Her Royal Highness, should be conferred on the Duchess of Windsor – but her mother would not hear of it. Every time the matter was discussed, Elizabeth would listen and say, 'It's

Mummy that matters. We mustn't do anything that hurts Mummy's feelings.' So nothing happened.

In 1962, Elizabeth provided a permanent private office for the Duke of Windsor and invited him and the Duchess to London for the unveiling of a memorial plaque to Queen Mary. But the offer of an HRH was not forthcoming and so the Duke returned to Paris and to exile.

Ten years later Elizabeth and Philip paid a state visit to France. The timing was impeccable, though accidental, for the Duke, then 78, was dying of cancer. Elizabeth went to the Windsors' home and after taking tea with the Duchess she went to see her uncle. He had refused to see Elizabeth in his pyjamas, linked up to tubes and drips, and insisted the nurses dress him and prop him up in an armchair. When Elizabeth entered she found him sitting in his favourite chair smartly attired in a tie, blazer and grey flannels. He couldn't stand and could hardly talk. After 30 minutes, Elizabeth bade him farewell, kissing him on the cheek. She knew he was at death's door. Ten days later he died.

Elizabeth arranged for his body to be flown, in a coffin of English oak, to London and from there to Windsor for burial. Mountbatten was asked to take care of the Duchess of Windsor during her short stay in London. He was the natural person to do so for he had been the special negotiator between the royal family and the Duke after the abdication.

The Duchess was concerned about coming to London for the funeral. She told Mountbatten, 'I am worried about Elizabeth, the Queen Mother, who never approved of me.'

Mountbatten reassured her saying, 'She will welcome you with open arms. She is so deeply sorry for you in your grief and remembers what she felt like when her own husband died.'

When she stood in St George's Chapel, at Windsor Castle, where the Duke lay in state, the Duchess said, 'He was my entire life. I can't begin to think what I am going to do without him. He gave up so much for me, and now he has gone. I always hoped that I would die before he did.'

Mountbatten commented later, 'I must say I feel desperately sorry for her. She is so lonely and sad, and yet kept saying how wonderful the family were being to her, and how much better the whole thing had gone than she had expected.'

However, the Duchess of Windsor commented some time after she had returned to Paris, 'The queen, Prince Charles and Princess Anne were polite to me, polite and kind, especially the queen.' But she added, 'Royalty is always polite and kind. But they were cold. David always said they were cold.'

That was probably a harsh judgement. Elizabeth nearly always appears cool during her official duties as monarch, and to a great extent she has to behave that way. She often seems distant when chatting to people but not to those she knows really well. And yet it would be untrue to say she is cold and distant for she can show great enthusiasm and a great sense of fun whenever the mood takes her. But that is a private side of her life that very few people witness.

After the Duke's funeral, Elizabeth went out of her way to make life as comfortable as possible for his widow who lived the invalid life of a recluse for many years before her own death in April 1986 at the age of 90. Elizabeth ordered that her body be flown to England and laid to rest beside her husband in the grounds at Windsor. Almost thirty years earlier the Duchess had persuaded her husband to buy a burial plot of enormous size in Green Mount Cemetery, Baltimore, in the United States, because she was convinced the British, and especially the Queen Mother – her arch-enemy – would attempt to achieve in death what they had singularly failed to achieve in life, their separation. Elizabeth however had informed both her uncle and the Duchess that she would provide a burial place for them both at Frogmore in Windsor Great Park and she kept her promise.

6. FRIENDS AND LOVERS

Prince Philip is the most fiercely competitive of men and a most macho figure. Yet for 50 years he has been forced continually, in public, to walk at least two paces behind his wife. And, as if to add further insult to his pride, Philip does not constitutionally exist at all. Nor can he be involved in any way in his wife's role. These factors have only aggravated Philip's natural aggression, leading to irritation, impatience and, on many occasions, bloody-mindedness.

For one, Philip is forbidden from seeing state papers. Once, shortly after Elizabeth became queen, Philip was offered the right to peruse them but turned down the privilege on the grounds that it would restrict his own freedom of speech. Since that time, it has been accepted that Philip never sees or reads the papers.

In fact, however, Philip enjoys having it all. Throughout most of Elizabeth's reign, Philip has always read, and still does read, whichever papers he wishes to, and has readily discussed them with Elizabeth. Indeed, she respects his views and opinions and throughout her reign has used her husband as a sounding board. However, since Philip maintains he never sees government papers he feels free to comment upon any subject he wishes.

When King George VI finally gave his consent to the marriage between Elizabeth and Philip, he appointed Philip to the Privy Council, a body of royal advisers originated in England in 1070 which later became the chief governing body, the forerunner of the cabinet of ministers. However, its powers, now purely formal, involve only royal proclamations and orders-in-council. Membership is an honour granted automatically to cabinet ministers and others who have held high political, ecclesiastical or judicial offices in Britain and the Commonwealth. Because no discussion ever takes place Philip has never attended. In fact, the meetings are so brief that neither the queen nor her representative, or anyone else, ever sits down.

King George also honoured Philip in other traditional ways. On the morning of the wedding, King George created Philip Duke of Edinburgh and he was given a new armorial bearing. The arms seemed most appropriate, showing hearts, lions, a cross and a castle; supporters being a golden lion with a ducal coronet on its head and a naval coronet around its neck, and the hero Hercules complete with bulging muscles, bushy blonde beard, lion-skin around his waist, and cudgel. Philip was also created a Knight of the Garter for protocol's sake, one week after Elizabeth had been given the same honour.

Philip's life changed dramatically from that day in February 1952 when King George VI died and his wife became queen. Philip had been head of the family for more than four years and, by nature, he loved being in command of anything, whether captaining a cricket team, a ship of the Royal Navy, a polo team or his own family. At a stroke his days of leadership were over. Sometime later he revealed his disappointment, 'Until that point I was head of the family. Within the house, whatever we did, it was together. I naturally filled the principal position. People used to come to me and ask me what to do. After the king's death the whole thing changed very, very considerably.'

It took some years for Philip to come to terms with the fact that, although he was head of the family, he was all but superfluous as far as the royal household, government ministers and the Establishment were concerned. And he was given short shrift by many members of the aristocracy, treating him as 'Phil the Greek'. Others called him 'a German princeling', which in the years following the Second World War, was a considerable insult.

Lord Charteris, who was appointed Elizabeth's first private secretary in 1949, observed Philip's attitudes during those awkward few years. He commented, 'I think Philip might have tried a little harder to accommodate the views of the royal household. Because of the way he was treated, especially before his marriage, he had a certain amount of prejudice against the old order. He thought it was stuffy and needed shaking up. He became the consort of the sovereign as opposed to the husband of a princess, with a certain amount of antipathy and impatience. He sulked quite a bit.'

Mike Parker noted, 'I felt that Philip didn't have many friends or helpers in the palace. There were people who were in a position to give a helping hand and who, it seemed, were reticent about doing so. Some of the British Establishment were hidebound and prejudiced. Some among the senior household members were affected to find the Duke 'teutonic' and there was also the business of all his German relations. We had just been through a war and Germans were Germans.'

Prince Philip never wanted to become Prince Consort, as his great-great-grandfather Albert did after some years of marriage to Queen Victoria. The title would have emphasised his official status without underlining his human vocation. Philip believed that accepting the title of Prince Consort meant he would have reduced his role to that of a mere symbol. His instincts were to distance himself from the mystery of monarchy and to assert his rights and duties as a husband and father. Furthermore, in the far-off days of the 1940s, when they were married, Elizabeth herself insisted on promising to 'obey' her husband in her wedding vows, as virtually every woman who was married in the Church of England did.

It was Boothroyd who noted in an article he wrote for *The Times* in June 1981 that Prince Philip does not enjoy servants bowing and scraping before their superiors and certainly not to him. He has always seen himself first as a man, and secondly as a prince. Sometimes Philip would chastise a servant for opening a door for one of his sons, 'He's not helpless,' he would remonstrate in a harsh voice, 'he's got hands like everyone else.'

It was not only for humbling servants, however, that Philip earned his reputation as the impatient, irascible, abrasive, almost aggressive character the world has come to know. He has given many bureaucrats a tongue lashing, and has often exclaimed to many journalists and photographers, 'Why don't you fuck off?' He is often rude to strangers, bludgeoning them with a totally uncalled for opening remark, and setting the victim at a disadvantage, not knowing how to answer the queen's husband.

Philip has been equally abrasive and insulting to those in senior positions in the royal palaces, not just to servants. He would some-times describe royal servants as 'gormless twits' to their faces, knowing, of course, that he could get away with these comments because of his position. But it didn't earn him much respect. Quite the opposite, in fact. He still uses the expletives, many of them coarse and base, that he had learned in the Royal Navy.

And he loves to appear to be in control, especially of the queen. Particularly in his early years, when inspecting factories or shopping malls, Philip would snap loudly so everyone could hear, 'This is a bloody waste of time,' and even, 'Let's go'. It was of course an embarrassment to Elizabeth and she would usually cast a hard glance at him. Sometimes it worked, but on most occasions Elizabeth would smile and the visit would come to a fairly abrupt end. Invariably impatient, Philip didn't seem to care whom he upset, even his own wife.

Easily bored, frustrated and impetuous, Prince Philip has been a thorn in the side of many people, particularly officials. He will nearly always find fault when accompanying the queen, for example, on official walk-abouts, when the queen gently waves and smiles to those who have turned out to cheer her. He will often proclaim in a loud voice to no one in particular, 'Get rid of some of these bloody police officers, no one can see us.' Or alternatively he shouts, 'There are no bloody police officers here. Get the Home Secretary.'

At the same time Philip has often been helpful to his wife and, on occasion, they can be an enchanting double act. Ronald Allison, a former Buckingham Palace press officer, recalled: 'I've always admired the way the Duke supports the queen. They are very close and understand each other perfectly when meeting the people in whatever part of the world. On an engagement together the queen will be walking down one side and Prince Philip the other. She'll be quiet and smiling and he'll be cracking jokes and livening the atmosphere.

'I believe a good way of seeing how close a couple might be is in their desire to share things. A frequent memory I have of Prince Philip is seeing him – if he's spotted something in the crowd – drawing the queen's attention to it. "Oh, look there, darling", he'd say, making sure she had seen it. If you don't like someone very much you don't bother to point things out. You don't care whether they see things or not.'

Despite the bad times – and with Philip, Elizabeth has experienced many – there are those today in the palace who still believe she needs her husband's constant support. 'I dread to think what would happen if anything were to shorten his natural life,' commented a bishop who knew both of them well for many years. 'She would be absolutely shattered. I am not sure, even with her inner strength, that she would be able to recover.'

Soon after she became queen, Elizabeth realised that she had to find things to keep her mercurial, over-active husband from having too much time on his hands. She knew only too well that Philip was a man of action, with almost boundless energy. Unable to keep still for a moment, he had to find a way of releasing his considerable adrenalin, while engaging and challenging his intelligence and intellect. Boothroyd described his energy as 'numbing'. Elizabeth also fully realised that, like his father, he was very much a ladies' man and he had the ego, the self-confidence, the good looks and the natural sex appeal to make whatever conquests he desired. He would not let his natural attributes go to waste!

One of Elizabeth's first ideas to keep Philip occupied was to put him in charge of modernising Buckingham Palace, Windsor Castle and Sandringham, as well as making him Chief Ranger of Windsor Great Park. These were four major tasks which gave him, in essence, a new career in estate management. Philip came up with hundreds of new ideas – some good, some zany and some hopeless – which he wanted implemented immediately without discussion or debate. He refused to listen to the opinions of other people who had far greater experience. Nor would he take advice. Understandably, many of his innovations proved to be disasters. Whenever he's in charge, Philip becomes the captain of a ship in the middle of a battle, issuing orders from the bridge and demanding instant obedience. Often he brushes obstacles aside with a scorn that appears totally arrogant, and not very appealing.

Impatient with those who ran Buckingham Palace, and especially the queen's advisers, Philip was determined to drag the monarchy into the twentieth century. He believed, sometimes correctly, that the old fogies who ran the palace were the prime reason the British monarchy of the 1950s remained rooted in the nineteenth century. Philip wanted change, innovation, initiatives and he worked hard to get Elizabeth to go along with his ideas.

Unfortunately, Philip never realised that Elizabeth herself was also rooted in the nineteenth century despite the fact she was only a youthful 26 when she became queen. She had lived the life of a cloistered princess, surrounded by royalty, residing in palaces and castles, cut off from ordinary people, never mixing or meeting anyone who didn't first bow or curtsey to her. She had never gone shopping, never been to a market, never waited in a queue, never been on a crowded bus, train or underground railway. Nor had Elizabeth walked through crowded city streets, rubbing shoulders with people. She did not have the faintest idea how ordinary people lived in their homes. She had never had to do a day's work, never washed a dish or dusted or cleaned or even made a bed or a cup of tea or coffee, let alone prepare or cook a meal. She had no idea of the value of money for there had never been a need to know. And throughout her life she had been surrounded by servants and maids, living exactly the life of a princess in the court of Queen Victoria 100 years earlier.

Philip first set about Buckingham Palace, marching through its miles of corridors inspecting everything, including the servants' quarters, the kitchens, the cellars, the bathrooms, the electrical system and the plumbing, finding ways to modernise, if not revolutionise the workings of the vast building that had barely changed for more than a hundred years.

He came up with a hundred and one ideas but found it impossible to push through all but a handful of them. 'This bloody place needs a bomb underneath it,' he would shout, 'and so do most of the people who work here.' The staff would wince whenever Philip went on one of his 'inspections' because they knew full well it would end in yet more innovations and changes, something none of them wanted. He complained one day in a loud voice so that a number of senior courtiers would hear, 'It's more difficult to get Prince Charles's cot from Windsor to Buckingham Palace than to move an army across the Rhine.' A senior member of the household recalled, 'Prince Philip would walk briskly along the palace corridors, hands clasped behind his back to prevent round shoulders, long neck thrust forward, face inquisitive, frowning, aquiline, like a fierce quizzical eagle, snapping at servants, demanding answers to impossible questions. He was always challenging, sharp and, the staff believed, dangerous. But most of the time his bark was worse than his bite.'

But his efforts to modernise Buckingham Palace, though not sweeping, did produce some results. False ceilings were installed; the central heating was eventually overhauled; rooms were painted in brighter colours. He brought in modern office equipment, like electric typewriters, he streamlined the chain of command and installed an intercom system which saved footmen and pages miles of walking every day. And he did win a cheer for one of his suggestions which was immediately implemented – that footmen should no longer have to powder their hair!

His modernisation, however, also led to about one hundred firings and redundancies among the four hundred staff who worked at the palace, many of whom were pensioned off because they had, in fact, passed pensionable age.

A substantial proportion of palace staff are gay. For a good many years a number of senior advisers, as well as those with whom the Queen Mother likes to surround herself, have been notoriously gay. The Queen Mother, still charming, delightful and going strong in her nineties, enjoys their sense of humour and appreciates their dedication to duty. Philip, on the other hand, is not too happy about having the palace peppered with homosexuals. One day he noticed that a particular footman had been missing for some time and asked his page where he had gone.

'He was fired, Sir,' came the reply.

Understandably, Philip wanted to know why.

'I'm afraid he was found in bed with one of the housemaids, Sir,' was the reply.

'And they sacked him! An outrage,' Philip exclaimed. 'The man should have been given a bloody medal.'

As was the custom in industry in the late 1950s, Philip decided to undertake a time and motion study throughout the palace in an effort to cut staff and make the place run more efficiently. He called in Sir Basil Smallpiece, a successful British industrialist, and, after several weeks and a full report, a number of staff were let go. Philip commented later, 'I don't think it made any difference at all. There still seem to be far too many people doing far too little work.'

In his haste to create change he sometimes overstepped the mark. To brighten up the stuffy palace he 'borrowed' some paintings he had found in another part of the royal household and put them near their private suites. When Elizabeth saw what he had done, she was horrified, 'Those belong to the State collection,' she said. 'You'll get us shot. We can't touch them.'

At Windsor Castle, Philip's role of moderniser meant that wall lights were installed as well as some central heating and a great many more electric fires in place of fireplaces. In the 1950s, Windsor Castle was a freezing, draughty place in winter, having no central heating and only half a dozen or so electric fires in the entire castle! Heat came from coal and wood fires alone, which gave totally insufficient heating for the huge rooms. He also installed some modern bathrooms with hot water. So tiny was Elizabeth's personal bathroom at Windsor Castle that she could only climb into her bath from one end. In another innovation he replaced all the old, metal hot water bottles which were religiously put into beds each evening, introducing modern rubber ones. Philip wanted to install electric blankets, too, but Elizabeth refused permission, believing they would prove too expensive.

Philip had more success at Sandringham in Norfolk, 120 miles north of London, a house owned privately by the queen which she had inherited from her father. Buckingham Palace, on the other hand, is the property of the state. He decided Sandringham was to be run without pomp and ceremony with no flunkies bowing and curtseying. Sandringham would be the country house where Elizabeth, Philip and the children could relax and enjoy life as any ordinary British family. He fired many of the staff, deciding that the family would 'muck in' and sometimes cook and wash up and make tea themselves. He also decreed there would be no servants at table, not even a butler. Elizabeth of course had never experienced anything like it in her life. At first she found it all 'immense fun' making tea, getting the children to help serve and clear away dishes. But not for long. Within weeks the servants returned.

As a result, Philip's grand ideas didn't really achieve that much. The only changes were new kitchens, the instalment of a dishwasher and the family appearing for breakfast instead of having it served in their room. Yet Philip did transform the Sandringham estate from a rather run-down farm to a modern, profit-making enterprise. Despite the fact Sandringham was privately owned by Elizabeth, he still had to cut through mountains of red tape to introduce more modern farming techniques. The queen's own 3,000 acres, which are not let to tenant farmers, produce pigs, turkeys for Christmas and mush-rooms and blackcurrants for market. Everything is now sold, usually at a profit. Even Elizabeth's personal interest, the breeding of gun dogs, which she treats as one of her favourite hobbies, is run at a profit. And at Windsor, Philip introduced efficient production of milk, cream and free range eggs. Most of this first-class produce goes to Buckingham Palace for Elizabeth and her guests as well as to a fortunate few senior courtiers.

In 1956 Philip launched a grand idea to foster leadership, self-discipline, enterprise and perseverance among young people from all backgrounds. As with everything he proposed at that time, Philip was not surprised when the Ministry of Education took a dim view. Some described his plan as 'square'. But he persevered. Philip wanted young people, boys and girls from 14 to 23, to develop a sense of service, coupled with fitness, something which gave purpose to their lives. He devised the programme which became known as The Duke of Edinburgh's Award Scheme. He has personally raised hundreds of thousands of pounds to ensure its success and the programme is, even today, the only one that bears his name. Since its inception more than 2,700,000 young people, from 55 countries, all volunteers, have taken part from all walks of life – from the middle classes to the poorest in the land, as well as those who have served time in remand homes and jails.

Bearing the imprint of Dr Kurt Hahn, the German founder of Gordonstoun, the scheme permits young people to tackle anything they wish as long as it is different from their ordinary life. Some will win awards, for example, for working a year in a mental hospital, trekking across 50 miles of country in the winter, clearing canals or helping the sick, the disadvantaged or the old. Young people are intended to enjoy the scheme. Some will win awards for learning to play the flute, passing a car maintenance course or playing football. Philip still attends the six award ceremonies every year, still raises money for the programme, and loves to talk about it to all the young people he meets. He has always been a great supporter of helping young people mature into well-disciplined, hard-working, responsible adults. Forty years later it is still going strong and, whereas the majority who took part were originally young men, the sexes are now more evenly balanced. Prince Edward has taken over much of his father's work but Philip still supplies a constant stream of ideas, advice, help and encouragement.

Ten men and one woman, all volunteers, now form the Duke of Edinburgh's Award Scheme special projects group. Chaired by Prince Edward, the committee is the think tank whose job it is to devise and run fundraising events for the scheme. Big business and the government help financially but most of the money is raised by the committee.

Philip also originated a plan to improve Britain's industrial relations. He founded the National Playing Fields Association in 1947 and, in 1961, he joined the World Wildlife Fund, a scheme for the protection of endangered species. Both have been hugely successful, partly due to Philip's drive and energy.

Throughout his life Philip has loved serving on committees and in particular chairing them. To many he is a very good chairman, but others say he is far too dominant and interfering, demanding to have his own way, rather than letting the committee decide democratically.

He was heavily involved in Britain's Automobile Association for many years, spouting his views which usually brought short shrift from motorists. He has been heavily involved in polo and carriage driving, not only actively participating himself, but also chairing and sitting on committees that govern the sports. From time to time Philip has also chaired various committees involved with education and the universities, housing and the environment.

'I happen to find myself in rather an individual position,' Philip once explained. 'I am involved in the activities of a great many groups but the sheer number of these groups makes it impossible to belong completely to any one of them. Furthermore in many cases my involvement is as an active or titular head and that in itself tends both to isolation and objectivity.'

Despite a lifetime spent accompanying the queen on official royal engagements across Britain and around the world, as well as his involvement in many causes and committees, Prince Philip has always found plenty of time to indulge in what appears to be one of the great passions of his life, that is, enjoying the company of beautiful women.

To those few people who know Philip well, fascination with women has probably been one of Philip's interests from his days as a young naval officer during the Second World War through his polo-playing years and well into his sixties, if not his seventies. Even today, at most functions, Philip can always be found chatting to one or other of the most attractive women in the room, flirting with his smile and his piercing blue eyes, and laughing and joking.

Two of the women with whom he had close friendships early in his life have written books about Philip but neither has revealed any suggestion of an affair. Indeed, they protested their innocence so strongly that many readers took it for granted that both women had probably flirted with him from time to time. The first was Queen Alexandra of Greece with whom he had a two-year friendship; and the second the cabaret artiste Hélène Cordet, the daughter of the Foufounis family, old friends of his mother, who lived near the family during their exile in Paris. Hélène recalls that she and Philip used to play doctors and nurses together when they were children. Hélène also recalls the two of them playing a game together called 'The king, the servant and the pig'. She explained, 'Philip always volunteered to play the pig. No one wanted to play the king. Philip would refuse to play the king saying he feared he would have his head chopped off.'

For some extraordinary reason, Philip had a 'thing' about pigs. At Hélène Cordet's home in Marseilles, in the South of France, Philip, when he was ten years old loved to spend time with the pigs, walking around them, cleaning and feeding them and even cleaning out the pigsties. But he never explained the reason for his fascination with his four-footed friends.

In Queen Alexandra's book there is even a hint of jealousy as well as strong resentment towards Dickie Mountbatten, suggesting he may have interfered with her friendship with Philip. However, the lovely Alexandra eventually married King Peter of Yugoslavia after numerous youthful trysts with Philip whom she first got to know when he was a youthful 17. Their love blossomed in 1940 after Italy invaded Greece. Both were then 19. Alexandra wrote, 'Suddenly Philip arrived in Athens, gay, debonair, confident . . .' Philip was to spend a considerable amount of time in Athens, almost always staying with Alexandra. She told stories of air raids: 'In the evenings the family often gathered either at the palace with the king or at one of our homes. We never knew when Philip would join us. When the air raids began we were supposed to go to a shelter . . . but instead we went to the roof-garden and watched . . . Philip contributed a running commentary amid the bark of ack-ack guns, the flutter of searchlights and the roar of bombers.'

Relentlessly, Philip pursued the delectable Alexandra. She revealed that Philip sought her out after she and her family had fled to the comparative safety of Cairo. She wrote, 'Philip soon tracked us down to Shepherd's Hotel. In his little wasp of a car we went out to the Ghezira Club, swam in the pool or just talked through the long, lazy afternoons when he was off duty. We explored the old bazaars and the magnificent botanical gardens together.'

As if by accident, Philip even turned up in Cape Town on board a troop-ship just weeks after Alexandra and her family had sought refuge in South Africa. The love affair was on again. Back in London the following year Philip was a constant visitor to the family house and dated Alexandra frequently. She wrote, 'I best remember Philip on furlough, Philip dining and dancing and confiding.' They spent weekends at the country home of their cousin Marina. Despite her denials, Alexandra was one of Philip's earliest serious passions. He thought she was wonderful.

The other woman in Philip's early love life was Hélène Foufounis, the petite, attractive, vivacious girl, his childhood sweetheart, who would become a well-known nightclub singer and a television personality of some fame in post-war Britain. Hélène had two children out of wedlock, Max and Louise, an act of courage at a time when the middle-classes of Britain still frowned on such 'anti-social' behaviour. Most middle-classes, church-going men and women in post-war Britain considered a child born out of wedlock brought absolute disgrace to the family, and believed that as a consequence the young mother would never find a husband.

Hélène and Philip spent a good deal of time together in Britain during and after the war, and they have remained good friends through the subsequent decades. During those years there was inevitable gossip about the paternity of Max and Louise, some suggesting different lovers.

Hélène Cordet was to marry twice. Her first marriage took place when she was 20 and Philip was four years her junior. At the time she proclaimed happily, 'Philip was the best man at my first wedding. He also gave me away. My mother didn't realise someone had to give away the bride so Philip volunteered. He was wonderful.' It was not long, however, before that marriage was to end in divorce. Her second marriage was celebrated during the war, when she married a French air-force officer by the name of

Marcel Boisot who deserted her only a few months afterwards.

Yet the relationship between Hélène and Philip has always remained close. Philip helped pay for her son's education at Gordonstoun, the school he had attended and to which, in turn, he sent Charles, Andrew and Edward. And it was Philip who suggested Gordonstoun to Hélène. Even today, Prince Philip still keeps in touch with Hélène's son Max, now a successful 55-year-old businessman living in China. Philip even went to see Max when he visited China on an official royal visit with the queen and disappeared mysteriously for some hours after taking the traditional walk along part of the Great Wall.

Hélène Cordet still keeps in touch with Philip and has occasionally visited Buckingham Palace, taking tea or having a meal there with him. She has also met Elizabeth, although it was a very brief encounter. Elizabeth smiled sweetly and said to her, 'Oh, I've heard so much about you. How nice to meet to you at last.' There was no further conversation.

Throughout her life, the ever-faithful Hélène has always defended Philip, frequently commenting in her lovely French accent, 'Of course he likes women. He is like his father was. I know he has this reputation. But if a man doesn't look at a woman, what happens? Let us not forget that some people say other things, completely the contrary, and that is terrible. What the hell can he do to have a decent reputation? If he doesn't look at women, they say he likes men. He likes women. So what? It's a good thing.'

In October 1956 Elizabeth and Philip were approaching their ninth wedding anniversary and finding life somewhat testy and difficult. Rumours circulated, particularly in the continental press, that their marriage was going through a rocky patch and that Elizabeth was fed up with her husband's aggressive attitude, glum appearance and bad moods. Elizabeth realised that Philip needed to get away from London. It had already been decided that Philip should open the 1956 Olympic Games in Melbourne, Australia, so, encouraged by Elizabeth, Philip proposed he should visit other Commonwealth countries on his return trip. Philip loved getting away from London, away from the strict confines of the Palace and the members of the royal household, with whom he was constantly at odds. It was therefore decided he should leave Melbourne on the Royal Yacht HMS *Britannia* and return via New Zealand, Malaya, the Gambia, Antarctica, the Galapagos Island and the Falklands. It was a mammoth tour. Altogether, he would travel 39,000 miles and be away for four months.

As his Private Secretary and equerry, friend and confidant, Commander Mike Parker went along too. Towards the end of the trip, word leaked out that Mrs Eileen Parker, Mike Parker's wife was suing for divorce. Philip and Mike Parker were known to be very much alike and to have enjoyed life together during the war and in and around London ever since. They went to parties, travelled the world, played squash and badminton, and often ate together. During his four-month trip Philip missed not only his ninth wedding anniversary but also Christmas with the children and the winter break with Elizabeth at Sandringham. Nor had he been in Britain to be at the queen's side during the 1956 war over the Suez Canal when Britain, France and Israel joined forces and attacked Nasser's Egypt.

But Philip did send his wife two dozen of her favourite white roses on their wedding anniversary and he did talk with her and Charles and Anne on the radio-telephone from the Falkland Islands on Christmas Day. The future president of the World Wildlife Fund also went crocodile shooting and bagged one with his first bullet. Philip arranged for the six-foot length of handbag to be sent back to Buckingham Palace, tanned and cured, to make beautiful leather presents for the royal ladies.

As Philip and Mike Parker sailed back to Britain, newspapers speculated daily on the status of the queen's marriage. All the signs pointed to a crisis. Word had leaked out that Mike Parker's wife Eileen was suing for divorce and now the newspapers sensed Elizabeth's marriage was in trouble. Speculation about the marriage became so intense that Buckingham Palace chose to issue a denial, an action totally without precedent in those days. Elizabeth's Private Secretary Sir Michael Adeane issued a statement to the press, which said in its entirety: 'It is quite untrue that there is any rift between the queen and the Duke of Edinburgh.'

Understandably such a dramatic statement, delivered with the full authority of the queen and her most senior advisers, only served to fuel the rumours. Then Mike Parker's solicitors issued a statement that said: 'We are authorised to state that Lt Commander Parker has tendered his resignation as Private Secretary to the Duke of Edinburgh and this has been accepted. The existing circumstances of his marriage make it impossible for him to carry on with his present occupation.'

The newspapers scented blood. They believed Parker was taking all the flak, in effect covering up for problems within the royal marriage. 'Parker of the Palace Quits', 'Grim Duke Sees Off His Friend, Parker', 'The Duke's Friend in Sensation', screamed the headlines. Over the radio-telephone to HMS *Britannia*, Elizabeth urged Parker to stay on and so, of course, did Philip who had no wish to see his greatest friend removed from his side. Despite rumours and headlines, many in the Establishment believed there was no need for Parker to resign at all. It was the palace courtiers – members of the household – who had secretly made the decision which would not only end Parker's career in the royal household in a rather abrupt and unwelcome manner, but also sever his close relationship with Philip.

For some time, palace courtiers had indicated their concern. They knew from intelligence reports that the two men often had a wild time in and around London, living life to the full, going to different parties. They feared that once the press began to dig deeper they might unravel the secrets of Philip's flirtatious activities which could cause great embarrassment to the queen. They were not prepared to take the risk.

Elizabeth, meanwhile, was kept in the dark as to what was really going on. The courtiers had no wish to add to her marital problems and general stress by telling her everything they knew. Her senior advisers believed that by placing Mike Parker fair and square in the limelight they could perhaps save Philip's reputation and, by degrees, paper over the cracks they knew were ripping Elizabeth's marriage apart.

In the midst of the chaos, it was suggested that Parker should not remain as Philip's secretary on account of his impending divorce action – but this, in fact, could hardly be the case. At that time, the Prime Minister himself, Sir Anthony Eden, was a divorced man who had married again. And another senior cabinet minister was also divorced.

At a Guildhall lunch which was held to mark his return from his long world tour, Philip tried to re-establish his reputation with the general public and excuse his actions – he suggested that he was forced to be away from Britain for such a long period of time as an act of duty and service to the crown. He told the assembled privileged guests, 'I believe there are some things for which it is worthwhile making personal sacrifices, and I believe that the British Commonwealth is one of those things and I, for one, am prepared to sacrifice a good deal if, by doing so, I can advance its well being by even a small degree.'

It was, of course, spinning. Certainly Philip had carried out his duties overseas with enthusiasm but he had thoroughly enjoyed his four-month jaunt, a never-ending round of parties, of meeting pretty women, drinking champagne and living a totally self-indulgent life with his best friend. Indeed it was Parker, forced to resign, who had been sacrificed. It was somewhat far-fetched for Philip to say later, 'Parker had to go.'

After his boisterous wartime experiences, Philip simply could not settle down to a life of apparent boredom, confined to Buckingham Palace. He welcomed the suggestion by Mike Parker that they join an exclusive, secret and select gathering of like-minded men called The Thursday Club, so named because the few members always met on a Thursday. Their idea was to bring the weekend closer and have a real bash, usually at Wheeler's, the fish restaurant in Old Compton Street, Soho.

Philip and Parker joined shortly after the Second World War and were still members 12 years later when the Thursday Club, fed up with bad publicity, dissolved itself to re-emerge secretly in Kensington as the Monday Club. (Not, however, the Conservative Party Monday Club!)

Philip had been introduced to the club by his cousin David, the Marquis of Milford Haven, who had remained a close friend since their schooldays in the 1930s. Other club members included the editor of *Tatler* magazine, then an up-market periodical for the aristocracy; a brilliant young Tory politician Ian McLeod who would become Chancellor of the Exchequer; and a well-known, irascible television personality, Gilbert Harding.

Many members of the Thursday Club came from the press, yet they too kept the club a secret. Press members included Arthur Christiansen, editor of the *Daily Express*, the paper Philip was to describe as 'that bloody awful rag'; Frank Owen, the legendary editor of the *Daily Mail*; Harold Keeble, a senior executive who worked on several national dailies; Lord Glenavy, better known as the famous columnist Patrick Campbell; Compton Mackenzie, the author; and legendary British actors like David Niven and James Robertson Justice. Remarkably, it was seven years before knowledge of the club became public.

There were others. One was the infamous Stephen Ward, the son of a canon at Rochester Cathedral, a well-known osteopath and portrait artist who was to cause the biggest political scandal to rock post-war Britain; the other was the famous photographer, Baron. Both men were heavily involved in dubious sexual activities.

Mike Parker accompanied Philip to those Thursday gatherings. The Thursday Club was all-male and needed to be. As well as enjoying good food and excellent wine during the three- and four-hour lunches, members would make amusing and risqué speeches. Much of the talk would be lewd, the jokes usually sexually explicit. The visitors' book was filled with vulgar humour. But the members loved the informal luncheons. There was much loud laughter and revelry. The club survived for over a decade.

One telling incident involved Prince Bernhard of the Netherlands who was invited one Thursday to attend the lunch. When Bernhard was leaving, a slightly drunk Prince Philip knelt down on the floor, made a lavish slave-like bow, and said, 'Give my regards to Her Imperial Majesty.' It was a most significant remark, for Bernhard, too, was consort to his wife Queen Juliana and shared with Philip the predicament of always being number two, of not existing constitutionally and always having to walk the prescribed two paces behind his wife. It may indeed have been a spur-of-the-moment joke but it nevertheless spoke volumes of Philip's deeper feelings towards his role.

Sometimes the club members would leave Wheelers and move on to a luxurious apartment in Grosvenor Square, near the American Embassy, where Philip would sometimes be asked to attend. It was here that the fun really began. The evening would usually start off with card-playing and then, when the drink had flowed for a good while, girls would be brought in. At this point, the eight or so men at the party would start betting on the women in games with names like 'Chase the Bitch' and 'Find the Lady'. Whoever won would then go off to one of the adjoining bedrooms with whichever woman he fancied to the cheers of those left behind. It is not known whether Philip ever did attend such parties but rumours began to spread over the licentious behaviour of some of his Thursday Club friends.

Elizabeth finally came to learn of the goings-on at the Thursday Club through the tabloid press. Desperate in her determination to trust her husband, she did just that. She had read a number of scurrilous stories in the newspaper hinting that Philip and Mike Parker were partying and womanising wherever they went. She asked Philip about the stories and he just dismissed them with a wave of the hand as 'nonsense'. He also suggested to her that the stories about him were part of the continuing campaign by those who had opposed their marriage. His argument made sense and Elizabeth believed him.

To reassure herself, Elizabeth turned to her maid and great confidante Bobo and asked her advice. And Bobo did reassure her, dismissing the stories as 'newspaper rubbish' and 'tittle tattle'. One of her famous remarks was often, 'You would think there were more important things for them to write about.' And she would leave it at that.

When more detailed accusations against Philip were made Bobo would tell Lilibet, 'Don't you worry your head about such things. We all know that boys will be boys; they will always get up to some mischief.' And on almost every occasion, Elizabeth's naïvety and infinite trust would lead her to accept Bobo's advice and forget the incident.

Elizabeth, of course, had no previous experience whatsoever with the opposite sex. As a child she had never been in mixed company – indeed, the two sexes had been deliberately segregated. As a teenager she had never mixed with boys, never attended teenage parties, and it was not until she was 18 that young men were invited to her birthday parties. In turn, Elizabeth only attended parties that were strictly chaperoned affairs where the young men would have been checked for their suitability and adults would always be in attendance to see that nothing untoward, like kissing or drinking, took place. Elizabeth never had a teenage romance, never had a boyfriend other than Philip, and during her teenage years he had been away most of the time in the Royal Navy.

Philip had told her, ever since 1946, that the Thursday Club was just a gentleman's luncheon club where a few chaps relaxed, told a few stories and had a good meal once in a while. He went along for the relaxation and to enjoy men's company. He claimed it was just like being back in the wardroom aboard ship.

Obviously Mike Parker totally supported his friend and boss saying, 'We've been given the reputation of being wild but the truth is that we enjoyed fun and going round with people who knew what was going on. The Thursday Club was a great sounding base and the idea that it was a drunken orgy was absolute rubbish. People got very merry but never drunk. As far as being wild, not guilty. As far as hanging around women, not guilty.'

In 1982 Parker's first wife Eileen wrote *Step Aside for Royalty* in which she revealed that Philip and her husband were in the habit of slipping out of the Palace at night on clandestine jaunts under the pseudonyms 'Murgatroyd and Winterbottom'. She did not reveal what the two got up to, but she had opened a Pandora's box. She left the readers to use their imagination. When asked about the allegations in the book, Philip commented, 'I had no idea that Eileen had written a book. Now that you have mentioned it I have no intention whatever of reading it.'

Perhaps he was wise not to do so, for Eileen Parker, who knew her husband had been involved in a steamy affair, wrote, 'There had been a number of people in high places before Michael whose marriages had ended and who had continued with their careers. My first instinct was to blame sheer panic for Mike's abrupt decision. But on reflection I started to wonder if his resignation was a smokescreen for something, or somebody, else.'

There were, however, other more serious scandals in which Philip's name was banded about. There were rather unusual parties to which Philip and Mike Parker were sometimes invited, thrown by the legendary photographer Baron Nahum, who had taken pictures of the royal family and who had been an enthusiastic member of the Thursday Club. Baron and Philip became close friends and were both, for a time, on the organising committee of the Thursday Club. Eileen Parker, however, knew something of Baron's secret, more scandalous parties. Baron was no model of sexual propriety. His sexual proclivities were bizarre, to the say the least, and he revelled in the reputation.

Baron was a society photographer with a withered arm which caused him to crouch in a crablike manner when taking photographs. and which gave him a somewhat sinister appearance. Philip had met Baron through Uncle Dickie who had wangled Baron the job of royal photographer. It was he who took Elizabeth and Philip's wedding pictures. Baron, however, was not only famous for his outlandish dinner parties but also for the intimate private parties that were held at his apartment, during which anything went. There was sado-masochism; whippings performed by men on girls and girls on men; bondage; girls who served the drinks and the food dressed only in masonic aprons; and, on some occasions, group sex. The guest list was kept secret, however, and those who attended were few in number. The aforementioned Stephen Ward, one of Baron's friends, was one of several who, as well as attending, also provided girls, mistresses and prostitutes for the influential and powerful.

Philip's passionate interest in polo evidently brought him into frequent contact with many beautiful women as well. And as a result, his name became linked with numerous women. In the late '50s and early '60s, Philip was playing polo two and three times a week. Most of the women he met were married to other players. More often than not the women would turn up at Windsor Great Park and Cowdray to watch their husbands play. Elizabeth, too, enjoyed attending polo at Windsor on Sunday afternoons after lunch at the castle. Occasionally, she would invite the players to Windsor Castle for a swim in the pool and she too would change into a one-piece bathing suit and join the men.

As well as playing at Windsor and Cowdray, Philip would often take part in polo tournaments which always ended with champagne and parties and often a dip in a swimming pool. One of those who was attracted to him was the late Susie Ferguson, former wife of Major Ronald Ferguson and mother of the irrepressible Sarah. Undoubtedly their marriage was shaky and the beautiful Susie left Major Ron for the handsome Argentine polo player and wealthy land owner Hector Barrantes because she would no longer put up with her husband's philandering.

As a wealthy patron of a number of polo teams during many seasons in the '60s and '70s recalled, 'Philip attracted and was attracted by a number of polo wives. How many I don't know, but at least a dozen or more during those years. It was a well known fact. I would watch him chatting to them after play, perhaps over champagne or a beer. He had them eating out of his hand. They were attracted to the macho image of the game and Philip was always a strikingly handsome man. In his polo gear, even more so. These matters were well known and yet, to his credit, he was most discreet and, it must be said, the women have behaved impeccably, never kissing and telling.'

Philip's favourite polo tournaments, however, did not take place in Britain but in France. They were held each year in the 1960s at St Memse, near Orly Airport, usually at the end of May. They were held at a stunning chateau owned by Robert de Balkany, a millionaire Romanian of humble origins who, after a Yale education, made a fortune from real estate. Once married to Maria Gabriello, daughter of Italy's ex-King Umberto, Robert de Balkany had built a great polo field on his estate where he kept 50 ponies and about two dozen grooms. The chateau also contained a beautiful cobbled courtyard with stables on two sides. A millionaire who attended several tournaments at St Memse said:

'Four or five teams and their patrons would be invited for the weekend and I saw Prince Philip there on a number of occasions. Before arriving one would be phoned and asked if we were bringing a lady or would prefer to take pot luck. There was nothing crude. The ambience was relaxed and wonderful, the food was exquisite and the wines superb. The parties were held in this fabulous bar and large room and we would be given bedrooms above this long hall. There was also an enormous shower room where everyone could shower at the same time and, of course, a number of individual bathrooms.

'The ladies present were wonderful and always so very sophisticated. Philip used to enjoy himself immensely as did everyone who attended. The queen certainly never accompanied him on those weekends and I don't remember him ever arriving with a lady. I think he preferred to take pot luck. As far as I remember he spent a lot of time chatting to a number of the ladies. It was all so discreet. I remember that Princess Grace Kelly used to attend the weekends occasionally and would often chat with Philip. But she was only interested in one man, David Niven, the actor. They had a remarkable relationship; David Niven was undoubtedly one of the great loves of her life, she adored him. And when you saw them together it was magic.

'The young ladies who were invited for the weekend were known of course, most of them friends of friends. The patrons would arrive on Friday, the players on Saturday and we would fly home on Sunday evening. It was the perfect polo weekend.'

Besides the passing romances Philip enjoyed throughout his polo-playing years, there were a number of well-known women with whom Philip became friendly. Perhaps one of the best known was the beautiful actress Merle Oberon, but these women apparently enjoyed flirtatious romances with Philip which went on for a number of years. Merle Oberon was 45 when she first met Philip, (she was ten years his senior) but she looked as though she was still in her twenties. Petite and slight with dark, smiling, almond-shaped eyes, an olive complexion and an engaging personality, she appealed enormously to Philip's idea of the perfect woman. They met through Dickie Mountbatten. From the moment he was introduced to Merle in 1956, Philip was smitten. He thought her one of the most beautiful women he had ever met.

Merle Oberon, who died in 1979, was a remarkable woman. She was born of mixed race in the slums of Bombay in the days of the Raj but was determined to end quickly her life of poverty. Her fine features and natural beauty helped and she never revealed her humble background, taking her secret to the grave. She told the world she was the daughter of an army officer, born in Tasmania. In reality Estelle Merle O'Brien Thompson was the daughter of a mechanical engineer from Darlington, England, and her mother was a nurse, part Irish, part Sinhalese with some Maori blood. Her parents nicknamed the lovely Merle, 'Queenie'. Her father returned to England, deserting Merle when she was still a child and leaving her to be brought up alone by her doting mother.

Merle Oberon obtained her first film part in 1929 and her career took off in the 1930s after meeting Alexander Korda, one of Britain's great moviemakers. They became lovers and eventually married. But like many movie marriages it was not to last. In all, Merle married four times but always kept a soft spot in her heart for her blond Viking Prince, Philip.

Secret dates were organised and Philip and Merle became close friends. At the begining of the '60s, a two-week holiday was arranged at Merle Oberon's beautiful house in Acapulco where she lived with her husband, the multi-millionaire Italian–Mexican Bruno Pagliai whom she had married in July 1957. Lord Mountbatten went there for a holiday with his secretary John Barratt and Philip accompanied him.

Miss Oberon had designed the magnificent house overlooking Acapulco Bay. A built-in waterfall cascades towards the swimming pool by the sea, and exotic flowers fill the beautiful, large garden. Philip and Merle would often eat alone in the open under a canopy of tall trees overlooking the bay, considered one of the most romantic places in the world. Merle had named the house 'Ghalal', the Mexican word for love. When she decided to sell her home, she commented, 'Many people are going to be sad about me selling the house because we threw some wonderful parties. When Philip heard the news he phoned to say he felt a pang in his heart at the thought of the house being sold.' According to John Barratt, Mountbatten's private secretary and confidant for 20 years: 'There was obviously great sexual chemistry between the two and Philip spent most of the time in her company. It seemed her husband was away. At night we would often leave the two of them alone and they would go for walks together in the moonlit gardens. It was a most romantic atmosphere.'

Indeed, they met quite frequently after that. On one occasion Philip was aboard the Royal Yacht *Britannia* when it sailed into Acapulco Bay. He ordered a five-gun salute to be fired in the direction of Miss Oberon's house giving further rise to the speculation of an affair.

At the beginning of 1962 Philip travelled 58,000 miles through South America visiting more than a dozen countries. The official records of that remarkable trip, officially sanctioned to 'stimulate British commercial relations' should have been released in 1993 under the government's 30-year rule, but the Foreign Office has instructed that they remain sealed until 2023. A Foreign Office spokesman said, 'The tendency is to release all papers after 30 years, unless things are terribly sensitive.'

Philip's trip apparently developed into a roisterous affair. Philip managed to play a few games of polo in Argentina and spent most evenings being entertained in every capital city. An Argentine polo player commented, 'All the beautiful women of Buenos Aires were at Philip's feet.'

Before his visit to Argentina in the last week of March 1962, the Peronists had won a landslide election victory and the senior Argentine army officers were apoplectic. All in the capital believed that a military coup was imminent. Because of Prince Philip's visit the military agreed to postpone the coup until Philip had left the country and the British Embassy was informed.

Philip's official visit to Buenos Aires went well with flag-waving crowds turning out to cheer. Then Philip travelled to La Concepción for three days of rest, recuperation, polo and partying. He stayed with the wealthy Blaquier family, the epitome of Argentine high society, combining historic and social credentials with great wealth.

In the early 1960s, Malena Blaquier, a beautiful, stylish widow in her early forties, owned La Concepción, following the death of her husband Silvestre in a plane crash. Malena was the social megastar of Argentina who threw the most fabulous parties of the social set. She happily agreed to act as hostess to Philip for his three days' rest and gave him the run of the place, then the centre of Argentina's polo-mad aristocrats.

The enchanting Malena had an outrageous reputation and she and Philip spent the three days enjoying La Concepción and its famed hospitality. During the day Philip enjoyed polo and lazing around the swimming pool with Malena; at night, grand balls, dinners, barbecues, midnight swims and walks through the warm late summer evenings. 'For most of the time Malena was at his side,' recalled a guest.

So enchanted did Philip become that he stayed an extra day at La Concepción. Philip's motorcade was making its way to Buenos Aires airport when the scheduled military coup began and tanks and thousands of soldiers were on the streets to prevent any rebellion against the new military junta who had seized power. And yet, such a detail would not have made it necessary for the Foreign Office to insist on hiding the state papers for a further 30 years. Although the real reason remains a mystery, it is widely accepted that Philip is involved.

Details of his long tour are sparse. Indeed, most British newspapers at the time praised him for his flag-waving trip while recognising his failings. As the *News of the World* reported in April 1962, 'His enemies say he is arrogant, overbearing and has an exaggerated idea of his role in the monarchy. His friends describe him as loyal, highly intelligent, hard-working, with a deep desire to do the job to the very best of his ability.'

The editorial continued, 'His friends say he has travelled the world showing the flag. His enemies regard these trips as junkets, highly relished by someone they still regard as an extravagant play-boy.'

The person who terrified many people was the seedy Stephen Ward, the man at the centre of the Profumo Scandal which electrified Britain during the early '60s. Ward, who had been trained as an osteopath in America, became a minor celebrity among the rich and famous for successfully treating their back problems. His list of patients included Philip's cousin, David Milford Haven, Winston Churchill, Averell Harriman, Danny Kaye and Elizabeth Taylor. But there were secret aspects of Stephen Ward's life which were to shock the nation.

Ward, then in his fifties, would bring pretty young women, some of them call-girls, to Cliveden, the home of Lord Astor, for weekends of sex, revelry and debauchery. Ward had been loaned a cottage on the Cliveden estate and would frequently stay there during the summer. A talented artist and portrait painter of some repute, Ward was granted the rare privilege of an exhibition at Leggatt's, the queen's personally authorised dealers in art, under royal patronage. Ward's subjects included Labour leader Hugh Gaitskell, Prime Minister Harold Macmillan, Cabinet Minister Duncan Sandys, Lord Boothby, Douglas Fairbanks and Sophia Loren. Ward went on to paint the Duke of Kent, Princess Margaret, Lord Snowdon, the Duke of Gloucester and, of course, Prince Philip. He was on first name terms with everyone who attended the parties, though they didn't realise that he was the supplier of the enthusiastic young 'amateur' prostitutes who were also invited for weekends at Cliveden.

The nubile young girls, including the famous Christine Keeler and Mandy Rice-Davies, both teenagers at the time, would serve drinks to the gentlemen, serve at table and indulge in whatever sexual kicks the Cliveden set requested.

A City millionaire who attended three Cliveden weekend parties in the early '60s recalls: 'I remember standing by the swimming pool one lovely summer's evening and this attractive young girl came up to me wearing nothing but a maid's white hat and a tiny apron which did not even cover her pubic hair. Her breasts and everything else were naked. She asked me what I wanted to drink. It was, in fact,

Mandy Rice-Davies. A little later another girl, dark-haired, came out to announce that dinner was served. She was wearing just a little hat and long thigh-high black boots and nothing else whatsoever. In her hand she carried a long whip. Very sexy. And that was Christine Keeler.

'About a dozen men were at dinner and about six or seven girls would serve the wine and the food, the girls virtually naked. It was after dinner that the fun and games began and, of course, most of the girls would end up in bed with one or two of the men. It was accepted practice. The girls would be well paid I suppose, but I never saw any money change hands. I suspected that for most of the time they did it for fun. They revelled in the champagne, the high-life.'

It was at one or two of these weekend parties for the rich and famous that John Profumo, who was then the Tory War Minister, met Christine Keeler and they had an affair. She was also having sex with the Soviet naval attaché to Britain, Captain Yevgeny Ivanov, who had also attended parties at Cliveden. In a sensational news-paper article Keeler confessed that she had been urged by Stephen Ward to obtain from Profumo the delivery date of US warheads to the West German Army. Nuclear warheads had in fact been in Germany since 1958, according to a NATO secret document, but US officers in Bonn were in charge of them, not the German Army. Ward's request to Keeler for information from Profumo was made at a time when the War Secretary was discussing the matter in the House of Commons.

Ward maintained he had become involved with top-level espionage in an effort to stave off a possible nuclear war at the time of the Cuban missile crisis of 1961 and 1962. Three days after Keeler's bombshell story hit the headlines, Ivanov, who was known as a Soviet spy by MI6, fled to Moscow, never to return to Britain.

A bon vivant and multi-millionaire of Italian descent, Profumo had married the talented actress Valerie Hobson. He first tried to persuade Christine Keeler to remain silent about their affair and then stood up in the House of Commons and denied he had ever had sex with her. He went to see Prime Minister Harold Macmillan and told him there was no truth in Keeler's story. An angry Ward was determined the truth should come out and began informing London society that Profumo had lied. In an effort to silence him, the Establishment decided Ward had gone too far and arranged for his arrest. He was charged with obtaining illegal earnings from prostitution. Ward's arrest failed to stop the rumours and two months later Profumo confessed.

Eventually Ward stood trial on living off immoral earnings, and

Keeler, as well as three other call-girls, testified that they had given part of their immoral earnings to Ward. No one would speak in Ward's defence despite the fact that many titled people, a number of cabinet ministers, as well as members of the Establishment, knew him well. That hurt Ward and he allegedly took an overdose of barbiturates while on his way from jail to court on the very day the jury was to announce its verdict. He never recovered consciousness and never heard he had been found guilty. He would have been sentenced to about 14 years' imprisonment.

Since then, suggestions have been made that Ward did not commit suicide but was murdered by Britain's security services, fearful that he might tell all at a later stage about his involvement with MI5 and MI6. Removing him once and for all would not only save the reputation of the security services, but the good names of many of Britain's rich and famous. At the time, Premier Macmillan wrote in his diary, 'Partly by the blackmailing statements of the call-girls and partly by Soviet agents exploiting the position, more than half the cabinet were being accused of perversion, homosexuality and the like.' Macmillan went to the grave believing the entire Profumo affair had been engineered by the Soviets to remove one of Britain's foremost pro-nuclear ministers.

Elizabeth, of course, knew of every detail of the scandal. She read of the facts in her dispatch boxes, and in the newspapers, as the story unfolded. Elizabeth never put all the blame on Profumo, preferring to believe that Profumo's only sin was that he had been found out, not that he had been living an adulterous, scandalous, sexual life with young prostitutes, and thereby putting national security at risk. Indeed, Elizabeth chose to remain on friendly terms with Profumo and many years later was smiling happily with him when she awarded him a medal, Companion of the British Empire, for charitable work with London's poor.

Some suggest that Elizabeth is incapable of seeing the bad side of anyone's character, that she always gives them the benefit of the doubt, no matter what the judgement of their peers, or even of the courts. She also seems to believe that much of life is simply bad luck in being caught out, and staunchly believes no one would deliberately put at risk their marriage, their reputation, or in Profumo's case, national security. It is as if she has a blind spot in her character, perhaps because she has known so very few people particularly well in her life. Those she has known well, such as her beloved Bobo, she has trusted implicitly. Having met perhaps hundreds of thousands of people and made many acquaintances, real friends are very few and far between. Naïvely, perhaps, she believes that those with whom she comes into daily contact, her family, her few close friends and her advisers, will always tell her the truth.

But the rumours surrounding Philip about his alleged affairs with a number of women continued to be the stuff of gossip, though the newspapers were careful never to reveal such tantalising stories. However, some of his alleged escapades reached the ears of newspaper magnates and, as a result, some allegations were passed on, most diplomatically, to government ministers.

Occasionally Philip was even invited to attend the infamous wild Italian sex parties that were held in Rome in the '60s and on which the film *La Dolce Vita* was based. Between a hundred and a hundred and fifty people would be invited to the Palazzio Borganza in Rome, the perfect setting to throw sensational parties. The parties were held on the first Monday of each month for most of the year. The invitation list read like a *Who's Who* of the international jet-set, people who wanted to enjoy their lives to the hilt and had the money and the connections to do so. Many well-known Americans were invited, like Harry Winston and Charlie Robson from Revlon, the Agnellis and a few of the European royals like Prince Philip. The Sicilian Massimo brothers were also involved. Those who attended were mostly Italian, French and American financiers, bankers and socialites as well as international polo players, tennis stars and generally those who had the money to fly to Rome once a month just for a party.

A French millionaire who went to a few parties recalled: 'I was totally taken aback the first time I attended one of the Borganza parties. I had heard rumours of the goings-on but wow, these parties were fantastic, unbelievable. There were really two parties going on, the one for men only which was strictly a stag party and the other for men and women. Sometimes a group of gays would hold their own party upstairs.

'Everyone wore dinner dress and about fifty or sixty men would be chatting and drinking cocktails or champagne waiting for dinner. Just before dinner a bevy of perhaps fifty beautiful young women would walk down the central stairway. They were naked except for outrageous hats, and sometimes masks.

'They would go into the dining room and disappear. Before dinner the men would be invited to take off their trousers and leave them, walking into dinner immaculately dressed, but with no trousers. They would sit down to dinner at this magnificent table and hidden beneath the tablecloth were the girls who spent twenty minutes or so taking care of the men. Outrageous but wonderful!

'After dinner there was gambling: roulette, blackjack, chemin de fer, poker, whatever; well organised and very civilised. And, naturally, the champagne and wine would flow. At the end of the evening the girls would reappear. They would all take part in what was called 'The Rome Olympics'. Twelve girls, all naked, would lie down on the floor in the beautiful drawing room, and the men would be invited to lay bets, not on the girls but on the men. The competition was to see which man could have sexual intercourse with all the girls without ejaculating and, of course, the girls were encouraged to really make love, to be seductive and vigorous in their love-making. And each man had to stay with each girl for at least seven minutes.

'It was hilarious. Most of the men failed after two or three girls and I hardly ever saw one man complete the task. To enter the competition each man had to put a thousand dollars into the kitty and was then permitted to take part. Whoever completed making love to all twelve girls first, won the jackpot. Usually twenty to thirty men took part. At the same time, however, tens of thousands of dollars were wagered in side bets by those simply watching. The trick was to select a man who was not very well endowed and not very young. Experience told. I actually won the pool a couple of times. Today it sounds dreadful but it was great fun. Those parties in Rome had style; they really were the dolce vita.'

And at the end of the evening, after more drinking and hilarity, the girls would join some of the visiting men, either staying the night in one of the many bedrooms or in the visitors' hotels.

The festivities came to an abrupt end in the summer of 1969 after one of the girls who had attended the party was found dead outside. She had not only indulged in a great deal of intercourse but she had died from an overdose of drugs. When the police began to investigate they discovered some of the names of the people present and the possibility of a scandal finished everything.

Similar parties were also held at Estoril in Portugal, and that too attracted many jet-setters. But these too came to an end at about the same time after a young fisherman's son was found dead on the beach having been raped. The party had been thrown by the King of Italy. One diplomat from the British Embassy staff in Portugal was brought home immediately after the incident because he had attended the party. It is known that Prince Philip attended one or two parties hosted by European royalty but there is no record of him ever participating in any of the sexual frolics. There is no record of his attending the parties at Estoril.

It is alleged that Philip sometimes visited the infamous Directors Club in London's Duke's Yard, off Jermyn Street not far from Piccadilly with his side-kick, Mike Parker, but there is no record of this either. A drinking club for the privileged, it was visited by more than half the cabinet, members of the House of Lords, financiers, bankers and those members of the aristocracy who liked visiting London for a night on the town. One room had been converted into a small theatre with a tiny stage. Late at night girls would arrive to titillate the sexual palates of the members and perform the most way-out kinky acts on stage to the cheers of the male audience. As a British tycoon commented: 'I went there quite often during the late 1960s because the people who frequented the club were among the most influential in the land. But the sex acts were worse than anything I had ever seen, worse even than those in Marseilles brothels, which had a dreadful reputation. In the Directors Club they even introduced a donkey on stage for the girls. It really went too far.

'It has always been said that the night the club was raided by the police there were 105 people there; half of them said they were named Smith and the others said they only spoke German. If they had arrested everyone in the club that night there would have been hardly anyone at the next day's cabinet meeting for most of the government ministers were there.'

Because of Philip's naturally boisterous character and his service in the Royal Navy, it is not surprising that he would occasionally enjoy wild, risqué parties. Understandably he had to be most discreet and, it must be stressed, he has always been so. Indeed, it is remarkable that so little has been written in books, newspapers and magazines about Philip's rather exuberant life during the past 50 years, proving perhaps that discretion had become his watchword. As a Royal Naval officer, Philip would have understood that whatever his private life he should not under any circumstances run the risk of embarrassing Elizabeth, his children, the monarchy or the nation. Despite Philip's vigilant awareness of the need for prudent behaviour, he has nevertheless been involved with a succession of married women throughout his life, some of a platonic nature but certainly not all. One can hardly doubt the enormous risks which, if publicised in the national press, would have caused severe embarrassment to Elizabeth and the entire family.

Even before Elizabeth had been crowned queen, Philip's name had been linked with other well known British stars and artistes including the beautiful Pat Kirkwood, known as the Champagne girl of the '50s, who was unofficially engaged for a while to the photographer Baron. But she denies any involvement with Philip, despite the fact she and Philip were seen dancing for hours on end one night at the Milroy Club, one of London's brighter nightspots of the 1950s.

But Pat Kirkwood did happily reveal how Philip loved to let his hair down and really enjoy himself. She also gave an insight into how Philip reacted to women he really liked. She recalled, 'We stayed dancing for ages. He was fantastic, dancing foxtrots, sambas, quick steps. It was ballroom dancing in those days. We got on like a house on fire. He told me not to bother saying Sir or Prince Philip or your Highness or anything. The dance floor was packed and everyone was coming on just to see Philip dance so wildly with me, Pat Kirkwood.'

Pat Kirkwood, Baron, Philip and another naval officer, Captain 'Basher' Watkin, who was also present, stayed at the club until the early hours, leaving only when the staff were placing the chairs on the tables. The four of them then went to Baron's apartment where he cooked scrambled eggs. The party didn't break up until 5 a.m. when Philip took a taxi home. That night Elizabeth was at Balmoral in Scotland. But it wasn't long before she knew of her husband's wild behaviour.

News of Philip's night on the tiles reached the newspapers within twenty-four hours and reports were on the desks of senior members of the household the following day. King George was not amused. He was incensed at the thought of Lilibet's husband acting in such an outrageous manner, dancing through the night with cabaret stars and drinking at London nightspots. He flew into one of his violent tempers instructing his staff to have Philip carpeted immediately and to remind him in no uncertain terms that he was now married to the future queen of England and that he had better learn to behave himself.

Within hours, a senior member of the royal household had called on Philip and warned him of the king's displeasure. He also ordered him to keep out of nightclubs, stay out of the limelight and not put Elizabeth's or the family's reputation at risk in the future. He was also informed that the warning came on the direct orders of the king who had been appalled by his behaviour. Philip learned fast. Never again was he seen in public acting in such a manner with any other woman. Indeed, he learned the lesson so well that despite his philandering and love of partying, something that went on for decades, only a handful of people knew of it. And they have kept their silence.

Pat Kirkwood's detailed account of her night with Prince Philip in 1949 reveals how Philip loved to escape the confines of the palace, even in the early days of his marriage to Elizabeth, at a time when she was unburdened by the responsibilities of the monarchy and Philip and Elizabeth had been married for less than two years. Affairs, however, would continue to form part of Philip's life for decades.

7. PHILIP'S SECRETS

Perhaps the best kept secret in the hearts of most members of the royal family, including Elizabeth and her four children, has been Prince Philip's 20-year friendship with one of Britain's favourite princesses, the lovely Alexandra of Kent, daughter of the late Duke and Duchess of Kent.

The late Duke, a handsome and talented artist, was the younger brother of King George VI. Until the lovely Marina, Alexandra's mother came along, the bisexual Duke of Kent had shown a greater interest in men than in women. The Duke would, on occasion, appear at private dinner parties wearing lots of make-up and sometimes dress up in women's clothes. His sexual appetite was legendary, and not without foundation, and he did not much mind if his partner of the night was male or female.

Marina, a snobbish and stunningly elegant woman, was an exiled, penniless Greek princess with Teutonic arrogance, and a cousin of Prince Philip. Marina boasted that she and her husband George were the most royal family in the land and would refer to Queen Elizabeth (the Queen Mother) and Margaret, the queen's sister, as 'those common little Scottish girls'. The comment was reported to Queen Elizabeth II who understood the comment was an insult to her mother. She was not amused.

Born in 1936 and 15 years younger than Philip, Princess Alexandra is perhaps the most natural of all the royals. With her fun-loving personality, she is undoubtedly one of the nation's favourites, endearing herself to everyone with her natural, warm smile and gentle character; rather like the Queen Mother who always seems so pleased to meet and chat with everyone.

As a schoolgirl in the '40s and early '50s, she had a reputation as a gregarious, happy girl, popular with everyone. Even in those days she admitted she was fond of Prince Philip, telling school friends, 'When I marry he must be rich, madly in love with me and he must be tall.' Alex, as everyone calls her, grew to be five feet ten inches tall. As for the requirement of wealth, all her classmates knew that Alex was always dressed in secondhand clothes, usually hand-me-downs from her cousins Elizabeth and Margaret.

The man who had courted Alex for eight long years, Angus Ogilvy, belonged to one of Britain's most prestigious aristocratic families, the Airlie family. Angus was tall, handsome and highly intelligent; and he was madly in love with her. Unfortunately, Angus wasn't very rich and never has been, even after a lifetime of working in the City.

Angus Ogilvy did not want to become a part of the royal family though his own family had been senior members of the royal household for generations, and still are. He knew the problems of marrying into the royals. Ironically, it was Elizabeth who came to the rescue declaring that while her first cousin, Princess Alexandra, would still be expected to continue her royal duties, representing the queen on occasion and chairing charities, Angus could continue his career in the City. The marriage finally took place in great splendour in Westminster Abbey in 1963. More than 1,500 guests attended the reception held at Windsor Castle. Elizabeth herself led a private bus tour of Windsor Great Park.

At the start of their marriage Alexandra seemed very happy and appeared to friends to be deeply in love and overtly sexually attracted to Angus. Lord Rupert Nevill, who had become Philip's Private Secretary following Mike Parker's resignation, gave a great dinner party to celebrate the marriage. A guest recalls, 'Alexandra was her charming, smiling self as ever but all she wanted to do was to leave and take Angus home to bed. She used to say quite openly that they could not stay out of bed.'

Angus and Alexandra had two children, James born in 1964 and Marina, named after her grandmother, in 1966. And, of course, since their father was not a member of the royal family, they have no titles – one of the snobbish reasons Alexandra's mother, Marina, did not want her to marry a commoner. But Alexandra didn't mind at all.

The relationship between Alexandra and Prince Philip began some time in the 1950s when Alex was in her early twenties and Philip in his late thirties. She had had a twinkle in her eye for Philip from the day she was a bridesmaid at his wedding in 1947, when she was just eleven years old. She never lost it. As a teenager Alexandra was mature for her years.

As she grew into a beautiful young woman, Alex saw Philip frequently, on royal occasions and at family gatherings. In 1953, when just 17, Alex joined Elizabeth and Philip on a rare spring cruise in the Mediterranean on board the Royal Yacht, *Britannia*. She came to know Philip really well when she would join him for the famous Cowes week regatta each year. The royal family had traditionally attended Cowes week since the reign of George V, who loved his week of competitive sailing. The Royal Yacht would drop anchor in the harbour and the festivities would continue every night after the serious business, the yacht races, were over for the day. The tradition was continued by Mountbatten and by Philip. It was during these weeks at Cowes each year that Philip and Alex became more involved.

Philip loved messing about in small boats, something he had learned to enjoy at Gordonstoun in the 1930s. He had continued pursuing his love of sailing at Dartmouth Naval School and his years in the Royal Navy had given him the opportunity to take part in sailing competitions. Philip was a good sailor and with his natural aggression and competitive spirit, he won many races.

In 1947, the Island Sailing Club of Cowes, on the Isle of Wight, gave Philip and Elizabeth a Dragon-class yacht as a wedding present. The yacht was painted dark blue and Philip christened her *Bluebottle* ('Dragonfly' . . . 'bluefly' . . . 'bluebottle' . . . was Philip's line of thought). For years he sailed her competitively during Cowes week with his regular crew which included the colourful local boat builder Uffa Fox. They made a great sailing team for Fox knew all the problems of sailing around the island waters. He later persuaded the people of Cowes to give Philip one of the first Flying Fifteens racing yachts which he had designed. Prince Philip named her *Cowslip*.

Elizabeth went to Cowes for only one year and did not enjoy the experience too much. She preferred large boats like the Royal Yacht *Britannia*. And it wasn't just the yachting she disliked. A country woman throughout, Elizabeth did not feel at home 'on water' with the informal sailing clique at Cowes who spent the entire week either on the water or talking about boats and the races over a drink at the end of the day.

On the other hand, Alexandra would join Philip on board *Britannia* every year. In the evening she would act as hostess when the sailing fraternity and the local dignitaries came on board for drinks and dinner. There would be party games and dancing which went on into the night. Alex was a most popular and natural hostess who fitted into the informality of the yachting fraternity. In turn, they all loved her and thought it wonderful that Princess Alexandra, who had never seemed interested in sailing, would come to Cowes for their most important week of the year. As Unity Hall stated in her book, *Philip, The Man Behind The Monarchy*: 'In court circles it is common knowledge that they have always been close . . . It is said that she and Prince Philip have come to rely on each other for friendship and support . . . Alexandra's husband is said to feel pangs of jealousy at the depth of the friendship between the two of them, but it is accepted in the royal family that Alexandra and Philip have a special relationship.'

Whenever Elizabeth was away from Buckingham Palace, Alexandra would arrive at the palace or Windsor Castle where she and Philip would swim together. A retainer who has been with the royal family for more than a generation commented, 'You could set your watch on a Thursday afternoon, because at 2.30 p.m. precisely Princess Alexandra would arrive at the palace in her car for her afternoon swim with Prince Philip. The pool was always reserved for Philip for an hour every Thursday afternoon and the entrance to the pool was locked whenever they were in there together. We supposed they didn't want to be disturbed by any other people, members of the family or of the household who were also permitted to use the pool.'

A member of the royal household who was aware of the relationship between Alexandra and Philip was heard to remark on one occasion in the 1970s, 'I don't know how those two manage it – they spend so much time together.' Those who have seen Alexandra and Philip together also note how close they are; the way they talk to each other, the body language, the acknowledged, natural intimacy.

Mountbatten wrote to Philip at the time saying, 'I do hope you will be more discreet in your relationship with Alexandra.' He then pointed out that, as his second cousin, Alexandra and he were 'too close'. Mountbatten also cautioned, 'If news of this affair should enter the public domain you must realise the reflection this would have on the whole family and especially on Lilibet.'

The storm that erupted at that time between Mountbatten and Philip nevertheless had one favourable outcome: Prince Charles, who had always enjoyed a rather good relationship with his great-uncle, now became much closer. Indeed, as time wore on, Mountbatten virtually took over the role of father figure.

When George VI died Elizabeth was only 24 and, almost immediately, Mountbatten became a surrogate father to her, advising, helping and supporting her in every way possible. He revelled in his new role. Mountbatten had become obsessed with Lilibet and would frequently be found expounding on Elizabeth's character, or personality, or her role as sovereign. Repeatedly he declared, 'She is intelligent, bright and undoubtedly the best monarch Britain has had for two centuries.'

How Elizabeth discovered Philip's affair with Alex is not known. But the answer lies in the strange way palace politics work. There are two schools in the palace. The larger one supports the queen, because she is the monarch. A smaller, more aggressive faction supports Philip. Whenever there is a tasty morsel of gossip that either side believes should be passed to their respective leaders, there are always people prepared to put in the knife and deliver the message.

It is not known what conversations passed between Elizabeth and Philip, or her reaction, when she discovered the affair but it can be guessed by what she confessed to Uncle Dickie. Distressed, miserable and unhappy, Elizabeth turned to the only person she could rely on – Mountbatten. Elizabeth had had her suspicions about Philip's possible philandering, but the news that he was involved with Alexandra, a young woman ten years her junior, whom she had always counted as a close friend, hit her hard.

Mountbatten told her that he expected it was just one of Philip's flings and that it would soon be at an end but Elizabeth was not so sure. She had seen the two of them together and had sensed they were indeed close. But now she feared for her marriage and the effect such a revelation would have on the monarchy. Mountbatten assured her that there was no question of Philip leaving her and setting up a discreet 'alternative' home with Alexandra.

Always a gentleman, Mountbatten felt that the hapless Angus Ogilvy, a kind and generous man who suffered for much of his life with severe arthritis, had been badly treated – he had behaved with remarkable loyalty and deference to his wife even if he did believe Philip had behaved like a cad.

Elizabeth also turned to Bishop Mervyn Stockwood, for many years a counsellor and adviser to members of the family, especially to Elizabeth. She discussed the matter with him. It is not known whether the Bishop also discussed the matter with Philip.

It is extraordinary that an affair that involved two members of the royal family, one of whom was married to the queen, has remained a secret for so many years. To the nation and to their beloved Commonwealth, the royals have purported to set an example for all their subjects. Yet the husband of the Head of the established Church of England, whose views on adultery were strict and unwavering, has lived an adulterous life for most of the 50 years he has been married to the queen.

Alexandra's daughter Marina came close to revealing the secret during the family rift in 1989 when, though unmarried, she became pregnant. She was so angry with the reaction of her parents, who urged her to have an abortion, that she threatened to reveal all to a newspaper. Fortunately for her parents, and particularly for Elizabeth and Philip, caution prevailed and, as a result, the long-standing affair remained a closely-guarded royal confidence, known only to a very few.

Time and again those close to the royal family have admitted that, according to the royals themselves, the sin is not in doing something that is morally wrong, but in being found out. Britain's strict libel laws have been instrumental in keeping Philip's adulterous life private. Many newspaper and magazine proprietors also feel that to reveal Philip's behaviour would be to humiliate the royal family and perhaps threaten the monarchy. As a consequence they do not want their journalists to enquire too closely or dig too deeply for fear of what they might discover.

In his bid to enjoy life with as little risk as possible, Philip sought to be invited overseas where he could behave with far more freedom. A favourite jaunt involved the famous Bohemian Grove, deep within the Californian redwoods, 65 miles north of San Francisco. Each summer a thousand or more VIPs – the decision-makers and opinion-moulders of the western world – would meet in mid-July to relax, attend lectures and debates and enjoy themselves for three weeks.

For decades the Bohemian Grove retreat was the major social event of America's male power élite and their overseas friends. And for decades those who frequented the retreat each year went there in secret; another reason why Philip, as well as many others, loved to attend. Herbert Hoover called Bohemian Grove 'the greatest men's club in the world'.

The 2,700-acre Grove, on the banks of the Russian River in Northern California, comprised 128 small camps, each operated by 20 or 30 members. These camps bore such names as 'Wild Oats', 'Woof', and 'Toyland'. The claim to fame of President Reagan's camp, 'Owl's Nest' is a gin-fizz breakfast. Most of the time members sit around and chat, discuss politics, business and deals. They also hunt, fish or just stroll around, going from camp to camp for a drink, a meal and a chat.

Women were not permitted anywhere near the Grove. Even the waiters and kitchen staff were all male. One of the reasons women were banned was because a number of members 'jump the river' when they visit the Grove. They quietly leave their sacred enclave in favour of a trek to nearby Guerneville.

And there were other overseas parties Philip loved to attend. John Barratt, Lord Mountbatten's much maligned private secretary for 20 years, told of one club in Nassau in the Bahamas which Dickie Mountbatten and Prince Philip used to frequent: 'I would sometimes go with Mountbatten but not always. He liked to go and let his hair down there. He rather enjoyed the raunchy atmosphere. So did Philip. It was a place for wealthy, as well as famous, people because everyone was so discreet. One had to be a member or be invited. It was a high-class dive, with lots of heavy drinking, drugs and, of course, high-class whores. The girls waiting for wealthy clients were all very good-looking, usually white, but there were some coffee-coloured girls as well.

'When Mountbatten and Philip were in Nassau they would stay with Sybilla Clark and, more often than not, whenever Philip was in Nassau Christina Ford, Henry Ford's former wife, would be there. Sybilla was an attractive, vivacious American–Italian, bubbly and bright. With her stunning figure and blonde hair, Sybilla was the perfect-looking woman for Prince Philip – exactly his type – and he loved the mini skirts she wore during the late '60s. Philip thoroughly enjoyed his visits to Nassau.'

And yet Philip has been so discreet that he believes he can laugh off any suggestion he has ever been unfaithful to Elizabeth. In December 1992, Philip gave an interview to the *Independent on Sunday* in which he was asked about long-standing rumours that he had had affairs.

He burst out laughing and said, 'Have you ever stopped to think that for the past 40 years I have never moved anywhere without a policeman accompanying me? So how the hell could I get away with anything like that?' Some noted, however, that Philip's wording contained no outright denial.

Prince Philip's relationship with the British press has, to say the least, been chequered. Prince Bernhard of the Netherlands told of one incident during a dinner in New York when he had had to physically restrain Philip from wanting to 'sort out' photographers whom he believed were coming too close.

When press photographers arrived at his meeting with Prime Minister Nehru in New Delhi, in 1959, Philip snapped, 'Who are all these damned people?' And in a direct insult to the impoverished Indian economy at the time, he added, 'I thought there was supposed to be a film shortage in India!' Later, when touring the beautiful Taj Mahal, he shouted at one photographer, 'Get on with your bloody business and stop talking.'

At a horse show in Lahore, a Pakistani photographer he had never met slipped off a flag-pole and fell to the ground. Philip yelled, 'I hope to God he breaks his bloody neck!'

At a famous occasion in Gibraltar, Philip remarked, in reference to the famous apes that inhabit the rock, 'Which are the press and which are the bloody apes?' That remark did not go down at all well with the British press corps. They never forgot his remark and they cetainly never forgave him.

During a state visit to China with the queen in 1986, he referred to his Chinese hosts as 'slitty-eyed'. He was furious the following day when he learned that his remark, made to touring Scottish students, had been plastered all over the British press and several editorials had lambasted him for his offensive remark. Philip's response was to lay the blame at the newspapers' door for reporting his remark at all. On that occasion it is known that Elizabeth became furious with her husband for bringing her, the monarchy and Britain into such disrepute in front of their hosts, the Chinese leaders, making her look foolish and Philip an extremely rude and ill-mannered guest.

Sometimes he couldn't care less if his 'gaffes' were reported or not. In October 1993, at the age of 72, Philip attended a cocktail party in Toronto in aid of the World Wide Fund for Nature. He asked fashion writer Serena French, 'I suppose you'll be looking out for people wearing mink coats then?' She told him, as politely as possible, that no one would wear fur to a wildlife fund event. Philip replied, 'Well, you never know what they're wearing underneath,' and put his hand on the girl's arm. He leaned forward and asked her, 'You're not wearing mink knickers, are you?' He winked at her and roared with laughter at the hilarity of his question.

Sometimes when Philip hurls abuse and swears at the press it is within hearing range of Elizabeth. She generally responds in one of two ways: she either looks the other way and pretends she didn't hear his offensive language or she gives him a hard, cold stare. Philip usually bites his lip, but never replies.

There have been occasions on royal tours when Philip has lost his temper with Elizabeth, complaining bitterly to her about her devotion to duty. Former *Time* photographer Peter Jordan recalls one such moment. Touring the island of Grenada in 1985 Philip exclaimed at Elizabeth, 'Your bloody obsession with shaking hands with everyone. Why do you have to do it? Let's go.' Jordan noted that the queen took not the slightest notice of his outburst and made Philip wait until she had completed her full round of farewells. Philip looked petulant and impatient but gritted his teeth and said nothing more.

Through the years the British press has shown Philip little courtesy; they have taken great delight in poking fun at Prince Philip and deliberately baiting him because they know he will often respond with impatience, irritation and anger, and frequently a number of choice expletives. They want Philip to respond angrily, providing them with good pictures and the journalists with front-page headlines.

In Trinidad in 1987 he turned on reporters and, to their amazement, he snarled, 'You lot have ruined my life.' With a view to making him look ridiculous, the newspapers responded with a description of Philip's life: a young man who arrived in Britain homeless and penniless, now living a life of absolute privilege, with an income at that time of £200,000 a year, palaces and castles to live in, 16 weeks' holiday a year and an army of servants to care for his every whim. Not exactly a life in ruins.

At times Philip totally misjudges his position and the privileges he believes he is automatically entitled to simply because he is married to the queen. Some of his actions have appeared remarkably naïve considering his undoubted intelligence. On one occasion, for example, Philip needed to travel from Holy Island in Scotland to Windsor to play in a polo match later that day. In order to get to Windsor in time he demanded, and was provided with, a naval launch, a destroyer of the Royal Navy, a car, an aircraft of the Queen's Flight and another car at the other end of the trip. He arrived on time thanks to the taxpayer, of course, who had footed the bill which ran into thousands of pounds. And yet Philip thought those demands were perfectly reasonable. He was outraged the following day when newspapers attacked him for wasting so much taxpayers' money so that he could enjoy a game of polo.

Despite all the press criticism, Philip has remained relatively popular with some sections of the British public. In 1969 the *Daily Telegraph* ran a competition to discover whom the British thought would make the best dictator. Prince Philip won handsomely. In many respects Philip would probably have revelled in the role of dictator, for he would have been able to give vent to his modernising ideas; his push for greater scientific and industrial advancement in Britain; for more efficiency in all walks of life; for his ideas for the armed forces, or the way in which to bring up the younger generation.

Throughout his entire adult life, Philip has felt fettered and, as a result, he has become frustrated and angry. Even in the late '80s, when he was over sixty-five years of age, he was not permitted to move some of the royal horses which he uses for carriage-driving from the Royal Mews at Buckingham Palace, where they are kept for state occasions, to Sandringham, 150 miles away. He wanted to build an enormous ménage or arena for schooling horses, as well as extra stables, while running a school from there for Britain's carriage drivers. Philip had designed and organised everything and the money was to be donated by Patricia Kluge, who for ten years was married to John Kluge, one of America's richest men.

Patti Kluge and Philip were to form a close working relationship. Like Philip's, hers too has been a rags-to-riches story. The daughter of an English Arabist, Edmund Rose, and an Iraqi mother, Patti was born in Baghdad and spent much of her youth there. As a teenager she worked as an erotic dancer in a Baghdad night club. At 19 she moved to London and began her working career as a belly dancer at the Labyrinth Club in Bayswater, London. There she met her future husband Russell Gay. She not only began posing nude for his soft-porn magazines but allowed him to write a column of explicit sex advice to readers under her name. In 1973, Patti married her soft-porn publisher.

Three years later Russell Gay moved to Monte Carlo while Patti took off for New York. In 1976 they divorced. It was in New York that she met John Werner Kluge – 30 years her senior and five inches shorter than the statuesque Patti – a man born in Germany, who had come to America as a German immigrant at the age of eight. After attending Columbia University on a scholarship, he became a captain in army intelligence during the Second World War. As a civilian he began buying and selling small radio stations and in the '60s he started to collect TV stations, founding Metropolitan Broadcasting, which became Metromedia. In 1985 Kluge sold Metromedia to Rupert Murdoch for £1.3 billion.

After their marriage in 1981 Patti Kluge began spending, something which continued until the couple separated in 1991. During those ten years Patti was determined to use her husband's enormous wealth – estimated at £3 billion – to achieve her great ambition of becoming involved with Britain's royal family. For some unknown reason the House of Windsor intrigued her.

John Kluge had become a good friend of Armand Hammer, the wealthy American businessman who founded Occidental Oil and maintained strong business and political connections with the Soviet

Union. Then in his eighties, Hammer was also a major philanthropist to his young friend Prince Charles. Some years previously Hammer had persuaded Charles to become patron of the United World Colleges, a group of charitable, multi-national, multi-racial colleges for teenagers which aspire to develop world understanding by breaking down racial prejudices and national barriers.

In November 1985 Hammer organised a charity dinner to raise money for the colleges in Florida and he invited Patti Kluge to become chairwoman of the gala ball. That meant she would meet both Charles and Princess Diana. But just before the ball was due to take place, Patti's 'past' was mysteriously revealed and John and Patti Kluge decided to take an impromptu world cruise instead. However, Patti did receive a letter from Charles spelling out his unhappiness and sympathy at the way she had been treated. As Charles said at the time, 'I can't see what all the fuss is about.'

As if to prove his point, Charles later accepted an invitation to go aboard the Kluge yacht, *The Virginian*, and spent some time with John and Patti Kluge during his Majorcan holiday in 1987. Diana was also invited, but she declined. Despite that small setback, Patti Kluge's determination continued apace. She invited one of Charles's best friends, the wealthy Duke of Westminster, and his wife Tally to live on *The Virginian* during a week of fundraising in New York in aid of leukaemia research. And another of Prince Charles's close royal friends, King Constantine of Greece, attended a weekend house-warming party at the Kluges' 4,000-acre Virginia estate in 1986. Prince Andrew and Fergie went to lunch with them and Charles and Diana returned the Kluges' hospitality by inviting them to dinner at Highgrove.

In the mid-'80s Patti Kluge, now approaching forty, decided to take up competitive carriage-driving, a very expensive and a most difficult sport, one in which Prince Philip had first participated only a few years earlier. During those years Philip spent a great amount of time perfecting his driving and schooling his horses, and he saw a lot of Patti. Physically, Patti was Philip's type of woman: a tall, shapely, good-looking, athletic woman with a charming personality, smiling eyes and a most attractive face.

She came to Britain in 1985 and met Philip while discussing carriage-driving with 30-year-old David Saunders, Philip's coachman at Sandringham. During that year Patti volunteered to fund the building of the royal ménage at Sandringham and set up a comprehensive carriage-driving centre. Philip was delighted. Patti Kluge bought six magnificent horses and stabled them at Sandringham at a cost of £50,000 a year.

Philip decided to move his royal horses from London to the centre and as was customary, he put forward his idea for moving the horses from Buckingham Palace to Sandringham to the members of the royal household who have to pass such ideas, those, that is, which involve the monarchy and the state. They rejected his plan even though it would have cost the taxpayers nothing. They argued that the royal horses had always been stabled at the Royal Mews next to Buckingham Palace and there they would stay.

One of Philip's close friends described his reaction when news of the decision reached him. He said, 'I was involved with the development of the idea and Philip phoned me one day to tell me what had happened. I have never heard or seen him so furious in my life. He was outraged. He went absolutely berserk.'

Eventually Philip took the problem to the only person who could help – his wife. She told him she was just as hide-bound by the rules as he was, and that there was nothing she could do. Elizabeth told him that if 'they' – those who ran the palace – decreed the horses could not be moved then there was nothing whatsoever she could do about it.

This decision highlighted once again for Philip the total lack of power and authority he has been permitted by the Establishment throughout his entire life. After Philip had been refused permission to keep the royal horses at Sandringham it was announced that the Sandringham Driving Centre would be closed down and that Mrs Kluge would take her horses away.

During her relationship with Prince Philip, Patti persuaded her husband John to spend £7 million to buy Mar Lodge, a Victorian mansion set in a magnificent 77,500-acre estate that had been built in 1896 for Edward VII's daughter Princess Louise. The neighbouring estate was Elizabeth's beloved Balmoral Castle. Patti's husband spent another £6 million renovating the dilapidated mansion and constructing a modern stable yard complete with a harness room which featured a crystal chandelier! She also persuaded John to fund, for five years, the Royal Windsor Horse Show which is run every year from the Mews at Windsor Castle. While Elizabeth was prepared to accept £50,000 a year from Patti Kluge to sponsor the Royal Show, she hardly ever met her, even during the Horse Show that she was sponsoring and that Elizabeth graced with her presence.

In 1988, Patti's team of American greys won the major trophy, the Harrods International Driving Grand Prix. Patti climbed into the royal box beside her driver, ready to be officially introduced to the queen and receive the prize from her. But Elizabeth hardly looked at her, and handed the prize to the driver instead.

Prince Philip's adult life can probably be divided into two rather distinct periods: pre-1957 and post-1957. By 1957 Philip had been married ten years and Squadron Leader Henry Moresby Chinnery replaced Mike Parker as his Private Secretary. In an interview with the *New York Post*, Parker's estranged wife said, 'My advice to Mrs Chinnery is that it would be better if she lived in London. Then she would be sure of seeing her husband fairly often.'

The relationship between Alexandra and Prince Philip began to fade somewhat in the 1990s and they drifted apart, though they continued to see each other from time to time. It was at about this time that Philip turned his attention to Lady Penny Romsey, who in 1979 had married Norton Knatchbull, Philip's godson. Norton, who became Lord Romsey, was the grandson of Earl Mountbatten.

Penny, who has been described as gorgeous, startling, pretty and beautiful, has captured many hearts with her great sense of fun, her quick wit and intelligence. Her father, Reginald Eastwood, the man who founded the Angus Steak House restaurant chain, wanted the very best for his bright daughter. Penny was educated at the Lycée Française in Kensington and attended the exclusive Le Rosey finishing school on the shores of Lake Geneva. On her return, however, she wanted none of the debutante season and chose instead to study at the London School of Economics. She first met Prince Philip at Windsor Great Park when Prince Charles took her along one day to watch polo. She was introduced to Philip who immediately insisted that she come and sit next to him in the royal enclosure. Apparently, they got on famously. She was just twenty. The bond between Lord and Lady Romsey and the royal family deepened following the death from cancer of the couple's five-year-old daughter Leonara in 1992. Since then, Philip has not only given great comfort, described as 'her pillar of strength', but he also advised her when she decided to set up a cancer charity in memory of Leonara. The fund has raised hundreds of thousands of pounds for research. (It was not the first time tragedy had struck. In 1979 Lord Romsey's brother, Nicholas, along with Lord Mountbatten and his grandmother Doreen had been killed in Ireland by an IRA bomb.)

It was in 1994 that Philip and Penny began seeing more of each other when the prince introduced her to his favourite sport, carriage-driving. It seems that Penny showed skill at the sport and has spent many weekends with Philip competing in trials and competitions all over the country. Philip usually handles a pony-class team of four horses while Penny competes in the pony-tandem class, driving two horses. They often train together at Windsor, Sandringham, Balmoral and Drumlanrig, near Dumfries, one of the historic houses of the Duke of Buccleuch, with the help of Philip's coachman, Micky Flynn. Penny Romsey, now 45 and still youthful and engaging, is permitted to travel on royal yets and helicopters when flying to join Philip.

It appears that since 1998 Penny and her husband have been drifting apart and friends are worried that their marriage may be going through a rocky period. In July 1998 neither she nor Philip attended the wedding of Mountbatten's grandson, Timothy Knatchbull, though Elizabeth, Prince Charles, Princess Margaret and Lord Romsey were at Winchester Cathedral. Instead Philip and Penny, the bridegroom's sister-in-law, chose to spend three days in Scotland at a carriage-driving competition. In the summer of 1999, Lord Romsey accepted an invitation to cruise around the Greek islands with Charles and Camilla but Penny preferred instead to stay in England.

In 1957 Elizabeth decided to make Philip a Prince of the United Kingdom. Previously, Philip had been only a Prince of Greece but had been permitted to use the title 'Prince' as a courtesy. Queen Victoria had bestowed the same dignity upon Prince Albert some seventeen years after their marriage. Henceforth, Philip's official title would be His Royal Highness Prince Philip, Duke of Edinburgh.

As noted earlier, Philip became involved in both the International Equestrian Foundation and the World Wildlife Fund. He continued to travel widely, throwing himself more into his royal duties. He has done so ever since. Even in 1991 at the age of 70, Philip spent nearly eight weeks abroad on numerous royal duties and, again, in 1999, aged 78, he visited both South Korea and then Saudi Arabia in the space of four days, a gruelling effort for a man of his advanced years. As James Orr, who later became his Private Secretary, said of him, 'He was a real self-driver. He would go on till he dropped.' Today, he still continues to push himself hard.

It was with the same enthusiasm and determination that Philip also expected his polo ponies and driving horses to follow his example. During the years he played polo, Philip was renowned for being hard on his ponies, treating them harshly, in contrast to his son Charles who always treats his polo ponies with far greater care. Because of an arthritic hand, Philip gave up polo at 48 and took up carriage-driving in the 1980s. He has become remarkably adept at the sport and, once again, always pushes his horses hard in his determination to win.

It was with the same urge to succeed and set an example that Philip took a close interest in Britain's manufacturing and scientific industries, seemingly desperate to help wherever possible to expand his country's industrial prowess and its exports. Despite his disappointment at having to leave the Royal Navy at such an early age, Philip continued to show a keen interest in the Royal Navy and in the new innovations introduced to all aspects of the senior service.

But perhaps his greatest achievement has been the creation of the Commonwealth Study Conferences which have helped members from all over the world understand better the relationship between industrial relations, the community and the individual. However, according to those involved in the conferences, Philip's earlier enthusiasm became somewhat overshadowed by his arrogance and forceful personality and, as a result, he was sidelined by those wishing to run a more democratic ship. Indeed, many in the royal household who have known Philip for a number of years believe that Philip would have achieved far more if he had bothered to win the respect of those senior advisers who work at the palace, rather than by his usual policy of trying to brow-beat people.

He does, nevertheless, run the most efficient, highly computerised office in Buck House despite the fact that he had to wait until the mid-'80s before being permitted to purchase computers and word processors for his highly motivated staff of three senior officials plus four secretaries. Brian McGrath has served as Philip's private secretary since 1982. McGrath, Eton, the Irish Guards and the wine trade joined Philip at the age of 56. He succeeded Lord Rupert Nevill with whom Philip had had a very close relationship for twelve years as his treasurer and later his private secretary. As a stockbroker, Lord Nevill also helped manage the queen's extensive stock portfolio. Philip also has an equerry, Lt-Commander Malcolm Sillars and the administration is in the care of Jimmy Jewell, a former Guards sergeant-major.

As someone who is highly critical of the programmes on television, Philip does enjoy reading, particularly books which he believes will further his knowledge and his education on any number of diverse subjects. He boasts a personal library of some 9,000 books, including 600 books on birds, 500 on religion, 400 on horses and riding and 350 on the Navy and ships. There is more poetry than fiction, which only accounts for about 200 books. The library also contains a further 200 books on humour. In addition, he has a collection of 200 cartoons from various artists, every one about himself.

At 70 Philip still enjoyed flying aircraft. An extremely able pilot, he has piloted more than 5,000 flying hours in many types of planes including Concorde and a Vulcan bomber, and at the controls of aircraft of the Queen's Flight. He has also flown helicopters. A keen photographer and talented water-colour painter, Philip believes painting helps him relax.

Throughout his life, Philip has enjoyed being a busy-body, invariably telling other people what to do. As a member of the International Equestrian Federation put it, 'Many believe it would be better if the Duke simply chaired meetings instead of arguing every item on the agenda and trying to ram his ideas down everyone else's throat.'

And yet there is a side to Philip which runs contrary to his brusque personality. He has shown an abiding interest in religion and philosophy which began in the early 1960s when the Rt Revd Robin Woods was appointed to the Deanery of Windsor.

According to Woods, 'At first the Duke had absolutely no time for the Church of England.' Apparently he did not even want Prince Charles confirmed and during the service read the Bible instead of paying attention. Afterwards, the Archbishop of Canterbury Dr Michael Ramsey, said, 'That was bloody rude of the Duke.'

Philip's religious upbringing had been chaotic. He had been brought up in the Greek Orthodox Church, become involved with German Protestantism as a teenager, and had ultimately married the Head of the Church of England, which entailed becoming a practising Anglican. From his teenage years to the 1960s Philip became disenchanted with all religion, even cynical towards church teachings. At other times deeply agnostic, he occasionally professed to being an atheist.

Despite Philip's attitude towards the church and religion, he and Woods grew closer as Philip supported a plan to raise £500,000 to convert the existing deanery college buildings at Windsor into a residential conference centre. As a result they became friends and Woods would be invited to drop in at Windsor Castle at weekends for a cocktail before dinner.

On Woods's promotion to the diocese of Worcester, Philip wrote to him saying, 'It has been simply marvellous having you at Windsor and your help and guidance for us and for our children has been invaluable but, frankly, I think the Church needs your services more urgently than we do.' It was a genuine letter built on eight years of friendship. Five years later, in 1975, Bishop Dudley Mann, who was a suffragan to Robin Woods at Worcester, took over the Windsor post.

Philip's involvement with the church continued. As a result of talks with Bishop Mann, Philip wrote a collection of essays of a philosophical nature, which were published in book form in 1982 entitled *A Question of Balance*. The Dean edited them. Philip began with a textual analysis of Karl Marx's *Communist Manifesto*; other chapters included, 'Truth', 'Clashes of Interest', and 'Community Health'.

Two years later he wrote *A Windsor Correspondence*, in which Philip and Bishop Mann argued in a series of letters about Sir Fred Hoyle's theory entitled 'Evolution from Space', suggesting science and Christianity might be moving closer together.

His third philosophical work is called *Survival or Extinction* and subtitled *A Christian Attitude to the Environment*, which he wrote with Bishop Mann as co-author. In it the two men try to persuade the Church to take a greater interest in the conservation of nature.

As a result of his dialogue with Woods and Mann, Philip grew closer to the Anglican Church and came to enjoy the philosophical discussions of religion and the church. It seems, however, to have led to more of an intellectual interest since he has not as yet embraced the faith as a true believer.

As the years have taken their toll on him, Philip – while still crusty and acerbic – has become demonstrably more contemplative and reflective. During his youth and middle-age Philip was a restless, impatient, curious man, as well as a man of action. Now he seems to prefer wrestling with questions about the meaning of life and the existence of a Supreme Being. Bishop Mann said recently, 'I believe the Duke has acquired a peace of mind that he did not have earlier in his life. But there's a worm inside the man that drives him on. I don't know that he would ever feel fulfilled, though he might feel content.

'The problem with Philip is that he could never accept anything until he had gnawed it and chewed it to pieces. When he's in a corner and he's lost a point in an argument he doesn't stop like other people and say, "yes, well, maybe you're right". He goes shooting off on something else . . . and usually he will go away and come back later having accepted the point. When you're actually in an argument with him, he will never admit that he's being convinced. You know if he has been convinced if he's changed the subject or changed the line of questioning. He would find it very difficult to say, "I'm sorry, I'm wrong."'

Mann believes a person who can admit errors has no need to constantly bulldoze people in discussions and arguments. In 1990, Tim Heald watched Philip at work over a period of months before writing his biography, *The Duke*. He wrote: 'Still he puzzles me. Real humility sits uneasily alongside apparent arrogance; energy and optimism co-exist with sudden douches of cold water; real kindnesses are mingled with inexplicable snubs; certainty and uncertainty, sensitivity and insensitivity, walk hand in hand. He is gregarious, he is a loner; he loves arguments, he cannot bear to lose one . . . His apparent inconsistencies certainly make him intriguing, but they also make him exasperating. He is energetic, mercurial, quixotic and ultimately impossible to pin down – partly on purpose.'

He rarely makes jokes at his own expense but sometimes a little humility does appear. At one time he signed his name for membership of the Imperial Poona Yacht Club, which wasn't really a club but an excuse among friends to get together for an occasional drink. Philip signed himself as 'The Maharaja of Cooch Parwani' which translated means 'Maharaja of not a lot'!

Despite Philip's love of travel, excitement, sport, action and women, he must ultimately be judged on how well he has fulfilled the job for which he accepted responsibility when he married Elizabeth, not simply as her husband but more importantly as consort to the Queen of England. It is true that ever since her coronation in 1953 Philip has been always at her side, photographed on thousands of royal occasions, resplendent in naval uniform or an elegant, well-cut suit or evening dress, as though a fixture, a rock of support for her to lean on. And the pictures show this to be the case.

But away from the flash bulbs and the photographers Philip has in fact led the solitary existence of a bachelor, doing the things he has always wanted to do, from painting to polo, from sailing to shooting and carriage driving. He has also single-mindedly pursued knowledge and is not the 'ignorant bum' he once described himself as being. He has organised and chaired meetings, spoken his mind and involved himself in his interests of science and engineering and whatever else has taken his fancy. To his great credit he has never shirked his duty in carrying out prodigious amounts of royal work, engagements, functions and speech-making. For years he has been the hardest-working royal, attending more royal occasions and events than most other members of 'The Firm', including all the younger ones.

At the end of several months of working on Philip's biography, Tim Heald wrote, 'The consensus among those I consulted is that the Duke has pulled this off.' If Heald had written his biography a couple of years later when the monarchy had plunged into crisis, perhaps the consensus may have been rather different.

Unfortunately, Philip seems to have failed in most of the important aspects of his life. He has certainly not been a faithful husband; the support he has given his wife Elizabeth in her life's work has been little more than marginal; and in the one area in which he had been determined to carve out a substantial role for himself as father to his children, he has been negligent.

As Philip once said, 'I am not really interested in what goes on my tombstone.' As it happens, his epitaph may not be too flattering.

8. INTIMATE FRIENDS

Throughout the 1950s, Elizabeth found herself turning increasingly to Uncle Dickie for advice, comfort and support. He proved a valuable adviser, not only concerning government policies and foreign affairs but on more personal matters too. At first, most of his advice was professional. It was only later, when they had become more closely acquainted, that Uncle Dickie advised Elizabeth on a whole raft of matters, and particularly on family problems. She put her trust in him and he replied with honesty, sympathy and under-standing.

Mountbatten began to advise Elizabeth when the Soviet leaders, Bulganin and Kruschev, visited Britain in 1956, and he spent many hours with her through the dramatic days of the Suez Canal crisis of 1956 when General Nasser of Egypt, dictator of Egypt since his coup in 1952, nationalised the canal because America and Britain had refused to fund the building of the Aswan Dam, which was essential to the economic development of his country. This flagrant violation of international law infuriated western public opinion. It alarmed France and, even more so, Israel. Britain, France and Israel sent in troops, ostensibly to recapture the canal but in reality to overthrow the dictator Nasser.

As First Sea Lord, Mountbatten, who was also at the time chairman of the Chiefs of Staff Committee, was intimately involved with planning the Suez invasion though personally he was passionately against the military operation and told Prime Minister Anthony Eden as much. He explained his opposition to Elizabeth and urged her to try and persuade Sir Anthony against using force. Elizabeth totally accepted Mountbatten's line of argument, took his advice and, using her right as monarch, advised Eden to take the greatest care before taking direct military action.

Eden went ahead in secret, however, and Britain, France and Israel seized the canal which Nasser promptly blocked by scuppering ships still in the canal. Only at the last moment did Eden inform Elizabeth the invasion would take place. Of course, Elizabeth had no authority to stop the military action and had to accept Eden's decision. Mountbatten was furious for he feared a debacle. Eden had gone ahead without even informing United States President Dwight Eisenhower or Secretary of State John Foster Dulles of the planned invasion. He was wary of the United States taking action to thwart the invasion. Eden hadn't even informed the United Nations.

Within hours of the invasion, the United States applied the strongest possible pressure to halt the military action, ordering a run on sterling and the French franc and cutting off all credit. Two more weeks and Britain would have been financially ruined. Eden had to back down. The invasion had openly divided the nation, Britain lost power and prestige and Sir Anthony, mentally and physically ill, resigned.

No documents exist in the public domain concerning Elizabeth's role in the Suez crisis. Before the invasion, however, Elizabeth had been asked to sign, as a matter of urgency, a Proclamation authorising Eden to call up reservists. For some reason she did not sign that Proclamation when asked to do so but waited until the following day. Elizabeth, of course, could not constitutionally have refused to sign the document but the delay appears to have been on account of her desire to discuss the matter first with Mountbatten. But she could not tell Eden, or anyone else, the reason why she did not wish to sign immediately. She knew there would be the most extraordinary furore if she was seen to be taking advice from a mere naval officer rather than accepting the advice of her Prime Minister.

But the Suez débâcle cemented the working relationship between Elizabeth and Mountbatten and throughout the following years Elizabeth came to respect Mountbatten's opinions and would heed his advice. She also came to depend on him to a remarkable extent.

Louis Francis Victor Albert Nicholas, 1st Earl Mountbatten of Burma, the great-grandson of Queen Victoria and Albert born in 1900, was of course distantly related to Elizabeth for she was Victoria's great-great-granddaughter. During the Second World War, Mountbatten achieved a meteoric rise to power and authority, from a senior naval officer in 1940 to Supreme Allied Commander South-East Asia by 1943. Appointed the last Viceroy of India to oversee the rapid transfer of power in 1947 until 1952, he returned to naval service as 4th Sea Lord and Commander of the Mediterranean Fleet. In 1955 he became First Sea Lord and four years later reached the pinnacle of power in Britain's armed forces, becoming Chief of the Defence Staff. The result was a vast wealth of experience and knowledge, which neither Elizabeth nor Philip could begin to match. And the rascally, manipulative Mountbatten was only too happy to be Lilibet's confidant and counsellor. He loved the role. Mountbatten encouraged the relationship and he thoroughly enjoyed the power of influence it gave him. From the time of the Suez crisis, Mountbatten, then 56, became a father figure to the 30-year-old Elizabeth, and the two were to remain close until Mountbatten's untimely death.

Mountbatten not only had access to many world leaders and power brokers in many Western democracies including the United States, he also enjoyed talking to the common people, to shopkeepers, to naval ratings, to soldiers, to people he met in everyday life – and, more than that, he listened to what they had to say. From these meetings and odd chats to ordinary people, Mountbatten had his finger on the pulse of the nation and knew how people felt towards the monarchy and the royal family; and he would pass on much of this to Elizabeth who, throughout her entire life, has been closeted in palaces and castles segregated from her subjects.

Following the Suez crisis Elizabeth was catapulted into the most serious political decision of her reign, a decision which would have considerable consequences: the selection of prime minister to follow Sir Anthony Eden. She was advised that Harold Macmillan should be invited to form the new government, a decision which came as a great surprise to the public at large and even more so to 'Rab' Butler whom most MPs believed would have been invited to take over. A political storm in which the queen was involved struck both parliament and the press. It was believed by the country at large that the selection of Macmillan, whose wife's family were royal courtiers, was a victory for the Tory aristocracy over the progressive middle-class Conservatives such as R. A. Butler.

In fact, Elizabeth had taken advice from others – besides the two leading aristocratic Tories, Lord Salisbury and Lord Kilmuir – and history shows that Elizabeth's decision at that crucial moment in the country's history had been based on the views of other leading Conservatives. But only time revealed Elizabeth's impeccable handling of that situation, in which she showed remarkable maturity and common sense for a thirty-year-old woman.

Some of the press criticism was not directly aimed at Elizabeth, but rather at the Tory aristocracy. In one respect the media were right to question the background of those to whom the queen had turned for advice. Indeed, the number of ordinary people Elizabeth has ever had serious conversations with throughout her entire life can probably be counted on the fingers of both hands. It was one of the reasons she clung to Bobo for so long because Bobo understood what the common people thought – and told Elizabeth so. In that respect Bobo became invaluable.

John Barratt, Mountbatten's trusted Private Secretary and close companion for 20 years, believes Dickie Mountbatten became too involved with Lilibet through the late '50s and '60s. He commented, 'In some ways I thought their relationship became too close; he became too obsessive towards her and too possessive of her.'

Elizabeth would talk to Uncle Dickie about Philip; indeed, Mountbatten would ask her in general terms about the relationship. More often than not Elizabeth would be non-committal; on other occasions she would confide her innermost thoughts to him.

Mountbatten had realised quite early on in their marriage that Elizabeth was overawed by Philip. Sometimes at dinner Philip would shoot his wife a severe look and she would suddenly become quiet, dropping the subject she had been speaking about. After only a few years of marriage, Philip would tell Elizabeth to, 'Shut up', on occasions, and she would obey immediately, embarrassed to have been addressed in that way in front of the family.

Sometimes when staying the night as house guests, Philip would abruptly stand up and say, 'Time for bed' and Elizabeth would immediately leave whatever she was doing and would retire with him, without any argument.

Amongst the family, Philip generally played the heavy male with his wife, especially during the first years of their married life, and even after Elizabeth had become queen in 1952.

During open discussions at table, Philip would always state his views most forcefully, often disagreeing with his wife's argument, telling her bluntly, 'Do keep quiet', if he wanted to make a point. He was particularly firm when speaking to Charles, often criticising him for no apparent reason and deliberately taking the opposite stance to his son's.

Philip also had a rather unpleasant way of putting his wife down, making her feel small, and those comments were usually made in front of the family. John Barratt recalls, 'It was as if Philip got some pleasure from treating his wife like that, deriding her, telling her she didn't know what she was talking about, ridiculing her views and her opinions. He intimidated her. He always did. And she accepted the position most of the time. As far as I can recall she always did as he said.'

Uncle Dickie was also aware of the way in which his nephew treated Elizabeth and he didn't like it one jot. In the early days he had talked to Philip about his relationship with Elizabeth, suggesting kindness and consideration, but the more Philip became involved in sexual adventures, the less he permitted his uncle to enter into his personal matters.

As a result, Uncle Dickie began to show more warmth towards Elizabeth. He would be attentive towards her, asking her opinions and views and listening to her arguments, something which he knew Philip hardly ever did. Throughout the '60s and '70s Elizabeth and Mountbatten would frequently go for walks together at Broadlands or Windsor. She seemed to gain confidence and comfort from Uncle Dickie which helped her in both her public and private life. Mountbatten wanted to be close to Elizabeth and they did indeed become very close.

This became evident when Elizabeth struck up a friendship with Henry George Reginald Molyneux Herbert, 7th Earl of Carnarvon, grandson of the 5th Earl who discovered the famous Tomb of Tutankhamun in the 1920s. He had first met Elizabeth during her teenage years. Indeed, they had danced together on a number of occasions and Harry was one of the young men her father had suggested as a prospective husband. Harry was then known by his courtesy title, Lord Porchester, and affectionately referred to as 'Porchy'. It became his nickname.

Elizabeth and Porchy became close friends in the '50s due to their keen interest in horse racing. In 1956, Porchy married an American girl, Jean Wallop, eldest daughter of the Hon. Oliver Wallop and Mrs Wallop of Big Horn, Sheridan, Wyoming in the United States. Lord Porchie, two years older than Elizabeth, was a racing man all his life and became at different stages chairman, and later president, of the Thoroughbred Breeders' Association, President of the Amateur Riders Association, a member of the Horseracing Betting Levy board and chairman of the Jockey Club's race planning committee. In December 1969, Porchy became racing manager to the queen.

Throughout the late '50s and '60s, however, Porchester and Elizabeth spent many, many hours together, discussing every aspect of racing: Elizabeth's horse studs, stallions, brood mares, blood lines, purchases, sales, race meetings and her string of race horses currently in training. It was from Porchy that Elizabeth gained some of her considerable knowledge of the race game of which she is now considered a fine judge.

But there was more to the relationship than racing. In public,

Porchester always called Elizabeth 'Ma'am' or 'Your Majesty' and showed her every respect, but in private he called her 'Lilibet' and she called him 'Harry'. It was fortunate for Elizabeth that Porchester was not like his father, who had boasted of making love to more than a hundred women in his life. His adulterous life nearly came to an untimely end when, at an advanced age, he was found locked in the arms of the Earl of Craven's wife Wilhemina, a gorgeous redhead. Her husband burst through the door brandishing a loaded revolver. Porchester's father beat a hasty retreat through the bathroom with bullets ripping into the door behind him.

Since his father's death in 1987, Harry Porchester enjoys the magnificent Highclere Castle, set in 6,000 Hampshire acres, not far from Broadlands. Harry Porchester's upbringing was that of the typical English aristocracy – he was educated at Eton where he was captain of boxing; he trained at Sandhurst; he served in Egypt with the First Household Cavalry and, after becoming disabled, was released by the army. He took up farming. But his love has always been racing and he spends a great amount of time and effort on his stud, though, to his credit, he has spent many years in local government having failed to gain a seat in the House of Commons in 1953.

A tall, well-built, good-looking, distinguished man, Porchester appears to be ten years younger than his near-four-score years. He is described by friends as 'charming, polite, with a good sense of humour and a twinkle in his eye'. As a young cavalry officer, and the son of the Earl of Carnavon, Porchy was much sought after by ambitious mothers wishing to marry off their daughters to a member of the aristocracy. But Porchy rebelled against tradition and fell in love with a lovely fresh-faced Wyoming girl when she came to England aged 21. In an interview given in 1989, Harry provided some evidence of his happy family life, saying, 'We're a very lucky family. My wife and I are very lucky to have our children and grandchildren and each other.'

Many people might suggest that Porchester has been most fortunate in his close working relationship with Elizabeth, one reason being the remarkable way in which she has kept faith in his capacity as her racing manager, for he has hardly been a great success. Despite Porchester's official role as her manager he is not of course responsible for training any of the horses, but is responsible for sending the horses to appropriate trainers. Throughout Elizabeth's abiding love affair with the race game, she has, like many owners, always dreamed of winning the English Derby, the Blue Riband of racing. But the chances of doing so seem to be drifting further away, not closer. Indeed, during a seven-year lean spell in the '80s, the queen did not even have a three-year-old good enough to enter the race, let alone win it.

The queen spends a small fortune, about £200,000 a year, on her string of race horses and her own stud and she is in constant conversations with Porchy. She always has a say in which mare to put to which stallion and she religiously studies their blood lines. She also involves herself, almost daily, with the more mundane task of deciding which horse should participate in which races. Consequently some, if not much, of the blame for her lack of success at the very pinnacle of racing must be down to her selections of stallions and brood mares. Through studying books and computer print-outs, she constantly educates herself on every aspect of the race game, as well as spending hours discussing with experts the breeding programme of the royal stables. And yet, thus far, she has been unable to achieve the greatness she yearns for in breeding top-class colts.

During the 1960s, Elizabeth began to spend a great deal of time with Porchy and they would frequently meet at Broadlands, where Uncle Dickie would act as their host. They would ride out together, walk for hours with the dogs and sit and chat late into the night. Mountbatten paid close attention to their relationship with some trepidation, his attitude to their friendship somewhat tinged with jealousy. At one stage, Mountbatten became concerned that Elizabeth was seeing too much of Harry Porchester. After months of deliberation Mountbatten took the extraordinary and unprecedented step of writing her a letter of warning.

John Barratt read the letter, as he did all Mountbatten's correspondence, whether private, public or official. It was one of his important daily chores. He recalled: 'Mountbatten would dictate most letters but he always wrote his private ones to Lilibet by hand. He always showed me all the letters he wrote prior to posting them so I could check them over, make a suggestion or point out any possible errors.

'I remember very well the letter he wrote to Elizabeth about Porchy. It was in the late 1960s. As usual the letter began "Dear Lilibet", and he went on to say, "I urge you to be more discreet in your relationship with Porchy".

'I think there was also a sense of jealousy. But because of his close involvement with Elizabeth, Mountbatten was genuinely concerned that she and Porchester were spending too much time together at Broadlands. He told me so on more than one occasion. He used to shake his head about it, not knowing how he should tackle the situation. Elizabeth was so animated when Porchester was around and they got on so well together.'

Elizabeth appeared to take little notice of Uncle Dickie's letter for she continued to work with Harry Porchester, but the couple were to spend fewer weekends at Broadlands. Later they would travel abroad together on racing business and spend weeks together. Philip hardly ever accompanied his wife on such overseas trips for he was not a racing man. Since 1975, Elizabeth and Porchester have frequently visited Kentucky together during the spring for the yearling sales. They nearly always stay at the Versailles, Lexington, farm of one of America's most wealthy and secretive multi-millionaires, William Stamps Farish III, a good friend of former President George Bush.

Born in 1930, Will Farish had a grandfather who founded Humble Oil, which later formed the major part of Exxon; his other grandfather was chief executive of Sears, Roebuck. His father died in a flying accident in 1934 when Will Farish was just four. Will Farish married Sarah Sharp, daughter of Bayard Sharp, a du Pont heir and horse breeder. Polo-mad, Will and Sarah loved horses and have taken a great pride in breeding the finest thoroughbreds in America. As President of the US Jockey Club, Will Farish met Elizabeth during a polo match and they got on so well he invited her to stay with him and Sarah during the Kentucky horse sales one year. For Elizabeth, the Farish hideaway – Lane's End Farm – was a perfect location, cut off from prying eyes and in the heart of racing country.

During a visit in October 1984, Elizabeth became fascinated by a revolutionary computerised bloodstock service installed at Corporate Center and spent some time watching the screen as stallions' bloodlines were analysed and re-analysed along with those of selected mares to ensure a perfect mating and a good chance of producing foals that would prove winners of Group 1 races. During that visit Elizabeth attended a special meeting at Keeneland, probably America's most beautiful race track, where the Queen Elizabeth II Challenge Cup Stakes served as the highlight of the day's racing. Today, Elizabeth keeps some of her brood mares in Kentucky, breeding from the plentiful supply of top-class stallions at the Farish and neighbouring studs.

One of those neighbouring stud farms is owned by Senator Malcolm Wallop, grandson of the Earl of Portsmouth, who owns a magnificent ranch at Big Horn. More importantly, however, he was the brother of Jean Wallop, now Lady Porchester, and therefore

Porchy's brother-in-law. During their 1984 visit Elizabeth and Porchy stayed there for a couple of nights.

Porchy had every good reason to accompany Elizabeth to Kentucky for she needed his advice. But it did mean they spent a week together enjoying life away from the strictures and disciplines of Buckingham Palace. All the people she met during her visits to Kentucky remarked how relaxed and happy Elizabeth appeared whenever she visited Kentucky. Away from the pressures of life back home, she could enjoy the never-ending subject of racing and race horses, the perfect holiday for the horse-mad Elizabeth.

Twenty years later Elizabeth and Porchester enjoy each other's company but most of their business is now conducted by telephone. Nevertheless, they do see quite a lot of each other when planning the queen's racing calendar and any possible sales or purchases of stallions and mares.

Mountbatten's jealousy towards Lilibet manifested itself in odd ways. He had a most remarkable collection of pornographic books, mainly sado-masochism, at Broadlands, though he also kept some at his London home in Kinnerton Street. In one of his favourites, *The Riding Mistress*, the eponymous heroine makes her recalcitrant young riders sit astride a wooden horse while she whips them. His favourite photographs – transparent coloured slides which he would look at through a viewer – nearly always depicted young women, fully dressed for riding in tight breeches or jodhpurs, usually wearing knee-high riding boots and carrying a whip.

Barratt recalled, 'I saw the slides once. There was nothing pornographic about the ones I saw. All the women were dressed and all in riding gear.' Barratt revealed that Mountbatten achieved sexual satisfaction on his ponies, most of which were retired polo ponies. He also revealed Mountbatten had a special relationship with one of his grooms, Mary, a lovely young girl with a boyish figure. In her contract she had to agree to go out riding twice a week with Mountbatten. Physically, Mary was Mountbatten's ideal woman: young, slim, boyish, attractive and a good horsewoman. The gossip at Broadlands was fed by the fact that whenever Mountbatten rode out with the lovely Mary or any of his other girlfriends, he always wore a condom, and all the staff knew this. Mountbatten only wore his spurs when riding out with a woman, not when he was riding on his own. He would achieve sexual satisfaction by fiercely spurring his ponies, using sharp rowels of the spurs to drive them faster, which frequently caused the ponies to bleed.

One of Mountbatten's great joys was to ride out with Lilibet whenever she visited Broadlands. They would usually go out once or twice together during a weekend, when they would school their ponies, like all polo players, riding them in circles and figures of eight. Barratt however has no idea whatsoever if Elizabeth ever knew of Uncle Dickie's secret sexual proclivities or whether indeed any of the girls or young women he rode out with ever knew.

There has forever been a question mark over Mountbatten's sexuality. Barratt, an open homosexual, lived and travelled the world with Mountbatten for 20 years. He swears that his Lordship was never interested in men, young or old, and to his knowledge never had a homosexual relationship, nor ever wanted one. He maintains that Mountbatten was openly heterosexual and nearly always attracted to young, slim women with boyish hips.

Philip Ziegler, Mountbatten's noted biographer, is convinced that Mountbatten was never gay despite his former naval valet's being madly so and his close relationship for many years with Peter Murphy, a highly intelligent Irishman who had served in the Irish Guards. A noted homosexual, as well as a brilliant linguist and pianist, Murphy was denounced as a communist agent in 1952. The fact that he was homosexual and a communist placed Mountbatten, one of Britain's most senior naval officers, in an awkward position. Western intelligence agencies, particularly the CIA, had become highly concerned about possible communist infiltrators. Mountbatten asked the British Security Services to investigate Murphy's alleged communist sympathies and they cleared him of any involvement with the Communist Party. This clearance was passed to the CIA, which accepted that Mountbatten was no security risk.

In his biography, Ziegler details a number of Mountbatten's affairs both before and after his marriage to the highly sexed Edwina, all of which were with women and good-looking, intelligent ones at that. Both Ziegler and Barratt agree, however, that Mountbatten, though he liked to portray himself as a sexual athlete, was not a very highly sexed man.

In 1975, a series of articles in the *Daily Mirror* revealed details of a homosexual ring centred on the Life Guards' barracks in London. A number of young guardsmen claimed that Mountbatten was involved and they gave details and signed statements of alleged visits to his Kinnerton Street home. Later, however, Mountbatten recorded in his diary, 'I refused to take this allegation that my name was mentioned in connection with this ring seriously and I said that I might have been accused of many things in my life but hardly of the act of homosexuality.' As a result of an internal investigation by the army, five Life Guards officers and 36 guardsmen were found guilty of being involved in homosexual activities and dismissed from the regiment.

Sir Robert Scott, Permanent Under-Secretary at the Ministry of Defence in the 1960s, and a friend and colleague, remembers Mountbatten saying to him about the same allegations, 'Edwina and I spent all our married lives getting into other people's beds.' According to Ziegler, however, Mountbatten exaggerated and conducted only two long extramarital affairs, both with women, and to the apparent satisfaction of all parties. He was never promiscuous, though – it was Edwina who was boundlessly promiscuous.

The closer Mountbatten became to his beloved Lilibet the further he became estranged from Prince Philip. Having spent years working to arrange the marriage of Philip and Elizabeth, Mountbatten now turned against Philip, primarily it seems because he was no longer able to influence his nephew, and because he had failed to prevent him from leading a sexually amoral life.

In private conversations with John Barratt, Mountbatten would occasionally say, 'Philip can't take this life. There are too many restrictions for him. He can't toe the line. It would have been much better if he had gone off and married some rich American lady. Then he could have had the time of his life without risking himself or Lilibet to public shame.'

It was on the advice of Uncle Dickie that Charles went to Gordonstoun, the school of which Mountbatten was a governor. There were endless discussions, even rows, about Charles's education. Elizabeth did not know whose advice to accept because she herself had never been to school. She ended up accepting the recommendation of Uncle Dickie and Philip that it should be Gordonstoun, despite strong protests from the Queen Mother who believed Charles should be sent to a traditional English public school like Eton.

The argument against Gordonstoun was that Charles would be encouraged towards more radical ideas which might manifest themselves later when he became Prince of Wales. The Queen Mother feared that Charles might take after his uncle, Edward VIII, someone for whom she had not the slightest respect after his decision to abdicate and go off 'with that Simpson woman'. She and other senior members of the household preferred schools like Eton or Harrow. They had severe reservations about Gordonstoun and the effect it might have on a child like Charles who did not have his father's strong, rebellious, aggressive character.

The Queen Mother warned of the danger of Charles becoming a free-thinking, extremist reformer or a radical philosopher. The arguments between the traditionalists and the radicals became intense on occasion as discussions raged for months over his education. And it can be seen that Charles's interests have been far more varied, radical and, some would say, downright odd, as a result. As yet, however, no one has any real idea of what changes, if any, Charles would make if and when he becomes king.

Elizabeth's other close friend was Patrick Plunkett, probably her favourite courtier. She loved having Patrick around the palace, not simply as a highly intelligent adviser but as a friend and a soul mate. Patrick Terence William Span, 7th Baron Plunkett, was two years older than Elizabeth and came to royal service when appointed as equerry to King George VI in 1948. From the start, Elizabeth had responded to Patrick's sweet nature and when she succeeded to the throne in 1952, Patrick continued as equerry until she promoted him two years later to deputy master of the household, a post he held until his tragic death in 1975 at the young age of 51.

He never married, yet when he first arrived on the scene in the late 1940s, he became so popular with the king and queen, indeed the whole family, that there was hope that he would marry Princess Margaret. A slender, good-looking man, with thinning dark hair and an aristocratic profile, Plunkett had inherited his handsome looks from his mother, the daughter of Fanny Ward, the famous American actress known as 'The Eternal Flapper'. His grandfather, Joseph Lewis, became a celebrated diamond magnate in the Transvaal in South Africa. Brought up by his aunt after his parents died in an air crash when he was 14, Patrick was never very interested in women. Indeed he seemed ambivalent to sexual matters for he wasn't interested in men either. He far preferred the arts world, enjoying opera, classical music, the theatre, the cinema and particularly the world of fine art. Despite rumours, gossip and innuendo, the people who knew him well believe that, basically, Patrick Plunkett was asexual.

His friendship with Elizabeth began after the war, in which he served as a Lieutenant-Colonel in the Irish Guards before being wounded. They would go riding together, a pastime which they continued to do frequently throughout the next 20 years. Patrick not only rode with Elizabeth, but frequently went shooting with Philip, fishing with the Queen Mother and occasionally escorted Princess Margaret before her marriage to Tony Armstrong-Jones.

Charming and witty, he came to be treated almost as one of the family, but he became close to Elizabeth. The whole family showed him warmth and true friendship which gave him emotional security and a feeling of belonging. In return, Patrick gave dedicated service. An aristocrat by birth, and inclination, educated at Eton and Cambridge, Patrick brought a touch of elegance, taste and a detestation of the second-rate to all he did. Elizabeth found his personality so warm and so very different from her relationship with Philip.

Elizabeth needed someone of Patrick's warmth, generosity of spirit and light-heartedness to counteract the forceful nature of Philip's full-blooded nature and meteoric changes of mood. Patrick had a knack of diffusing awkward situations and bringing harmony where there was so often discord and argument, something Elizabeth appreciated enormously.

Patrick also had a genius for entertaining and the family often asked him to join their parties. He had the knack of making everyone relax and enjoy themselves, something which many members of the royal family find surprisingly difficult to do. Elizabeth would frequently roar with laughter at Patrick's antics, throwing back her head, tears of pleasure streaming down her face. He was one of the very few men that could bring that reaction from Elizabeth and, understandably, she loved him for it. The family nicknamed him 'Master of the Revels' for he understood better than anyone how to mix informality with splendour.

And Patrick had other talents. He had a sure sense of decoration and an instinctive appreciation of quality in works of art. Patrick enjoyed moulding Elizabeth's rather philistine understanding of anything artistic which she appreciated. Her education had been utterly lacking in the arts and although she has never shown any real interest in them, a point of considerable criticism in some artistic quarters, she did want to learn more, primarily because she had found someone whom she trusted, and liked, and who made art a fascinating subject. Patrick, more than anyone else, inspired and developed the Queen's Gallery at Buckingham Palace which has proved such a success.

Patrick's relationship with Elizabeth became remarkably close. In private he would greet her with a kiss on the cheek, which she welcomed. In full view of members of the household, Patrick would always address her as Ma'am, though she invariably called him Patrick. And Philip was not in the least jealous of the relationship, indeed he seemed to welcome having Patrick around nearly as much as Elizabeth because it relieved him of all the duties which he was not really very good at, such as being naturally pleasant, understanding, comforting and cheerful.

For more than ten years, throughout the late '60s and early '70s, Elizabeth and Plunkett would go out secretly together, to dinner, the cinema and, occasionally, the theatre. They would have supper together, enjoy a glass of champagne, with no one being aware of their identities. Frequently on a Monday evening Elizabeth and Plunkett would leave the palace in Elizabeth's old Rover car. She would dress in an ordinary coat and wear a scarf over her head to conceal her identity.

They would often visit a cinema, usually the Odeon Cinema in King's Road, Chelsea, two miles from Buckingham Palace. Plunkett would pay, always securing two seats at the back of the auditorium, though at that time there were no assigned seats. After the show they would sometimes walk across King's Road to Raffles Club, a highly respectable dining and drinking place, which was decorated like a library and not frequented by the aristocracy. They would ask for a table at the back of the dining area, the darkest spot in the club. Together they would enjoy a light meal and a glass of champagne or wine before driving back to the palace around midnight. Apparently no one recognised Elizabeth – perhaps because they would never expect to see the sovereign in such places.

Occasionally, Elizabeth and Patrick would take long walks together in Windsor Great Park, sometimes alone, but, more often than not, with the corgis. They loved one particular spot: the beautiful, secluded Valley Gardens overlooking Virginia Water which sported white delphiniums and peonies. The flowers became Elizabeth's favourites. After Patrick's death from cancer in 1975, Elizabeth placed a wooden seat in his honour in the Valley Gardens which today still holds a special place in her heart.

These secret outings were an absolute joy to Elizabeth. They were the only moments in her life when she could be among ordinary people, unrecognised and unknown, enjoying the mundane life like everyone else. Though their relationship was almost certainly non-sexual, in many respects Elizabeth loved Patrick Plunkett in a way that she had never loved anyone else. She responded to his warmth and kindness, his patience and sincerity. And she felt closer to him than to any other man in her life, including Porchester and Prince Philip.

Elizabeth not only liked having Patrick around her most of the time but relied on him greatly, not just for advice but for moral support. He was a kindred spirit who understood Elizabeth better than anyone could, and probably far more so than Philip.

Patrick Plunkett was not, however, simply fun to have around.

Elizabeth sought his advice in many areas. He was astute and articulate; he understood people and their politics, whether the politics of members of the household or the politics of government. Perhaps his greatest attribute, for which he has not been given sufficient credit, was his understanding of people and their motives, which proved invaluable to Elizabeth, since recognising baser motives has always been foreign to her nature.

Without personal ambition, Patrick seemed happy as a courtier with a remarkable degree of objectivity, perhaps one of the great criteria for counsellors to the powerful. In return for the happiness Patrick brought to Elizabeth's structured life of service, she showered rewards and titles on him whenever possible, always bestowing on him those honours which were in her personal power to grant. In 1955 she made him a Member of the Victorian Order, Commander of the Victorian Order in 1963 and Knight Commander of the Victorian Order in 1974 when she knew he had not long to live. Elizabeth could give no higher personal honours.

In 1971 Patrick learned he was suffering from cancer and told Elizabeth of his illness which, he had been informed, was incurable. His illness put such a strain on Elizabeth that she too became rundown and ill. She was due to undertake an extensive 47-day-long tour of South-East Asia with Princess Anne but decided to postpone it so she could stay in Britain with her beloved Patrick. He would not hear of it and persuaded Elizabeth that she must carry out the tour. The trip was not successful, the heat unbearable and Elizabeth suffered from stress. She phoned Patrick each and every day.

Patrick fought his four-year illness with humour and courage. When he became seriously ill, Elizabeth was a frequent visitor at his bedside but his long illness affected her enormously. When he died in June 1975 she wept openly.

Another man close to Elizabeth through the '60s, '70s and '80s was Sir John Miller, Crown Equerry from 1961 to 1987 and appointed an extra equerry from that date, when he reached 70 years of age. No man made Elizabeth laugh so much and no man seemed to be able to get into as many scrapes.

Sir John Miller had served as an officer in the Welsh Guards throughout the Second World War and had stayed on to command the 1st Battalion, the Welsh Guards from 1958 to 1961. Horses were his lifelong fascination and his love of them cemented a strong and lasting relationship with Elizabeth. Since retiring from the army, Sir John has been president of many British organisations, societies, clubs and associations, all concerned with various aspects of horses, ponies, riding and carriage-driving. He has also been in charge of every royal procession for nearly thirty years.

Sir John summed up his 30-year career as Elizabeth's equerry in a fashion that was typical of the man, 'I am what they call the Crown Equerry, which means I am in charge of all the horses and carriages. The cars as well, come to that. I've got a lot to be blamed for.'

The queen was often exasperated by the ever-faithful Sir John. Elizabeth's typical cries, heard frequently in intimate royal circles were, 'Where, oh *where* is John Miller?' or 'That man always disappears when he's wanted.' And yet another variant, 'You make me so cross, John.'

When called, Sir John would emerge as if by magic, perhaps from under a carriage or from behind a horse, resplendent in his black bowler, his pince-nez on the end of his nose: 'You called, Ma'am,' he would say and, on most occasions, Elizabeth could only smile and shake her head. He is a lovable, thoroughly charming character whom many see as the quintessential English aristocrat and member of the royal household.

Unmarried, Sir John has devoted his life to Elizabeth and to royal service, accompanying her whenever she goes to stay anywhere in Britain, on hand for every eventuality. They would often have supper together and Elizabeth used him for many years as a sounding board. A rather pompous man with a dreadfully limp handshake, Elizabeth could rely on Sir John to state his views honestly and openly. And there were never too many such people with the courage to do that in Buckingham Palace.

Once, in the 1960s, Sir John's name was romantically linked with a lady-in-waiting at Buckingham Palace and there was gossip of a romance. Sir John's answer was typical of the man, 'When you're a bachelor you have to take someone to a dance. I have known this young lady for many years. But talk of an engagement is absolute bunkum and rubbish.' And so it has remained.

Another loyal servant, but a totally different character, is Sir Matthew Farrer, private lawyer to the queen since 1965. Elizabeth has come to be more and more dependent on Sir Matthew's opinions and advice and, as a result, Elizabeth has made him both a Commander of the Victorian Order and, in 1983, a Knight Commander of the Victorian Order.

Sir Matthew is an extremely able lawyer held in the highest repute. His family firm, Farrer & Co, founded 250 years ago, has been the sovereign's advisers for generations. Many of the nation's aristocratic families and members of the Establishment come to Farrer & Co to sort out their legal matters. Yet the man who holds all the queen's secrets is the most retiring, if not secretive, of men. There is, for example, no official photograph of Sir Matthew in the public domain.

Born in 1928, he now flits between his homes in London and Sussex. His office is in Lincoln's Inn Fields and, increasingly of late, through the gates of Buckingham Palace. No chauffeured Rolls-Royce transports Sir Matthew to and from work, however; he usually goes by bus. And none of his neighbours in London or Sussex have even met him though he has lived in the same houses for decades. During the past 15 years, since the problems over the marriages of the younger royals, Elizabeth has turned more and more to Sir Matthew Farrer, the lawyer she has come to regard with admiration and who many believe is now one of her principal, though unofficial, advisers.

It is not without irony that Farrer & Co also carry out vast amounts of legal work on behalf of those sections of the British press which have exposed the royal family to so much embarrassment – *The Sun* and the *News of the World*, *The Times* and the *Sunday Times*, all owned by Rupert Murdoch and all of which have espoused republican sentiment.

Sir Matthew had not only been responsible for seeking solutions to the marital problems of Princess Diana and Sarah Ferguson, but before that of Princess Anne and Princess Margaret. He was deeply involved in 1992 and 1993 in the issue of Elizabeth's decision to pay income tax and spent many days and weeks in high-level discussions with the queen as well as her senior courtiers.

Elizabeth's close relationship with Sir Matthew goes back to the time of her sister's separation from Lord Snowdon over which Elizabeth spent many sleepless nights. It was not for the first time that her sister had caused such heartache. One of the most emotional times in Elizabeth's young life concerned Margaret, with whom she had shared a most happy, and extraordinarily care-free childhood. Privileged and pampered, cut off from the world and ordinary people, their mother Queen Elizabeth, a stout, warm-hearted woman from Scotland, had been determined, and succeeded to a great degree, in allowing them remarkable freedom.

Over time, that freedom has seemed all the more precious to Elizabeth. Ever since she became queen, Elizabeth has had such little freedom, her life dictated by protocol, duty and service, and those never-ending boxes of papers which she must read, day and night, seven days a week, 52 weeks a year.

9. A FAMILY DIVIDED

For better or for worse, Elizabeth's life has been dominated by one man, Prince Philip. The teenage Elizabeth fell in love with her blond, handsome prince and, despite her father's objections, married her dashing young naval officer. She certainly did not believe at the time that he would be a cantankerous, unfaithful husband and heartless father.

Yet Elizabeth managed to come to terms with Philip's character and inconsistencies. Very few rich and powerful women would have put up with the pain and anguish which Elizabeth has managed to do for nearly fifty years.

She has shown remarkable discipline regarding her own personal life under the most severe strains – imposed on her almost solely by her husband. At the same time she remains genuinely fond of him despite her admission that 'sometimes he riles me' and on other occasions, that 'he infuriates me'.

Elizabeth had known that Philip flirted and chased other women. It was Dickie Mountbatten who put it in perspective, telling her of his own marriage in which his wife had openly enjoyed liaisons with both men and women including the Indian Prime Minister Pandit Nehru. Mountbatten talked to Elizabeth of the pain he had suffered at his wife's hands before her early death in 1962. In a sense they were brought closer together for they had both suffered at the hands of unthinking, selfish partners. One of the earliest lessons of Elizabeth's married life was learning to adopt the same attitude to Philip's affairs as Mountbatten had had to his own wife's. He told her that he used to say to himself, 'Oh, let her get on with it.'

Mountbatten also explained to Elizabeth, 'Philip knows on which side his bread is buttered. Don't worry, he'll be back.' Mountbatten knew how Philip thought for they had had many talks together in the days when Mountbatten had planned his nephew's marriage to the future queen.

When Elizabeth feared losing whatever love Philip had to give, she would seek Mountbatten's advice. On those occasions Mountbatten would discuss Philip's personality and character. He would remind her that Philip was only manifesting his natural sexual aggressiveness, and that he was not capable of falling deeply in love.

John Barratt recalled, 'Mountbatten knew Philip so well. He knew Philip was just sowing wild oats with no real emotion attached. He would say to Elizabeth "Don't worry, he'll get over it."'

Mountbatten was right, but Philip's affairs took a considerable toll on their marriage and, inevitably, on Elizabeth's love for him.

In those first happy years while Elizabeth was still a princess, Philip did take a strong line as head of the household. He was in his element making decisions, whether choosing the colours for their home or bossing the servants. He enjoyed that role. During those five years Philip assumed a dominant position in his relationship with Elizabeth, who accepted a subservient role, seemingly happy to let the man she loved take responsibility.

But everything dramatically changed on the sudden death of King George in 1952 when Elizabeth became the queen and Philip was relegated to the role of consort. The sudden change proved difficult enough for Philip but the reversal of roles also proved extremely difficult for Elizabeth, the more so because of Philip's aggressive attitude to everyone and everything.

Those close to Elizabeth have often heard Philip shout at his wife, even in company. During a visit to Broadlands in the 1970s John Barratt was in the room with Mountbatten, Elizabeth and her husband when Philip said to his wife, 'I'm thinking of going out for a stroll. Care to come along?'

Politely, Elizabeth replied, 'No thank you, I think I will stay in. But you go if you wish.'

Barratt recalled, 'Philip gave Elizabeth a piercing look of anger and stormed out of the room shouting at her, "Don't come, then. Go to hell."' There are countless other stories of Philip's aggressive attitude towards Elizabeth. Barratt recounted an occasion when Mountbatten witnessed the relationship between the couple: 'The three of them were driving down to Cowdray Park where Philip was due to play polo. As usual, Philip, who had a notorious record of minor motoring accidents, was driving accompanied by a police car. Worried about the speed at which Philip was driving, Elizabeth began to tense up and draw breath at critical moments. Mountbatten told me that eventually Philip turned to her and said, "If you do that once more I shall put you out of the car". She immediately stopped. Later, when Mountbatten asked her why she didn't protest, because Philip was indeed driving too fast, Elizabeth replied, "But you heard what he said." '

Philip frequently swears using phrases and expletives he first heard in the Royal Navy: *damn* this, *damn* that, and the word *bloody* most of all. He seems to think swearing is a manly virtue but Elizabeth, though she puts up with it, doesn't relish his bad language which she finds coarse and uncivilised.

Those who have known both Philip and Elizabeth recall that whenever they have heard discussions or arguments between them, nine times out of ten Elizabeth gives way. Elizabeth learned early on in their marriage that Philip is not only obstinate but hates to lose any argument on any subject with anyone, including his wife.

Philip's relationship with Elizabeth has been markedly different from that of Prince Albert as consort. Albert believed his own individual existence should disappear into that of Victoria's; 'He should aim at no power by himself or for himself; should shun all attention, assume no separate responsibility before the public, but make his position entirely part of hers and fill every gap which as a woman she would naturally leave in the exercise of her regal functions.'

Philip believes nothing of the sort, although when he and Elizabeth are among anyone other than family, Philip always acts with the utmost decorum towards Elizabeth, treating her more as the queen rather than his wife. He will stand behind her, never in front; and he will usually heed her conversation when in company rather than speak his own mind. On one occasion at Balmoral, where the family was on holiday, he arrived late for drinks before dinner. There were ten guests present and yet Philip entered the room, bowed to his wife and said with no sarcasm, 'I'm very sorry I'm late,' before going and helping himself to a drink. And he would never leave a room before Elizabeth, even when on holiday.

Nevertheless, within the royal household Philip has tried to overcome his subservient role and demanded he be treated as 'Head of the Family', particularly with regard to the upbringing of their children. It is not known when Elizabeth allowed Philip back into her bed but, in 1960, seven years after the coronation, Andrew was born and their youngest son Edward four years later.

Philip had been raised without a real father, as his was away during the critical years of his childhood and youth. He was therefore determined to be a strong father figure in his own family. Prevented from continuing his career in the Royal Navy after the death of King George VI Philip felt there were precious few other jobs for him. Given Elizabeth's many duties and responsibilities, Philip decided that he should be both father and mother to their children.

From the moment Charles was born in November 1948, Elizabeth was all too happy for others to care for him and even more so when Anne came along two years later. Elizabeth never changed a nappy or bathed any of her children. They were always brought to her sitting room at the appointed time and she would hold and talk to them while nanny would report on their progress. Then Elizabeth would hand them back. Her children were only ever a small part of her life. Once they became teenagers, a standing joke among the four children was always how difficult it was for any of them to see their mother on her own, and impossible to see her without the dogs being present. Yet when all her children had grown up Elizabeth did confess, once: 'I came to the throne when I was very young, and I never had the opportunity to bring up my children. The Crown separated them from me. It is something that I have regretted all my life, and I am determined that Charles shall not be put in that position. I want him to be a father to his children, because I was never allowed to be a mother to mine. '

Elizabeth was being less than honest for when Andrew arrived in 1960, eight years after she had come to the throne, and Edward four years later, Elizabeth was once again happy to have them cared for by nannies and maids. Times had changed by the 1960s, and Andrew and Edward suffered much less discipline than Charles or Anne. They were given more freedom and their relationship with both Elizabeth and Philip was more open. On one occasion Anne was asked if she had left her children with her mother to care for when she had to be away. Anne replied, 'Leave the children with mother? You must be joking. That's the last thing she would want.'

Philip himself believed that Charles, his first born, should grow up to be a man's man, and would do so by becoming a naval officer, thus equipping his young son for his role as the next king of England. He believed that a normal schooling would also help Charles understand his fellow citizens rather than living a cloistered existence, cut off from the outside world, as Charles's mother had done. Philip failed, however, to take note of Charles's character.

Prince Charles is a far more sensitive person than his father, instinctively shy and retiring with none of Philip's brash self-confidence. Still, Philip disciplined his son from a very young age as though he was a junior naval rating rather than a beloved first-born child. Philip's attitudes toward child rearing verged on the Victorian: Charles was to remain quiet at all times, unless asked to speak; sent to his room for the least misdemeanour and threatened with a good 'thrashing' for the slightest infraction.

As royal biographer, Ben Pimlott, wrote in his biography *The Queen*, 'Philip was a martinet not just with his children, but with the queen.'

Philip would not only speak sternly to his young son, but frequently administer corporal punishment, usually with his hand on Charles's backside. Later, Philip would use a slipper or a tennis shoe to beat his young son. Philip once gave him a spanking for sticking out his tongue in public, another time for slipping an ice cube down a servant's neck. In yet another instance he was spanked for being rude to guests; and he was always beaten for not immediately obeying his father. All these beatings took place before Charles had turned six.

Charles's first governess, Miss Catherine Peebles, a good-hearted, no-nonsense Scots woman, nicknamed 'Mipsy', believes that Prince Philip was partly responsible for Charles's nervous, over-sensitive personality when she arrived at the palace to care for him when he was five. Charles was nervous of coming forward, afraid to say anything, for fear of the retribution he would receive from his over-bearing father. Charles's governess recalled, 'If you raised your voice to him, he would draw back into his shell and for a time you would be able to do nothing with him.'

At first, Elizabeth tried to intervene to protect her son from Philip's strict discipline but he would not hear of it, telling Elizabeth, 'The child must learn to obey and I intend to teach him.'

Mipsy however did have some kind words for Philip. She said, 'The Duke of Edinburgh was a marvellous father. He used to set aside time to read to Charles and Anne, or help them put together those little model toys. And he taught them practical jokes, like putting dead birds in guests' beds or feeding visitors tadpole sandwiches.'

Charles grew up believing his father to be good, brave and invincible. He imitated his walk, with his hands behind his back, hoping to please him, and yearned one day to grow up to be just like his Papa. He desperately wanted his father's praise and his love. But Philip knew from the beginning the life Charles, as future king, would enjoy, and resented it. Instead of encouraging his son, Philip subjected him to a regime of obedience, trials and punishment. The man who should have been proud of his son's achievements hardly ever gave him praise and whenever he failed at anything Philip was quick to condemn him. Throughout Charles's childhood and teenage years Philip ignored his son's needs because he was driven to prove himself right and clever. It was most certainly true that Philip taught his son to stand on his own two feet, but at a price.

Philip would refuse Charles help when he needed it; refuse Charles advice when he sought it; and, more importantly, turned his back on his son when Charles yearned for paternal love. The adoration and love Charles bore his father gradually turned to estrangement and fear in the face of icy contempt. As Charles became a teenager and closer to eventual power, Philip found himself demanding still more obedience from his son, the heir to the throne. He still insisted on the uncritical worship of a disciple but could not bring himself to ever embrace that disciple. In recent years Charles has talked of his relationship with his father. He told one of his close friends: 'I can never remember my father ever telling me he loved me; I can never remember him ever praising me for anything; I can never remember him putting his arms around me and giving me a hug. It was all very sad. It has taught me that I must never be like that with my sons. I want them to know that I love them and to let them feel that I do.'

Charles attended a fee-paying preparatory school and, at 13, after much fierce argument in the family, Charles was sent to Gordonstoun. Philip was convinced that the Scottish school would 'make a man' of him. Philip instructed the headmaster Robert Chew to treat Charles with more severity than the other boys.

Charles received canings and other disciplinary measures from Chew and his housemaster and he was alternately teased or left alone by the other boys. Charles would tell his grandmother, the Queen Mother, that during his first year at Gordonstoun he cried himself to sleep most nights. In an effort to bring some comfort to his miserable life, the Queen Mother took pity on him, frequently inviting Charles to her Scottish home, Birkhall, on the Balmoral estate not far from Gordonstoun. Charles, suffering from homesickness and loneliness, found a sympathetic and comforting shoulder to cry on. The Queen Mother has always had a soft spot for Charles, and understood the ordeal of this quiet child in an alien world.

'He is a very gentle boy with a kind heart which I think is the essence of everything,' she once said. The Queen Mother believed Charles would have been happier and more confident if he had gone to Eton. She also knew that Elizabeth would have much preferred Charles to attend that quintessentially élite school because it was close to Windsor Castle, but Philip and Uncle Dickie had won the argument and Charles went to Gordonstoun.

Charles enjoyed his three years at Cambridge for he could behave as he wished and was able to strike up a number of happy relationships with people of different ages. Moreover, he was spared the school discipline which his father believed would be the making of him. Charles also enjoyed his time in the Royal Air Force, where he learned to fly and, later, pilot jets and helicopters. Nevertheless, he was disenchanted when Philip, backed by Dickie Mountbatten, decreed that he must spend some years in the Royal Navy. He joined the guided-missile destroyer, HMS *Norfolk*, in November 1971 at 23 and so miserable was his life on board with 33 stuffy British officers that he confessed to spending many nights in his tiny cabin, sometimes crying himself to sleep.

One officer on HMS *Norfolk* who became a close friend recalled, 'He really was so very unhappy during the nine months on *Norfolk*. He felt alone and miserable. It is not an exaggeration to say he hated most of his time in the navy. Once again he felt people didn't want to chat with him or become his friend because he was heir to the throne.'

Charles had hoped his fellow officers would have been able to cope but they were scared their naval careers might be adversely affected if they as much as argued with him. Indeed, it was only after taking command of the tiny minehunter HMS *Bronington* for ten months in 1976 that Charles began to enjoy his days in the navy.

Chief Petty Officer Michael Colborne, who would later work with Charles as comptroller of his private office, saved Charles's sanity during those first five years in the Royal Navy. Charles admired Colborne's honesty, common sense and understanding of life and people. There was a natural empathy between the two men even though Colborne was 14 years older. Unlike any other older man he had ever met, except perhaps for Mountbatten, Colborne was warm and open, honest and straightforward – all the qualities Charles admired but had never found in the people that surrounded him, especially in the one person he longed to embrace him, his own father. His friendship with Michael Colborne would become one of the most important relationships of Charles's life.

By the side of his bunk Charles kept only one photograph, that of Princess Alexandra, who had always shown him kindness and friendship. It was an odd choice, since he certainly knew of his father's good friendship with her, but it is interesting that there was never a photograph of his mother at his side.

Charles's relationship with his mother has been described by family counsellors as 'unhealthy' because he was expected, even by his own father, to treat Elizabeth as the queen rather than as an ordinary boy would treat his mother. Throughout his life Charles has shown his mother the utmost respect, adhering to all her wishes and demands. He was brought up never to argue with his mother, never to be critical, and to accept all she had to say. It was a point that Diana could not bear. Time and again Diana would have violent arguments with Charles because he would refuse to disobey his mother or even argue with her. Diana became infuriated with Charles because he would not express his own opinion but would agree with his mother's point of view even if it was diametrically opposed to his own.

The truth is that he always found his mother rather cold towards him – he can never remember being held or comforted by her throughout his boyhood. Charles also tried to please his mother in whatever way he could but today he simply cannot recall his mother praising him or even being interested in what he was doing.

In an effort to emulate his father in everything, Charles tackled all that his father had done during his life and more. As a result, the adult Charles shares many interests with his father: they both sailed small boats and captained Royal Naval ships; both played polo well; both shot deer and birds and fished expertly; both stalked deer; both flew aircraft and helicopters competently. But Charles excelled in some of these activities in which his father was often only competent. Charles was a far better pilot than his father, particularly at flying helicopters; Charles flew fighter jets at speeds exceeding Mach I, and parachuted from aircraft, both of which Philip has never done. Charles also snow skied much better than Philip, he snorkle dived, team-raced on horseback and hunted deer and fox, all things Philip had never done.

Both men paint, particularly water colours, and both are talented. They are avid readers and involve themselves in the serious side of life, sharing, for example, a fascination for philosophy and religion. But Charles loves music and the opera, whereas Philip has no interest in either art. In different ways, both are highly intelligent men though neither would suggest for a moment they are intellectuals.

And in their baser interests they are so very different, particularly involving the opposite sex. All his life Philip has felt the need to prove himself with women, chasing, flirting and bedding them while Charles, on the other hand, has always enjoyed far deeper, meaningful relationships with women.

In his bachelor days Charles did enjoy sowing some wild oats but those sexual relationships were few and far between. And yet on the occasion of Charles's 50th birthday in November 1998, the *Daily*

Telegraph wrote a scandalous article claiming that it was easy for Charles to attract women. All he had to do was raise an eyebrow or flick a finger, and almost anyone he fancied would oblige. Even some modest women, who were already married, would fall like ninepins, and the article inferred that he'd have needed to have been very strong-minded to resist women who offered themselves like that.

The same article also claimed, 'Those who know him well say that, during the 1970s, the number of his amours ran high into double figures.' Those *Daily Telegraph* claims, allegedly made by an anonymous former courtier, suggesting that Charles had nearly one hundred lovers during those years were at best highly speculative, at worst pure fiction, a tissue of lies. Those who were close to Charles during those years including Sir David Checketts, Michael Colborne, his personal bodyguards Chief Inspector John McLean and Chief Inspector Paul Officer testify that such claims are a nonsense, a fantasy.

Far more important to Charles was the relationship with his father which, to this day, still arouses feelings of rejection and pain. Those who know Philip and Charles well – and there are very few people who do – believe that Philip's attitude to his eldest son has been dictated by a deep-seated resentment that his eldest son would be more privileged, accepted, honoured and respected simply because he was the future king, a position which Philip would never achieve. Some believe Philip's bullying attitude to his son was based on jealousy which was to have a damaging effect on Charles's life.

Princess Anne was much like her father. A girl with guts and courage, she had a forthright attitude, a no-nonsense approach to life which Philip greatly admired. Anne would be rude to people in public and behave stubbornly in private. Philip would laugh and forgive her though Elizabeth tried to control her wayward daughter who was far more challenging than Charles had ever been.

During her teenage years at Benenden, Anne had, on occasion, been rude and difficult to the teachers but she had made some firm friends. She was spirited, vigorous and, some complained, even pushy. But she spoke her mind and stood her ground whenever challenged. At 16, she would become captain of her house and housemother, both positions of responsibility.

Nevertheless, Anne was no beauty: in fact, if she had not belonged to royalty most would have called her a 'plain Jane'. At 16 years of age, she lacked confidence in herself, believing she looked ugly, with a protruding nose, eyes too close together and overweight; and she hated her hair which her mother said made her 'look like a sheepdog'. Anne would use her beautiful, thick, long hair as a shield against the none-too-friendly world, brushing it forward over her forehead.

Philip told her that character and personality were far more important than looks, a piece of advice she would remember when the beautiful Diana arrived on the scene. Her father talked to his polo-playing friends, who had sons and daughters of Anne's age, and suggested she should enjoy their company. A flood of invitations – to balls, dinner parties, weekends away and barbecues – arrived, and at 18, Anne finally began to enjoy what had been difficult teenage years.

Philip wanted to be a responsible father and would take Charles and Anne away once every month or six weeks for a weekend on their own, usually to Sandringham. Later, Andrew and Edward would also attend his family weekends. Elizabeth, however, hardly ever attended these occasions for they were reserved for Philip and the children. They would eat together, go for walks, sometimes shoot, ride, play games, watch a film and, more importantly, talk together. The purpose was to resolve problems that might be unique to them because they were royals. However, most of the time Philip would not discuss matters with them; rather he would lecture his children, telling them what they were doing wrong and instructing them how they should behave in future.

Philip intended the weekends to be fun, an opportunity to relax and enjoy each other's company away from the strictures of royal life at Buckingham Palace. He wanted his children to be like ordinary youngsters for those two or three days. Instead, Philip spent much of the weekend getting rid of his own tensions, demanding the children's obedience and absolute attention. These weekend retreats went on for years until Charles and Anne had reached their late twenties and decided they no longer wanted to go. What is surprising is that the children continued to attend for as long as they did.

Philip also insisted that his offspring should learn to appreciate their privileged life, pull their weight and not just carry out royal duties. During his bachelor days, Charles would take a dozen or so people to Sandringham twice a year, usually for a few days or a weekend shoot in September and January. He and his guests would have the run of the place, shooting during the day followed by boisterous dinners where the wine flowed.

Then Philip suddenly decided that his son should bear the cost of such treats and from then on, Charles was ordered to pay the going rate for the shoots. Philip decided on the amount to be paid.

Charles's friends had no idea that he had to pay to use the family home but in the late '70s and '80s Charles would contribute £1,500 to £2,000 to the Sandringham coffers for the weekend house parties. That was why he later gave up the parties, not because he could not afford them; Sandringham was one of the sovereign's personal homes, nothing whatsoever to do with the state. But Philip wanted to be sure his children realised they had to pay for things in life; that nothing came for nothing.

In 1977, when Charles was 29, Philip simply stopped communicating with his son. During the 1970s Philip saw Charles becoming a likeable, well-rounded young man who was respected and popular with the British public and eventually Charles's privileged position along with his popularity consumed Philip.

Philip's phone calls ceased and, what was worse, Philip gave orders that he would not accept calls from Charles. He ordered his own staff to stop liaising with Charles's office unless it was absolutely necessary for logistical reasons. When entering a room Philip would deliberately avoid Charles, never looking in his direction, pretending he wasn't there. Only in public would he address Charles but the smile was glacial and he spoke no more words than were necessary. From 1977 onwards Philip went out of his way never to be with his son so that they would never have to speak. There are virtually no photographs showing the two men alone together in that period although 1977 marked the queen's Silver Jubilee, celebrated by walkabouts throughout the land with Elizabeth going out to meet the British people surrounded by her ostensibly loving family.

Charles simply could not understand why his father had turned against him. In vain he tried to speak to him, to ask him why he had stopped talking to him as though he longer existed. The only response was silence. When Charles tried to raise the subject whenever the whole family met at Windsor weekends or Balmoral holidays, Philip would simply ignore Charles and speak to his other three children.

Charles spoke to his mother about the problem asking her whether, in his father's eyes, he had done anything wrong to upset him. Elizabeth could not help. It seems she had not realised the deep-seated resentment Philip felt towards Charles. Elizabeth told her son, 'You know what he is like. He will get over it soon enough.' But he didn't.

Charles would ask his staff and friends about their relationships with their fathers, whether fathers generally cut their sons off. The replies Charles received differed greatly but he found no one whose father had cut his son out of his life so completely and for no apparent good reason.

Once again Charles turned to Uncle Dickie. They talked for hours about Philip. Mountbatten was open and straightforward. He told Charles that Philip was jealous of him, that he would be the next king no matter what happened, and that Philip had never been able to succeed in a career because he had never been given the chance.

Elizabeth also talked to Uncle Dickie about the problem and asked him to try to persuade Philip to think again about his attitude to Charles. She told Mountbatten, 'I have tried to talk to him about it but he won't listen to me.'

Mountbatten urged Philip to rekindle the relationship with his son but Philip refused, saying, 'It's none of your business. Mind your own business and keep your nose out of my family affairs.' As a result of this setback in Philip's relationship with Uncle Dickie, they drifted even further apart. By the time of Mountbatten's assassination in August 1979, the two hardly ever spoke.

The effect of his father's behaviour has been emotionally devastating to Charles. To this day, he has been far more wounded by the break with his father than most people realise.

Elizabeth, however, had always known of Philip's attitude to Charles. She saw it when Charles was a child, seeing how Philip deliberately criticised his son when he was growing up, rarely displaying affection or praise for anything. She noted how Philip had pushed Charles, ridiculing him without encouragement, not giving him the confidence he craved. Elizabeth was aware that when anyone made a fuss of Charles, Philip would instantly counteract it.

Worried that Philip's attitude would cause unbreachable divisions in the family, Elizabeth remained concerned about Charles throughout his childhood and teenage years. She had known that Charles was not a strong character but she hoped Philip's treatment of him would help him grow up with the determination and strength he would need as king so that the monarchy would survive and prosper in the new millennium.

Elizabeth always wanted to know how Charles was coping. She asked schoolmasters, senior officers, polo players, friends and colleagues whether her eldest son was coping and enjoying life. In the words of one polo patron: 'In a way she was a bit of a mother hen with Charles. She worried about him, even asking if his ponies were fast and safe. She asked whether his flying was competent or whether it was wise to permit him to fly helicopters or particular aircraft. She even worried when he went skiing and hated the idea of him parachuting. Yet she never wanted to stop him actually doing anything. And I always noted that whenever the queen did ask me such questions, Philip was never around.'

In the early 1980s when Charles was having marital difficulties he appeared to lose interest in his royal duties. He had become disillusioned with everything and everyone. He still absolutely respected his mother but there was little affection. None had ever really existed. His father had turned his back on him and Charles had lost all respect for him. Dickie Mountbatten, always a source of consolation and affection, had been murdered by the IRA in 1979. His death was a tragedy not only for Charles but for the entire royal family.

Because Princess Anne was a girl she did not encounter the same pressures from her father as Charles had done before her and as her two younger brothers would. Most people who know the four children well say that Anne seems to have more macho instincts than any of her brothers. Some believe her intelligence, sense of humour, down-to-earth approach to life and natural aggression would make her an excellent heir to the throne. Philip adored his only daughter.

After shaking off her teenage lack of confidence, Anne enjoyed the company of several young men before she met her husband-to-be, Mark Phillips. She had friendships with former Scottish racing driver Jackie Stewart and the young English polo player Sandy Harper.

Anne had wanted to marry Sandy Harper but he didn't want to become involved with the royal family and the two drifted apart. As a polo pal put it, 'Sandy was worried shitless of what he was getting involved with, the royals and everything; he didn't want to know. But Anne and Sandy had a jolly good ding-dong going for some months.'

Louis Brown, the late owner of the Valbonne nightclub in London's West End, would tell of the nights that Anne visited his club with Sandy Harper. He recalled, 'Understandably, they would always ask for a table in the darkest part of the club and I always tried to make sure their privacy was respected. They would indulge in the most passionate embraces most of the night as they had a meal and listened to the music until the early hours. It was an opportunity for the princess to let her hair down.'

Both Elizabeth and Philip were surprised when they finally met Captain Mark Phillips, for he wasn't at all the sort of young man with whom they had imagined their daughter falling in love. Yet the Queen Mother believed the couple were a perfect match, suggesting even that a computer would have selected them. Elizabeth found

Mark quiet and unassuming and knew immediately that it was Anne who would be the dominant partner. Philip found Mark rather dull and boring and told everyone so whenever they discussed the marriage.

Mark is shy and relatively inarticulate, whereas Anne has the quick-witted intelligence of her father. When the couple appeared on a television talk show at the time of their engagement, Mark barely spoke a word while Anne controlled the interview. The royal family gave Mark the nickname 'Fog', suggesting he was not very bright. After an affair that began over their love of horses, Anne, 23, and Mark, 25, were married in November 1973.

Anne had won the admiration of her parents with her spurs, eventing horses and winning the 1971 European Championship on Doublet, a pony Elizabeth had bred to join Philip's string of polo ponies. Doublet became a brilliant eventer instead. Mark Phillips had been a member of the British eventing Olympic Team in 1972. Horses were their lives.

Mark insisted he did not want to join The Firm under any circumstances and turned down a title offered by the Queen. Anne was pleased because it meant their children would grow up as commoners, only distantly related to the royal family. She believed that as a result, they would be happier and more free. Mark recognised that Philip thought little of him and therefore made it known he did not like visiting Sandringham, Windsor or Balmoral for family weekends and holidays. In contrast, Anne thoroughly enjoyed holidays at Balmoral especially when her children were growing up.

By refusing a title, Mark Phillips would not have to undertake any royal functions and the two happily went off with their horses to live in the country, in a lovely Gloucestershire mansion, Gatcombe Park, which the queen gave Anne as a wedding present. The fact that Mark did not want to know about his wife's family, however, did not augur well for their future. Philip did not care if he ever saw Mark but Elizabeth became upset when her son-in-law showed no enthusiasm whatsoever in becoming part of her family.

At first Anne and Mark were inseparable, either at equestrian events around the country or working together at Gatcombe Park. But following the birth of their son Peter in 1978, Anne and Mark began to drift apart. Anne would come to rely on her detective, Sergeant Peter Cross, and when Mark learned of it later, it was the beginning of the end.

In 1983, two years after the birth of Zara, Anne told her parents her marriage was all but over. Neither expressed surprise. Philip had never believed Mark was an ideal husband for Anne and Elizabeth felt Mark had never made the effort to become one of the family. Elizabeth told Anne, 'I think it will be terribly sad for Peter and Zara.'

Peter had become Elizabeth's favourite grandchild. She used to walk slowly along the corridors of Buckingham Palace holding his hand, even when he was only three and four years old, pointing out to him the names of the men and women in the huge portraits that hang in the palace corridors. She would spend twenty or thirty minutes explaining the relationship of the various people, as though giving him a history lesson. And Peter, who obviously had no idea what Elizabeth was talking about, was happy to toddle along holding his grandmother's hand.

Anne, who has always been open about her mother's lack of maternal feelings, commented, 'The first time I saw them together I couldn't believe my eyes. There was my mother with my child behaving as though she was really enjoying herself with Peter. I've never seen her ever spend more than a minute with any child.'

Understandably, both Philip and Elizabeth were easier on their younger sons, Andrew and Edward. Both were given much more freedom of expression and behaviour than Charles or Anne, though Philip made sure they were obedient to both him and their mother. Rumours have spread suggesting that Andrew or Edward, or both, were fathered not by Philip but by men such as Porchester or Patrick Plunkett. I have researched these claims as far as is possible and can find nothing at all to substantiate them. They are the stuff of royal gossip, with no substance in fact.

Prince Andrew rebelled more against his mother than his father. He was less deferential than his elder brother Charles but he quickly understood that he had to obey him. Andrew would even be rude to his mother in a playful way but he was never chastised as was Charles when he was a child. Andrew, aggressive, strong and opinionated, took after his father and emulated many of the same boorish habits. Elizabeth took it for granted that at least one of her three sons would be like their father.

Andrew also took after his father in his aggressiveness with women during his late teens and twenties. He became unpopular with most of those he tried to date and then bed, because they knew they were only being asked out so that Andrew could add another notch to his belt. The actress Koo Stark was typical of the sort of girl that attracted him: sexy, raunchy, daring, a girl whose love for

Andrew was ruined by the press, simply because she had appeared in a soft-porn movie. She was in fact intelligent, and a most pleasant young woman. She helped Andrew and he became so smitten with her that he wanted to set up home with her and, so he said, eventually marry her.

Philip intervened personally, advising his son that although Koo Stark was a lovely girl, she was not quite right for him, the family and his mother especially. A friend of Philip's commented, 'It was as if Andrew had to be reminded that his mother was the queen.'

Andrew was determined to enjoy himself and did so just as his father had done a generation before. He was frequently in the news where his romantic escapades became the stuff of gossip. Once he turned up unexpectedly at the home of a girlfriend, Katie Rabett, a lovely young blonde who, unknown to her parents, had been working as a nude model. It was Andrew's birthday and he went to see her. Katie Rabett's parents, who lived in an ordinary, sober middle-class area of London, entertained Andrew to a meal and drinks. The next day pictures appeared showing Andrew and Katie kissing goodnight on the doorstep and also raunchy pictures of her in the nude. Her father, who had had no idea his daughter was a nude model, was utterly infuriated.

Andrew also dated Noelle Williams, daughter of singer Andy Williams and Claudine Longet, during a trip to Los Angeles. He also liked to attend School Dinners, a London Club whose members were punished by attractive young waitresses wearing maid's black dresses, white aprons and black stockings – only these girls' dresses were very short, revealing black suspenders, lots of bare thigh and their knickers. The waitresses would punish the members – all of them men – by making them bend over and caning their backsides. Andrew loved it.

Both Elizabeth and Philip were informed of the treatment Prince Andrew received at the hands of his fellow officers on the aircraft carrier HMS *Invincible*, as the ship steamed towards the Falkland Islands in the spring of 1982. Prince Andrew, who piloted a Sea King helicopter, had joined the British Task Force dispatched by Prime Minister Margaret Thatcher to evict the Argentines after they had occupied the British base in the south Atlantic. An officer on board *Invincible* recalled: 'Andrew was being a real pain to everyone, throwing his weight around as though he was the ship's captain rather than just a 22-year-old sub-lieutenant, a helicopter pilot, like the rest of us. After we had sailed more than halfway towards the Falklands many of us were heartily fed up with him. One night, after a few drinks, he was invited on deck and we beat the shit out of him. So that no one would get into trouble a number of us had a go at him. We had just had enough of his bragging, treating us like dirt.'

The punishment meted out to Prince Andrew seemed to work wonders for the young man. *Invincible*'s captain heard about the beating young Andrew had been given and secret messages were flashed back to London, asking if any action should be taken against those responsible. The matter was eventually passed on to Elizabeth and Philip. The captain reported that Andrew seemed to be suffering no ill effects and Philip informed the Admiralty that no action should be taken against the officers unless the ship's captain thought differently. No action was ever taken against the young officers. Andrew has never been told his parents were informed of the incident. The officer commented later, 'It was the best thing that happened to him. After that he was a different chap. He took it and learned the lesson. As far as I understand there were no hard feelings. He knew he was being a pain.'

Like many mothers, Elizabeth treated her youngest child, Prince Edward, as her perpetual little boy, causing him many personal problems. Philip, however, treated all his children from a very young age as though they were all young adults. It was the same with Edward who, to a great extent, had the same shy, retiring nature as Prince Charles.

As a result, Elizabeth felt more maternal to Edward than the rest of her children. She felt that she should have been more protective to Charles than she had been in his young days, protecting him from his father, and she determined that the shy Edward would be given greater protection. Edward was a delightful child, always smiling and loved by everyone. Still, Philip determined to make a man of his youngest son just as he had done with Charles. Philip believed that because Edward appeared weak and quiet, even an introvert, he had to apply more pressure to make a man of him.

Prince Philip once said that his sons had few possibilities: if they did not go into the armed services, then a career in the church remained the only alternative. For Philip, a man with a purely intellectual interest in religion, entering holy orders meant retreating from life.

Like Charles, Edward had been unhappy at Gordonstoun, for he was not really cut out for the tough spartan school. Undeniably, Edward would have been far happier at Eton or Harrow or any public school which did not put so much emphasis on the hard life of cold showers and morning runs through snow and ice, dressed only in singlet and shorts. But Philip decreed that he had to follow in his footsteps and those of his two brothers.

Philip had been honoured by the Royal Marines by being invited to become Honorary Captain General, and he decided that as Charles and Andrew had both seen service in the Royal Navy it would be an excellent idea for young Edward to join the Royal Marines instead. Philip could not have chosen someone less suited to the rigours of such a life. To succeed in the marines a young man needed the aggression and confidence of a man like Philip, not Edward's weak and retiring disposition. Edward himself always wanted a career in the arts, preferably in the theatre. What he didn't want, after the ordeal of Gordonstoun, was a life in the Royal Marines. He had enjoyed his three years at Cambridge where he had become involved in amateur dramatics, and felt music, the opera, theatre, ballet and dance were his metier.

One of Philip's proudest moments as a father took place in October 1986 when Edward began his training at the marines' headquarters. It was not to last long. By Christmas, Edward had confessed to his brothers that he found the course 'too hard and too rigorous', the discipline 'too strict' and much of the training 'mindlessly boring and juvenile'. He also talked over the matter with his father telling him that he felt he did not belong in the marines and had no intention of making the Royal Marines his career. Philip tried to understand, believing his son was just going through the usual doubts of young men when they enter an extraordinarily tough regime. He had no doubt that by the end of the six-month course Edward would have thoroughly enjoyed the experience and look back on the training as 'not all that bad'. But Philip was wrong. He had failed to notice that his son was looking nervous and tired, and that his spirits were low.

But Elizabeth had noticed. And she was worried. She was worried that Philip refused to understand the character of his son, determined to make sure a son of his would finish the course come what may. Elizabeth talked to Philip but he would not hear of Edward withdrawing. 'I am absolutely determined that he'll finish the course,' he said, 'It'll make a man of him. Edward needs a bit of toughening up.'

So Edward, his stamina flagging and feeling miserable and alone, returned to barracks. A month later, in January 1987, Edward quit the marines in a blaze of anguish and acrimony from his father. He had tried to complete the training schedule which even the marines admit is 'bloody tough'. More importantly, Edward had wanted to prove to his father that he was indeed a real man, but the rigours of the training and the mental anguish had been too much for him.

In the bitter family row that followed, Elizabeth seemed determined to challenge her husband. When Edward arrived home, the outraged Philip accused him of letting down the family, of being a 'quitter' and a 'coward'. For three hours Philip raged while Edward cried and stammered trying to explain why he had walked out. Philip didn't want to know.

In turn, Elizabeth became angry with Philip. A member of the household who overheard one of the violent arguments between Elizabeth and Philip, recalled, 'I had never heard the queen raise her voice like that before. I had never heard her challenge her husband in that way, accusing him of being responsible for Edward's decision to quit because he had never bothered to try and understand his sons. The queen let Philip have it with both barrels.'

The following weekend Elizabeth's anger with Philip boiled over, this time in public. They were attending a pheasant shoot for local farmers at Sandringham and Elizabeth was not at all pleased with her husband's behaviour. She decided to show Philip, the man who prided himself on being great at everything, that he wasn't the Mr Wonderful he thought he was. In a loud voice, so all could hear, Elizabeth accused him of mishandling the gun dogs and of being 'ignorant'; she accused him of failing to arrange the shoot properly, telling him that it had been his responsibility. Never before had anyone witnessed Elizabeth criticising Philip in public, ridiculing his competence in front of his social inferiors.

Philip retaliated with a colourful string of expletives and Elizabeth, her face filled with fury, strode away from the shoot.

The drama over, Edward made Elizabeth realise how wrong she had been to leave the children's upbringing to such a narrow-minded man, while failing to become involved herself. She realised how much more difficult life had become since the death of Mountbatten who had been so understanding, not just for her but also for the children. There was no one to whom she could turn for advice. She believed her mother, then 87, and her ever faithful Bobo, 83, who had proved so helpful in the past, were too old to trouble with family problems.

She determined to take a closer interest in her children. But she feared it was too late, that the damage had been done, although in 1987 the full extent of its repercussions could never have been imagined.

Despite the problems within the marriage, Elizabeth happily

recognises that by far the most important person in her life has been Philip. As Kenneth Harris wrote in his biography, *The Queen*: 'She has proved herself to be a woman of unique charisma and professional skill who deserves the admiration and affection . . . of the people of this country. It is mainly the product of the queen's own personality and manifest sense of duty. But it is in great measure the result of her relationship with her consort. The Duke of Edinburgh has been a powerful husband to her. He has not been the easiest man to live with: he is short-tempered, brusque and self-willed with his wife as he has been with everybody else. But he has loved her, revered her and supported her – sometimes imparting valuable advice – from the earliest days of their marriage.'

But Philip has never seen himself in his true light, preferring to believe that he should be remembered only for the good things that he has achieved in his 78 years. He puts his role as supporter to the queen at the top of his list of achievements. Of second importance is the highly successful Duke of Edinburgh Award Scheme which he had started in 1956 and has since spread to 56 countries worldwide involving two-and-a-half million young people. He is also proud of his close involvement with The World Wide Fund for Nature which has grown from a commitment to the conservation of natural habitats to championing global environment issues. Likewise, the Commonwealth Study Conference which meets every six years to discuss advancements in work and the changing demands of industrial society is a source of pride to him. He is also content by his fundraising powers although, as we have seen earlier, he is not a particularly good chairman. Since Elizabeth became queen, Philip has taken part in 586 overseas visits to 137 countries on behalf of the United Kingdom and the Commonwealth.

In 1999, Philip talked to a friend and admirer, Gyles Brandreth, about his life and his relationships with his children and other family members, claiming, 'I'm not vindictive . . . Our children come and stay. The atmosphere is very happy. We are a happy family.'

Asked about his differences with Prince Charles, Philip commented, 'Charles is a romantic, and I'm a pragmatist. That means we do see things differently. And because I don't see things as a romantic would, I'm *unfeeling*.' And he laughs.

Philip's efforts to gloss over his 'unfeeling' image cut little ice with his three sons. Prince Charles still suffers emotionally from the cold, unforgiving way in which his father had brought him up.

Now Charles, Andrew and Edward are the new men in Elizabeth's life, but she sees little of them. The divisions within the family have never healed because of Philip's attitude to his three sons. Elizabeth had hoped that Charles and Andrew would have had the strength of character to cope with married life but neither man has shown they possess the personality that Philip has revealed in his marriage. Elizabeth hopes and prays that the cool, mature Sophie, who married Edward in the summer of 1999, will have the understanding, temperament and character to make a success of their marriage.

10. STORM CLOUDS

Most of the major crises that have plagued Elizabeth and the monarchy throughout nearly fifty years on the throne have not been political, constitutional or affairs of state. To her great embarrassment, they have been personal family matters involving all that she finds deeply disturbing and abhorrent: adultery, separations, divorce and re-marriage. These problems have given her much heartache and personal grief and, in her view, undermine the monarchy and the role people expect the royal family to play in the affairs of the nation.

Elizabeth has been held in the highest esteem by the great majority of the British people, and no one has been able to point an accusing finger at her for the way she has gone about her life's work. But there is a feeling throughout the nation that she has been let down personally by her immediate and extended family. And in nearly every case it has been 'sins of the flesh' that have been at the root of the problems she has tried to solve, virtually single-handedly.

Throughout much of her reign, Elizabeth has seemingly been engaged in a titanic struggle to stop, or certainly slow down, society's changes in practice and attitude to the moral absolutes which she knew as a young woman. Since 1950 in particular, she has witnessed radical changes concerning the values of matrimony, divorce, 'living in sin' and having children out of wedlock. Elizabeth has valiantly fought against these great social changes by promoting the Christian and Victorian principles she was brought up to believe are sacrosanct and which, in her view, are necessary to a healthy, stable society.

At the start of her reign her attitude toward divorce reflected her grandmother Queen Mary's profound belief that it should never be tolerated under any circumstances. Now Elizabeth is simply surrounded by divorced people, with a third of British marriages

202

ending in divorce and, in her own family, marriage after marriage has ended in disaster. Elizabeth knows that Queen Mary would never have tolerated such behaviour, but she is no longer able to pretend these changes have not occurred.

In the early 1980s the *Sunday Times Magazine* published an alphabet of 'The Greatest' people in the world at that time. Under 'Q' the magazine selected Queen Elizabeth II, explaining, 'So much dignity in presiding over the dissolution of the Empire . . . the demonstrations of loyalty at her Silver Jubilee in 1977 and the unrivalled interest aroused by her and her family all over the world.'

The queen's policy of a slightly more open monarchy seemed to have hit a rich vein at the beginning of the 1980s; after a fairytale romance, Charles had married Diana, the young woman who had captured the western world's heart, and had presented the royal family with an heir, Prince William.

In her celebrated biography, *Elizabeth R*, published in 1982, Elizabeth Longford wrote: 'The monarchy has grown smarter, the courtiers shrewder, and the megastar status of the royal family has given it immense international interest and prestige. With so much popularity – and with the royal income automatically adjusted through the Civil List – the monarchy has made itself virtually invulnerable to politics and politicians.

'But the true measure of Elizabeth II's extraordinary achievement is that, for all the changes which have happened in her reign, she has surrendered nothing of the essence of the royal myth which she accepted as a sacred trust from that dedicated king, her father . . .

'As a human story and a super-human dream remorselessly conveyed throughout the world by all means of modern mass communications, the monarchy is more than ever indispensable, and probably immortal . . .

'At the same time the queen's younger children have shown themselves impressive additions to the "Royal Firm", Prince Edward teaching for two terms in a New Zealand school and Prince Andrew establishing the traditional connection between the monarch and the people in time of war. Prince Andrew's performance in the Falklands task force on HMS *Invincible*, where his Sea King helicopter was used as a decoy for an Exocet missile, proved to be an irresistible mixture of the heroic and the human . . .

'Whether or not Elizabeth II speaks her mind on any particular occasion, the nation is fully aware of her standards and deeply felt religious beliefs. After 30 years she is intuitively understood and whole-heartedly respected. Against the hurly-burly of national life her thoughts have become a kind of ideal voice-over, no less moving and effective for being often unspoken.'

This idyllic, perhaps idealised, view of Elizabeth, her character and her close family was shared at that time by the great majority of the British people, from the highest to the lowest in the land. The following decade would see a series of scandals that would strike at the very heart of her family and would radically alter people's perceptions of the monarchy and the role of the royals. Indeed, the nation's loyalty to the Crown itself would be brought into doubt.

But it wasn't just during the 1980s that the House of Windsor suffered disruptions and divorces. Since she has become queen, scandals involving the royals have plagued Elizabeth; and although many of the influential élite have been well aware of their existence, until now the public has not known about them.

From the moment she became queen, Elizabeth wanted her family to be the epitome of a loving, caring nuclear family, a beacon of moral example to the British people. She wanted to emulate Queen Victoria, seen as a paragon of morality and whose virtuous life set an example to the nation. Elizabeth understood that two disastrous world wars had weakened the people's moral fibre as well as their sense of duty, obligation and observance of the values of the earlier part of the century.

Throughout her reign Elizabeth hoped and tried, by her example, to restore that sense of responsibility, of bounden duty to family life. Certainly during the first half of this century, divorcées were treated by the royal family like lepers and ostracised by the court. Once again, it was the strict moral code of Queen Mary, George V's wife, which had laid down the royal family's rules on morality, sex and divorce. During Queen Mary's 26 years on the throne it became an article of royal faith that divorced people would never be allowed in the presence of the monarch. Moreover, any divorced person, either man or woman, or even the wronged party in a marital dispute, would not be allowed to be presented at court or to meet any members of the immediate royal family. So strict was Queen Mary's adherence to the sanctity of marriage that divorcées were even forbidden entry to the royal enclosure at the races. It was Wallis Simpson's status as a divorcée that ultimately cost King Edward VIII his crown.

The 1960s brought dramatic changes in society. This was the Swinging '60s, the time of The Beatles and the sensational introduction of the contraceptive pill with its revolutionary effect on the sex lives of the younger generation as well as their marital practices. Divorce and infidelity became widespread. Elizabeth tried desperately to hold the line against social change, and her attitude to divorce was still unforgiving as late as 1967, the fifteenth year of her reign. In a remarkable demonstration of her principles and beliefs in the old moral code, Elizabeth acted with dramatic, if not draconian, fashion towards the divorce of her own cousin, with whom she had been most friendly, indeed on close family terms, for most of her life.

In 1967, the beautiful, famous concert pianist Marion Stein divorced her husband George Lord Harewood, Elizabeth's first cousin. Marion was the daughter of Erwin Stein, a Second World War German-Jewish refugee and one of the world's most respected musicians. Before marrying Marion in 1949, Harewood, then eighteenth in line to succession to the throne, had to obtain permission from the queen. (Even today, all in line to succession have to do so.)

The Harewood marriage disintegrated in 1959 when Lord Harewood met Patricia Tuckwell, a beautiful Australian model known as Bambi because of her dark, doe-shaped eyes. They fell madly in love and Bambi had a son by Harewood in 1965, although the world knew nothing about the child until Harewood's divorce from Marion in 1967.

Harewood went to see Elizabeth, explained the situation to her and asked her permission to divorce Marion and marry Patricia Tuckwell, the mother of his two-year-old boy. At first Elizabeth refused outright, suggesting in the strongest possible terms that Harewood should leave his mistress and return to his wife. Harewood explained that his marriage to Marion was over, and had been for some years.

Elizabeth, who had always been on friendly terms with her cousin, never cared for the young Countess Marion Harewood, the title she was given upon her marriage. Once Elizabeth said of her, 'Marion is the only woman I know who can make me feel like the cook!'

Determined to save the marriage, Elizabeth called in the then Prime Minister Harold Wilson and the Archbishop of Canterbury in an effort to gain their support. She was adamant that no close member of the royal family should be allowed to divorce. It was a matter of principle which, she said, the House of Windsor would always uphold.

After much discussion, Elizabeth was finally persuaded that, in the circumstances, it was perhaps better to agree to the divorce mainly because the woman Harewood intended to marry had already borne him a son. But she warned Harewood in a stinging meeting before granting him the divorce that he and his second wife would have to bear the consequences. He would be banished from court. And Elizabeth kept to her word. It was a prime example of Elizabeth's iron determination to remain loyal to the moral principles she had learned as a child from Queen Mary and her own mother when her uncle had decided to renounce the throne for the love of a divorced woman. Elizabeth saw her banishment of Harewood as a warning to the rest of the royal family, as well as the aristocracy and others, that divorce would not be tolerated by the House of Windsor. Those who wished to divorce would have to accept the consequences.

Harewood's total ostracism ended much of his public life. On instructions from the queen, neither the wretched Lord Harewood nor his wife were invited to the funeral of his uncle, the Duke of Windsor, in June 1972, something which hurt Harewood deeply. Nor were they invited to Princess Anne's wedding in November 1973.

On Elizabeth's explicit instructions, Lord Harewood was made to retire early from his position as Chancellor of York University and even as artistic director of the famous Edinburgh Festival. Both institutions were persuaded to do so by the queen's advisers at the Palace.

But Elizabeth's staunch views and draconian treatment of Lord Harewood could not prevent the changes demanded by all sections of the population. Finally, in 1968, and much against Elizabeth's wishes, the politicians realised they had to bow to the inevitable. After much debate, Parliament passed the 1969 Divorce Reform Act which permitted much easier and quicker divorce with no blame attached to either party.

The Divorce Act meant that for the first time in Britain the sole ground on which a petition for divorce could be presented to the court by either party was that the marriage had irretrievably broken down. As church leaders feared, and sociologists suspected, the 1969 Act was the catalyst for a dramatic upsurge in the number of divorces.

Despite the new Divorce Act, Elizabeth continued to make Lord Harewood unwelcome for ten long years before she finally relented. In 1977 Elizabeth deemed Harewood had completed his penance and allowed him back into the royal fold. He and his second wife were invited to take part in the Silver Jubilee celebrations. Elizabeth, however, had little or no option but to forgive her cousin, for in 1976 she had been forced to accept that her own sister's marriage had failed and had agreed to a separation. Ironically, adultery and divorce which Elizabeth so abhorred would envelop her life and her family.

In the early 1970s Elizabeth learned that the marriage of her sister appeared to be in trouble and that both Margaret and her husband, the photographer Lord Snowdon, the former Anthony Armstrong-Jones, had been seeing various people. Margaret and Tony had been married in traditional royal splendour at Westminster Abbey in May 1960, the first great family occasion since the coronation seven years before. The procession of horse-drawn coaches down the Mall was greeted with great cheers and flag-waving. Two thousand people attended the wedding and Margaret and Tony were loaned HMS *Britannia* for their honeymoon cruise. A year later, their first child, David, arrived, and in 1964, Sarah.

Margaret and Tony's marriage had been a hectic affair, laced with passion, violent rows and remarkable individual freedom. When Margaret told her sister Elizabeth of their marital problems, the couple had already been unhappy together for some years. Nevertheless, Margaret's confession alarmed Elizabeth who feared the rumours would become the stuff of gossip and end up splashed across the pages of the dreaded press. Margaret could see nothing wrong in what she was doing and in a remarkably open discussion between the two sisters at Buckingham Palace in 1971, she told Elizabeth that she and her husband Tony had been having an 'open' marriage and had both become close to others from time to time during the past few years. Elizabeth was shocked that her own sister could behave in such a manner.

Elizabeth also feared that Margaret's 'indiscretions' would become public knowledge and that the royal family's stance on adultery, morals and sex outside marriage would be held up to ridicule. Furthermore, Elizabeth believed that such revelations would seriously damage her personal standing in the nation's opinion of her.

In fact, Elizabeth had no knowledge of the life Margaret had led ever since she had been forced by those grey men in the Palace to end her relationship with the love of her life, Group-Captain Peter Townsend. The enforced end to that relationship had made Margaret realise that if she could not marry the man she wanted, because of her position as sister to the queen, then she would make sure she enjoyed her life. And she did.

Margaret and Tony Armstrong-Jones appeared to be happy for the first five or six years – the couple seemed ideally suited. But problems soon emerged and Margaret's rather raffish, even bohemian love of life, led her to seek out and form relationships with other men. It was the London of the 'Swinging '60s' when the sophisticates spread the gospel of free love and Margaret wanted to live life to the full.

The brilliant theatre critic and writer, Kenneth Tynan, who died tragically of a rare disease when only in his fifties, told me decades ago of blue films Princess Margaret asked him to arrange and show for her. Tynan said, 'There would only be eight or ten of us at each showing and she would have a few drinks and smoke cigarettes with that remarkable long holder which became a sort of symbol of her rebellion. The films were quite raunchy, with everything including lesbian scenes and, of course, masses of straightforward heterosexual gyrations. She loved it all. And when she was leaving she would always say on the way out. "We must do that again, it is most exhilarating." And she would disappear into her chauffeured car with whoever was escorting her. Sometimes she would even become a little tipsy but never drunk.'

By the mid-'60s both Tony and Margaret had become involved in full-blown love affairs with people outside their marriage and they decided that an agreement should be made between them to make sure their children would not suffer and that their indiscretions would not become the stuff of gossip columns. They both knew there would be serious repercussions if Elizabeth heard of their affairs.

They were being naïve. As a matter of security, their private detectives had to report back to their superiors the names and, if possible, the addresses and backgrounds of all their friends and acquaintances. More importantly, it was *de rigueur* that the detectives should pass on to their superiors the names and relevant details of lovers, or potential lovers, because they could always pose serious problems when members of the royal family were involved. Yet neither Tony nor Margaret seemed to have taken that channel of communication into consideration when they decided to actively enjoy an open marriage. Either they didn't worry or, as some suggest, they had decided to live the lives they wanted to and damn the consequences.

Princess Margaret became involved with a number of men. One of the first, Anthony Barton, a tall, dark handsome wine importer, was known to Tony from his days at Cambridge. Margaret and Tony, and Anthony and his Danish wife Eva, became close friends and would holiday together. Anthony Barton became godfather to the Snowdon's daughter Sarah. Then Margaret, who found Barton very sexy, fell in love with him and the two became lovers in the mid-'60s. However, Margaret felt guilty about the affair and, inexplicably, phoned Barton's wife Eva and confessed, telling her, 'I have to tell you what has been going on because I feel so guilty.' Eva had been totally oblivious to her husband's affair. Understandably, Margaret's adultery with the handsome Barton soured the relationship between the four and there were no more combined family holidays, but Margaret and Barton continued seeing each other for a while longer.

Holidays had always been one of the problems between Margaret and Tony. At first they had both enjoyed their joint misery when expected to holiday at Sandringham or Balmoral and they contrived to avoid such events whenever possible. Margaret preferred lying around in the sun on hot beaches far from England, while Tony, who never liked sunbathing and swimming in faraway places preferred quiet holidays in the English countryside. Silly, frivolous rows over where to spend their holidays and weekends proved to be one of the main reasons their marriage drifted apart, perhaps as much as the affairs they seemed to need outside their marriage.

Tony had found a ramshackle, uninhabitable cottage on a 30-acre estate near Nyman's in Sussex, about 40 miles from London, which had been handed over to the National Trust some years before. Called Old House, the building had originally been woodsmen's cottages and dated back three centuries. Tony planned to modernise the building, which had no running water, and make a lake in the middle of which he planned an island with a pagoda to be reached by a replica of a gondola.

While his new holiday home excited Tony, Margaret was annoyed that he could spend so much time, and nearly all his savings, on Old House. They fought relentlessly about it because Margaret wanted to build a weekend home near Sunninghill, not far from Windsor, where she loved to water-ski. Margaret was to say later, 'Tony was responsible for breaking up our marriage by insisting on buying and living at Old House as much as he did. We had agreed to build a house at Sunninghill where we could water-ski together, but without even discussing the matter with me, he simply went off and bought those dilapidated old cottages. I knew nothing until after he had bought the place. That was stupid and it was the beginning of the end.'

But Tony remained adamant, determined to keep his independence. During the first few years of marriage many believed Tony was just a royal hanger-on, having an easy life of luxury, occasionally accompanying Margaret on official functions and walking, just like Prince Philip, a few yards behind his wife, his hands clasped firmly behind his back. Because he was a relaxed, serene character most people believed he loved the role. In fact, he hated it.

The more time Tony spent at Old House the more Margaret socialised in London. She rekindled an old flame, Robin Douglas-Home, whose uncle Alec Douglas-Home had been Prime Minister of Britain in 1963. Robin was a gifted piano player, and he and Margaret shared a love of classical music and ballet. Again, Margaret fell in love and again she indulged in a passionate love affair which most of London society knew about because of the time the two spent openly in each other's company.

It seemed that Margaret was capable of falling in and out of love quite easily and was sometimes accused of playing on men's emotions. Robin Douglas-Home, who had one failed marriage, asked, indeed repeatedly pleaded, with Margaret to divorce Tony and settle down with him, perhaps even marrying at some later stage. It was obvious that Margaret and Robin had much in common and were very close, but Margaret's good sense prevailed.

Margaret told a friend, 'I can't even think of divorcing Tony, my sister would simply not tolerate it. Whatever happens between Tony and me, she would expect us to stay married for the sake of the monarchy.'

As a result, Margaret realised she had to end her relationship with Robin and tried to do so. Emotionally unstable and madly in love with Margaret, Robin could not get over their affair. He would write her endless love letters which, in the end, Margaret threw away unread. Robin began talking openly of suicide and, in 1968, one year after Margaret had finally spurned him, he did indeed take his life at his country cottage. Margaret was devastated.

But Margaret had been trying for more than a year to put her marriage back on track. She had returned to Tony and they tried to make the marriage work. They still found each other sexually exciting and Tony was able to satisfy Margaret's sexual demands. But Tony continued to insist on his independence. He wanted to prove himself as a great photographer and he spent more time pursuing his career, and gaining a worldwide reputation, often to Margaret's annoyance.

The film actor Peter Sellers, a close friend of Margaret's, suggested they should all travel to the Costa Smeralda in Sardinia for a long summer holiday with his beautiful young Swedish wife Britt. They would be accompanied by Kirk Douglas and his wife Anne. Tony would come too as well as Princess Alexandra and her husband Angus Ogilvy. It was a great success and Margaret and Tony seemed happy again. But their happiness would not last.

That holiday convinced Margaret that she wanted a private, sun-drenched holiday home to which she could escape and enjoy herself. She loved to laze around in her swimsuit, smoking and drinking, swimming and water-skiing and spending the afternoons and evenings relaxing, usually with a large gin and tonic. Fortunately, at the time of her wedding, Margaret had been offered the gift of a home on the tropical isle of Mustique in the Bahamas from a wealthy British socialite friend. Now she decided the time had come to accept the proffered gift and contacted Colin Tennant, who would become Lord Glenconner, an old friend from her bachelor-girl days.

Happily he agreed and a site above Gelliceaux Bay was selected. Margaret had asked her husband, who had studied architecture at Cambridge, to design the house but he steadfastly refused telling her it was a stupid idea to have a holiday home so far from Britain. This disagreement led to more rows between the two. However, Tony's uncle, Oliver Messel, a well-known theatrical designer who for reasons of health lived in the Caribbean, agreed to take over the project. When it was completed, with stunning views over the sea, Margaret named it Les Jolies Eaux, so beautiful were the waters below the house.

By the late '60s, the couple were spending more time apart, Margaret escaping to Mustique whenever possible and Tony living at Old House where, after a few visits, Margaret refused to go, let alone stay for a night or a weekend. Tony, who had become a keen shot under the tuition of Philip, decided to end relations with the royal family, and he stopped shooting. It was obvious to their friends that they were living separate lives and were so open and outrageous about their various liaisons that it appeared they were trying to vie with one another for attention.

Among Tony's coterie of friends were various gay men whom Tony would occasionally entertain at Kensington Palace and Old House. Margaret would frequently ridicule Tony about them, calling him 'a pansy' and 'a faggot'. One night in the late 1960s Margaret arrived home to find Tony dressed in one of her ball gowns, dancing on the dining room table with three of his gay friends. It had all been innocent fun but Margaret virtually chased the men out of her home and a ferocious row took place in which Margaret called her husband 'a queer' and Tony called his wife 'a drunken slut'.

At the time Tony, who had been given the title of Lord Snowdon after his marriage to Margaret, was seen among the young social set as a man-about-town, the husband of Princess Margaret and a man with an eye for a pretty girl. He had numerous liaisons, some with former debutantes as well as young career women working for glossy magazines. Tony was enjoying his independence.

Tony's neighbours at Old House were the Marquess of Reading, a wealthy aristocratic stockbroker, his wife Margot, their two sons and their lovely daughter Jacqueline, then in her early twenties. Tony frequently visited his new-found friends and in 1970 he and the lovely Jackie, as everyone called her, became lovers. Tony had become so confident in himself that he would take Jackie to parties and dinners at Kensington Palace at which Margaret was also present.

For more than a year Tony and Jackie continued their outrageous affair all over London. Tony was flattered by the passionate love of young Lady Jacqueline and she was hopelessly in love with the famous royal photographer and husband of Princess Margaret. Jackie told a close friend in 1971, 'I love Tony; I love him with all my heart. And he loves me; he wants to marry me.'

When news of the affair hit the front pages early in 1971, Lord Reading called Tony to his house, Staplefield, and demanded an explanation. An amazing scene took place, just like something from a bygone era. In the drawing room of his home, Lord Reading, apoplectic with rage, accused Tony of seducing his daughter, of ruining her chances in life and of acting like an absolute cad. He banned him from ever entering his house again or setting foot on his estate. He also warned him never to see his daughter again.

Margaret, who had spent the last months happily entertaining such men as Peter Sellers, her cousin Lord Patrick Lichfield, the royal photographer, as well as others including an old friend, Jocelyn Stevens, became angry as she felt her husband's affairs were making her a laughing stock.

Unhappy in her marriage, and disgusted at being held up to ridicule, Margaret went to see her sister to discuss the possibility of a separation. Elizabeth told her it was out of the question for someone so close to the monarch. Elizabeth also told her to arrange a reconciliation because attacks being made on her marriage were damaging the influence of the crown, which Margaret had to realise was vital to Margaret as well as to the queen.

Margaret felt trapped in a loveless marriage, and became alternately angry and miserable that she could not separate from, or divorce, her errant husband. She saw nothing wrong in the illicit affairs she herself had indulged in during the marriage. So Margaret continued to enjoy herself, but with as much discretion as possible. She had affairs with other men, like Dominic Elliot, an old friend, and others. But Margaret did not just need a man, but a man she could love.

Enter Roderick Llewellyn, the younger son of former Olympic horseman Colonel Harry Llewellyn. In the early 1970s Margaret met Roddy, a happy-go-lucky minor socialite who had tried to become an up-market gardener to the rich and famous. He had also tried his hand as a pop star and for a while was involved in a hippie commune at Surrendal in Wiltshire, a hundred miles west of London.

Margaret took a distinct fancy to young Roddy, with his raffish clothes, long, shaggy hair and soft voice. And she was flattered by the fact that an attractive man 18 years her junior had shown such a physical interest in her. She liked his sense of fun, his humour and the fact that he refused to be subject to the usual boring social constraints. In a matter of weeks the two had become lovers. There was another, more personal reason for this affair.

Tony was now spending more time apart from his wife and children, leading a very independent existence. Ostensibly, Tony still lived with Margaret at Kensington Palace, but they rarely shared a bed together. Both were drinking heavily. Margaret had just turned 40, drank too much and had become a heavy smoker. She craved companionship and, because of her age and the fact that she was putting on substantial weight, she luxuriated in the friendship of young people around her, particularly a handsome young man who adored her and wanted to be her constant companion and lover. It didn't seem to bother Margaret that once again she was courting scandal. Eyebrows were raised in the same way as when she was courting Group-Captain Peter Townsend, when she married Tony Armstrong-Jones and now when she was dating a hippie gardener.

Elizabeth cautioned Margaret to tread carefully for fear of further scandal. She would phone her sister and try gently to influence her. Margaret told one of her close friends, 'My sister keeps trying to rule by life, telling me what I can and cannot do. I have to listen to her of course but I don't have to take her advice; I have to lead my own life.'

Margaret had always been headstrong; Elizabeth knew that only too well. Margaret continued to lead the life she wanted to lead. Throwing caution to the wind she even visited the hippie commune, sometimes secretly staying the night. In Britain, as it was elsewhere, of course, commune life in the 1970s was associated with free love, nakedness, flower-power and marijuana, all of which were celebrated by Roddy's group. Indeed, Margaret seemed to get a nefarious thrill whenever she visited the commune, with everyone eating, drinking, smoking and chatting together, and watching topless young women gardening. Nights in the commune reverberated with the noise of couples making love.

Ignoring advice from her sister and palace advisers, Margaret was determined to enjoy her new young, virile lover and pay no attention to the press and the *paparazzi* photographers. The more her life with Tony drifted apart, the more Margaret seemed to need the emotional and physical security she had found in Roddy. Their affair became public knowledge but there was no proof for the newspaper editors who felt certain they had come upon another royal scandal. Then Margaret invited her beloved Roddy to Mustique in January 1976. They were 'snapped' eating lunch together in the lovely sunshine of the tropical island.

It was an innocent enough picture but to the British, suffering the January snow and frost, the picture conjured up sun, sea, golden beaches and, more importantly, sexual innuendo. Margaret Rose was not the most popular royal in the 1970s. She was seen as the dream princess, with every privilege and no responsibility, prepared to live off the taxpayer and give very little in return.

For many years some newspapers had seen Princess Margaret as a legitimate target whenever the debate over royal finances – the Civil List – came before Parliament for reappraisal each spring. Since her marriage to Tony Armstrong-Jones, Margaret had received just £15,000 a year in order to pay the wages of her nine staff. In fact, Elizabeth had been secretly funding her sister, paying for all her clothes and air fares. Her ten-roomed apartment in the Clock House at Kensington Palace was provided free. And yet in 1972, when the government put forward plans to increase her allowance to a more respectable £40,000, some members of Parliament put forward a motion to axe Margaret's allowance altogether. They believed the queen's sister was not earning her keep, not carrying out enough royal duties. The motion was eventually defeated by 148 votes to 34. In the 1970s, Margaret was awarded £50,000 a year, and this was steadily increased, mainly due to inflation, to about £85,000 by 1980.

At that time Margaret employed a first-class private secretary, a former Guards major called Nigel Napier whom she paid the miserly figure of £10,000 a year; a butler, John Leishman; a housekeeper, Mrs McIntyre; a ladies' maid, Mrs Greenfield; a chauffeur, Griffin; a cook, two daily maids and her personal lady-in-waiting Lizzie Paget; she had to pay them all. Many in Britain argued that Margaret had no need for such a large staff to care for her needs, but she believed that, as the queen's sister, she was entitled to privileges, including sufficient staff to make her life comfortable. In Margaret's estimation, she certainly does not have too many staff; quite the contrary, in fact – it is hardly sufficient to keep her in the style in which she believes the sovereign's sister should be expected to live.

As the debate on her allowance raged in the press and the House of Commons in 1979, Margaret commented at the time, 'The increase of £10,000 this year hardly pays for the postage stamps. Don't people realise that all my income goes on the staff that I have to employ?'

Comparisons were made between Margaret's workload and that of her sister Elizabeth, and she was found wanting. Throughout the whole of 1979, Princess Margaret made only 113 official public appearances while the queen, with a much greater load of official business, had undertaken 325 royal functions. Prince Philip had carried out 243. Some newspapers criticised Margaret for 'not pulling her weight' and 'dereliction of duty'.

The winter that Margaret's photograph was taken with Roddy on Mustique, the public found itself gripped by a fit of moral indignation aimed directly at Princess Margaret. They believed that in return for her life of privilege and luxury she should at least follow the dictates of conventional morality and remain loyal to her husband, especially since she was a member of the first family of the land, who were meant to set an example. Here was Margaret flouting those conventions by taking as her lover a man eighteen years younger than her, and openly disporting him on her tropical Caribbean island hideaway. Feelings were running high which palace advisers faithfully reported to Elizabeth. They also advised her that she would have to put a stop to Margaret's flagrant disregard for the moral codes which, if permitted to continue, would bring the crown into severe disrepute.

The picture of Margaret and Roddy, splashed on the front page of the Murdoch Sunday paper, the *News of the World*, made Elizabeth realise that the scandal she had feared had arrived with a bang. After all the pleas for discretion she had made to her sister, Elizabeth had had enough. Urged on by her advisers and for the first time ever, Elizabeth issued her sister an order. She told her to fly back immediately to London, and leave the wretched Roddy on the island. From the tone of her voice Margaret knew that on this occasion she had to comply with her sister's orders. She flew back alone.

Elizabeth did not know what to do about these unseemly events. As in previous scandals involving her sister, she hoped the matter would soon disappear from the headlines and be forgotten. She kept reminding herself, as the papers also wrote, that Margaret was not really likely to ever ascend to the throne, and therefore it was not that important to the monarchy if her renegade, independent-minded sister did sometimes bring disrepute into her own life. But worse was to follow.

For some time Tony had wanted out of the marriage and had openly told friends that despite the strict understanding that no member of the immediate royal family would ever be allowed to divorce, he believed that one day he could permanently leave

Margaret. He realised that Margaret's stupid indiscretions with Roddy had made things easier. The day following the *News of the World* photograph showing Margaret and Roddy together, he telephoned Elizabeth and asked to see her.

Elizabeth met her brother-in-law a few days later in her drawing room at Buckingham Palace. She had hoped she could persuade him to overlook this latest escapade, pointing out that to do so would be for the greater good of the family. But Tony had other ideas. Elizabeth was rather taken aback that Tony seemed so determined.

He told her, 'I am being made to look a fool. I have put up with her behaviour for some years. You must have known what's been going on. But I cannot take any more. The world believes I am just a cuckold and it is ruining me, my reputation and my photographic work. The time has come for us to separate.'

Tony went on, 'I am sorry, terribly sorry that our marriage has come to this but I am left no alternative. Please sort something out.'

Elizabeth was sympathetic and said that she could not give him an answer right away but would think about it. Tony had the final word, 'You will have to think of something because I won't go on like this.'

Elizabeth seethed with rage at what she saw as her own sister's stupid behaviour. She told her so when they next met. Elizabeth realised that Tony was using the bad publicity to obtain a divorce. She said nothing to him but Elizabeth knew the fault did not only lie with her sister for she had been kept informed of Tony's sexual adventures.

Reports of that extraordinary meeting show that Elizabeth kept asking her sister, over and over again, 'How could you? How could you do this to me, to the family, to the monarchy? How could you have been so silly?' She buried her head in her hands.

Elizabeth implored her sister to try to save the marriage. She asked Tony to come to Buckingham Palace where she appealed to him, for the sake of the royal family, to give the marriage 'one last try'. She assured him that Margaret was willing to give the marriage 'another go', a true reconciliation. But Tony remained adamant. He had had enough and was determined to take the opportunity Margaret had presented. Tony sat on a sofa, shaking his head, and saying, 'It won't work. It's over. It's unfortunate, but it's finished.'

Elizabeth knew she had no option but to give way. After calling in royal advisers and lawyers, she told Margaret and Tony that she had agreed to give permission for a parting of the ways but she was adamant on one point. No divorce.

Tony, however, had not been completely frank and Margaret knew it. Some months before, Tony had told her of his affair with a young woman called Lucy Lindsay-Hogg, who lived in a small apartment just five minutes' walk from Kensington Palace. Tony had fallen in love with Lucy, a brunette divorcée in her thirties, during a film trip to Australia in 1975 when she had spent weeks with him in the outback as his photographic assistant. Lucy had previously been married for four years and her divorce, some years before she met Tony, had been amicable.

After a discreet lapse of time – a couple of months – the queen gave permission for the official announcement. On 18 March 1976, three months after the scandal had become public knowledge, a simple statement from Buckingham Palace read: 'Her Royal Highness the Princess Margaret, Countess of Snowdon, and the Earl of Snowdon have mutually agreed to live apart. The princess will carry out her public duties unaccompanied by Lord Snowdon. There are no plans for divorce proceedings.'

Tony was given £100,000 from Princess Margaret's personal small fortune to enable him to buy a London home and the couple were allowed the freedom and the independence they had both wanted. Tony celebrated his freedom with champagne and Lucy, while the wretched Margaret felt lonely and cheated. Tony had ended his relationship with Margaret as a highly successful, world-acclaimed photographer and was seen as one of the world's ten sexiest men. He had been given a lovely home and the woman with whom he wanted to share his life. Margaret, on the other hand, had been practically forced to give up young Roddy. She commented, 'The only consolation I have at the end of my marriage is a bottle of gin and packet of fags.'

But the feeling of humiliation was Elizabeth's alone. From those far off childhood days when Uncle David had renounced the crown for a divorced woman, poor Elizabeth had clung to the stern words of Queen Mary that divorce would never be tolerated in any circumstances, and especially in the royal family. To Elizabeth, divorce had always been considered a curse more than a failure. She viewed divorce as a blight upon her family and the monarchy itself, and Elizabeth saw her sister's separation as a visitation, a warning of dire punishment to come for the family and the crown. To uphold the monarchy was the one principle, above all else, she was determined to perpetuate, and now the threat of divorce had arrived at the very gates of Buckingham Palace.

Prince Philip tried to encourage his unhappy and dispirited wife, pointing out that both Margaret and Tony were independent and wayward individuals. He urged Elizabeth not to blame herself for her sister's and Tony's refusal to subordinate their personal preferences and selfish wishes.

After the heat of the separation had died down, Margaret began dating Roddy Llewellyn once more and for the next two years they were treated as a couple. But Roddy was never accepted in royal circles – his career continued to go downhill, his gardening ambitions turned to nought and his new career as a pop singer with the support and enthusiasm of Margaret, proved painfully unsuccessful. The press once again pointed the finger at Margaret and what they saw as her 'lack of dedication' and her 'love for a worthless young layabout'.

In May 1978, Princess Margaret announced that she was to seek a divorce from Tony but had no intention of remarrying. Seven months later Lucy discovered she was pregnant and, though unmarried, was thrilled and delighted. She had always been told by doctors that she could never have children. Without a second thought, Tony immediately asked Lucy to marry him. Weeks later, on 15 December 1978, they married quietly at Kensington Register Office and a daughter was born the following July.

Tony's wedding and the news of the baby upset and angered Margaret. She thought it was disgraceful that Tony had neither told her of the forthcoming child nor of his intention to marry Lucy. And, as Margaret pointed out, he hadn't even told their own children, David and Sarah. Tony's behaviour surprised his friends who would have expected him to break the news of his marriage to his teenage children, rather than leave them to learn about it, and the expected baby, by reading it in the newspapers.

Margaret sought solace from Roddy and tried to persuade Elizabeth that she must allow Roddy to accompany her, even when she was staying at royal palaces. Elizabeth adamantly refused, informing her Private Secretaries that Mr Roderick Llewellyn was not to be included in any royal party nor invited to any royal occasion.

One day, however, Elizabeth did meet Roddy under the most bizarre and embarrassing circumstances. As Nigel Dempster related in his biography of Princess Margaret *A Life Unfulfilled*, Elizabeth was staying at Royal Lodge, when Roddy, dressed only in shirt and underpants, burst in on Nanny Sumner to have a button sewn on. Standing there, chatting to her, was Elizabeth. Roddy blushed and stammered, 'Please forgive me, Ma'am, I look so awful,' as he froze to the spot not knowing how to hide his embarrassment.

'Don't worry. I don't look very good myself,' she replied, and put him at his ease by smiling as she left the room.

The next day they were formally introduced by a rather mortified Margaret after church in Windsor, for Roddy was not meant to have been staying at Royal Lodge that weekend. Margaret had become accustomed to taking Roddy with her whenever she was invited to large mansions for weekends and he would keep discreetly out of the way though the servants and maids would know he was staying overnight.

But Roddy was still not invited to any royal occasions. Events proved the decision was a wise one when torrid revelations of Roddy's past were revealed later in the *News of the World* by his older brother Dai. In a series of articles, Dai recounted numerous suicide attempts by Roddy and revealed that he had indulged in homosexual affairs.

Yet Roddy, then 33, was changing. In the early 1980s he met an old flame, Tania Soskin, a freelance travel writer and he found himself falling in love with her. Eventually he summed up the courage to tell Margaret of his intentions to marry. Margaret was said to have commented, 'I was shocked to start with but I welcome the news with a sense of relief. I have spent so long mothering that boy. In any case I couldn't have afforded him much longer.'

Margaret even threw a lunch party for the couple at Kensington Palace and would have attended the wedding in June 1981 if it had been possible. Following Roddy's marriage, Margaret felt free once more and began enjoying her more lonely but independent life. She also hoped Charles and Diana would start a family shortly after their marriage, demoting her further down the line of succession, and still further out of the royal limelight. Since those hedonistic days Margaret has lived a quieter, more serene life, but has never found another man to settle down with.

In 1980, just two years after Margaret and Tony's official divorce, Elizabeth had to face yet another problem. Anne had become close to her police bodyguard. Sergeant Peter Cross, a handsome, blond but balding man in his late thirties, had bright blue eyes and a great deal of charisma. Two years older than Anne, Sergeant Cross's own marriage had ended a few months after he became her bodyguard. His wife explained their marriage had come to an end because he was never at home, working day and night at Anne's Gloucestershire home, Gatcombe Park.

Mark Phillips sensed that his wife was becoming emotionally dependent upon her bodyguard and decided that he should have Sergeant Cross removed from duties at Gatcombe Park. He believed Anne had changed towards him during those few months, becoming more hypercritical of whatever he said or did. And he had noticed the way Anne and Cross talked to each other and acted towards each other whenever they were together. Mark may have been given the unenviable nickname of 'Fog' but he was nobody's fool.

Mark informed Commander Michael Trestrail, the queen's personal bodyguard and the man in charge of the Royal Protection Squad. Other officers were ordered to investigate the complaint, and phone calls to and from Gatcombe Park were tapped. Because Anne was then sixth in line to the throne, Trestrail informed the queen. He informed Elizabeth that the problem had been going on for some months and asked if any action should be taken. The queen asked for a watch to be kept on the couple and for Trestrail to keep her informed. When Mark reported back that he feared the affair had become serious, Elizabeth, without informing her daughter, agreed that Sergeant Cross should be transferred immediately from Gatcombe Park and all royal duties. Her actions may have been ruthless, but she dreaded another marriage split, another scandal affecting the family.

Assistant Commissioner Wilford Gibson, the officer in charge of Royal Protection, summoned Sergeant Cross to Scotland Yard while Anne was abroad on royal duty. Commander Trestrail was also present. Cross was told that his 'conduct did not come up to the standards expected of police officers who guard the royal family'. He was also accused of drinking on duty. Amazed at such an accusation, Cross replied, 'Everyone drinks on royal duty when invited. But I've never been drunk on duty.'

Gibson continued, 'I didn't say you had been drunk, only that you had been drinking.' Of course drinking on duty was considered a serious offence in the police force but Gibson raised the matter for technical reasons, just in case Cross should object to his immediate transfer. To make sure Cross realised the authorities knew about his phone calls, Commissioner Gibson told him, 'We've heard rumours that you have been over-friendly with the princess.'

Gibson informed Cross he would be transferred immediately to Croydon, south of London, as station officer, – a dramatic demotion which some considered to be an insult, especially to an officer of Cross's ability and past record. Princess Anne, meanwhile, returned home two days later to be informed that a new personal bodyguard had been appointed to her and that Sergeant Cross had been transferred.

Anne was absolutely furious. She immediately phoned Trestrail at Buckingham Palace and, in an outraged voice, asked, 'I would like to know why my personal bodyguard, Sergeant Cross, has been trans-ferred and on whose authority?'

Later in the conversation Anne shouted, 'How dare anyone remove my bodyguard without my permission and without any reason being given whatsoever!'

She slammed down the phone, after telling Trestrail, 'Do not believe this is an end to the matter.'

That night, Anne turned on her husband Mark and accused him of telling tales behind her back. Mark stumbled and stammered but Anne knew that her own husband had initiated the complaint that had led to Cross's forced removal. She appeared to consider her behaviour blameless and despite Mark's attempts to quiet her anger she remained in a fury over what had happened.

That Christmas, Anne sent Cross a signed photograph through a police friend, Inspector Colin Hayward-Trimming of the Royal Protection Squad. Later, Anne sent a message through the same officer asking Peter Cross to visit her at Gatcombe. Cross waited in the library and Anne walked in, looking heavily pregnant.

Anne said, 'How lovely to see you. You can see I'm pregnant, five months.'

Anne took the initiative by asking whether he wanted to continue to meet. He replied that he did, very much so – Cross had resigned from the force shortly after being transferred and was therefore absolutely free to visit Anne whenever she invited him.

Some details of Cross's relationship with Princess Anne were printed in a series of articles in the *News of the World* in the autumn of 1985, four years after Anne's blue-eyed, blonde-haired daughter Zara was born. For a substantial sum of money, Cross agreed to tell something of their relationship but he revealed nothing of an intimate relationship with Anne. He did tell the readers, however, that within minutes of Anne giving birth she had phoned him to say she had a beautiful daughter.

He told of how their close relationship began in early 1980 after he had worked as her bodyguard for just a few months: 'I well remember the first evening Princess Anne and I began to confide our problems to each other. Mark was away and I was doing my last chore of the day, setting the security alarms.

'I was in the kitchen of the Gatcombe Park house. Suddenly I was aware that Anne had come in and was going round turning off light switches. I had to smile. She might be a member of one of the richest families on earth, but the princess had a real thing about saving electricity.

'We started to talk. Then, somehow, we were sitting together on the backstairs, which led from the kitchen to my room. We sat there for two hours. I was on a higher step than Anne. Her arm, I noticed, was leaning against my knee. But that didn't concern me.

'I was too busy that evening thinking about my personal problems, for my private life was in turmoil. I'd left my wife Linda and our two girls because our marriage was over. I had an Iranian girlfriend with whom I shared an apartment in London on my off-duty times, but that relationship too was running into trouble.'

Peter Cross went on to say that he had often had such conversations with Anne and she had told him that she talked to her mother about how well he and Anne got on, confiding in each other. Then he described how their intimacy began in the summer of 1980: 'One night Mark and Anne both had to go to Salisbury, Anne to attend a dinner and Mark to train for the Olympics. As usual we were late starting and Mark drove like the wind. I found it really difficult to match his speed in my car for I was meant to be escorting them.

'Later Anne told me she had asked Mark to slow down because I couldn't keep up. He apparently retorted, "Who are you worrying about – the car, or the man driving it?"

'After the dinner Anne and I drove back to Gatcombe. When we arrived we stood chatting in the hall. I was acutely aware of our closeness. It seemed we were standing there for hours . . . Then we sat down. I flopped down into the armchair and she sat on the carpet at my feet . . . Suddenly she turned and looked at me, our hands brushed and for a few seconds we were like statues looking directly into each other's eyes. Then suddenly we kissed. Within minutes we had moved to the library and there we embraced.'

After Zara's birth, Anne and Peter Cross continued to see each other, occasionally at the home of a friendly police officer in Surrey and at an unused cottage on the Gatcombe estate. Anne would phone Cross where he worked as an insurance salesman, using the name Mrs Wallis. (It was Anne's mischievous idea to use the name of the most famous adulteress known to the House of Windsor, Wallis Simpson.)

The whole business ended in 1983 when Peter Cross told Anne that he had fallen in love with another woman, a dental nurse. Devastated, Anne realised their meetings could not continue without something dramatic happening. In her heart she realised they could never lead a life together.

But it all spelt the end of her marriage to Mark Phillips. For some time, Mark had worked hard to establish a bank balance for himself for he had never liked the idea of sponging off his wife or the royal family. To maintain his independence, Mark had always refused a royal title, which meant that Princess Anne's children were the first royals of the House of Windsor not to have titles of some kind, something Anne entirely approved of.

As a former Olympic Games rider, Mark had an excellent reputation as a horseman and he began to give riding exhibitions, mostly abroad. He also lectured at equestrian weekends and was sponsored by the famous British four-wheel drive car company, Land Rover. In addition, he ran Gatcombe Park's farm, often working 16 hours a day.

Between April 1988 and April 1989, Anne and Mark spent exactly 40 days together with their children. It was a sign that the marriage was going nowhere. But it was not only Mark who was away working. After the birth of Zara, and the end of her meetings with Peter Cross in 1983, Anne threw herself into royal engagements. She had been criticised in the press over the years for her relationships with the press and with people, her rudeness and lack of dedication to the royal family. Some sections of the press suggested that she showed little devotion to her royal responsibilities.

Like her father, Anne's relationship with the press had often been prickly. Some tabloid newspapers went as far as to describe Princess Anne as rude and arrogant and as a result, she had been given a hard time by the press. She decided to start a new life and eagerly accepted the challenge when offered the job of President of Save the Children Fund.

The job proved a watershed for Anne and her relationship with the press and the public. She was seen frequently on television, dressed in a shirt and jeans, helping, encouraging, inspecting and working in the field; she visited the famine areas of Africa, India and many third-world countries actively helping aid workers as they cared for starving children. Overnight, the public's image of her changed and she won almost instant praise.

But this was no momentary change in Anne's behaviour. She has proved a remarkable president for the charity, spending many weeks every year overseas, travelling tens of thousands of miles, heavily involved with the world's underprivileged children. She also spends many weeks a year raising money on behalf of Save the Children. Anne became the first royal to clock up 500 engagements in a year, and then she increased that to 600.

Elizabeth was proud of her. Anne had realised all her mother's dreams, surmounting her greatest expectations, and shown the nation that the royal family worked hard for good causes; that they did not sponge off the nation but gave of themselves, selflessly, for charities. In recognition of her work Elizabeth bestowed on Anne in 1988 a title which she believed she had earned, that of Princess Royal. Until Elizabeth gave her the title, Anne's correct form of address had been a mouthful, 'Her Royal Highness the Princess Anne, Mrs Mark Phillips'. Now she would be called, 'Her Royal Highness, the Princess Royal'. The title also means that, at any time in the future, Elizabeth can bestow titles on Anne's two children.

But the title made little real difference to Anne's way of life. Her life at Gatcombe had always been the same: down to earth with no ostentation. Her home, like any other working farmhouse, has chickens running everywhere, dogs in the kitchens and the courtyard, and the main hall cluttered with dirty boots, weatherproof Barbour jackets and old macs. The grooms, most of the staff and Princess Anne walk around all day in jeans, sweaters and trainers.

Still, Anne's new title brought with it another implication: by making her daughter the Princess Royal, Elizabeth was ensuring her daughter's elevation to the second lady in the land, immediately beneath the queen herself. Until then, Diana had been the second lady because she was married to the Prince of Wales. Now Elizabeth had promoted Anne above Diana whose rank comes only from her being married to Prince Charles and not in her own right. Accepting the title was something Anne relished, for she believed Diana to be somewhat of an upstart whom Charles should never have married. Almost from their first meeting Diana and Anne had taken an immediate dislike to each other though it was never evident to the public.

In 1989, less than a year after accepting her new exalted title, Anne was at the centre of another love affair.

Her marriage to Mark ended quietly in contrast to Margaret and Tony Snowdon's, Charles and Diana's, and Andrew and Fergie's. Mark never argued or shouted. Whenever Anne tried to pick an argument he would say nothing, leave the room or go out to work on the farm. The two simply drifted apart.

Most of the family, including Elizabeth, realised that the marriage between Anne and Mark was over months before the press wrote about it. But Elizabeth had hoped that like many other royals, as well as many aristocratic families, the couple would go their separate ways, live different lives but appear together for occasional royal functions. Elizabeth believed she could count on her only daughter to abide by the unwritten Windsor rule: no divorce. Occasionally her mother had talked to her of divorce, at the time of Margaret's separation, and

Elizabeth of York in 1931, aged five

20 November 1947, Elizabeth's wedding day at Westminster Abbey. The future queen looks radiantly happy while Prince Philip appears nervous and apprehensive

Returning from Kenya after the death of her father, King George VI, in February 1952

Elizabeth with Prince Philip at her coronation, 1953

Elizabeth and Philip on holiday at Balmoral with
their three children, Anne, baby Andrew and Charles,
September 1960

The same Charles a few years later: one month after
his engagement to Lady Diana Spencer, Buckingham
Palace, March 1981

Elizabeth with her prime ministers, July 1992

Greeting friends at the Royal Windsor Horse Show, May 1994

With the Brownies during a royal tour of Belize, February 1994

In the House of Lords for the State opening
of Parliament, November 1995

With the Queen Mother at Royal Ascot, June 1997

Attending the annual Garter Ceremony at
St George's Chapel, Windsor, June 1998

Inspecting the mountains of flowers outside Buckingham Palace
following the death of Diana in 1997

Anne had seemed to understand the damaging effects of royal divorces on the family and on the respect the nation gave to the royals.

In 1988 Anne, at the age of 38, confided in her mother that she had become involved with a young naval officer five years her junior, Commander Timothy Lawrence. A tall, handsome man, Lawrence had been Equerry to the Queen since 1986.

An equerry's job is roughly the male equivalent of a lady-in-waiting and invariably goes to someone from the three services and lasts for just three years. Considered a position of privilege, it nearly always ensures rapid promotion after the three-year stint. Lawrence looked the quintessential equerry in his naval commander's uniform, an important element of his role as young man always on show walking one or two paces behind the monarch.

On royal occasions a tall, elegant man in naval uniform, complete with sword and medals, appears considerably more distinguished than a fellow in a lounge suit. Lawrence had come to the queen's attention when he had been on duty on the Royal Yacht *Britannia* some years before. When the call from the palace came in 1986, Lawrence was in command of his own vessel, HMS *Cygnet*, a coastal patrol craft. He had followed in the footsteps of Major Hugh Lindsay, killed in the avalanche that narrowly missed Prince Charles at Klosters in March 1988. So Lawrence became part of the royal household and Anne caught his eye.

Elizabeth knew only too well the attraction of equerries. She had tried to comfort her sister Margaret 30 years before when Margaret had fallen in love with Group-Captain Peter Townsend. She cautioned Anne about becoming too involved with Commander Lawrence, a quiet, respectful, unassuming man. She hoped their relationship would not mean that Anne would decide to end her marriage to Mark, for the sake of the two children and more importantly, for the well being of the monarchy.

In April 1989, however, the nation awoke to news of a fresh scandal. A mystery man had handed *The Sun*'s royal correspondent four letters written to Princess Anne over a period of 18 months. The letters had been taken from the briefcase she kept either with her or in her private suite at Buckingham Palace and as such were stolen property and legally belonged to the writer. Because of those facts, the editor of *The Sun* immediately returned the correspondence to Princess Anne, and agreed not to divulge the contents.

The Sun then checked to see whether the letters were genuine, and having discovered the writer was Commander Timothy Lawrence, they decided to splash the story on the front page. Buckingham Palace immediately issued a statement: 'The stolen letters were addressed to the Princess Royal by Commander Timothy Lawrence, the queen's equerry. We have nothing to say about the contents of personal letters sent to Her Royal Highness by a friend, which were stolen and which are the subject of a police investigation.'

Before issuing the statement Elizabeth phoned her daughter and asked her about the letters. Anne immediately went to see her mother and explained that her relationship with Commander Lawrence was serious and she believed the two of them might have a future together.

Elizabeth's heart sank. She said to Anne, 'You do realise what all this means, to all of us. You do realise what effect this could have on the family.'

But Anne told her mother that her marriage to Mark had been over for some years and that they only stayed together, not just for the sake of the children, but because it seemed the correct way to behave. Furthermore, neither of them had met anyone they seriously wanted to settle down with. Three times during their conversation Elizabeth asked her daughter, 'You are sure about Commander Lawrence?' Three times Anne replied, 'Yes.'

Elizabeth had feared something like this would happen but she had hoped and prayed that nothing would come out into the open.

Minutes after her meeting with Anne, Elizabeth called her Private Secretary, Sir Robert Fellowes, and instructed him to issue a statement to the press. She had hoped Anne would be able to continue her relationship with Commander Lawrence and remain married, but it was obvious that Anne had determined that she wanted an open, honest life, and that meant bringing Commander Lawrence and their relationship into the public domain.

During his two-and-a-half-year tour of duty as her equerry, Elizabeth had found Commander Lawrence a most likeable and amiable young man who had not only carried out his duties impeccably but had also endeared himself with his tact and friendliness to various members of the family. So very different from Mark Phillips.

Once again, Elizabeth realised she had to face facts and agree to her daughter divorcing her husband of 15 years. She did not like the idea at all. On the other hand Elizabeth had been unable to have any sort of relationship with Mark, whom she believed had never wanted to be part of the royal family, and, indeed, he spent little time in the presence of his in-laws. Elizabeth sensed that Mark had distanced himself from her and the rest of her family. He would seldom holiday with Anne and the children at Balmoral, always having reasons to stay away. Elizabeth had noted that he was distancing himself, not only from her and Philip but more especially from Anne. Elizabeth felt his attitude and actions revealed an absence of the properties due to the monarchy, the family and her personally, which she never forgave. Despite those private thoughts, however, the queen always behaved correctly towards Mark.

None of these personal thoughts worried her now. She was far more concerned about the effect a divorce in her immediate family would have on the people's reaction. She knew that if Anne was indeed in love with Tim Lawrence then she would demand a divorce from Mark and, understandably, want to marry again, and soon. And yet, only 40 years before, Elizabeth had tried to comfort her distraught sister Margaret when she was forbidden from marrying an equerry to their father simply because Townsend was a divorcée. Now she had to contemplate what it would mean to the monarchy for her own daughter to divorce and marry again. She knew full well what her grandmother Queen Mary would have said to that. Elizabeth was aware that Anne's remarriage would be historic, the first time since the days of Henry VIII in the sixteenth century that anyone so close to the throne had remarried after being divorced.

Elizabeth told Anne that she must wait a respectable length of time between the embarrassing revelation of the love letters and the date when Anne should finally decide whether her future did lie with the dashing Tim Lawrence. But Anne was impetuous.

In August 1989, only four months after the love-letters scandal had broken, an official announcement came from Buckingham Palace that Princess Anne and Captain Mark Phillips had formally separated. Nothing was said of divorce and Tim Lawrence, having completed his three years as equerry, had apparently returned quietly to naval life, being handed the command of HMS *Boxer*, a coastal craft. But he did not remain in the background for long. In the same month Lawrence was seen at the queen's side while on holiday at Balmoral, when there was no need for Lawrence to have been in attendance at all. The gossip writers scented further revelations.

The last word in discretion, Lawrence also had a knack of quietly disappearing from public view for months at a time while, unknown to Fleet Street, his affair with Anne became more intense. Finally, in the spring of 1992, Elizabeth gave Anne her blessing, and the princess royal appeared publicly for the first time with her Commander. Pictures were taken at the Royal Caledonian Ball showing a very happy Anne dancing the eightsome reel with the new love of her life.

Anne's second wedding, in December 1992 – the year of *Annus Horribilis* – was a stark contrast to her first in 1973. Instead of a magnificent theatrical tableau in Westminster Abbey which was televised around the world as a showpiece of British pomp and royal tradition, Anne and Lawrence were united in the tiny, plain Scottish Presbyterian kirk (church) of Crathie near Balmoral.

Anne had wanted a strictly private wedding ceremony, held at the private chapel in Balmoral Castle, away from the cameras, the photographers and the public gaze. Elizabeth, however, would not allow it because she did not want the nation to believe the royal family were ashamed of what was happening, or be accused of trying to make it appear that the wedding had never taken place. Anne relented but insisted the ceremony remain simple and private. Elizabeth agreed.

There was another reason, however, for choosing a Presbyterian church in Scotland. With no episcopal hierarchy to trim its ministers' sails, the Church of Scotland had for years taken a more liberal approach to second marriages and tended to leave the decision to the discretion of individual clergy. On the other hand, the Church of England still frowned on marrying divorced persons, although many parish priests of the Church of England were happy to do so. For Anne to have married in an English church would have exposed Queen Elizabeth, Head of the Church of England, as condoning divorce, for she either had to be sitting in the front pew at her daughter's second marriage or not attend at all.

Another alternative would have been a civil ceremony, but once again only in Scotland. For the Royal Marriages Act of 1772 debars a child of the sovereign from a civil wedding, as does a law from Victorian times which forbids any member of the royal family from marrying in a registry office in England and Wales.

Elizabeth decided that Anne's marriage should take place in Scotland on the advice of the Archbishop of Canterbury, Dr George Carey, who, in turn, had taken soundings from other senior bishops. Crathie Church was the perfect diplomatic solution. It also let Elizabeth off the hook.

Permitting Princess Anne to remarry was undeniably a major landmark in the royal attitude to divorce and in Elizabeth's views towards the once taboo subject. By the time that decision had been taken in late 1992, Elizabeth already knew that two of her sons, Charles and Andrew, had separated from their respective wives. She was also aware that a chance, a very good chance, existed that they would one day want to remarry.

By allowing Anne to divorce and remarry, Elizabeth and the senior bishops of the Church of England had permitted a vital precedent to be set that would be of dramatic and significant importance if Prince Charles, the heir to the throne, ever contemplated remarrying. The precedent also helped the royal family skate over the once sacrosanct concept of marriage for life.

The marriage of Anne to Commander Lawrence was even more interesting than many supposed. For Tim Lawrence was of Jewish descent. It was a remarkable *coup de théâtre* for two reasons: Tim's paternal great-great-grandfather was called Joseph Levy, the son of Zaccaria Levy, a merchant of Venice who had changed his name to Lawrence in 1826. And Tim's paternal great-grandfather was a Church of England clergyman, the Reverend Percival Lawrence. The Jewish connection is an interesting addition to royal genealogy, but not the first. Lord Snowdon's mother was a Messel, descended from Aaron Messel, a famous banker of Darmstadt.

Princess Anne became Mrs Timothy Lawrence on 12 December 1992, after the simplest royal wedding in history. It lasted only 20 minutes. Elizabeth was happy too. Nearly 20 years before Anne had arrived at Westminster Abbey in a horse-drawn glass state coach, 40,000 spectators cheered her procession through the streets of London, 1,500 guests packed the abbey and millions had watched the ceremony on television.

By contrast, just 30 family members and friends attended Anne's second marriage and not more than three hundred spectators turned out in freezing weather. The bride travelled not in a state coach but in a four-wheel-drive Range Rover. Anne and Tim Lawrence promised to stay 'loving, faithful and loyal . . . until God separate us by death'. After the ceremony the couple left in their Range Rover, with Tim driving Anne and Anne's children Peter and Zara in the back. Behind them in the kirk remained the busts of Queen Victoria, King George V and her grandfather King George VI staring down stonily on the empty church from the plinths near the stained glass window. Nobody was guessing what the stern Empress Victoria would have said – the sight of a divorced Princess Royal remarrying in a Scottish church would have been beyond her comprehension.

The wedding breakfast was also a quiet, rather quick affair, held at Craigowan Lodge on the Balmoral estate. After champagne, a light snack and the cutting of the cake, the guests left within the hour.

Among the guests was every member of the immediate royal family except two, Princess Diana and Sarah, Duchess of York. But they had decided earlier that year to walk out on their royal husbands. That royal wedding day Diana was photographed, a lonely, solitary figure flying to London. She did not even smile for the cameramen.

All Elizabeth's compassion and diplomacy had been called upon in yet another royal scandal. In 1987, Princess Alexandra's daughter Marina, a talented pianist of 21, fell in love with Paul Mowatt, a young photographer of 24. For the first three months Paul had no idea of his girlfriend's royal connections.

Marina had always been the royal rebel, headstrong, self-willed and extremely independent. As a teenager she had a strong social conscience, dedicated to helping youngsters in trouble with drugs and crime. While still in her teens, she worked as a shorthand typist to raise the £2,000 needed for a trip to the West Indies where she helped to build a new school – she worked to save the money because she refused to ask her parents to finance her life.

Calling herself 'Mo', Marina Ogilvy lived the life of a tomboy. She attended Outward Bound schools, dressed in jeans and sweaters and shunned royal protocol, describing it as 'stuffy'.

In December 1988 Paul and Marina began living together in part of Paul's mother's semi-detached house in Kingston-upon-Thames only a few miles from her parents' lovely country home Thatched House Lodge in Richmond Park in south-west London. Alexandra and her husband Sir Angus, wanting to show they were modern parents, turned a blind eye to their daughter's new arrangement. Marina auditioned and won a place at the prestigious London Guildhall of Music to study singing and piano but after only eight months she quit, telling her parents she wanted to spend more time with her live-in lover and that she was dedicating her life to rock music.

The real shock came in October 1989 when Marina told her parents she was pregnant, and determined to have her lover's baby. She had no intention of getting married. Marina, a cousin to the queen and 24th in line to succession to the throne, was to give birth to the first royal baby born out of wedlock for 150 years. (Scores of royal children have, of course, been illegitimate. Very few, however, were officially recognised. Usually the scandal was hushed up and the mother paid a handsome maintenance allowance. The last officially recognised illegitimate British royals were the ten children of King William IV and his mistress Dorothea Jordan, a famous actress. In 1830 King William gave titles to all ten.)

Alexandra broke the news to Elizabeth by calling the queen at Balmoral where she was holidaying. She was not very pleased and told Alexandra and Angus to sort the matter out with as little fuss as possible. But the stubborn Marina wasn't open to calm, rational argument.

In a newspaper article before the baby was born, Marina claimed that her mother had given her two alternatives: either have the baby aborted right away in Harley Street or get married by special licence. To this Marina replied, 'My mother gestured with her fingers in front of my face and told me, "It will only be about that big. You are a healthy young girl and you will conceive easily again."

'I couldn't believe she could talk like that, so coldly about my baby and her grandchild. Paul and I were horrified. And she said the same the next night when Paul was with me. I am still shocked about it. My father was furious and my mother's mouth turned into a kind of snarl. I have been scared on a few occasions that my father might hit me. I have always been a bit frightened of him.

'I asked him what came first, "Your daughter or queen and country?" He replied, "Queen and country."'

Marina claimed that her parents cut off her allowance of £250 a month after she refused either to have an abortion or to agree to a shotgun wedding. She said, 'All my life I have heard my parents talk about the image they must have before the public. My mother has this public image of being serene and composed. But I know she was desperate for this not to come out.'

Shocked and angry, Marina wrote a six-page letter to Elizabeth which began, 'Dear cousin Lilibet.' In it, Marina asked for her help and wise guidance. She explained everything that had happened between Paul, her parents and herself and outlined her love for Paul, their desire to marry one day and her parents' ultimatum. She said in a newspaper article, 'I wrote to her hoping that she could make my parents see sense and help us reach a compromise. I know the queen likes me and I like her. The queen is a warm, caring person and I know she will listen to my plea for help.'

What worried Alexandra, Angus Ogilvy, Elizabeth and Philip was the danger they feared of public exposure and shame if Marina told the world royal secrets of which she was fully aware.

Elizabeth knew she had to use her influence with Marina to bring her back into the family and stop her talking to the press. She told Alexandra and her husband that whatever she arranged, they had to agree to go along with it, whatever their private thoughts. Elizabeth knew that the royal secrets Marina could reveal would cause irreparable damage to her personally and the monarchy. Deep down, however, Elizabeth was furious with the young recalcitrant

Marina for what she believed was nothing short of treachery, accepting £100,000 from the Murdoch *Today* newspaper to reveal details of the row between her and her parents in which she humiliated them, revealing the 'abortion or marriage' threat. Indeed, not only did she humiliate her parents but the entire royal family as a direct consequence.

The queen, quite at a loss as to the best course of action, called Marina to Buckingham Palace for a heart-to-heart chat. Elizabeth knew that the only chance of heading off potential disaster was to talk to Marina, woman-to-woman. And that is what she did. She persuaded Marina that it would be best for herself, her unborn baby and the royal family if she would agree to marry Paul, the man she loved, before the baby was due. Only after much thought and many comforting words from a sympathetic Elizabeth, did Marina agree and take the queen's advice.

In February 1990, Marina walked down the aisle on her father's arm in St Andrew's Church in Ham, Surrey, near her home. She was dressed all in black, and her long velvet dress revealed only a very slight bulge. There were no flowers and no bridesmaids – it was all so very, very different from her mother's glittering wedding at Westminster Abbey in 1963.

Giving his daughter away was about the only thing Sir Angus did for his daughter that day. Both he and Alexandra refused to attend the small reception afterwards. Marina wanted to invite 150 people to the wedding breakfast but her parents refused. And when Marina asked that some relatives should be invited to the celebration, Alexandra refused, telling her not to be so ridiculous, that they would be far too embarrassed to have anything to do with the wedding.

The royal family were among those who shunned the wedding. Only Fergie contacted Marina, in fact, and when they met they spent time chatting to each other about the family problems. Much of their talk was about babies since Fergie was also pregnant at that time with Eugenie.

The crisis for the royal family had passed but the Ogilvy family continued. After Marina's daughter Zenouska was born, Princess Alexandra went only once to see the baby, for twenty minutes, during the first two years. In June 1992, Marina said in a newspaper article: 'I have everything a woman could wish for. I have a husband I adore and who loves me in return, a beautiful daughter who is healthy and happy and my career as a musician. I know the family consider Paul to be the "wrong sort". But what is the right sort? I'm sure my parents would have been happier if I had married into the aristocracy but it just wasn't for me.'

Elizabeth survived the Marina problem, but the personal lives of the younger royals continued to cause untold anxiety and trouble for her and the family.

11. A WORKING WOMAN

At 7.30 every morning of the week a tap on the door of Elizabeth's private bedroom heralds the start of a new day for Her Majesty. It is one of her personal maids, dressed in a maid's black dress with a small white apron, bringing her morning tea. The tea is served in a sterling silver pot, with milk and a bone china cup and saucer. In the saucer is a sterling silver teaspoon.

'Good morning, Ma'am,' are the maid's only words as she enters, and Elizabeth's response is nearly always the same each day, a plain 'Good morning'. Having placed the tray on a side table the maid may comment on the state of the weather as she goes to the huge windows and draws the long drapes, bringing light into the room. No further conversation takes place then, because Elizabeth has already started her day by listening to the radio which she still insists on calling 'the wireless' – sitting up in bed. Each morning she turns to BBC's Radio 4 programme *Today*.

Meanwhile the maid draws a bath in a large Victorian-style white enamelled bath tub, resplendent with large brass taps, then retires leaving Elizabeth to get up at her leisure. While she continues to listen to the radio, Elizabeth usually has two cups of tea and bathes and dresses. The previous evening she would have selected the clothes she is to wear the next morning and these would been laid out in the adjoining dressing room which is lined with cupboards, drawers and a number of walk-in wardrobes.

Elizabeth's bedroom is only 16ft x 12ft and dominated by the blue counterpaned, queen-sized bed and a beautiful Georgian chest of drawers on which stand silver-framed photos of her children and grandchildren. Crisp white cotton sheets are changed daily and traditional pure new wool blankets have never been replaced by a duvet.

Nearly all her married life Elizabeth has slept alone while Philip occupies another set of rooms further down the first-floor corridor, both suites of rooms overlooking Constitution Hill and The Green Park. Philip is wakened at the same time but he is served coffee not tea, and he too listens to the *Today* programme. If neither of them has any engagements which necessitate early departures they usually meet in the breakfast room.

Philip used always to enjoy a typical English breakfast of bacon, eggs, sausages and toast but more recently he has joined Elizabeth in taking fruit juice and toast with marmalade. There is virtually no talk at breakfast, both preferring to read the selection of newspapers laid out immaculately on a separate table. Though they may flip through the sensational newspapers, they read the more serious journals with a keen interest. All the national newspapers are there, including *The Sun*, the *Daily Mirror* and the *Daily Star*.

Having finished her breakfast before nine, Elizabeth returns to her private rooms, brushes her teeth, and then makes her way to her suite of offices on the same floor overlooking the Green Park. Whenever she moves from one floor to another she usually walks down the sweeping staircases, and only occasionally takes the ancient, slow lift, with its mirrored walls and wood panelling.

The pattern of her working week has hardly changed in 40 years. Many people overlook the number of times, in one day, that Elizabeth has to have a complete change of clothes. Depending on the royal functions she has to attend, Elizabeth may have to change three or four times a day. For someone who is not particularly keen on clothes, changing so often becomes a real bore. In contrast, Princess Diana used to treat choosing each outfit as a pleasurable experience.

By nine each day her senior advisers, who have their offices on the ground floor, would have held their first meeting and decided on what items are to be given priority. Then it is time for her personal private secretary, Sir Robert Fellowes, who is married to Princess Diana's sister Jane, to have his first meeting of the day in the queen's office.

Elizabeth's office, which is in effect her private sitting room, has an elegant, though homely atmosphere. There are nearly always fresh flowers, usually pink carnations or, in season, lily of the valley, and bowls of sweet-smelling potpourri. She sits on a stunning Chippendale elbow chair with a tapestry seat and the room has exquisite, delicate furniture, though it is all functional and not just for display; for this is very much a working room. Her desk is a mass of photographs of different sizes in silver frames, nearly all of them members of the family, though there are some of horses and dogs. The walls of her sitting room, as to be expected, are hung with fine paintings, some lovely horse paintings by Hondecoeter and others given to her personally by friends.

As with all her staff, Sir Robert always calls Elizabeth 'Ma'am' but invariably refers to her in conversation as 'Her Majesty'. This formality is never broken, because one of the rules is that the dignity of the monarch must never be put in jeopardy. Elizabeth, however, calls all members of the household by their first names from the first day of their appointment because she wants a happy, relaxed, friendly atmosphere in the palace.

Elizabeth goes out of her way to provide an atmosphere in which her senior staff enjoy working. Words and phrases like 'fascinating', 'inspiring' and 'hard work', as well as 'privileged', are used to describe what it is like being in the queen's senior employ. There is a feeling of camaraderie though Elizabeth will be curt with anyone if and when things go wrong. All seem to agree she is a most compassionate woman. If any member of staff has personal problems, or anyone in their family is ill, then Elizabeth will always give advice, console and help in whatever way possible.

Sir Oliver Millar, who was appointed Surveyor of the Queen's Pictures in 1972, said, 'She is an inspiration. When one talks to her about one of a variety of things, one is always sharply impressed by an astonishing mixture of common sense and an extreme niceness. No time is wasted, but everything is friendly and unpretentious. I always leave wishing I could see more of her.'

Other courtiers speak of her strong dislike of snobbery and the fact that she shows no favouritism to any member of her court. And deliberately so. Others speak of the queen's sense of dignity. Lord Charteris recalled, 'I've known the queen for 40 years and I've never seen her lose her dignity, ever. Whether she's coming into the house wet and covered with mud from deer-stalking, or coming down the steps of the aircraft in her dressing-gown to give me a message, she's always the queen.' Charteris believes Elizabeth would have made a very successful businesswoman.

And she loathes unpunctuality; she considers it a cardinal sin. Mountbatten would recall the day he feared he might be late for an appointment – and it is a perfect indication of how strict she can be: 'I left home knowing I would be late. I told my driver to go like hell and he drove the wrong way round a traffic island and the wrong way down a one-way street in a bid to save vital minutes. We arrived in a cloud of dust and I ran up to her room, arriving about ten minutes late. I was huffing and puffing when I arrived. The queen looked me up and down and said rather curtly, 'Nice of you to decide to turn up; perhaps we can meet another day', and walked out of the room. I felt so small. But never again was I ever late.'

Unless something arises of the utmost importance, Elizabeth's first working conversation of the day will involve the press, radio and television reports of that morning. On her desk she will find reports and newspaper clippings and these will be read, re-read, discussed, debated and, if necessary, acted upon. Elizabeth knows that the press, which she often refers to as 'the dreaded press', is the nation's link with the monarchy.

Not only that. The other reason is the power and influence of the press in Britain. Unlike the United States, Britain has a strong *national* press, with five serious, quality newspapers each day as well as five tabloids of varying seriousness and flippancy. And these are all distributed and sold the length and breadth of Britain, all available by breakfast time.

These ten newspapers are read by more than 20 million people a day, 70 per cent of the adult population. That is a remarkable reader profile for a national press and it is also why Elizabeth rates the media as being so important.

Most mornings the decision is taken, usually by Elizabeth, not to issue any press statement concerning reports in the media. Even when stories are untrue, libellous or worse, the queen issues no denials or even permits any off the record comment. The reason is simple: if the Buckingham Palace press office issued a statement of denial for every piece of incorrect tittle-tattle that was written, it would be forced to issue a neverending string of comments. Moreover, if the palace failed to comment, the press and the public would believe that particular piece of information was wholly accurate.

Only in extraordinary circumstances does the royal family take newspapers or the media to court to sue for libel (and undeniably they could have done so during the recent past) because it would necessitate the cross-examination in open court of that particular wronged royal person, perhaps even the queen herself.

On one occasion the queen took legal action against a newspaper. In February 1983, *The Sun* printed an exclusive story about Prince Andrew and his girlfriend at the time. The source of the allegations was a former employee, a junior storeman who had quit after two years. All royal employees, from the highest to the lowliest, have to sign an undertaking not to disclose any information they may acquire while employed at the palace. The storeman had broken that rule. The queen applied for an injunction in the Royal Courts of Justice to prevent any further articles being published. Of course, because the storeman had broken that agreement, the queen was granted the injunction and no further stories appeared.

The next most urgent matter for Elizabeth is the daily report, prepared specifically for her by the Vice Chamberlain of the household, on the previous day's parliamentary proceedings which she will often discuss with one or two advisers. She will sometimes make a note to remind herself to discuss a particular matter during her weekly Tuesday-evening chat with the Prime Minister.

Early in the day, too, the menu book is presented to her. This is a small, leather-bound red book with a pencil that runs through the front which acts like a latch. The book contains the chef's suggestions for the day, written in French, though nowadays there are no French chefs in the kitchens. Every day she crosses out the dishes she doesn't fancy for lunch and dinner and never leaves it to the chef's discretion. Her food is simple and straightforward. She does not enjoy caviare and foie gras and never drinks champagne for dinner. Elizabeth would think all three an absolute waste of money. Most of the food Elizabeth likes is moderated nouvelle cuisine, nutritious ingredients, perfectly balanced and attractive to the eye as well as the palate.

But she is extraordinarily fussy about her food. Virtually every piece of food is cut to the same size; each slice of carrot will match the next; each sauté potato will be of equal thickness and diameter; each cube of deep-fried potato is identical in size. The food is always decorated with greenery and no piece of fish is served without garnish. And all the food is prepared by hand by the chefs who have all trained at Buckingham Palace, so they know exactly the queen's likes and dislikes.

By mid-morning Elizabeth will have been briefed by her duty lady-in-waiting. For the past few years, Lady Susan Hussey has become one of Elizabeth's principal advisers and now wields amazing power inside the palace. She speaks with the same authority as Sir Robert Fellowes and those who work near the queen realise that a word from Susan Hussey carries the authority of the queen.

Susan Hussey has became the queen's most powerful adviser, in reality the only woman to attain such a prominent and influential position since Bobo McDonald. Until only a few months before Bobo's death in September 1993, Elizabeth occasionally sought advice from her old nanny though she was then in her late eighties. Elizabeth not only promoted her but the two have become almost inseparable, so much reliance does Elizabeth now put on her advice.

At some time during the morning the letters need to be read. More than one hundred thousand arrive each year addressed to 'Her Majesty, The Queen'. A task force of three people read, sift through and reply to them all, as well as decide which should be sent through to the private secretary or Her Majesty to read herself. Private letters to Elizabeth are always carefully initialled by the sender in the bottom left-hand corner of the envelope and these are sent through unopened. However, because of the ever-present threat of terrorism nowadays, a team of three men, equipped with the latest X-ray machinery, checks every item of mail that comes into the palace. Elizabeth invariably begins by reading those from personal friends. After that is done she will sift through her mail, deciding at random which letters to read. As well as the personal letters, she will, given the time, peruse twenty to thirty letters from the general public every morning. That provides her with a valuable cross-section of opinion.

One of Elizabeth's little foibles concerns 'thank you' letters. She is most particular about who writes them. After each and every gathering she attends Elizabeth insists that every letter of thanks that arrives at the palace is read personally. As a former lady-in-waiting commented, 'She simply wants to know, for future occasions, who has written to thank her and those who have not. And, let me say, she knows the names of those people who have not written. My advice to everyone who is ever entertained at Buckingham Palace or anywhere else by the queen, is to write and say thank you. If no letter of thanks is sent, it may be a very long time before that person is again invited.'

Throughout the day there is an inescapable neverending supply of official boxes, the leather-covered briefcases inscribed in gold lettering with the words 'The Queen'. The boxes contain government papers, including papers from No. 10 Downing Street, the Cabinet Office, government departments, ambassadors, government ministries as well as the incessant requests to visit factories, hospitals, shopping malls, business parks, museums and countless charities.

These boxes arrive throughout the day and night at the palace or wherever the queen is in residence. They are called 'red boxes' simply because originally they were all red, but nowadays they may be any colour. Briefing papers on particular matters, such as necessary backgrounds on foreign affairs, will also be sent to her. As monarch, Elizabeth is the only person other than the Prime Minister who receives all the information from every government department. In addition, she receives the same type of information from every

Commonwealth nation, which the British Prime Minister does not. She spends many hours in arduous reading each day, much of it tedious. The same material is also sent to Prince Charles, as heir to the throne.

The tradition of the monarch being given access to all state papers goes back to the Bill of Rights of 1689 which established parliamentary supremacy in England. In effect, that Bill transferred most political power from the sovereign to parliament. Agreement was reached, however, that the sovereign would be informed of everything carried out by his ministers. As we have seen already, Britain has no written constitution; it consists of an accumulation of customs and precedents which have arisen through history. It is accepted the sovereign has three rights under Britain's constitutional monarchy – the right to be consulted, the right to encourage and the right to warn. It has been customary that these rights should also include the right to know.

For the first two hundred years after 1689, very little government business was conducted, parliament hardly ever sat, very little legislation was passed and the time taken for information to arrive by ship from overseas took weeks. There was not much paperwork for the sovereign to read. But the explosion this century in information technology, in the speed of transmission and the amount of government work has meant the papers forwarded to the monarch have risen tenfold. Compared to her father George VI, who reigned from 1936 to 1952, the number of boxes delivered each year has trebled. Many people believe Elizabeth does not in fact bother to read many of the boxes sent her. It would, of course, be impossible for the queen to read *every* paper – her private secretaries sift through the boxes selecting the more important items for her to read – but Elizabeth is diligent in what she regards as an important part of her job, keeping herself informed of what is happening. She reads more than is imagined.

Some Prime Ministers have, on occasion, been caught out for Elizabeth has known more about some matters than they have. By reading those government papers she possesses a unique knowledge of what is happening in all the most important matters of state, including the armed forces and the secret services, MI5 and MI6. A former private secretary said, 'A box of work sent up in the evening, even as late as 10 p.m., is invariably read, signed where necessary and back waiting on one's desk with comments first thing in the morning.'

Many ask why the queen bothers to read all these documents

when she has no political power. It is true that the knowledge she gains from the boxes is of no direct help in her role as queen and she wields virtually no political power within Britain's constitution. The principal reason Elizabeth devoutly reads so many government papers is because it is her duty to do so. She was instructed as a teenager, and later when she became queen, that it was her daily duty to read and understand all she could about her government. And that knowledge is contained in those boxes. Elizabeth believes that held true 40 years ago, and still does today. There is no question of her not attending to her boxes. And she prides herself on the knowledge she has accumulated over the decades. The other reason is that Elizabeth must accumulate as much knowledge of government affairs for the occasion when she might need to 'encourage or warn' her ministers. As Lord Charteris commented: 'In 40 years of doing business with her I have never seen her enthusiasm waver. She wastes no time but gets on with the work in hand. She is a very quick reader and very quick to spot possible mistakes in planning. Her transparent honesty is so encouraging. You need have no hesitation about telling the queen about anything. Never need to wrap anything up, whether it's about her children's behaviour or whatever. All you say is, "Ma'am, this is what people are saying". She listens carefully and is glad to be informed, usually.'

Under the unwritten British constitution, many in Britain – let alone overseas – ask the same vital question, 'What real power, if any, does the queen hold today?'

The quick answer is 'very little', but that is an over-simplification. Elizabeth is Head of State but cannot order or command her prime ministers to do anything. She is Commander-in-Chief of the Armed Forces but she cannot declare war or indeed take part in any battles without the permission of the prime minister. She cannot levy taxes, create her own private courts, maintain her own standing army, or suspend obedience to Acts of Parliament.

Elizabeth can, however, still exert enormous influence behind the scenes, through senior members of her household who have powerful friends in every area of society but particularly in government, industry, Britain's financial centre and the aristocracy who still retain the great majority of the nation's wealth.

Normally, Elizabeth has read through her first box of the day by ten o'clock and her first appointment begins between ten and twelve o'clock. Unless she has to attend a royal engagement, most of her appointments now take place at Buckingham Palace. She also likes to check, on her computer, everything that is being carried out that day by all the other members of 'The Firm' so that she knows who is doing what, where and at what time. Until the first computers were installed in the late 1980s, no one really knew exactly what any other member of the family was up to, which sometimes led to chaos as well as misunderstanding.

Elizabeth will usually eat a light lunch, often alone but occasionally with Philip or one of her senior advisers. The meal will often consist of fish or an omelette, or perhaps a salad with cheese, and she will drink only still Malvern water – certainly no alcohol at lunch. Elizabeth will, of course, sometimes host a luncheon party for perhaps ten people. Then lunch is a more formal affair.

The guests are 'commanded' to arrive at 12.30 p.m. and car stickers are provided for windshields to pass gate security. A footman escorts them to the Bow Room, painted cream and gold, where they meet a lady-in-waiting and an equerry who puts guests at their ease over a pre-lunch drink. After everyone has arrived the queen walks in quietly with usually a number of corgis at her heels. She meets everyone in turn.

Lunch is served promptly at 1.10 p.m. The palace steward slips into the room, catches Elizabeth's eye and announces, 'Luncheon, Your Majesty'. There is a seating plan outside the dining room, the 1844 Room. The queen always sits in the middle of the table, opposite Philip or Prince Charles. The most important guest is on the queen's right and if there is a lady present, she will sit on Philip's right. During the first and second courses the queen will chat to the guest on her right, and during the third and fourth courses, to the person on her left. Towards the end of the meal she will talk to others around the table. No one is ever neglected. At these luncheons lamb cutlets are popular; so are escalopes of veal and salmon on a bed of rice. Nothing messy or difficult to eat is ever served, to save any possible embarrassment to her guests.

Weather permitting, Elizabeth will usually take a walk after lunch in the palace gardens, often with some of her innumerable corgis, all of which she knows by name. After lunch she will sometimes take a short half-hour nap or lie down on a sofa with her feet up, reading or studying her favourite subject of horse breeding.

At some point during most mornings or afternoons the queen will have to meet officially ('receive' is the official royal word that is always used) some dignitary, official, ambassador or some representative, and probably a number of them. She may also have appointments with groups of people, from a drove of diplomats to a gaggle of Girl Guides. These meetings usually take ten to fifteen minutes at the very most and the queen always tries to involve everyone in the conversation, though the topics are invariably extremely dull.

On several occasions throughout the year the queen will hold investitures at Buckingham Palace when those who have been honoured are invited to the palace to receive their awards personally from her. There will usually be around 150 people receiving honours at any one time, yet she will chat to each individually for a moment or so without giving any impression of being hurried.

When meeting groups of people Elizabeth will have been briefed on the group she is to meet and will ask basic questions of them. She will often ask diplomats, 'How long will your stay in Britain last?' and she will usually ask whether they have brought their families with them. And there will often be a remark comparing London's weather to that of the diplomat's own country.

If meeting groups from Britain she will ask about their work, their role in the organisation and their length of service. She will never become involved in contentious issues, deliberately avoiding problem areas, for that might draw the monarchy into a question of politics. And that the queen will always steer clear of.

It is amazing that Elizabeth remains so animated and shows such interest when she must be so thoroughly bored with those she is chatting to. Yet there is never an indication of it. Indeed, she has trained herself to appear to be exactly the opposite.

It is not often that humour interrupts such occasions but when something untoward occurs Elizabeth will often find difficulty in smothering a smile. On one occasion at Balmoral when a privy councillor was walking away from her backwards, he knocked into a table, sending a book flying. Elizabeth went red in the face. Later, the councillor apologised to her. 'I could hardly contain myself,' Elizabeth told him later, 'I wanted to burst out laughing.'

Without exception, it seems, everyone who meets Elizabeth is impressed, and the vast majority leave her presence with the same words, 'She is really lovely, so interested, so knowledgeable. She made me feel great.'

Each day Elizabeth spends at least an hour discussing her future diary with her private secretary, planning dates and times of official visits, functions and meetings, all of which have to be attended to with military efficiency. Elizabeth pays great attention to overseas visits, particularly to Commonwealth countries. She is not head of this great family of nations by right of succession, in the manner by which she came to be queen of England, for she was appointed to the position by common consent which fills her with pride and which she takes most seriously.

From the earliest years of her reign Elizabeth came to see the Commonwealth as her own special responsibility. As former Prime Minister Harold Macmillan observed, 'The Commonwealth offered Elizabeth opportunities for a monarchical role, carved out for herself, that the United Kingdom could not provide.'

And as Elizabeth proudly pointed out when opening the new Commonwealth Institute building in Holland Park, London, in 1962, 'I suppose that, between us, my husband and I have seen more of the Commonwealth than almost any people alive.'

It is said that the queen is 'wedded' to the Commonwealth and that she believes she is the personalised symbol of all that unifies it. It is generally accepted that there could be an elected president of the Commonwealth, but that the queen, being non-political, does the job better.

As former Prime Minister James Callaghan (1976–79) commented, 'She really does know more about Heads of Commonwealth than any prime minister, because she has travelled so much and over such a long period. She really knows them, and about them.'

Another former Prime Minister, Lord Home (1963–64) said, 'The queen does a great deal to make the Commonwealth work.'

During every biennial Commonwealth Conference, which the queen always attends, she has private one-to-one discussions with each and every leader of the countries attending. Leaders remark that those discussions are 'informed and sympathetic'. Familiarity with Commonwealth leaders, who are often longer in power than British ones, encouraged Elizabeth's interest which she believes gives the palace an important Commonwealth perspective that was separate from that of the British governments which advised it.

Elizabeth's diary is not as heavy as it used to be during the early years of her reign. And yet in the 1990s she still averages about four hundred official engagements a year and that does not include overseas tours. Now the younger members of the family share the work load, as well as Philip's prodigious participation in royal duties.

At five o'clock there is tea, a most important part of Elizabeth's daily routine. She usually takes tea in the main drawing room. The tea is in fact a special blend, a mixture of China and Indian teas, designed by R. Twining & Company of the Strand in London. But anyone can buy the blend from Fortnum and Mason in Piccadilly. She takes her tea with cold milk but no sugar and most afternoons she eats thinly-sliced cucumber sandwiches and occasionally her favourite Dundee cake.

For some years now Elizabeth has been 'banting', the word Elizabeth and other members of the family use instead of the more common word 'dieting'. The word actually derives from a man's surname, an English undertaker and dietitian of the nineteenth century named William Banting, whose treatment for obesity was abstinence from sugar, starch and fat. When asked if she would like a slice of cake, Elizabeth will usually answer, 'No, thank you very much, I'm banting.'

And she will often challenge friends with a slight admonishment, coupled with a smile, if she sees them munching sandwiches at tea time: 'Are you supposed to be eating that? I thought you were banting.' Elizabeth watches her weight all the time and becomes quite frustrated with herself if she finds she is putting on too much weight. It is not, however, for reasons of vanity but for her own health, for she is determined to live as long as her mother, who is nearly a hundred and still going strong.

Often hovering around the tea table, hoping for tidbits, are a few of her favourite corgis. This 30-minute interlude for tea and relaxation is followed by the ceremonial feeding of her pets – and, on occasion, Elizabeth has had as many as 13 dogs. These ever-present corgis spend the time yapping and squabbling between each other and fighting for favour from the royal hand, be it a stroke, a pat or something to eat.

Incredibly, Elizabeth knows the names and ages of all of them, despite the fact that they look so alike. They are not all corgis, however, for she also owns what are called 'dawgies', an unplanned cross between corgis and dachshunds. Elizabeth adores them all, even though they can be infuriating little animals, difficult to discipline.

Every afternoon Elizabeth feeds them herself. For Elizabeth, the Queen of England, the crowned head of the greatest surviving monarchy in the world, the afternoon ceremony of feeding her pet dogs is one of her most important events of the day. Elizabeth's dogs form as integral a part of her life, if not more so, than her children.

Liveried footmen are called in when Elizabeth rings the bell and tells the maid it is time for the dogs' evening meal. Firstly they put down a green plastic sheet over the rather threadbare carpet and then return and place the line of dog bowls, each with the dog's name inscribed on it, in a long row. Meanwhile the excited dogs, keen for their food, scamper around her legs, barking and yapping. A great bowl is brought in and handed to Her Majesty who then proceeds to the end of the row and begins to scoop the food into each bowl.

Every dog knows its bowl and the footmen stand by in case a greedy one tries to steal another dog's food rather than waiting its turn. If that should happen, Elizabeth issues a cross word and a footman steps in, picks up the offending animal and, at the risk of getting nipped, holds the dog until its bowl has been filled. Only then is the wayward canine permitted to eat his or her food. In fine weather the ritual takes place on the terrace, but Elizabeth always tries to be on hand to feed her dogs every day.

For the footmen involved, however, the task is sometimes not without risk. As one confessed on camera, 'When they occasionally fall upon one another, whoever is present on duty is expected to haul them apart at whatever risk to hand and foot.'

After the dogs have been fed, it is time, weather permitting, for a walk in the garden. Elizabeth leads them downstairs, all yapping with excitement, and out into the beautiful garden where they run and fight and chase tennis balls and spend their 'pennies and tuppences' as the queen delicately puts it, while she walks around playing and chatting and talking to her beloved animals. Generally speaking, the dogs are fairly well behaved mainly because of the rigorous training they are given as puppies at Sandringham. Occasionally, however, massive fights do break out during which one poor dog may be virtually torn to pieces by the others.

There are always piles of dirty towels kept on radiators, or left on the floor near the garden entrance into Buckingham Palace, the queen's personal front door. The footmen use them to clean the corgis' 52 tiny muddy paws. Throughout the day Elizabeth likes to have three or four of the older, better-behaved corgis in her suite of offices, lying around and waiting for a word or a pat from their mistress. They seem to comfort her and she loves their company, often chatting away to them while tending to the affairs of state. It is indeed most unusual if two or three corgis are not with her. And those privileged ones go everywhere with the queen, walking down corridors, up and down stairs, lying around while she reads a newspaper, watches television or talks with her advisers. Sometimes they lie under the royal table during meals waiting for the queen to secretly feed them the odd morsel.

Through the years, of course, the number of dogs has varied. In 1993 Elizabeth had only seven – Pharos, Phoenix, Myth, Kelpie, Fable, Diamond and Spark. At weekends, it is customary for all the dogs to pile into the Rolls-Royce and sit in the back with Elizabeth for the 30-mile ride to Windsor Castle. Like Elizabeth, they also enjoy the weekend away from 'the office' and know that at Windsor they will have more 'walkies' with their royal mistress and, with luck, occasional long walks in Windsor Great Park.

And yet, alongside what many people would consider rather eccentric behaviour, which the public and her subjects never witness, Elizabeth believes in running a tight ship and she is adamant that everything must be carried out correctly, with the preservation of the monarchy and the House of Windsor of paramount importance.

Sometimes this involves finding ways of getting out of many of the situations in which she finds herself. The satirical television show, *Spitting Image* was frequently most cruel towards Elizabeth because she is, of course, such an easy and obvious target. For years the single word she used repeatedly when talking to people was 'interesting', or perhaps she would vary the reply by prefixing it with the word 'very'. Then she would pass on to the next person and repeat the same words. It did make life easy for her but very boring for everyone she spoke to. As a direct result of *Spitting Image*'s mimicry, Elizabeth stopped using the word altogether. Even today, however, it still occasionally creeps in, particularly at the end of a busy day of meeting hundreds of people.

Elizabeth is the perfect diplomat, too, when it comes to avoiding awkward questions or embarrassments of any kind. During a conversation in which she does not want to answer a question or make a statement, Elizabeth will say quite spontaneously, 'Isn't it a lovely day?' Another favourite, which she employs as a polite dismissal, is 'I think I had better take the dogs out for a walk.' At which point anyone talking to her at that time knows the conversation is at an end. If someone persists, she simply turns and walks away, sometimes leaving people in mid-sentence. Since she is the queen no one dares to challenge her right to leave without answering.

As one of her former advisers said, 'She never likes to say "yes" or "no" to anyone or about anything so that she can never be accused of commenting on anything that might be political or cause offence. She never forgets she is the queen; never. It is ingrained in her.'

And yet Elizabeth loves to hear the palace gossip, about love affairs, marital rifts, scandals, accidents or anything amusing or funny and she hears it all from those staff close to her who are not of senior rank: her dressers, pages, footmen, bodyguards and chauffeurs. She has two special pages, officially called 'Pages of the Back Stairs' who act as the queen's official go-between with everyone else in the palace, running errands, taking messages or delivering and collecting documents. They are usually discreet, responsible men in their thirties and forties and, more often than not, gay.

One footman arrived to see a senior footman, John Davis, standing outside the queen's sitting room talking volubly to Elizabeth about the plight of a housemaid whose love affair had gone horribly wrong. He said, 'They looked like a couple of neighbours chatting over the garden fence. I waited and listened to Her Majesty wanting to know all the intimate details. She was fascinated and told him to keep her informed.'

There is one important phone call she makes without fail each day – to her mother who lives at nearby Clarence House. They chat for fifteen minutes or so. Indeed, Elizabeth is quite addicted to the phone. She has one in every room she uses and four on her office desk: one direct line to No. 10 Downing Street, in case of an emergency; an internal phone linking her with everyone in the palace; a scrambled line for personal calls; and another private outside line.

Elizabeth's day never officially ends but she tries to leave her office at around six once the dogs have had their run and she has received her final briefing of the day, and read some of the more important letters that have been written in her name or on her behalf. A few, usually the personal ones, she writes herself.

She will try to watch the *Six O'clock News* on television or listen to the news on radio so that she can keep abreast of the day's major events. She does take a keen interest not only in what has happened in Britain but around the globe. That is why she also enjoys listening to the BBC World Service programmes because they give a more global view of the day's events.

Often, and more so during the past few years, she and Philip dine together in the small drawing room and they always dress for it: she will often wear a smart short dress and Philip a smoking jacket and, usually, a bow tie. Occasionally a friend and his wife are invited to dinner. The evening is informal and the food is usually plain. The first course will perhaps be smoked salmon or a little terrine; the main course, lamb; and for the finish, there is always a proper pudding, something like apple pie. Of course there are footmen and a butler but most evenings Elizabeth does not drink at all. If she does drink at dinner, it is usually a little dry white wine. After dinner, they usually sit and watch the television, not unlike any other couple of pensionable age in Britain.

The queen and the duke are television fans, and some would suggest they have become addicts during the past few years. Elizabeth sees it as her one true means of relaxation after a day's work and she has a wide interest in subjects that fascinate and entertain her.

Understandably, Philip's television interests are different in that they are less serious, political and practical. He will often go to his study and watch what he prefers on another set. Sometimes they will spend the evening watching the latest film release, for Elizabeth in particular is quite a movie buff.

When their television viewing for the evening is over they will not see each other again until the following morning. Elizabeth may go to bed early, either to read a book or peruse the contents of the last official box of the day. She is not a great reader, but the executives of Hatchards, the booksellers in Piccadilly, continue to make up a selection for her and send them to the palace. Those she wants, she keeps; the others are returned. Elizabeth's reading interests are both varied and conservative. Preferring biographies, thrillers and current award-winning novels, she has no particular favourite author except for Dick Francis, whose speciality is thrillers revolving around horse racing.

For much of the year Elizabeth works tirelessly in what she sees as her duty to the nation. Indeed, there are those in the palace who believe she now works harder than ever. She had hoped that by 1990 she would have been able to take things more easily, to give most of her royal duties to Prince Charles, Anne, Andrew and Edward. And yet the traumas of the failed marriages have meant that Elizabeth has had to continue her duties far longer than she could have believed necessary. As a result, she continues to attend every royal engagement arranged for her.

A great amount of work goes into a royal visit, whether it be a grand royal tour to Australia or Canada or the opening of a new building 200 miles from London. The schedule must run like clockwork, not just for Elizabeth's own penchant for punctuality but for the local dignitaries and the hundreds who might turn out to see and cheer her; neither should the schedule disturb nor disrupt the daily lives of others for the sake of security. The palace can never forget the assassination of Mountbatten.

Elizabeth herself always checks the plans and the invitation list before final details of the visit are authorised and put into operation. She reads through the usually thick file of names and brief descriptions of the people to whom she will be introduced. And a note will be made of whether she has met them before. Buckingham Palace always asks those providing lunch or dinner for the queen to submit three menus so that the final choice is left to Elizabeth, which she will make three or four months in advance. And however she feels she will never change her mind or ask for anything else on the day of the visit.

Her selection of the clothes she wants to wear for the occasion will be made a week or so in advance in regular meetings with her dresser, so she ignores conditions imposed by the weather. In any case, the palace wet-weather programme – a number of umbrellas – is always at hand. Fortunately, Elizabeth rather likes rain, and certainly prefers it to hot weather.

Elizabeth used to enjoy frequent journeys on the royal train – at the taxpayers' cost of £1 million. She would travel by night, sleeping on the train in a siding somewhere *en route* to her destination. The dark train, crimson lined, has a carriage with sitting room, bedroom and bathroom for herself and a smaller compartment and bathroom for her dresser. She also takes her chef with her and eats extremely well; since the train is secure and easy to guard, she can work comfortably, reading her boxes or planning future engagements. Those courtiers accompanying her have their own coach with sleeping and working quarters. And there are two coaches for police and servants, footmen and pages.

The queen still resents the fact that the Queen's Flight has been abolished so that now she doesn't know the pilots or the crew who will be travelling with her as she did before. Travelling, which Elizabeth used to enjoy, being surrounded as she was by the coterie of faces she knew so well, has all become so impersonal that today she prefers to stay at home. If the engagement is near enough she will travel by Rolls-Royce. The Rolls is accompanied by a single patrol car and motor-cycle outriders but their sirens remain silent for Elizabeth cannot bear them.

Today, Elizabeth still draws crowds wherever she goes in Britain, though not as large as they used to be at the beginning of her reign. The average British man and woman still believes it a privilege, if not an honour, to meet, chat and shake the hand of the sovereign. Afterwards, they talk of their meeting with the queen for days and weeks, invariably describing her as 'wonderful', 'lovely' and 'understanding'.

Because her daily life has hardly altered in 40 years, Elizabeth cherishes her weekends away from Buck House. She has always tried to escape the confines of her office, either spending 48 hours at Windsor, the place she calls 'home', or with friends somewhere in the country, but never in London.

In the '60s and '70s she loved to spend weekends at Broadlands when Dickie Mountbatten was alive and spent more weekends there than at any other country home. She would usually arrive on a Friday morning and go riding with Mountbatten through his 5,000-acre estate. They would return for a light lunch and afterwards take Mountbatten's labradors for a long walk. Or they would fish in the River Test during the afternoon, depending on the weather.

Tea was rather a formal occasion and would be held in the Wedgewood Room. After tea she would rest or perhaps read for an hour and Philip would usually arrive in time to change and dress for dinner. Even at Broadlands, Elizabeth and Philip never shared a bedroom.

At eight o'clock everyone would gather in the drawing room dressed for dinner, the men in black tie and dinner jacket, the ladies in long dresses. All would be waiting for the queen. No one is ever permitted to arrive late.

While the queen may take a whisky before dinner and a glass or two of vintage wine during the meal, she has never appeared tipsy in anyone's presence and no one has ever seen her the worse for drink.

In private, Elizabeth really does have a good sense of humour. John Barrett tells the story of one dinner party at Broadlands when the butler, Frank Randell, well into his seventies, had taken a drop to drink. He recalled, 'It was an informal dinner but everyone was dressed as usual, the men in dinner jackets and black tie and the women in long dresses. Poor old Frank Randall, slightly the worse for wear that night, had been given the task of serving the soup and he spilled an entire bowful right into the lap of the queen. There was a gasp around the table and then Elizabeth looked up at Frank who was now in a terrible bother, and she roared with laughter. You have to have a good sense of humour when your lap is full of hot soup.'

Among the after-dinner games they play, charades remains one of her favourites. But there are others, including a tricky game played with string, to which a cork is attached. The object of the game is to put out a lighted candle placed on the floor. The string is tied around the player's waist and the cork dangles around the person's ankles. Each person has to bend over and try and put out the candle in the shortest possible time. Old Sebastian Ferranti, a friend of the royal family, used to chirp up whenever the ladies took their turn, 'Take care you don't get singed!' and everyone, including Elizabeth, would roar with laughter.

When everyone has had enough of party games, the group splits up, some going to play billiards or snooker, others to work together on a difficult jigsaw puzzle which Elizabeth enjoys tackling. Some watch television or a movie. Elizabeth usually goes to bed at eleven even if the party is in full swing.

At seven o'clock sharp the following morning a maid would bring

Elizabeth her tea tray and breakfast would be at eight, served at Broadlands in the shooting room. This was thought to be a very adventurous undertaking: trestle tables would be set up with folding wooden chairs for the guests and everyone including the queen would eat off plastic plates and drink tea or coffee from plastic cups, like school children enjoying a picnic in the garage at home. The food included freshly cooked bacon and eggs, or her favourite kedgeree, rice, fish and hard-boiled eggs mixed together. For decades, Elizabeth would always start Saturday at Broadlands with a picnic in the shooting room.

Afterwards she would take a walk with one of Mountbatten's labradors and the whole party would take off for the day's shoot. Elizabeth would always join in, not shooting herself but working the dogs, springing the birds and collecting them after they fall to the ground. Elizabeth had been trained to work gun dogs by the staff at Sandringham and takes great pride in handling them efficiently.

Rain or shine, the shooting party would venture out by 2.30 for the third stand of the day. All would return for tea at 4.30, once again taken in the Shooting Room, everyone standing around in their Barbours and muddy boots. Then Elizabeth would go to her suite for a bath and a rest, and would take the chance to look though some boxes that had arrived during the day, to check if anything of dramatic importance had occurred. After a four-course dinner, always taken with a good vintage wine, there would usually be a film, something light, like a comedy. Elizabeth would be offered a choice of films and she would decide on which one. Having made the decision she would ask everyone in the room, 'I would rather like to see this one unless anyone has any other ideas.' No one ever had any other ideas.

Sunday would start with the same routine followed by church, the family visiting Romsey Abbey for the morning service. Sometimes the house party would break before lunch, but Elizabeth always wanted to be back in London at Buckingham Palace by the early evening, fully prepared for work the next day.

Most weekends nowadays Elizabeth takes off for the 30-mile drive to Windsor Castle, the place she calls 'home', where she spends more than thirty weekends each year. She spent much of her formative years there as a child during the war and that is where she feels at peace. She arrives by car from London in time for afternoon tea on Friday, followed by a long walk with the dogs. Despite the fact that nearly one million people a year visit Windsor Castle, Elizabeth feels a far greater sense of privacy there than at the palace where tourists are only permitted during two months in the summer when the queen is away at Balmoral. At Windsor, the areas to which the public are admitted are isolated from the private areas where the family lives.

After a light, informal dinner Elizabeth and Philip will probably watch television or a film and early on Saturday, before breakfast, Elizabeth usually rides in Windsor Great Park. Sometimes, after a hearty breakfast, she will ride again or visit estate workers and their wives in their homes, chatting to them about personal problems or about their work. And she will always take the dogs for a good long walk, while reserving at least an hour for her boxes.

On a lovely summer's day both Elizabeth and Philip will spend the afternoon lying on loungers, enjoying the sun. If it is too hot, however, they will go back inside to read or browse through the newspapers.

Often, around teatime, other members of the family will drop by. Charles used to be a frequent visitor, although his many commitments make that more difficult nowadays. Anne, too, used to visit. During the past few years Andrew and Edward have spent many Saturday evenings with their parents, Andrew practising his golf on the nine-hole private course in the grounds.

Occasionally on Saturday evenings Elizabeth will organise a dinner party to which she invites betweeen ten and twenty people, friends, members of the household and their wives, sometimes MPs, cabinet ministers or members of the church. She prefers familiar faces for her Saturday dinners, people with whom she can relax and have fun. Usually, gentle or swing music from her favourite musicals is played.

But Elizabeth differs from most hostesses in one important respect: she never greets her guests. They stand around and wait for her to appear, usually at half past seven, perhaps an hour after they have arrived. Within the space of a few seconds, Elizabeth can look around a room and register those people she knows and those she doesn't. Indeed, she can do so when meeting more than a hundred people and she will, more often that not, remember where and when she met them. She likes to have people around her so that she can listen to the news from the gossip grapevine.

On Sunday morning, the queen never fails to attend the morning service at St George's Chapel, inside the castle walls. And whoever has stayed for the night is also expected to appear, and always does. After church there is a traditional Sunday lunch, sometimes attended by one or two children – and perhaps grandchildren – an afternoon walk in the park with the dogs, and most importantly, the reading of four heavy, quality broadsheet newspapers. At six o'clock most Sundays Elizabeth says farewell to Windsor and returns to the palace with her dogs for another week at the office.

As well as Buck House and Windsor Castle there are, of course, two other homes where Elizabeth likes to relax. And she has known both since childhood. Sandringham House in Norfolk and Balmoral in Scotland were both inherited from George V by his heir David. When he was forced to abdicate, Elizabeth's father bought them from him for £1 million. They were to become the beloved playgrounds for Elizabeth and Margaret and have always been considered special by them.

Elizabeth spent her first Christmas at Sandringham where she has continued the tradition. It was at Sandringham that Lilibet enjoyed many happy hours with her father. King George would take his beloved Lilibet wildfowling on the marshes and they would enjoy long walks together in the cold, crisp December air. She remembers with nostalgia her childhood Christmases at Sandringham where the family would all meet and lay out their presents on the dining room table on Christmas Eve, forbidden to open them until after Christmas dinner the next day. The tradition has not changed. And Elizabeth has also continued another royal tradition of making everyone give unusual, even odd presents at under £20 – but ensuring that gifts are thoughtfully chosen.

As though in a time warp, nothing has changed at Sandringham since Elizabeth's childhood and she intends to keep it that way. Nearly everything is the same as when it was first built at the beginning of the century: the country-style, old-fashioned furnishings and the net curtains on the windows, even though Sandringham House is isolated in the middle of the countryside, overlooked by no one. Even today, the central heating barely works and the big bathrooms are still cold. Indeed, the same jigsaw puzzle that Lilibet first played with 60 years ago can be found in the saloon. Every Christmas the family still spends time piecing it together.

Elizabeth's father died in his sleep in the early hours of February 1952 at Sandringham. Her grandfather George V also died at Sandringham in January 1936. It is as if Elizabeth wants to keep alive her childhood days at her Norfolk home where she still spends her six-week Christmas break.

A special pleasure awaits her black labradors and cocker spaniels whenever Elizabeth sets foot there – there is no doubt she has a special relationship with her dogs which seems almost uncanny. The gun dogs seem to know whenever she arrives at Sandringham where they spend most of their days in the care of their trainer Bill Meldrum. Gun dog trainer Martin Deeley, who has watched Elizabeth working her dogs, recalled, 'Observe her facial expressions and listen to her voice and you realise that here is a lady who is at home with animals. She knows how far to let them go, she can see when they are trying to please her or themselves and is at one with them at work or play.'

Sometimes Elizabeth is asked to judge novice and open Retriever Trials at both Sandringham and Balmoral but she finds the job nerve-racking and only occasionally will she agree to participate. It seems amazing that this intelligent woman who has a considerable knowledge of animals should be so nervous at judging them, while all the highly knowledgable gun dog breeders watch and wait for her decision.

Balmoral is the turreted, fairytale castle in the Scottish Highlands, close to Braemar with its 11,750 acres of grouse moor and five beautiful glens spread across 50,000 acres. It is there that Elizabeth takes her long annual break which stretches ten weeks from August to October. It is a magnificent estate which the queen adores to ride across most days during her long stay, enjoying the spectacular views as well as the peace and quiet of the countryside. She looks forward to that holiday to escape into another world.

And, unlike Sandringham, Elizabeth has made a great many changes at Balmoral. She has rid the place of Queen Victoria's mania for tartans and has put in their place homely, country-style decor and furnishings. There is always a special tang of wood fires, stags' heads and heather at Balmoral which visitors find relaxing. There is a wonderful ballroom, but no magnificent state rooms as you would find at Buckingham Palace. Balmoral is where Elizabeth goes to enjoy life.

She will invite friends to stay for a night, a weekend and sometimes for an entire week. But that seven-day stay is usually reserved for members of the family or very special guests such as senior ladies-in-waiting or old family friends. She always invites the Prime Minister of the day – and their spouses – to visit Balmoral for one weekend. On occasions, Prime Ministers from Commonwealth countries have been invited to enjoy the quiet.

Elizabeth's bedroom provides a haven of peace. It is filled with photographs of her parents, children, grandchildren and other relatives at various stages of their lives. In earlier years, during the long summer break, the castle would ring with the laughter and chatter of children and grandchildren whom she encouraged to use the castle as their family holiday home.

But no matter where she is, those official boxes keep arriving. Yet the few people who know the queen well report that she does enjoy her life and, despite the many family crises, has learned to relax at weekends, away from the pressures of work.

12. A COUNTRY GIRL AT HEART

Shy and retiring, Elizabeth would have far preferred a quiet life away from the centre of attention and the spotlight that has followed her since her childhood. But when her uncle King Edward VIII abdicated in 1936, her father was suddenly thrust from obscurity to become King George VI. The dramatic change proved a shock to him but he responded with remarkable courage.

For Elizabeth, then only ten years old, her father's ascendancy to the throne was less traumatic. She realised, however, that since her father was now to be king, that meant she would one day be queen. Before that moment arrived, she had believed she would marry a wealthy aristocrat, live in some fine stately home, raise a family and lead the quiet life of a privileged lady in the heart of the country.

Her passion for country life has never left her and it is this side of Elizabeth's life that the public occasionally glimpses and which this author has witnessed when the queen has taken walks in Windsor Great Park, attended horse trials or watched informal polo matches. Dressed in a large, dark green, weather-proof waxed coat which reaches below her knees, a bright silk scarf on her head and green Wellington boots, Elizabeth finds relaxation as she walks through a wet field with a couple of black Labrador dogs at her heels.

At Balmoral, Elizabeth can lead the country life she craves. The castle has always represented freedom for Elizabeth, a precious commodity for someone whose life has been so rigidly ordered and disciplined. It was there that Elizabeth and Margaret as young princesses rode their ponies over the moors alone, with no groom accompanying them. It was at Balmoral that their mother, sometimes accompanied by their father, would take them on picnics, both before and after the war. Elizabeth would happily wash the plastic dishes in a sparkling burn or stream before packing up the picnic hamper and heading back to the house. Since those idyllic childhood days Elizabeth has always loved to ride horses, and especially at Balmoral, with its rolling acres offering freedom, peace and solitude.

It was at Balmoral that Elizabeth began her life-long interest in stalking and where she shot her first stag at the age of 16. Since then she has brought down many a deer but she prefers stalking them. Every year Elizabeth stalks in the glens during her holidays at Balmoral – even today, though she is well into her seventies.

The royal party will take along a ghillie with a telescope, binoculars and rifles and a pony boy with a Haflinger pony, to carry the carcass down the mountain. As they walk up the slopes of the glen, Elizabeth is often the first to spot the herd of deer at the foot of a ravine. Together with the entire hunting party she will immediately drop down and make her way to the nearest boulder to hide and check the herd through her binoculars. If necessary, Elizabeth has been known to crawl on all fours through the rain-soaked heather.

To ensure a clean kill, they often leave their initial hideaway and make their way to a new position, sometimes walking for more than two hours. As the party moves through the heather and rocks, and across streams, they are barely visible as their tweeds blend in with the background. When in place, the ghillie will confirm which stag should be killed, usually an older one. He loads the rifle and passes it to Elizabeth who takes up her position to shoot. The rifle shot reverberates like a thunder clap around the glen and the stag lies where it fell.

Elizabeth's reputation as a crack shot is legendary and she takes a special pride in it, one reason being that she was taught by her beloved father. If ever a stag is not shot cleanly the party will not give up until the stag has been followed and killed. As one ghillie said, 'Her Majesty is a dead shot. I cannot recall seeing her miss though there will have been times when she did.'

Neither Elizabeth nor Philip is bloodthirsty about their shooting, nor are they sentimental. They know that deer have to be culled because if they are not properly farmed then the weak will suffer from malnutrition. Charles, Andrew and Princess Anne all enjoy stalking but neither Diana nor Fergie went hunting deer more than a few times, nor did they want to actually attempt to shoot one themselves. In the end, fed up after a day of hard walking across glens and through burns, often in filthy weather, they preferred to stay indoors. On a fine day, however, Diana and Fergie would happily arrive in time for the family picnic, even if the skies were overcast, because they knew they were expected.

Today Charles, accompanied by Wills and Harry, still visits Balmoral in the summer holidays and all three will sometimes go out together. More often than not, however, the queen and Philip like to join them. Charles has taught his sons the rudiments of stalking and shooting and he has ensured they have also learnt the discipline of the guns. From a young age, Wills and Harry happily joined in helping to pick up the fallen birds. They used to take along their toy guns and pretend to take part in the shoots. Since those early days both boys have now learned to shoot and have developed quite an expertise. And like their father, both Wills and Harry love to ride. There is every reason to believe both boys will become expert riders and already Wills has been taking polo lessons. Never having forgotten those idyllic childhood memories, Charles has certainly encouraged them to hunt foxes and deer on horseback. He recalls, 'The sound of a horn or hearing the hounds sent tingles down my spine as a child. I just knew I would have to do it one day.'

Today, Charles believes he has passed that same enthusiasm on to his sons despite the fact both boys understood that their mother did not approve of hunting and had no interest whatsoever in any field sports. Many of their earliest arguments concerned field sports, – hunting, shooting and fishing – but it was a battle Diana was destined to lose. In the early years of their married life, Diana tried desperately to persuade Charles to give it up. To keep the peace in the home he did for a while. But as their relationship became more difficult and they spent more time apart, Charles returned to the hunting field. Diana made it clear that she not only disapproved of hunting but found the great majority of people who went hunting undesirable company. She once said of them, 'They are so frightfully snooty. If someone doesn't like hunting they think they should belong on another planet, they're so stuck up.'

Diana once found herself in a serious argument with her mother-in-law during dinner at Balmoral. It was over hunting. Diana said she believed it was morally wrong and that she didn't want her sons indulging in such sports that, she believed, would soon be banned in Britain. Elizabeth took up the pro-hunting argument, explaining why it was necessary to hunt and shoot, to keep the foxes down and cull the deer. Much to the queen's annoyance Diana kept interrupting her, but the queen persisted in her argument, determined to make Diana listen to the points she was making. The queen is not used to anyone, save occasionally her husband, having the temerity to argue a point with her and she was not about to let her daughter-in-law shout her down. Finally, Diana flew into a rage. 'You don't realise how many people in this country hate hunting and shooting because it's so cruel!' Her voice reached a crescendo as she screamed, 'Would *you* like to be hunted and shot at?'

Elizabeth looked at Diana but said not another word. She then turned to someone else and began another conversation, leaving her daughter-in-law angry and embarrassed that she had lost her temper.

Charles understands that many people believe hunting to be cruel and that those who oppose hunting want him to set an example. 'I do not enjoy the killing but I know it has to be done,' he has said. 'I wish the anti-blood sports people could realise how much more painful and more horrible all other known methods of fox control would be.'

Charles's numerous injuries and falls on the polo field finally took their toll and in 1993 at the age of 44, he gave up high-goal polo, the sport's top grade, and now only plays an occasional charity polo match. But, like Camilla Parker Bowles, he still thoroughly enjoys a day's hunting which he believes helps to keep him fit. Sometimes Charles will hunt three times a week from November through March, riding with the Beaufort or the Berkeley near Highgrove; in Leicestershire with the Belvoir; and on Mondays and Fridays with the Quorn.

When Philip and Charles took part in the same shoot – which nowadays is very rare – there was a definite but unspoken competition between the two men to see who could bag the most birds. Nicholas Soames, a close friend of Prince Charles, said, 'Most people realise they are very competitive. Prince Philip always had a reputation for going for a big bag and Charles does the same. Neither want to go home with the smaller bag. No one said anything, of course, but the competition was sometimes intense. The Duke seemed to have to prove himself.'

That's at holiday time, however. For most of the year, Elizabeth relaxes quietly at home most evenings. At the end of the day, unless she must attend an official function or dine with friends, she likes to lie on a sofa in front of the fire reading a book or watching television, often in stockinged feet, just the way most of her subjects do.

In many ways Elizabeth has few complexities in her character. In many respects she appears a quite ordinary person, especially in her everyday habits, her likes and dislikes, her demands and preferences. She may be the wealthiest woman in the entire world, yet she hates wasting a single penny. She will go to great lengths to save even a few pounds. She orders curtains to be darned rather than buy new ones; she refuses to have new sofas and chairs when the upholstery is worn out and orders loose covers instead. But even then, if she believes the loose covers are too expensive she will have the old ones darned. When bed sheets wear thin and housekeepers ask permission for new ones to be purchased, Elizabeth usually refuses, telling them to re-sew them by exchanging the middle parts for sheeting at the edges. Carpets are hardly ever replaced, but simply sent away to be expertly patched and then put back again. Fitted carpets are re-sewn so that the old, worn areas are moved to the outside, providing a few more years' wear. And she usually orders carpets underlaid with canvas instead of the more expensive backing which the rest of the western world uses.

For decades every single light switch throughout Windsor Castle was marked with a small notice, 'Please turn off the light when you leave the room.'

Her frugal ways even extend to food. Leftover food from one meal will, if possible, be used the next day. She will always expect meat left over from a roast joint to be minced for later, and leftover smoked fish will be used in a kedgeree the following morning. Jam and marmalade left from one meal will be put back into the jar for consumption another day.

Lord Charteris, Elizabeth's first private secretary from 1949 to 1978, believes it was a privilege to work for the queen for so many years. He knows her character and personality, her foibles and failures: 'The queen is courageous, honest, humble, truthful, but mean. She is not a good giver and she doesn't particularly like saying thank you. Her mother is cornucopia. The queen, no. I don't know why. It may be shyness, but she doesn't get any pleasure out of saying thank you. I'm telling you this because the queen, like everyone, has faults. She has fewer than most in my estimation, but that is one of them.'

She did, however, say to Lord Charteris when he finally left her service, 'Thank you for a lifetime.'

'That was enough for me,' he said later. She also gave him an exquisite silver salver and two signed silver picture frames.

Elizabeth is even stingy with her own family. Prince Charles tells of one occasion after he had left Buckingham Palace to move into an apartment in nearby Kensington Palace where many other royals also live. Since he had no furniture he asked the store keeper at Buckingham Palace if there was any spare that he could have.

He was told the palace basement contained store rooms filled with furniture, most of it antique, which would be ideal for his new apartment. Charles knew he would have to obtain permission from his mother. 'No,' she told him bluntly. 'You can't have it, any of it.'

Telling the story, Charles said, 'I was flabbergasted that she refused.

That stuff had lain in the basement for decades, just gathering dust, but my own mother refused to let me have one piece. I argued but it was no good. "Buy your own," she told me, "that's mine."'

At least she extends her tight-fisted ways to herself as well as her children. All the queen's children wore hand-me-down clothes and, when they outgrew them, she would then hand over the clothes to Margaret for her children or any other member of the family who wanted them. She believed it wasteful to throw them out, or even give them to some deserving children's charity.

Elizabeth may have little freedom compared to the average man and woman, but she also faces no financial or other inhibitions in choosing and buying clothes. Many women would adore to be in Elizabeth's position, to be able to spend a fortune on clothes. But not so for the Queen of England.

Once, she set fashion trends. As a small child she wanted her nursery painted primrose and the British middle classes flocked to follow her lead. On her sixteenth birthday she appeared for the first time as Colonel of the Grenadier Guards and set an instant fashion: her green felt hat, beret-shaped, with the top jutting forward over a small peak was copied immediately and sold in shops across the land.

In 1948 Princess Elizabeth visited France, then the fashion centre of the world, and according to her nanny, Marian Crawford, her 'wardrobe sent a ripple of excitement through the fashion capital'. She even won praise from the famous Christian Dior himself who said, 'She is magnificent; I never knew from pictures that she could be so lovely or wear her clothes with such distinction.'

Three years later Elizabeth and Philip toured Canada and together they went square dancing, Elizabeth dressed in a brown-and-white checked shirt and steel blue dirndl skirt, Philip in jeans, loafers and a hastily purchased checked shirt. It still had the price tag.

Such informality surprised their Canadian hosts but the students at McGill University in Montreal cheered the princess on: 'Yea, Betty, yea Windsor, yea, yea Betty Windsor . . . rah . . . rah . . . rah.' Elizabeth flushed with embarrassment. She had never received such rapt enthusiasm for the way she dressed and behaved, nor had she ever been called 'Betty', a name she cannot stand.

Later Elizabeth and Philip flew to Washington. The *Star* proclaimed, 'The Princess ought to be told the simple truth . . . that she has charmed and captivated this city to such an extent that our oldest inhabitants, searching around their memories, are hard put to remember the name of any past visitor comparable to her.' Those were the days before Elizabeth took on the duties of monarchy.

In post-war America discretion reigned too. Elizabeth had to be careful. Coming from Britain, a country recovering from a devastating war, she did not wish to stun New York society with her outfits. Neither did she want to disappoint. Her day wear was based on a modified New York look, coats that flared, and skirts at mid-calf length. Evenings consisted of glittering occasions which she attended with embroidered dresses, tiaras and stunning royal jewellery. Dignity and comfort during the day and glamour at night, the formula Elizabeth has clung to throughout her public life.

As a child and as a teenager, Elizabeth had never been involved in choosing any of her clothes. She had always had all her clothes selected and bought for her. Each morning her nanny had laid them out. She accepted the fact that the clothes she was to wear would always be there. It never crossed her mind to become involved in any decision-making concerning the clothes in which she would appear. Crawfie, her first governess, wrote, 'The princess was always conservative about her dress and content to wear whatever was laid before her. Choosing a wardrobe was taken out of her hands by her dressmaker, shoemaker and milliner. The exact colour of the main garment was given to the tradesmen and then the accessories arrived, perfect, beautiful and costly, without the personal effort which makes shopping so large a part of the whole intriguing adventure of a young woman's life.'

Occasionally Elizabeth did protest but Crawfie was always on hand to advise. 'The princess had to remember', she wrote, 'that however she might long to wear a certain colour, she could not do so if it was a shade that would tone in and get lost among a large crowd and make it hard for her to be easily seen by the loyal crowd who congregated wherever she made a public appearance.'

Crawfie also added, 'There were also times when, in the interest of trade, she was asked to wear a certain dress material or shoe style to give a boost to the fashion so the whole world would buy it.'

Elizabeth's teenage years covered the war and its immediate aftermath, when the Government restricted clothing in Britain by issuing coupons to each and every member of the public, including Princess Elizabeth and the rest of the royal family, severely controlling all purchases. King George and his wife Elizabeth, determined to set an example, were never seen lavishly clothed nor did they permit Elizabeth or Margaret any excesses. Such experiences occurred from the time Elizabeth turned fifteen to her twenty-fifth year, when most young women love to experiment. These restrictions account to some degree for the queen's pragmatic approach to her wardrobe and her lack of any real interest in fashion.

During those years, some of Elizabeth and Margaret's dresses consisted of material from their mother's old, discarded clothes – including evening dresses and ball gowns – because the severe style of the late 1940s needed so much less material.

In 1952, British designer Norman Hartnell made Elizabeth's first-ever party dress. She had turned 26. Afterwards he said, 'She accepted the fitting as part of her official duties but one did not feel that she was interested in clothes as such or in creating or even following the latest fashions. Princess Elizabeth was happiest, one felt, in country tweeds or very simple things and always would be; even when choosing her trousseau she made few suggestions.'

Even after she had ascended the throne in 1952 and the government restrictions on clothing had been lifted, Elizabeth never indulged herself. Most of the time she relied on Bobo, then in her fifties and with no flair for fashion, to be her honest critic and together they would decide on her wardrobe. Indeed, Elizabeth insisted Bobo be on hand whenever she had to have new clothes made rather than the fashion designers who had been invited to the palace to advise.

For a while the young Elizabeth followed the example of her own mother and dressed in fussy hats, decorative trimmings, floating panels and soft pastel shades but they did not suit her or her character. For most of her life the Queen Mother has been dressed by the House of Hartnell, first by the late Sir Norman, and now by his successors. Most of her outfits consist of soft fabrics such as chiffon, georgette, organdie, silk and lace. They follow a generous but basic pattern and allow plenty of material for freedom of movement, as well as comfort. Pastel shades have always dominated: blues, pinks, yellows, greens, lilacs and mauves are constantly repeated. Her famous veiled hats never seem to change from decade to decade nor do her shoes with their slight platforms and four-inch heels – even in her nineties.

Elizabeth was gently advised that her mother's dress sense would simply not suit and so she reverted to her more traditional clothes. She met understandable criticism for looking more like 45 than 25. Elizabeth dressed older than her years because, she believed, it made her look more dignified, formal, elegant and more like a monarch.

Even the fashion trade saw that the young queen had a problem. As a young woman she was expected to enjoy clothes and dress in a casual and informal way but as queen, formality was considered essential to her role as the sovereign. She couldn't win. Normal, everyday wear totally defeated Elizabeth and she continued to appear frumpish and boring.

In evening dress, however, Elizabeth did look regal, the clothes a dazzling richness outshining other ladies who tried in vain to compete, especially since none could match her unrivalled, stunning jewellery in quality and quantity. In uniform, too, Elizabeth always looked splendid with her straight-back, low-bosom figure; in country and riding outfits she looked happy, relaxed and confident and any pictures on horseback show an accomplished rider of real ability.

Through the years, of course, Elizabeth has had to spend a fortune on clothes. Each day she probably changes her clothes three times and occasionally four or five. Indeed, if she had been fascinated by fashion, simply choosing her clothes, let alone buying them, would take most of her life.

Not until the 1960s did Elizabeth find the classic simplicity of line which suited her best and, to a great extent, she has stayed with it. But even when she occasionally became a slave to fashion she would save money by making her outfitters adapt and alter her existing clothes. It did not go unnoticed.

As the London *Evening Standard* reported in 1971, 'Up and down go the hemlines; while we plead with women to wear what suits them, they usually follow fashion . . . even the queen appeared at Smith's Lawn, Windsor garden party at the weekend in a raspberry-coloured suit which clearly had two hemlines – the old and the new. The skirt was originally made to reach the knee. But it had been let down by about three inches!'

The critics became bolder. In May 1972, the American fashion bible, *Women's Wear Daily* asked scathingly, 'Why does the queen dress so badly? Why must she be the nice queen in the nice little Chanel copy? And why does she need a dumb handbag? Is she trying to suggest that she's just like other women who have to carry money and identity cards?'

The same year, the usually pro-royal *Daily Express* commented, 'Even the most ardent royalist must grudgingly admit that some of the hats which have rested on the royal head are, to be polite, rather strange creations. Her shoes, somebody once said, were only suitable for retired schoolmarms. All clump and no glamour.'

Over the years Elizabeth became used to being attacked by the media for her view of fashion. In June 1979, the *Daily Mail* suggested the queen's carefulness with money was actually meanness, explaining, 'The queen wore a make-do-and-mend dress for the opening of Royal Ascot, with 24 inches cut off the hemline of a dress she wore in Saudi Arabia in February.'

The following day the *Daily Mail* returned to the subject, 'Our parsimonious monarch was at it again yesterday – she turned up at Royal Ascot in a printed chiffon dress in grey, pink and lavender, with a matching loose coat and lavender straw hat, created by Hardy Amies for the state visit to Denmark last month.'

Sometimes she won praise for her pragmatism. In 1979 the *Daily Mirror* commented, 'The chill winds of economic reality are blowing through the strangest of places these days – even the queen's personal wardrobe. In what is obviously an attempt to cut down on the high cost of her clothing – the annual bill is huge – she has just had four of her Norman Hartnell outfits (costing about £500 each) copied. In these inflationary times when things are so expensive it is probably very sensible of her.'

Elizabeth does, however, give far more attention to her outfits during overseas tours and royal visits where she is the object of minute attention by the media. Throughout royal overseas tours, daily briefings and handouts are given to the press which include a description of the clothes she wears and the name of the designer or couture house. Even during her early years as monarch, Elizabeth always tried to appeal to the local people. For example, during a visit to France in 1957 she wore an evening dress for the gala opening of the Opera House in ivory satin, thickly encrusted with pearls, topaz and gold, with *fleur-de-lys*, poppies and a tiny gold bee – Napoleon's symbol of industry. It was a subtle form of flattery the French appreciated and loved. For the same reason decisions on colours, fabrics and styles are taken after consultation with the host nation so that no one is embarrassed or any local customs offended. That is why great care is taken in particular when Elizabeth tours Muslim countries or visits the Vatican.

Elizabeth has devised certain rules for overseas visits. For example, outfits already seen in Britain are not normally worn on formal occasions in foreign countries. A dress worn for an important occasion in one major city during a tour will not be worn again in another city. The same holds true with different countries. Clothes worn on an important North American tour will never be seen on a tour of, say, Australia. But, in order to save money, such outfits can reappear on tours to less westernised countries.

During those trips, the queen wears clothes that make her look confident yet attractive but, most importantly, slightly distant. Over-excited foreigners rushing up for a kiss would never do. On the other hand her appearance must not be too formidable. Adherence to protocol must be tempered by a degree of friendliness and accessibility.

The planning, preparation and choosing of everything to do with overseas visits, not least the selection of all her clothes, requires enormous amounts of time and effort. Dresses and coats travel in large wardrobe trunks, dark blue and labelled 'The Queen'. Accessories are placed in separate trunks; hats are hung on suspended ribbons secured to the sides of trunks to prevent them being dented; shoes and umbrellas are packed separately.

For major overseas tours, Brigade of Guards Sergeant Major Ronald Lewis, her baggage master for 20 years, has at his disposal a separate aircraft which takes all the luggage in advance. In addition to the clothes she intends to wear, alternatives are packed against unforeseen emergencies, such as torrential rains.

Once the tour begins the queen's dressers are responsible for preparing every outfit, pressing, brushing and checking each item before each occasion. They lay out all the items which the queen requires for each change of outfit, from underwear to jewellery. Of course, they must know where every item has been packed and lists are essential. The contents of all trunks, cases and hat boxes are written in duplicate, one kept by the dressers and the other glued to the inside of the container's lid. To keep creases to a minimum, masses of tissue paper is used for each outfit; shoulders and collars are padded with tissue and every fold is interlined with several more sheets of tissue. Important evening dresses and state gowns travel separately on their hangers, shrouded in cotton wool and dark tissue paper (to prevent tarnishing) and zipped in plastic protective covers before being placed in individual containers. Such attention to detail keeps ironing to a minimum on arrival.

Some overseas newspapers like to criticise the queen when she visits their country. During a state visit to Canada in 1984, for example, the *Toronto Star* took Elizabeth, then 58, to task, criticising her 'unflattering round necks, long coats and awful hats' and 'her safe and round hairstyle, which makes her look like a grandmother'. That particular attack was rather unfair. Elizabeth had been a grandmother for seven years.

A year earlier, differences between the elegant, fashion-conscious emerging glamour girl of the royal family, Princess Diana, and what many saw as the fuddy-duddy Elizabeth, evoked comparisons and criticism. The *Daily Mail* commented:

> Princess Diana is said to be having a marginal effect on the queen's terrible clothes. In time, hopefully, she will persuade her to reject the double-breasted coat, the felt hat, the sensible costume, the bow-tied blouse. So the next time she goes through her mother-in-law's wardrobe, we suggest she persuades her to chuck out those frumpish stoles the queen is partial to clutching to her diamanté-encrusted evening gowns.

Newspaper attacks compared Elizabeth's dress sense with the fashionable Diana. The *Sunday Express* in 1983 said:

> There ought to be someone around to save the queen from wearing silly things . . . half Britain must have cringed with vicarious embarrassment when they saw on TV and in the papers the outfit the queen wore on Sunday at San Diego. Her fussy blue and white suit was bad enough, but the matching sailor cap she wore with it was gruesome. She ended up looking like a matronly cinema usherette, circa 1940.

Occasionally Elizabeth's fashion advisers urged her to try more outrageous clothes; to stun her audience with high fashion. It never seemed to work; Elizabeth has never been a fashion model. In March 1984 she attended a San Francisco banquet dressed in a frou-frou dress of taffeta and lace ruffles, cut with a voluminous skirt flounced from a dropped waistline. A flurry of gold lace ruffles decorated the sleeves, and giant candy bows perched on each shoulder. With the glittering tiara she wore 110-watt diamond drop earrings. It was a dreadful mistake which embarrassed Elizabeth and which she has, wisely, never repeated.

People continue to wonder about the queen's handbag. She has hardly ever been photographed without one, not even when strolling across the comparative privacy of her own front lawn. The handbags are invariably leather, highly polished, neat and buttoned up. But what is its function? The answer, quite simply, is psychological. She needs it. She feels an attachment to her handbag. A handbag is something to clutch when nervous, something to busy the hands with during long, awkward moments.

Her handbags are usually copious, always in top-quality heavy calf for daytime and silver tissue for evening, often black and occasionally white, and never without a loop to hang over her wrist. She has never considered a clutch bag or even a shoulder bag. Her handbags have ignored every change in fashion through the decades and have been a frequent subject of criticism if not open amusement.

And in her handbags? A lipstick, a small gold compact, her spectacles, a handkerchief and occasionally her favourite gold-plated camera. Nothing more. And never money. She never needs it.

It is the same with her gloves. The queen regards them as essential, not only as a sign of formality but a practical defence for a woman who has to shake so many hands. Elizabeth has deliberately perfected a rather limp handshake in order to protect her fingers, in direct contrast to Philip's very firm, manly grip. The gloves also help to protect her hands. Most of her gloves are not leather or suede but a suede fabric which can be easily washed, removed and dyed. That is the point – the fabric is far less expensive than real leather or suede.

This, indeed, is one particular aspect of Elizabeth's royal life that bores her to death: that is, the endless hours spent being fitted for the thousands of different clothes she needs. She tries to make her hours with dressmakers as relaxed as possible and has been known to perch on a chair, chatting and munching chocolate. She needs to be on good terms with her dressmakers because she sees them far more often than she does her children, her husband or indeed her personal maids.

It was Bobo who always made sure no one dressmaker became too powerful, distributing the queen's patronage carefully among a number of leading designers. If a couturier tried to make suggestions as to the queen's hats, handbags or shoes to go with a certain outfit, Bobo would always intervene, telling them in her Scottish accent, 'Ye know, ye're here for the clothes and not the accessories.'

And if Bobo disapproved of an outfit it would be put away, never to be worn again. Bobo was the only person who openly criticised Elizabeth's outfits, even in front of other staff or the designers and Elizabeth would take the criticism without comment, virtually always accepting Bobo's dress sense. There were some who regretted Bobo's influence on Elizabeth's fashions. Their joint policy on clothes was always one of minimum fuss.

All testify to Elizabeth's relaxed attitude and her understanding that since she has to have so many fittings she should enjoy them as much as possible. And yet even in this informal setting, she insists that the strict palace protocol must not be breached. The dressmakers are not, for example, permitted to speak unless spoken to; not allowed to turn their backs in the royal presence under any circumstances and, whenever leaving the room, the designers and dressmakers must walk backwards and bow to the queen when they reach the door, though she may be standing on a chair munching a biscuit at the time. And no one is ever permitted to sit during these fittings, not even on the floor, when working on her outfit.

The rewards and privileges are not great. When the fitting session is over Elizabeth departs and the fortunate workers are sent tea and cakes; if the fitting is before lunch a single dry sherry will be offered.

Elizabeth has her favourite dyes and, despite her age, can still look remarkable in bright, strong colours. She is not fond of navy blue and keeps black for mourning, despite the fact that she apparently looks stunning in black velvet. Her designers have two main considerations: to create the illusion that Elizabeth is taller than her five feet four inches, and to minimise the fact she is a 'clinger'. Due to her own static electricity her favourite materials – silk crêpe de chine and chiffon – have a tendency to cling, which is why she hardly ever wears them.

For the record, Elizabeth takes a size 12 dress; her weight fluctuates between eight-and-a-half and nine-and-a-half stone and she normally finds herself at the upper limit after her long vacation at Balmoral each summer. She keeps dress and skirt hems one-and-a-half inches below the knee and she still has long slender legs which maintain their shape by regular horse riding. And she wears nothing but beige stockings and tights. Shoes are usually black with chunky heels for comfort during long spells while standing still.

For relaxing in the country, however, Elizabeth invariably wears tweeds, warm sweaters and sensible walking shoes.

Surprisingly, members of the royal family do not confer with each other, nor do their dressers, when preparing for a family gathering, despite the fact that two or even three members may turn up in the same colour of outfit. Shortly after joining the royal family, Diana worried about appearing in the same colour as the queen. She raised the matter with Elizabeth's ladies-in-waiting and was told never to worry, Elizabeth wouldn't mind whatever colour she wore.

Prime Minister Margaret Thatcher once attended a function wearing the same colour of dress as the queen, which didn't bother Elizabeth one jot. The following day, however, Mrs Thatcher sent a letter to Buckingham Palace suggesting, rather preciously, that in future their offices should confer over choice and colours of dress in order to avoid possible embarrassment. Back came the stinging snub from the palace, obviously with Elizabeth's blessing, 'The queen does not notice what others wear.' Mrs Thatcher was livid.

Elizabeth enjoys nothing more than a day at the races, especially if one or more of her horses is running. And the famous Royal Ascot meet, held for four days each year in June, is the most stylish day at the races. The highlight is still the processional drive down the course in open carriages before racing begins each day and those invited to stay at Windsor Castle feel especially privileged.

The day starts with a ride across Windsor Great Park for all guests invited to stay overnight at the castle. Those who ride out end up on the adjoining Ascot race course where they compete in a special, private royal race – which is usually won by the queen.

The thirty or more guests will meet for pre-lunch drinks followed by a brisk, simple meal before stepping into a fleet of Rolls-Royces to be driven to the course, after which the royal party appear in the carriages at 2 p.m. Everyone who is admitted to the royal enclosure at Ascot must dress formally, in top hats and tails, and ladies in their best summer frocks. Even detectives and officials wear the Ascot rig and the ladies-in-waiting wear elegant summer wear.

Officially, anyone can gain access to the royal enclosure but every application has to be accompanied by a recommendation from someone who is already a member and the possessor of one of those prized enclosure badges. The royal box itself is off limits.

Elizabeth spends the afternoon literally running from the television set at the back of the royal box where she watches the early parts of the race, to the front for the final two furlongs which she watches through binoculars. Her face reveals the excitement, the ecstasy that grips her at great race meetings and close finishes. She has been known to jump up and down in excitement during the last yards of a race. Bets are laid on her behalf but, as far as is known, never more than £20 a time. Like everyone else, she is exhilirated when she wins and despairing when she loses.

Between each race Elizabeth and other members of the family will make their way to the paddock to inspect the horses before they run. It is a nightmare for police and her personal bodyguard, for Elizabeth walks among a thousand or more people, many of them total strangers, who will be standing inches away from her. On many occasions, especially when terrorist activity is at its height, Elizabeth has been warned not to take such a risk since she would be a certain target for a committed assassin. But she is adamant that there be no change to her schedule. 'If I cannot enjoy my day at the races,' she says, 'I may as well never leave the palace.'

In her own family Elizabeth is the most passionate about racing, an interest she inherited from her mother who still attends as often as she can, despite her age. Philip, on the other hand, cannot abide racing and attends only under sufferance, and while Elizabeth insists that he ride with her in the open carriage down the course, Philip indicates his annoyance by never showing his face in the royal box throughout the entire afternoon. In fact, he refuses to watch the horses run. He sits in a room below the royal box watching cricket on another television set, specifically installed so that Philip can watch something other than the racing. Prince Charles is no race fan either and when he had to attend, on his mother's orders, he was permitted to leave early to take part in polo matches which follow the end of Ascot racing each day. Andrew, Edward and Princess Anne have no real interest either.

Indeed, Elizabeth and Philip have very little in common. Even when they are in the country, Elizabeth will go riding while Philip fishes; Elizabeth will do some light reading while Philip prefers more serious literature; Elizabeth will go for a walk alone with her dogs while Philip sits and paints.

Even though Elizabeth attends the National Theatre on the odd occasion, neither Elizabeth nor Philip enjoy the theatre, the ballet or the opera. She has no real interest in art either, despite being the present owner of one of the most magnificent private collections in the world. Actually, the great majority of her collection has been handed down through the family over the generations. Elizabeth will sometimes purchase a painting for her collection – a Turner, for example – but mainly because she is advised its acquisition will help fill a gap or supplement a certain part of the collection, not because she is enraptured by a particular work or artist – any interest she once had was lost after the death of her beloved Patrick Plunkett who loved art and tried to educate and interest Elizabeth in her art collection.

Those involved in the arts in Britain have given up trying to persuade Elizabeth to be more involved. They argue that even if she is not terribly interested in the arts herself she could, and should, show more enthusiasm and give greater encouragement than she does, perhaps by making public donations or providing patronage. As far as Elizabeth is concerned, however, there is no point in being what one is not or feigning interest in something that does not arouse one's natural enthusiasm.

The monarch has taken little notice of Britain's struggling, or even successful, modern painters – so very different from years gone by when a reigning sovereign became the patron of a nation's aspiring artists. Sir Oliver Millar, Keeper of the Queen's Pictures, commented, 'I think the sadness as far as pictures are concerned is that the momentum which began in the early part of her reign, even on a small scale, of purchasing pictures by contemporary British artists, has not gone forward. It is a criticism ever since Prince Albert's day that there has not really been a royal involvement with good modern painting, either significant foreign or British work. But if you don't want to buy modern pictures, why should you? You can't do it as a duty. It has to be something that springs from the heart.'

On the other hand, Prince Philip, who enjoys painting as a hobby, has bought some modern art and he does support local artists. Each year, over the past twenty years, he has purchased privately a number of paintings by Scottish artists at the Royal Scottish Academy.

Elizabeth would never claim to be an intellectual, but she is certainly an intelligent woman. At heart she is a country woman, interested in country pursuits and she does not really care for the cultural life that cities offer. What seems extraordinary, though, is the loneliness of the lives Elizabeth and Philip lead. After a lifetime of meeting people, they now seem to have hardly any close friends with whom they like to spend time. Elizabeth has some friends in racing circles with whom she loves to chat about the sport. For female companions she relies on her ladies-in-waiting. Susan Hussey is always on hand, spending most of her life at the palace and often attending lunches or dinners as a guest while carrying out her duties and acting as a listening post.

There is also the lovely Philippa de Pass, whose husband Robert, now in his seventies, served as aide-de-camp to Earl Mountbatten. Uncle Dickie suggested to his Lilibet that Philippa would make an ideal lady-in-waiting and, in 1988, she became the official 'Lady-in-Waiting to the Queen'. This title means that the 'Lady' has become one of Elizabeth's principal advisers and unofficial close friends. Philippa, now in her fifties, held the job for five years before handing over to Lady Susan Hussey in March 1993. Both women remain close to Elizabeth and she values their advice and their friendship. They are her eyes and ears and she sounds them out on controversial matters, but neither woman feels she is really a close friend.

Even family gatherings are few and far between these days. Gone are the days she could summon her children to Balmoral for eight weeks every year where she would try to create a family atmosphere they could all enjoy. In any case, for much of the time there was little relaxation for anyone; they all had to behave as though they were on parade with set times for lunch and dinner and set games every night. And they still had to treat Elizabeth more as the queen than as their mother or grandmother. Nowadays, the children will drop by to visit their parents for the odd week or so but none hangs around.

Neither has Philip any close friends. The good pals whose

company he did enjoy, like Mike Parker and Rupert Neville, have been replaced in name but not as close confidants. Philip has acquaintances with whom he will enjoy passing the time of day, like those people he meets when carriage-driving, or shooting or sailing, but during the last few years Philip has preferred to spend more time by himself reading, painting, fishing or watching television.

Today Elizabeth and Philip spend more time together, like any other couple of pensionable age. But, unlike most pensioners, they lead extremely busy and full lives. In reality, very little has changed for them. Elizabeth has the neverending discipline of the boxes and, like Philip, she still carries out hundreds of official royal engagements every year.

This discipline which has ruled her life has helped Elizabeth come to terms with aspects of her marriage, for instance, which have been to her a source of considerable distress. By throwing herself at her toils of duty, she has succeeded in all but ignoring Philip's chain of amorous exploits, pretending not to know and, more importantly, not *wanting* to know, what has been going on.

To some critics that was the easy way out but, in Elizabeth's unique position, that was unfair for there was no other way out. She could never contemplate separation or divorce whatever sins her husband may have committed. She married him for her entire life in the same way that she was 'married' to the monarchy, 'until death do us part'. Elizabeth has always lived with those disciplines and whatever her unhappiness or anger at Philip's behaviour, there has never been the slightest consideration that she might discard him.

For some years during their marriage, after the birth of Edward in 1964, Elizabeth and Philip lived almost separate lives rather like 'ships passing in the night'. In that respect Elizabeth was fortunate. It was very easy for her not to see her husband for days and weeks at a time, depending on her mood. To Elizabeth that was nothing extraordinary; it was merely the normal arrangement for couples in her social stratum who had separate bedrooms, bathrooms and dressing rooms. Even today, it is not uncommon for Elizabeth and Philip not to eat together from one week to another for a variety of reasons. By deliberately ignoring him, Elizabeth displayed not only her strength of character but also her discontent and dissatisfaction with Philip.

Elizabeth is never alone unless she wishes to be. She always has her courtiers, her personal staff, footmen, pages, ladies-in-waiting and dressers on hand, 365 days a year. She still keeps in daily contact with her mother and can phone any of her children at any time. And when away at Windsor, Balmoral or Sandringham she is happy walking with her dogs or riding or indulging in other country pursuits. Her life is so full and busy, even today, that she has no need for the constant companionship of a husband.

Only on holidays are Elizabeth and Philip truly together and their lives are reversed. When out stalking or shooting it is Philip who strides ahead with the guns and the ghillies and Elizabeth who walks behind, in control of the gun dogs and picking up the dead birds. But she loves that role. The monarchy was thrust on her; she never asked for it, and sometimes she prefers to lead the more normal life of a woman with a determined and self-confident husband.

When holidaying together, Elizabeth and Philip give dinner parties and invite guests to stay for long weekends. People who attend these events report that during the past few years, just as during the early years of their marriage, Elizabeth and Philip laugh a lot together. One might suggest there is no better test of a good marriage than a couple being able to laugh together, especially after a marriage of more than fifty years.

13. ALL THE QUEEN'S MEN

Life stirs in Buckingham Palace at around six when the first of the three hundred people who work there arrive at the queen's official London residence. In reality the palace never rests, for men of various royal regiments take turns to guard their sovereign around the clock. Visitors see them at various palace entrances, and they provide the picturesque daily tourist attraction of the changing of the guard when a troop of the household cavalry, resplendent in their bright uniforms and matching coloured horses, parade down the Mall.

Some live above the shop and a number of single men and women have rooms in the palace while privileged courtiers and their wives are granted lovely free apartments, which in royal terms are always referred to as 'grace and favour' residences. These are provided only with the express permission of Elizabeth.

Officially, three separate royal bodyguards have different responsibilities for protecting the queen. The oldest is the Yeomen of the Guard, the most ancient military corps in existence anywhere in the world. It was founded in 1485 after the famous Battle of Bosworth in which Richard III was killed. He was the last English monarch to die on the field of battle.

The Yeomen of the Guard's original duty called for the protection of the sovereign, especially when he or she went into battle. They were also responsible for the more mundane protection at the royal palaces. Today, the Yeomen of the Guard consists of retired officers, warrant officers and non-commissioned officers from the army and Royal Air Force. On official occasions Yeomen stand closest to the queen and, by tradition, there are always six present.

Once they numbered 600. Now there are only 66 Yeomen. Most of today's Yeomen would be incapable of defending anyone, let alone the sovereign, for they are not allowed to join until they are over fifty and most are nearly seventy, the compulsory retirement age. Another requirement is that they be over five feet ten inches tall, so they still look impressive in their official scarlet and gold doublet, with breeches and red stockings, black buckled shoes, a ruff at the neck and a black velvet hat with ribbons of red, white and blue around the crown. They also carry a ceremonial sword which, by tradition, is never drawn.

They may look picturesque and odd but they have literally saved the sovereign's life in years gone by. Their most recent act of gallantry occurred during the reign of King George III around 1800. He survived three serious attempts on his life, all foiled by the quick thinking of the Yeomen of the Guard. How much quick thinking would occur today is certainly open to question, but their presence on state occasions has become part of tradition.

Today the physical protection of the queen is undertaken by a much more highly specialised group, officers of the Royalty Protection Department, who provide 24-hour security for every member of the royal family. The Royalty Protection Department is divided into two sections: those who wear uniforms number around sixty; they are responsible for security within Buckingham Palace. The plain clothes officers, numbering around a hundred, provide the royal bodyguards.

The Buck House police guards are based in a special bomb-proof police station which was built shortly after a man had broken into Elizabeth's bedroom early one morning in July 1982. For ten long minutes Michael Fagan, suffering from a mental disorder and in a state of severe emotional distress, sat on Elizabeth's bed, pouring out his problems to her. The nation was shocked and outraged that an intruder could so easily gain access to the queen's bedroom.

Michael Fagan, 35, was having domestic problems involving his wife, their four children, two stepchildren and their parents. Because of abnormal behaviour due to his mental condition, his wife wanted to leave him and take the children. For reasons that Fagan himself cannot fathom, he decided he had to share his troubles with the world and make front page news. He figured there was no better way of gaining the attention of the authorities than by slashing his wrists in front of the queen. He had also been suffering under the delusion that he was the son of Rudolf Hess, Hitler's former right-hand man who parachuted into Britain at the start of the Second World War, allegedly in a vain effort to bring peace to both countries. On that occasion Hess had wanted to appeal directly to King George VI, but was not granted permission for an audience and spent the war in a

British jail. Fagan decided he would fulfil his 'father's' ambition and see the sovereign himself.

At 6.45 on the morning of Friday, 9 July 1982, a man was seen climbing the palace railings by an off-duty policeman who telephoned the palace police. Two officers went to check but they discovered nothing. Then the alarm in the queen's Stamp Room, which had a reputation for being unreliable, sounded once. The sergeant on duty switched it off. A few seconds later it sounded again and the unnamed sergeant switched it off again, not bothering to check if an intruder had somehow gained access to the room.

Having entered the Stamp Room by simply climbing through the ground-floor window, Fagan had found that the door from the Stamp Room into the palace interior was locked, so he climbed back out of the window and searched for another way in. The on-duty police who had failed to discover any intruder went back to their room and had a cup of tea. Having tried other ground-floor windows, and finding them all locked, Fagan decided to shinny up a drainpipe and see if any first-floor windows were open. It was broad daylight and the palace was starting to buzz with all the staff coming on duty. No one noticed anything amiss.

Finding a first-floor window half open, Fagan climbed the nearest drainpipe and within a couple of minutes was inside the palace. For some unknown reason, he removed his sandals and socks before padding along the corridor leading to the queen's private apartments. He picked up a heavy glass ashtray and smashed it against the wall, holding on to a large jagged piece so that he could ceremonially slash his wrists in front of the queen. Incredibly, no one heard a sound. Fortunately for Fagan, the armed police officer who patrolled the corridors around the queen's private apartments had, as usual, gone off-duty at six.

While Fagan was quietly walking along the corridor in his T-shirt and jeans, holding the piece of broken glass, the queen's personal maid was cleaning up in a room adjoining her bedroom while the footman on duty had taken the corgis for their early morning walk in the gardens. Fagan popped his head into several rooms until he had found the queen's bedroom and saw her lying asleep in bed. Quietly, he slipped into the room and closed the door.

At 7.18 exactly, as the queen was to report later, she woke up as the long drapes were being drawn, not by her usual maid but by Fagan. Dressed in her night dress, she sat up and asked Fagan who he was and what on earth he was doing in her bedroom. Then she noticed his scruffy, dirty appearance and the jagged piece of glass. The dishevelled, unshaven Fagan, dripping blood from a cut on his thumb when he had smashed the ashtray, walked over to the bed and sat down just a few feet from Elizabeth.

She sat motionless as she watched the unkempt Fagan toying with the jagged piece of glass. 'I've got terrible problems,' he said, 'I've got to talk to you.'

Elizabeth said later that she realised as soon as the man sat down that she had to keep her nerve for she had sensed he was emotionally unstable. 'I realised that I had to keep him talking, to keep his attention. I thought that if I kept him talking he wouldn't become violent.'

Elizabeth invited him to talk through his problems with her – he appeared to be stumbling through his words as though he did not know what he wanted to say. As he began to speak more calmly she put her hand down by the side of the bed and pressed the emergency night alarm button connected directly to the police control room. She expected that within a minute or so the police would rush into her room. Nothing happened. The bell wasn't working.

Patiently Elizabeth waited, unable to understand why her panic alarm call had not been answered. She managed to keep Fagan talking about his problems as the blood from his right thumb dripped incessantly on her bedclothes. After a couple of minutes, as Fagan continued his rambling, incoherent story, Elizabeth decided to try another bell, the one she always pressed for her maid to answer. This bedside bell rang outside, down the corridor and Elizabeth was confident her duty maid would arrive within seconds.

No one came. The duty maid had failed to hear it because she was in a side room further down the corridor. Elizabeth became alarmed after the only two ways she had of contacting anyone outside her room had failed. She wondered whether Fagan had somehow turned off both bells, in which case she feared she was in a more serious predicament that she had first realised.

Fagan continued to talk, telling Elizabeth about his 'father' and his need to explain why Hess had flown to Britain in an effort to stop Germany and Britain from declaring war on each other. It was fortunate for Elizabeth that she had had so much practice at small talk, and with such a variety of people. She continued to ask Fagan questions and at one point commented, 'Then Prince Charles is a year younger than you.'

Realising that the man was seriously disturbed and a possible danger, Elizabeth knew that she must not frighten or alarm him, for fear of his potentially violent reaction. Throughout the ordeal she kept her eye fixed on the piece of jagged glass Fagan gripped in his right hand. She had worked out that if he tried to strike at her she would throw bedclothes over his arm and make a dash for the door.

As the minutes ticked by, Fagan began to relax and Elizabeth decided to risk another tack. She asked him if he would like a cup of tea, which he accepted. So Elizabeth picked up the telephone to order the tea. The call went directly to the duty palace operator and she asked him to send tea to her room, immediately. It was, of course, extraordinary for the queen to phone the palace operator to ask for tea, something she had never done before. Rather bemused, the operator thought it might be some joke so he didn't immediately react. To be safe, however, he put a call through to the queen's maid. Once again there was no reply; her maid had heard nothing.

Elizabeth was perplexed and now seriously worried when neither the tea nor the maid arrived. 'I kept wondering where on earth everyone was,' she said later. 'I kept wondering what was going on outside. What possible reason could there be for no one answering any of my calls?'

After a few more minutes had elapsed with Fagan continuing his rambling stories, Elizabeth decided she had to make one more effort to contact someone, anyone. Under the pretence of demanding the tea again, she phoned the operator once again and asked him to send up not only the tea, but also a policeman. She told later how her heart had beaten even faster when she quietly spoke the word 'policeman' into the phone. Fagan apparently did not notice that she had called for an officer. The operator thought the queen's request odd and phoned the police control room, telling them, 'Her Majesty would like a police officer to go to her room.' Not realising the alarm surrounding the request, although such a request was most unusual, the duty officer said he would notify someone later when more officers had come on duty.

Throughout her entire life, Elizabeth had only to ring a bell, ask for something, and within seconds her wish would have been fulfilled. Maids, footmen, police would come running immediately. Yet here she was in the most extraordinary and dangerous situation of her life, with a mentally deranged man armed with a jagged piece of glass sitting on her bed, and no one had answered her pleas for help. She began to worry if there was some sort of plot; if something had happened that she did not know about. She felt cut off, isolated and highly vulnerable.

Elizabeth knew that if no one was to come to her rescue then she would have to get out of the room – and quickly. She had no idea concerning the real state of the man's emotional stability but had to presume he could become violent at any moment. Why else would he have entered her room armed with a large piece of broken glass if not to threaten her, or worse, to use it? She was surprised that he had allowed her to make two phone calls without objection and she tried one last ploy. She asked him if he smoked and whether he would like a cigarette while waiting for his tea to arrive.

'Yes,' he replied. Elizabeth saw her chance but realised she had to remain calm and cool. She told him, 'I'm sorry, I have none in this room, I will have someone bring some for you. Will you wait a moment?'

Her heart thumping, Elizabeth slipped out of bed, all the time watching Fagan who was pacing around the room, still holding the broken glass. He was showing increasing signs of agitation. She put on her dressing gown, tied the belt and walked slowly out of the room. In the corridor she met her duty maid and told her to ring for the police immediately and tell them a stranger was in her bedroom. 'Bloody hell, Ma'am,' her maid exploded. 'He oughtn't to be in there.' Elizabeth replied, 'Shush, do as I say, and quickly.'

At that moment the first piece of luck occurred: the footman returned, walking down the corridor surrounded by eight of Elizabeth's corgis who, upon seeing her, started to bark. Hearing the noise and commotion, Fagan ventured out of the room, to the shock of the footman. Elizabeth still managed to retain her composure, and fearing Fagan might strike out at the footman, told him to get some cigarettes for her 'guest'. The footman called Fagan to the nearby pantry and gave him a cigarette.

Having seen the footman and the maid, and with the dogs yapping and barking, Fagan began to show signs of panic. He still held the broken glass in one hand as he nervously puffed at the cigarette with the other and watched as the queen tried to control the unruly dogs. He began to look around him but the footman, knowing the police would arrive at any second, enticed Fagan back into the pantry with the offer of food. Seconds later, the police came running down the corridor. Fagan was pinned to the floor, his arms stretched out, and never got the chance to use the glass.

It had taken nine minutes from the time Fagan had entered Elizabeth's bedroom to the moment the police arrived. Immediately after his arrest, Elizabeth went back into her bedroom but suddenly began to shake, her hands sweating. She suddenly felt traumatised by the realisation that she had faced at best, a weirdo, at worst, a man who was mentally ill and armed with a large, jagged piece of glass.

She almost fainted when her maid led her to her blood-stained bed to recover. For 20 minutes Elizabeth lay quietly, shaking nervously as she regained her composure. Tea was brought and she began to feel better.

More than anything Elizabeth wanted a bath to somehow wash away the feeling of this man who had sullied her bedroom. After that she felt well enough to dress and have some breakfast. Immediately afterwards she phoned her mother to tell her of the incident but assured her that she was fine.

The incident illustrated, not for the first time, Elizabeth's physical bravery and moral courage in the face of a serious, potentially dangerous situation. It also showed her remarkable presence of mind when, having woken from sleep and wearing only a nightdress, she had been able to take command of the situation and defuse it entirely by herself.

Mystery surrounds the whereabouts of Philip that morning whose suite of rooms is just along the corridor from those of Elizabeth's. When news of the incident was announced, Buckingham Palace reported that Philip was in his suite of rooms. No mention was made, however, of Philip's part in the affair. Despite the noise of yapping dogs, running policemen and the commotion caused by Fagan's arrest, Philip had apparently heard nothing. Subsequent reports suggested he had not been sleeping at the palace that night but had stayed at one of his London clubs. None of his friends can testify to that, however.

The Fagan incident showed very little security existed at Buckingham Palace at all. Inquiries were ordered into the incident from government ministers, Scotland Yard and the Royal Protection Squad. Some heads rolled; police officers were changed. One of the changes made the following day called for an officer to remain outside the queen's bedroom until Elizabeth went to breakfast. In the time-honoured way, those responsible decided that by throwing money at the problem everything would be solved – a new £1.5 million police control room, bristling with the latest electronic gadgetry, was built inside the palace grounds.

The pathetic state of security at the palace was revealed later when Fagan told police he had entered the palace a month before, on 7 June and had drunk half a bottle of wine before climbing out of a window and walking away. No one at the palace had even known of the incident until Fagan had admitted it under questioning and a butler had confirmed that half a bottle of wine had been found around 7 June and in the exact place Fagan had told the police.

Extraordinarily, the law of trespass did not permit Fagan to be prosecuted for his 'intrusion', so he was accused of burglary over the bottle of wine. The jury acquitted him but, after psychiatric reports, Fagan was sent to a mental hospital.

The Fagan débâcle had another, rather sad ending for one of Elizabeth's favourite police officers, Michael Trestrail. As well as being the queen's personal bodyguard, Trestrail had become a friend during the nine years he had served her. Then in his fifties, he was gay and for twelve years had had a serious affair with another homosexual. Following the Fagan break-in, Trestrail's lover had seen an opportunity to make some money for himself so he decided to try and put pressure on Trestrail despite the fact that the bedroom incident had nothing whatsoever to do with the police officer. Honourable to the end, Trestrail informed Elizabeth that his lover was trying to expose him and believed he had no alternative but to offer his resignation. Elizabeth reluctantly accepted it, knowing she had no other option. Nevertheless, she realised the ignominy that would follow for the trusted officer who had become her friend and confidant.

During his nine-year stint, Trestrail had travelled everywhere with Elizabeth, on all her overseas trips and throughout Britain, accompanying her on virtually every royal occasion. She appreciated his impeccable manners, his wit and intelligence and chatted with him, sought his advice, relied on his good sense and found his conversation highly amusing. There is certainly no suggestion of anything more than a close friendship between the two, but undeniably Elizabeth felt let down, taken aback that someone whom she had grown close to should have allowed a situation to arise which meant he could no longer continue the job, thereby putting their relationship at risk.

As a result of the Fagan incident the entire approach towards security of the queen and all other members of the royal family was re-appraised and dramatically upgraded.

Another more pertinent and far more dangerous reason for introducing change was the Irish Republican Army, which had carried out two audacious bombing atrocities in London in July 1982, in Hyde Park and Regents Park, both involving members of the armed forces and both close to Buckingham Palace and other royal residences. If the authorities needed further warning of the dangers to which the queen and other members of the royal family were exposed, these bombings concentrated their minds.

Prime Minister Margaret Thatcher gave orders for a general

tightening of security. The SAS was called in to advise on security and, as a result, every room in every palace and royal residence was photographed and the pictures filed in the palace control room and SAS headquarters, so that in an emergency SAS troops would know exactly the layout of any room and the position of all furniture, if it was ever necessary to carry out a raid or rescue mission. Fagan and the IRA bombers had shown how vulnerable the sovereign and her family had become and how easily determined bombers could penetrate the security. Mrs Thatcher recognised what an extraordinary coup the IRA would have achieved if they had managed to assassinate the queen or any close member of the royal family in the way they had murdered Earl Mountbatten in August 1979.

As a result, electronic equipment, which is relayed instantly to the palace control room, was installed not only at the palace but at all the other royal residences including Highgrove, the country home of Charles and Diana, and Gatcombe Park, Anne's Gloucestershire home. Now, even if main lines of communication should be bombed or blown up, other back-up systems ensure the royal homes are never cut off. As a further measure, every royal car was fitted with an electronic homing device so that the control room knows, at any precise moment, exactly where the cars can be located. But for an open monarchy like Britain's there is virtually nothing that can be done to stop an assassin from shooting or throwing a bomb.

The Fagan incident was more worrying, and severely embarrassing for the authorities, because it occurred only 13 months after a serious attempt had been made on Elizabeth's life in broad daylight. It was on 13 June 1981, during the Trooping the Colour birthday parade, just two years after the IRA had murdered Mountbatten. An unhappy youth of 17 tried to shoot the queen as she rode down the Mall on her black mare, Burmese, a 19-year-old charger presented as a gift from the Royal Canadian Mounted Police. Television viewers heard a number of shots ring out; they saw Burmese break into an instinctive canter; they saw Elizabeth lurch backwards as she moved to control Burmese – she was riding side-saddle, as she did on all official parades, making it much more difficult to control her horse.

Elizabeth turned a little pale; she reached forward and patted Burmese on the neck to reassure him and then Philip and Charles, on their horses, dropped back to form a barrier around her. Other mounted officers spurred their horses forward to shield her and police and members of the public dived on a young man who disappeared in a mêlée of arms and legs.

Later that day Elizabeth told guests at a Garter ceremony at Windsor Castle, 'It wasn't the shots that frightened Burmese but the sight of the cavalry, everyone rushing to shield me.'

In her Christmas message that year, which was the Year of the Disabled, Elizabeth played down her own courage while praising others, 'There is courage with its bold physical face, the courage of firemen and servicemen,' she said, 'but above all there is moral courage.' In this way she included the unshakeable will of the handicapped to endure. 'The golden thread of courage,' she quoted, 'has no end.'

As a result of the scare, members of the household, senior police officers and cabinet ministers prevailed on Elizabeth to abandon riding in public: they urged her to stop riding in slow, horsedrawn carriages and to start adopting more modern forms of transport which were not so vulnerable to an assassin's bullet or a bomber's aim. Many urged presidential-style protection, the queen riding in armour-plated cars with outriders and SAS soldiers in close attendance surrounding the vehicle. The debate raged in the press and throughout the media.

Elizabeth would have none of it. 'If my people cannot see their monarch on such occasions,' she said, 'then there is no point in having a monarchy. The debate is at an end.' The youth of 17, who had armed himself with six blank cartridges in a replica pistol, was jailed for five years under the Treason Act 1842. His reason: he wanted to be noticed.

The 160 members of the Royalty Protection Squad, like the Yeomen of the Guard, are all hand-picked and all volunteers. They have to endure a rigorous selection system – only one out of twenty volunteers is accepted – and they must be agile, fit and crack shots, as well as trained in unarmed combat. They all carry hand guns but also have immediate access to automatic weapons, and the queen's personal bodyguard, as well as all royal bodyguards, are under orders never to allow their charges to go out alone. Stories in the press that Princess Diana would drive off from Kensington Palace by herself are untrue because, no matter what the royal demands, the bodyguard is under the strictest instruction never to allow their personal royal out of their sight. And they never do.

Many of those who work in the nation's palaces carry out duties that have been performed by royal servants for centuries. They take great pride in the fact that they are part of privileged traditions and thoroughly enjoy their rather unusual jobs.

The duties of the colourful Yeomen, known as Beefeaters, are symbolic though they do have a function. They are Yeomen Warders, created by William the Conqueror in 1066 to guard state prisoners in the Tower of London while the Yeomen of the Guard protected their sovereign on the field of battle. Today they have no prisoners to watch over, but they do look after some two million visitors a year who flock to the Tower. Their photographs are taken hundreds of times a day.

There is also the Honourable Corps of Gentlemen at Arms, founded by Henry VIII in 1509 as a personal mounted guard. Their number has never altered – 10 officers and 27 so-called gentlemen, all hand-picked – but now they perform their ceremonial duties on foot. In Scotland, the Royal Company of Archers, founded in 1676, escorts the sovereign on visits to Scotland. Even today the 400 men have to be proficient with a bow and arrow up to a range of 180 yards.

Buckingham Palace became the headquarters of Britain's royal family in 1762 when George III bought the mansion from the Duke of Buckingham for £60,000 as a suitable London home for himself and Charlotte, his 18-year-old bride. In 1822 the famous architect John Nash was commissioned by King George IV to re-design the original building. It now has 19 magnificent state rooms, 52 bedrooms, 188 staff bedrooms, 92 offices and 78 bathrooms. In all, the palace has a grand total of 429 rooms.

It is here that Elizabeth, following the tradition of British sovereigns since George III, conducts the business of a constitutional monarchy. It is also where the queen receives foreign Heads of State, representatives of the Diplomatic Corps, her Privy Council and where she entertains groups of people to small, intimate lunches or holds magnificent banquets catering for more than a hundred guests.

Until August 1993, Buckingham Palace was a unique constitutional royal palace because it never opened its doors to the general public. However, since Elizabeth agreed to open Buckingham Palace to visitors for two months each year, anyone can now pay £8 for the privilege of viewing the magnificent interior. Paying visitors use a different entrance from visitors with appointments to see members of the household on official business.

Private, non-paying guests are still welcomed in the time-honoured manner. On arrival at the massive gold-topped gates at the entrance to the palace grounds, the invited guest is directed to the North Centre Gate by a police officer. One officer checks their identity and telephones a footman inside the palace to ensure that they do indeed have an appointment. They then make their way across the gravel forecourt to the Privy Purse Entrance which is on the right when viewed from the Mall.

The steps leading to the Privy Purse Door are carpeted even though they are exposed to the rain and snow throughout the year. Just as you arrive at the steps the door is opened by a liveried footman dressed in a dark green frock-coat, black trousers, white shirt and striped waistcoat. The footman addresses you by your name and invites you to wait in a tiny adjoining room furnished with gilt chairs covered in lime-green silk. There are two small, exquisite writing tables, an umbrella stand and another small table covered with newspapers. Three large paintings, which are regularly changed, hang on the walls.

A second footman knocks on the door, enters and asks the guest to follow him. Together they walk down long corridors, past a number of open doors which reveal lovely large rooms in which various people are working quietly. These are the offices used by the queen's most senior aides and, by tradition, the doors always remain open. The silent corridors are flanked by portraits of former senior advisers.

You are then brought to a simple room to meet the aide with whom you have an appointment. The chairs are upright and the desks leather-topped and wooden. There are also computers and copying machines and filing cabinets. There is, however, an air of serenity about the place.

By far the best way to see and appreciate Buckingham Palace, though, is to attend a State Banquet when all the State Apartments are in use; the servants are in their scarlet and gold livery and the guests are dressed either in their national costume or full-dress uniform with medals and sashes and the ladies in full-length ball gowns and tiaras.

To ensure the palace itself and the official ceremonies operate smoothly and efficiently, Elizabeth takes great pains to ensure suitable staff are employed at all levels. Save for young secretaries, footmen, junior clerks, kitchen staff, cleaners and gardeners, the queen herself interviews most prospective employees despite the fact they have all been checked out by other senior staff beforehand. She usually tells candidates at the end of the interview, 'Let's give it a try for a year. Then if we decide we can't stand each other we can let it go at that.' It is, of course, the perfect escape clause that applies to both parties.

As was the case centuries ago, the most rigid hierarchical divisions permeate the royal household. At the top are members of the household, the private secretaries and the assistant private secretaries, and the people who come into daily contact with Elizabeth in her official business. They handle and manage the daily diaries, attend royal functions, organise royal visits and advise the queen personally.

Their lives are spent in some luxury: they live in rent-free houses and apartments, called 'grace and favour residences', and it is Elizabeth who personally decides on the home to offer each royal servant. Even then, size and comfort depends on title and position. The highest paid earn £70,000 a year while the majority of the top advisers receive less than £50,000 and along with the various perks of the job, they tend to remain in the monarch's employ for decades. They can call on assistants and secretaries and have servants to pack, unpack and press their clothes, wait on table, run errands or pour a drink. Whenever they travel on the queen's business they will go first class, stay in the very best hotels and have chauffeur-driven cars.

All this pomp reflects the glory of the monarchy. It also enhances the reputation of those senior advisers who are 'close' to Her Majesty. Most of the people immediately surrounding Elizabeth are men but their wives seem to adore the prestige and glamour attached to the fact that their husbands work 'at the palace'.

Many who hold senior posts are former officers of the armed forces. They claim that they 'know the form', palace parlance for how to behave in the presence of Her Majesty. Just as important, Elizabeth, and more so Philip, are sticklers for planning, protocol and timing. Army officers believe they are uniquely trained for such duties which they maintain are all essential for the efficient running of the monarchy. Others, more critical, see it as 'jobs for the boys'.

Usually retired, the former officers are already in receipt of a service pension. The queen gives them a small salary, rent-free accommodation in the heart of London and a position of privilege which no other position can offer.

After the members of the household come the officials, those responsible for the efficient day-to-day running of the palace itself. They include qualified accountants who authorise payments, pay royal bills and decide staff levels and pay. These employees, with decades of loyal service, organise the royal functions and the feasts, the kitchens and the food, the gardens and the cars. Yet these men and women can never climb to the next rung on the ladder, they can never become members – that is, the officer corps of royal service. In most circumstances, they earn more than the members but do not receive as many privileges. In fact those I have spoken to show some jealousy towards their 'superiors' who, without their years of training, nevertheless have many of the perks and privileges without the burden of everyday responsibility.

Finally, the royal household staff make up the lowest grade. These are the two hundred or more workers – maids, domestic servants, junior clerics, labourers and other workers who live all their lives 'below stairs'. Here also, the pecking order is strictly adhered·to, just as it was decades ago. None of these people would ever address the queen or Prince Philip without first being spoken to. Indeed, they would hardly ever see the royal couple, and most would go out of their way rather than come face to face with them. At all levels there is unquestionably a determination on everyone's part to dedicate one's working life to the service of the sovereign and most believe they are part of a very large team, working together to ensure the monarchy runs like a well-oiled machine.

How the staff address one another provides the clue as to the standing of each, just like the armed services. Members address each other by their first names, no matter how junior or senior their position; yet officials are always addressed by their surname, preceded by Mr, Mrs or Miss but never Ms, for such a term is never permitted or accepted in royal circles. The officials always refer to the members by their titles, Sir so-and-so or Colonel so-and-so. The staff – the workers – call everyone above them Sir or Madam.

The queen's household is made up of six separate departments, the Private Secretary's Office, the Keeper of the Privy Purse, the Lord Chamberlain's Office, the Crown Equerry, the Master of the Household and the Royal Collection.

The most important person in Buckingham Palace, after the queen, is the office of private secretary to the sovereign, a far more important person in real terms than the titular head of the queen's advisers, the Lord Chamberlain, and more important than Prince Philip. This man (because thus far the position has always been held by a man) shares all the sovereign's secrets, reads all the secret state and government papers, and has access to every piece of information given to the queen. Provided with all that knowledge it is his duty to advise her.

The Right Honourable Sir Robert Fellowes, who is married to Diana's sister Jane, held that post from 1990 to February 1999, ending 22 years' service at the palace. His job has been taken over by Sir Robin Janvrin, whose background includes the Royal Navy and the Foreign Office before becoming deputy to Sir Robert some years ago. Sir Robert Fellowes had many of the right credentials for the post but many doubted whether he had the intellectual brilliance to carry out the job properly or the authority with the queen to push through the radical reforms the palace so obviously needed to haul it into the new millennium. He had two major problems: Sir Robert is 15 years younger than the queen with very limited knowledge of the workings of the monarchy; and secondly, his father Sir William Fellowes worked for the royal family for much of his life as their land agent at Sandringham, a job which some critics believe did not equip his son with sufficient credentials.

Still, Sir Robert's background is impeccable: educated at Eton, he gave service in the Scots Guards followed by nine years in the City as a director of a discount broker. At that point he was invited to join the palace staff in 1977 as an assistant private secretary. Sir Robert married Jane in 1978 and has a son and two daughters. Possessing all the interests of a typical English aristocrat – hunting, shooting and fishing – he belongs to the right clubs, Pratt's and White's, and loves watching cricket and occasionally plays a round of golf. But in no way does he have the look of a sportsman. He is tall, thin and bespectacled and those who have seen him in the presence of Elizabeth remark that he seems to be in awe of her, ready at a moment's notice to do anything for her, but not the type to challenge her particularly.

Sir Robert failed to make a marked impression in the BBC film *Elizabeth R* in 1991, an insight into a year in the working life of the queen. As the queen's principal adviser, he tried and failed to answer Elizabeth with any authority. He appeared to be poorly briefed, not sure of his facts and rather uninspiring. What he seemed to have in his favour was impeccable breeding and manners, an upper-class accent and fine dress sense, rather like the famous P.G.Wodehouse character Bertie Wooster.

Some of his colleagues credit him with a quick brain and a sense of humour, and he certainly got on well with the other courtiers. Others at the palace confirm him to be man of great integrity and high principles. But he is as streetwise in the ways of the world as an Australian aboriginal would be in New York. Apart from what he reads in the tabloid press, he has little idea of what the ordinary man or woman in the street thinks about.

And this of course must be an indictment of Elizabeth herself. Her previous Private Secretaries were the tried, tested and trusted courtiers of a bygone era but they did display great intellectual capability. Sir Alan Lascelles, Sir Michael Adeane, Sir Martin Charteris and Sir Philip Moore were all older than Elizabeth and she listened to their advice and learned from them. Sir Robert's immediate predecessor, Sir William Heseltine, who most at the palace called Bill, was an affable, rather aggressive Australian who would challenge the queen where he thought it necessary. He had been in closer contact with ordinary people before starting his career at the palace.

Today it seems that Elizabeth prefers to surround herself with people like Sir Robert Fellowes who make the monarchy run like clockwork, with everything in its correct place. Now over seventy, Elizabeth does not welcome change. Not many older people do; and yet this attitude exists at a time when the monarchy is under attack, when change is swirling around the Palace of Buckingham and many other British institutions. Elizabeth's hope is that by surrounding herself with those grey men the monarchy can ride out the storm of change.

The Private Secretary is in absolute command. He holds power over the queen's diary, the functions she attends, the visits she makes, the people she sees as well as serving as her guide in advising ministers of the crown, foreign statesmen and Heads of State. He also sees every piece of correspondence addressed to Her Majesty and has responsibility for drafting all her speeches and official letters.

Perhaps the most important part of the Private Secretary's job is that he is the principal link between the sovereign and the Prime Minister and all other branches of government. Well read in politics, he knows every one of the government's moves yet at the same time he must remain completely objective in his persuasion for the government may change from Tory to Labour and back again. He must be as absolutely impartial as the monarch. Many presume that all the royal family and their senior advisers must have a bias towards the Conservatives, after all the Conservatives are known as the hunting, fishing and shooting party. Most official biographers, however, suggest that they favour neither side.

The Private Secretary is the keeper of the queen's archives. He has overall responsibility for cataloguing and filing all Elizabeth's correspondence which is stored in the Round Tower at Windsor castle. These documents are watched over by the queen's librarian, a post now filled by Oliver Everett who was not only a good friend to Prince Charles for many years, and a polo playing pal, but also his assistant Private Secretary. Princess Diana came between them, however. Everett was one of those found wanting by Diana in the first years of marriage when she had found palace life difficult and demanded the removal of many of Charles's former friends and advisers. Charles asked Oliver Everett to take care of her and become her official secretary. Reluctantly, he agreed.

At first all was well, for Diana liked having the handsome, intelligent and witty former Foreign Office diplomat as her secretary.

Everett tried to help Diana come to terms with her new role as Princess of Wales after the birth of Prince William, and at a time when Diana had become more petulant and demanding. Some believe she was suffering from post–natal depression. She accused Everett of 'spying' on her at Charles's behest, and became paranoid about him, finally demanding that Everett leave. One morning she put a large piece of paper on Charles's desk with the words written in capitals: 'OLIVER MUST GO'.

Charles showed the piece of paper to his friend. They looked at each other, resigned to the fact that in the face of Diana's implacable hostility Oliver's only choice was to quit. Nevertheless, Charles was able to secure for his friend the key librarian's job at Windsor Castle and they continue to meet up.

The Private Secretary is also responsible for liaising between the queen and the armed forces. Throughout this century there has always been a close relationship between the House of Windsor and the military and many members of the family have served, and still serve, in the army, the Royal Navy and the Royal Air Force. As a result, the palace has its own Defence Services Secretary, the link man between the palace and all three services.

The single most important position of the Private Secretary, however, is his total responsibility for the Buckingham Palace Press Office, the link between Elizabeth, the press and the nation. The Press Secretary's job has become increasingly difficult since the tabloid press has shown few or no inhibitions in its coverage of the royal family, particularly the younger members. He must also contend with the *paparazzi*: while the British press claim they do not employ such freelance photographers, and never permit their own staff photographers to intrude in the lives of the royal family, the tabloids will nevertheless pay thousands of pounds to any photographer who turns up at their office with sensational, exclusive royal pictures.

A spectacular example involved the pictures showing a topless Sarah Ferguson, the Duchess of York, in St Tropez, kissing and frolicking in the pool with her 'financial adviser', John Bryan. The *Daily Mirror* bought these pictures, taken by a *paparazzi* photographer in the summer of 1992, just after the break-up of her marriage to Prince Andrew. The *Mirror* paid more than £75,000 for them and sold nearly one million extra copies of that day's paper. The public revelled in the scandal the pictures revealed and at a stroke, Fergie lost any remaining sympathy she had with the public because she had been captured on film making a spectacle of herself in front of her young daughters, Bea, then four, and Eugenie, two, who were also captured on film. Elizabeth was furious that she could have been so mistaken about Fergie whom she felt had let her down.

In November 1993 another set of royal photographs caused an uproar when the Mirror Group published pictures showing Princess Diana, dressed in a leotard and Lycra shorts, working out on a leg-press machine at a London fitness club. The photographs had been taken secretly by Mr Bryce Taylor, the New Zealander owner of the LA Fitness gymnasium in West London which Diana had joined in 1990. Bryce Taylor, a former squash coach, revealed how he had bought a Leica camera for £3,000 and installed it in the ceiling above the leg press, taking photographs of the princess on three separate occasions during the spring of 1993. He sold the photographs to the Mirror Group for £100,000 and his agent maintained he would make almost £1 million from worldwide syndication.

Diana expressed her 'distress and outrage' at the 'gross intrusion' into her privacy and ordered lawyers to sue Mirror Group Newspapers and Mr Taylor over publication of the 'peeping tom' photographs. She also won an immediate injunction banning publication of further pictures in Britain. The case against Bryce Taylor was eventually settled amicably.

The Mirror Group was condemned throughout the newspaper industry and inevitably and understandably there were renewed calls from members of parliament for laws to shackle Britain's newspapers by bringing in restrictive privacy legislation.

The palace Press Office also fields a thousand questions a week from journalists covering every aspect of the royal family. Many questions are on sensitive matters. Generally speaking the Press Office does not comment on stories that appear almost daily in the British national press because common consensus at the palace is that the best way to deal with these stories is to ignore them. As a result, the Press Office remains aloof to most absurdities: if Buckingham Palace denied every story put to them as queries, they would be denying stories every day.

This means, of course, that on occasion the royal family can appear less than candid. As I reported in my book, *Diana: A Princess and Her Troubled Marriage* in the autumn of 1988, Charles and Diana were living apart most of the time and a year later Charles had moved to his country home, Highgrove, while Diana stayed at Kensington Palace. And yet, even when my book was published with these revelations in the spring of 1992, Buckingham Palace still refused to comment. It was not until six months later, just before the official separation was announced, that the Palace hinted that there might indeed be problems within the marriage.

No information is ever released to the media, either in a formal statement or in any 'off the record' comment by the palace Press Office without the knowledge of the Private Secretary. Since 1990 Sir Robert Fellowes had exercised absolute authority over the press officers and responsibility for every statement made. But that does not take note of one vital and important aspect of life at Buckingham Palace.

Superficially all working relationships at the palace appear to be amiable. The senior advisers are expected to be cordial towards one another, seeing themselves as brother officers in the same regiment. In reality, ruthless power politics are the order of the day.

One example involved the separation of Andrew and Fergie in March 1992. Within hours of the official announcement, Charles Anson, the pleasant, affable and competent Press Secretary, talking to the BBC's royal correspondent, had attacked Fergie. He told the BBC that Fergie had ordered media leaks about her marriage, employed a high-powered public relations firm and, worse still, had revealed by her behaviour that she was not worthy of being a member of the royal family. No one in the media had ever heard of such a personal attack on a Royal Duchess of the House of Windsor on any other occasion for half a century.

The day after Anson made the critical remarks which were reported in television news bulletins and in the newspapers, Elizabeth ordered Anson to make an unprecedented, humiliating public apology to the Duchess of York and herself, both for the criticisms themselves as well as for suggesting that the criticisms had been endorsed by the queen. Anson said, 'I have apologised to the queen, and both Her Majesty and Her Royal Highness have been kind enough to accept these apologies.'

In fact, Anson had been briefed by Sir Robert Fellowes who had discussed with him the way in which he might suggest, off the record, the palace's view of the Duchess of York to a few selected journalists. Sir Robert had never felt any fondness towards Fergie. His attitude had been influenced by Major Ronald Ferguson's predilection for consorting with prostitutes and massage-parlour girls. He also had the reputation of trying to seduce the wives and girlfriends of friends he met in the polo world. According to Sir Robert, after his daughter's marriage to Prince Andrew, Major Ferguson had been told to forbear his lewd behaviour for fear he would damage his daughter and the royal family if his activities ever became public. Not surprisingly,

Major Ferguson's seamy adventures were reported in the the newspapers and, as a result, Ronald Ferguson lost his job with the Guards Polo Club, and his role as Polo Manager to Prince Charles. He later lost another £30,000-a-year job with the Royal Berkshire Polo Club. His behaviour brought disrepute on the entire royal family, and proved especially embarrassing to his daughter Fergie.

Sir Robert had formed the opinion that Sarah Ferguson's unsavoury 'past' made her an unsuitable member of the House of Windsor. He advised Elizabeth when it became apparent that Andrew and Fergie were becoming more than lovers. Sir Robert had hoped that Andrew's mercurial sexual adventure with Fergie would end – so he was not a little dismayed when it became obvious that Prince Andrew was to ask Fergie to marry him.

From the beginning of their marriage, Sir Robert put pressure on Fergie. He hoped that he could persuade the Duchess of York to behave in the way in which he wanted, but he was not prepared for Fergie's gutsy response. She was far less susceptible to his powers of persuasion than her sister-in-law Diana. In short, Fergie refused to be ordered about by Sir Robert and told him so in no uncertain terms.

A row occurred in 1989 when Fergie wanted to travel overseas on a holiday. There was no reason why she should not do so; there was no suggestion of any other man in her life and yet Sir Robert believed it was not good for the royal family's image at that time for Fergie to be taking too many overseas holidays. He asked her to see him in his palace offices and the meeting ended with Sir Robert shouting at the top of his voice when Fergie refused his request not to go.

From that moment, Sir Robert lost hope of any successful relationship with Fergie and, unfortunately from Fergie's viewpoint, she had made an enemy of the most powerful person in the palace. She feared he would make life difficult for her. And he did.

He put pressure on Fergie, demanding that she carry out duties, functions and visits which he arranged and which were all but impossible for her to cancel. He began to be more critical of her, pointing out that her speeches weren't good enough; that her dress sense was inappropriate on occasion; that her demeanour wasn't sufficiently royal. As a result, Fergie lost confidence in herself and began to rebel more openly against the system until she felt she simply could not carry on.

Sir Robert saw his chance the moment Fergie came to tell Elizabeth that she could no longer remain a member of the royal family, that the pressures had become too great and that reluctantly she had had to ask Andrew for a separation. He briefed his Press Secretary, the luckless Anson and the inevitable results were there for all to see.

The job of Royal Press Secretary was instituted in 1918 during the reign of King George V but 13 years later he had decided to dispense with it. In 1944, however, King George VI realised a press secretary could be useful in feeding information to the media and the post has continued to the present day. So far there have only been ten press officers. The Press Secretary is in direct contact with Elizabeth and, so that he can be contacted at any time, he is equipped with a mobile telephone. Elizabeth believes such modern contraptions are not necessary for those working at Buckingham Palace, but accepts that the Press Secretary should be permitted to carry one. Despite the direct access to Elizabeth, however, most contacts come through the Office of the Private Secretary.

The link between the royal family and the media has become so important that other members of the House of Windsor now have their own press officers, who all take their orders from the queen's Private Secretary. In addition to directing the press office, Charles Anson has been given special responsibility for the queen. His number two is responsible for Prince Philip and The Princess Royal, Princess Anne.

Another assistant press secretary is responsible for Andrew and Edward as well as Princess Margaret. Still another worked practically full time for both Charles and Diana, but after their separation they employed separate press officers. The Queen Mother has her own man at Clarence House while press matters involving the Duke and Duchess of Kent, the Duke and Duchess of Gloucester, Prince and Princess Michael of Kent and Princess Alexandra are dealt with by their respective private secretaries, but only after consultation with the Buckingham Palace press office or the Private Secretary.

The Private Secretary's responsibilities also include the Information and Correspondence section: besides all the official correspondence, the queen also receives from members of the public another 250 letters a day, close to 100,000 a year, all of which receive a reply. Sackfuls follow a visit by the queen to a part of Britain or after an overseas tour. There are daily requests for information on every aspect of the queen's life including her horses, corgis, wealth, homes, clothes and even her diet. A team of seven people sift, read and then reply to the ceaseless torrent of mail.

Officially, the head of the royal household and the man with overall responsibility for all its departments is the Lord Chamberlain. Since

Elizabeth came to the throne in 1952 there have been five and the present holder is the Earl of Airlie, a former chairman of merchant bankers Schroder Wagg. All were chosen for the job by Elizabeth herself and, undeniably, Lord Airlie has been most helpful recently with all the discussions and publicity concerning the queen's finances. However, the Lord Chamberlain, unlike the Private Secretary, has nothing to do with the day-to-day running of Buck House. Lord Airlie's duties range from ceremonial occasions to royal weddings and funerals and the care of the five thousand or so pictures in the Royal Collection.

The Lord Chamberlain has authority over many other senior royal appointees such as the Marshal of the Diplomatic Corps, whose prime duty is to keep happy all members of foreign embassies, consulates and delegations in their dealings with the palace; he is also directly above the Constable of Windsor Castle who has overall responsibility for the efficient running of the castle; the Clerk of the Closet and three Priests in Ordinary, all involved with the religious aspect of the monarchy; and the medical household, pharmacists who attend when necessary.

He must instruct, and as delicately as possible, incoming diplomats in the ritualistic customs associated with Buckingham Palace when they come to present their credentials to Her Majesty. All nations are treated as equal and some ambassadors of the smaller nations have a rather grandiose view of their own importance, which can cause problems. It is all done most correctly, starting with a ride in an open horse-drawn landau from the embassy to the palace, with much bowing and scraping as they enter the Bow Room on the ground floor accompanied by various royal officials. Then the ambassador and the queen are left alone to chat for five minutes before the ambassador's entourage is formally presented. Finally, the ambassador's wife is invited to join the group and curtsies when she meets the queen. In the late 1960s Elizabeth did away with one embarrassing point of protocol. Until then, ambassadors, their entourage and their wives had to leave the room backwards. Today, once they reach the doorway, they all must turn and bow. Everyone does.

The Lord Chamberlain is responsible for making sure that no 'undesirables' are allowed access to the court to meet the sovereign for fear the crown might be tainted by scandal. Of course, what constitutes scandal changes through the centuries but it was Queen Victoria, followed by the high-handed Queen Mary, who banished all divorcées from the palace or any royal gathering. Some time after Elizabeth came to the throne she relaxed the rule that forbade divorcees to enter her presence. Those divorced politicians who had to be permitted access to Her Majesty were only accepted in their 'official capacity', a typical yet neat British way of circumventing the problem. At first the queen only allowed 'innocent parties' of divorce cases to come to court and be presented to her but the divorce explosion in Britain has meant that the strict rules have had to be relaxed and they were quietly dropped in 1970. However, even today, no one is presented at court who has a serious criminal record or has ever been involved in a major scandal.

Three times a year the beautiful 40 acres of gardens that surround Buckingham Palace are thrown open to invited guests for the legendary garden parties where Elizabeth, Philip and often other members of the family mingle and chat with their privileged guests over afternoon tea. It is considered a special day for the ladies, some of whom spend a fortune buying expensive *haute couture* creations, and always with a hat, to parade before Her Majesty, the cameras and each other. Though debutante dances were cancelled in the 1950s as being *passé*, garden parties have somehow managed to survive the rigours of time and the changes in Britain's social structure.

The three parties are always held in the summer. Altogether around twenty thousand people attend. (There is also one garden party held each year at the Palace of Holyroodhouse in Scotland.) Each party costs about £50,000 and an outside caterer provides everything: 30,000 sandwiches, 18,000 cakes and 2,000 gallons of ice cream. However, while everyone else gorges themselves on food and drink, Elizabeth remains aloof. Her special tea with her favourite cucumber sandwiches are brought to her on a silver salver.

Every name on every invitation must be vetted, every person checked. But not for the all-important security reasons. Rather, palace officials go to great lengths to make sure Elizabeth will not be tainted by meeting anyone considered undesirable. For example, until recently, any person who had been found guilty in court, even of riding a bicycle without lights 30 years before, would be barred for life from attending a garden party. And there would be no appeal.

The garden parties are considered so important that a special Garden Party Office employs nine women for six months of the year to check invitations and people's reputations. The office contains cabinets filled with 'top secret' garden party files. They include thousands of names of people blacklisted through the years by the Lord Chamberlain's office. One strict rule, still applied, is that no one is allowed to *seek* an invitation to a garden party, either directly or through a third person. Anyone caught lobbying for themselves or for anyone else is barred for life, and so is the person for whom they are trying to secure an invitation. And should anyone make a false claim that they are related to a certain individual, or use a title or a decoration to which they are not entitled, they will never be invited.

A special file, known as the infamous black box, contains anonymous letters from unpleasant, jealous people, including those who are outraged that particular people should have received a garden party invitation. These letters invariably contain unsavoury allegations about individuals. The Garden Party Office must check out each one by judicious questioning of the appropriate authorities. If the allegations are well-founded that person will not receive an invitation or will have the invitation rescinded. Equally, care is also taken to ensure the innocent are not victimised.

Returning, however, to the Lord Chamberlain's duties, these include the Crown Jewels which officially come under his jurisdiction. So do the Royal Bargemaster and the Queen's Watermen, responsible for the sovereign's safety when on board a craft on the River Thames. But perhaps the most extraordinary group of men are the queen's Swan Uppers – who still carry out their task today – catching and inspecting all the young cygnets on the River Thames each year. Swans that belong to the queen are not marked, while every other swan must be identified. These men are called 'Uppers' because when they sight a cygnet they shout 'Up, Up, Up' as they move in to catch and inspect the new arrival.

The Lord Chamberlain is also in charge of the Lords-in-Waiting who represent the queen at funerals or memorial services and greet important visitors; the Gentlemen Ushers who conduct guests around at official royal functions, making sure everyone is in their right place; Serjeant at Arms, the oldest armed royal guard in England but now purely a symbolic post, awarded for long service; the Central Chancery of the Orders of Knighthood which provides employment to a dozen older men whose full-time job is to record and maintain the lists of millions of people awarded a medal, a gong, a decoration or any honour. The name of every single man and woman, living or dead, who has ever received an honour is stored there.

The Master of the Household is in charge of the three hundred men and women whom it is considered are necessary to take care of Elizabeth's domestic needs and all those who live and work at the palace. His job can be described as that of a head waiter, a major domo, a restaurateur, a head porter, a head butler, employer, housekeeper and bookkeeper all rolled into one. For all this work he receives only £40,000 a year.

He divides his kingdom into three categories, food, general and housekeeping. About fifty men and women work in the royal kitchens as chefs, under-chefs, pastry cooks, vegetable cooks, kitchen porters and dish-washers; and another eighty as footmen, stewards, pages, upholsterers, seamstresses and cellar men – their main concerns are the palace's furniture and fittings. The remaining fifty are maids and cleaners.

Actually, it's quite easy to get a job at Buckingham Palace, indeed there are frequent vacancies, even in times of recession and severe unemployment. Many people are simply frightened of the daunting prospect of life below stairs in Buckingham Palace. And the pay is poor. Before Britain introduced a minimum wage, maids, cleaners and dish-washers earned only £80 a week. They are provided with training, a uniform and free meals, but there are no tips. Unmarried people can live in, occupying single rooms on the top floor. The single bedrooms are sparse and the bathrooms are located at the end of each corridor. Until the 1960s young men and women slept in separate dormitories where up to twenty people would be accommodated. Fun, but not very private. It goes without saying that boys and girls were strictly monitored and the dormitories more than one hundred yards apart.

Working in the palace is not nearly as bad at the end of this century as it was at the end of the nineteenth century. Then they worked 14 hours a day, six days a week under very strict conditions. Today, alarm clocks ring at 7.15 a.m. Breakfast for all the staff is served from 7.30 to 8.30 a.m., all with strict adherence to seniority: the members in one dining room, the officials in another and the staff in a third. A full English breakfast of orange juice, porridge or cereal, bacon and eggs and tea or coffee is provided in all three dining rooms. It's all self-service. Even when the entire royal family breakfasts together, for example at Windsor or Balmoral, the morning meal is a self-service affair.

After breakfast each goes about his or her work as in any other large establishment with breaks for coffee, lunch and tea. But life in Buckingham Palace is different. The atmosphere is quiet, sombre, monastic, some would say funereal and there is, of course, never-ending obsequious behaviour at all levels, some long-serving and senior servants demanding such treatment from those they see as their inferiors. Elizabeth, it seems, treats all her servants (for that is what they are) as equal to each other, demanding the same respect from her most senior courtiers as from her most junior footmen.

Whenever a royal servant meets the queen in the palace he or she will either bow or drop a 'bob' curtsy but will never say 'hello' or 'good morning'. Every servant calls the queen 'Ma'am' and Prince Philip simply 'Sir'. If by chance a servant should meet Philip or any other member of the family while walking along a corridor the servant must wait until the royal person has passed by. Only then may they proceed. And under no circumstances must any servant talk to any member of the royal family unless spoken to. Still, my own experience of Buckingham Palace is that the attitude of all the staff, from the highest to the most junior, has been relaxed, none appearing nervous or agitated by their permanent proximity to the sovereign.

After dinner, at about 8 p.m., the footmen, pages and anyone else still working are finally free to come and go as they please. Friends are allowed to visit the palace but must be out by ten o'clock. Overnight visitors are strictly forbidden and, if a man or woman lets anyone, of either sex, stay overnight, they are fired.

Senior courtiers do enjoy some privileges which are not given to the most junior dish-washer. One is the palace indoor swimming pool. Senior members of the household can use the pool in the early morning but never when a member of the royal family is there. Indeed, if a courtier is in the pool when a member of the family wishes to swim they must immediately leave the pool. Princess Diana used the pool more than any other member of the family and she liked to have a good swim most mornings. She always swam alone.

The keeper of the privy purse looks after the queen's private financial affairs. He is also called her Treasurer and in that capacity keeps an eye, with her full permission, on her various bank accounts. His other responsibilities include the finances of the royal estates, the royal horse stud and the not inconsequential expenses of the queen's favourite hobby, horse racing.

The current keeper of the privy purse is Major Sir Shane Blewitt and is next to Sir Robin Janvrin in order of precedence. Now that the queen has agreed to pay income tax, like every other British citizen, Sir Shane will have to deal with the tax inspectors. The finances of the royal family, and particularly those of Elizabeth, are complex and have until now remained secret.

Sir Shane is the one man who knows how much the queen is really worth. For years it has been accepted that the queen is one of the world's wealthiest women. On the surface it does appear that Elizabeth is a billionaire many times over but that is a false picture of her wealth for the great majority of her surpassed fortune is not hers at all but owned by the state.

A committee for the crown lands published a special report in

1955 detailing the queen's estate. No list of the queen's English properties was meant to exist, yet the report contained one. It revealed she owned 2,000 buildings in London, among them part of Regent Street, office blocks, a number of embassies, hotels and stores including the famous Liberty's. Outside London she owned 400,000 acres of land, the bed of the sea three miles off shore and almost all foreshores. She also owns Buckingham Palace and Windsor Castle. Today, however, all these are classed as crown estates and none of the income goes to the queen. For most purposes, the crown estates are now state-owned.

The queen inherited the world's largest collection of jewels in private hands, the crown jewels alone being incalculable in value. She also inherited the greatest array of paintings in private hands including Canalettos, Holbeins, Leonardo da Vincis, Michelangelos, Raphaels and Van Dycks; a magnificent stamp collection, wonderful tapestries and a vast array of French antique furniture. But all these are the inalienable property of the monarchy which she could never sell.

Some newspapers have suggested she is worth £4 billion, others £7 billion. But that would include such items as the crown jewels, Buckingham Palace, the Royal Art Collection and other inherited wealth which belongs to the nation, and is only entrusted to the monarch for his or her lifetime. They too cannot be included in her fortune.

Elizabeth's *personal* wealth includes only her stock portfolio, Balmoral and Sandringham, which together are worth about £100 million along with her string of race horses. The only guideline ever volunteered came in 1972 when Lord Cobbold, then Lord Chamberlain, in evidence to a House of Commons committee examining royal finances, said, 'Estimates of Her Majesty's private wealth as being between £50 million and £100 million are highly exaggerated.'

At that time her stock portfolio was probably worth only £35 million. Sensibly invested in UK shares, it should have grown to about £600 million by 1999 if all dividends had been re-invested and the queen had not spent any of the capital. But she has spent most of the dividends and occasionally dug deep into her capital, mainly to help other members of the royal family and pay for the upkeep of her personal homes, Balmoral and Sandringham. Today, her stock portfolio is worth approximately £100 million, earning perhaps £7 million a year.

The queen's other private income comes from the Duchy of Lancaster. The Duchy consists of large tracts of land, farms and property in six different counties as well as the piece of ground on which stands the famous Savoy Hotel in London. Passed down from monarch to monarch since 1399 when Henry IV was on the throne, whoever becomes monarch automatically inherits all the Duchy and its wealth and property, tax free of course. This income, which amounts to about £1.5 million a year after all expenditure, is paid directly into Elizabeth's private bank account.

In reality, Elizabeth has at her disposal her income of about £5 million from stock investments, plus perhaps another £1 million from the Duchy of Lancaster, an annual income of £6 million. Her annual income goes on staff pensions, various amounts to minor royals for carrying out their duties, numerous charitable donations, her racing stables and string of horses, and her extensive wardrobe, which is absolutely necessary for her role as queen. In reality, Elizabeth is certainly not among the world's wealthiest women.

The keeper of the privy purse must check all the civil list finances, those monies voted to the monarch by parliament to enable her to pay her staff, run her palaces, operate her aircraft and boats; in other words the money needed to perform her duty as Head of State. The total cost for the queen, the royal family and the services it needs to function amount to approximately £9 million a year, of which about 70 per cent is spent on staff salaries.

The civil list does not include a salary for the monarch or any other members of the royal family. Every penny has to be accounted for: over and above the civil list, the government meets other royal expenses. In 1992–93, for example, the upkeep of the royal palaces – Buckingham Palace, Windsor Castle, Kensington Palace, St James's Palace, Hampton Court and Holyroodhouse – cost about £30 million; the Queen's Flight, about £8 million; the Royal Yacht *Britannia*, £10 million and the royal train another £3 million – a total of £51 million, all paid for by the government.

The crown equerry is another man of considerable importance. Officially responsible for the Royal Mews he is in fact in charge of literally everything that takes place outside the palaces. That includes the five Rolls-Royce limousines painted in Royal maroon and the chauffeurs, all the gardens and grounds, the horses and the priceless collection of state coaches, landaus and carriages. In Victoria's day there were more than two hundred horses in the Royal Mews at Buckingham Palace, and even today there are 20 – 30 bays and 10 greys – all used for ceremonial purposes. At first glance the job may not seem arduous. However, in addition to the normal daily duties, an average of 150 events take place each year.

Then there are those ubiquitous women whom people always hear mentioned but never seem to see – the ladies-in-waiting. All female members of the royal family have ladies-in-waiting but none are so vital or important as those who wait on the queen. Whenever Elizabeth sets forth from any of her palaces on any occasion, whether it be a ten-minute meeting or a full-blown month-long foreign visit, she is accompanied by at least one, usually two, ladies-in-waiting. They are the invisible but indispensable aides who smooth the way, chat to a dignitary, check the queen's dress and stand ready for any emergency.

Today Elizabeth has 14 ladies who take turns to be on call and who are on duty at all times of the day and night. It is the most extraordinary job which carries no pay whatsoever and no perks, except that their role is the most important position in terms of status in class-conscious British society. Ladies-in-waiting work, live and have the ear of the most important person in the land, the queen.

A good lady-in-waiting is discreet and tactful; she displays refinement, taste, a ready smile and the ability to conduct small talk with anyone. She must also know when to hold her tongue, which means most of her time on duty. She must know how to dress in such a fashion that she never detracts from Elizabeth's limelight. She must also learn to smile discreetly: on most occasions she will ride in the chauffeur-driven limousine sitting beside the queen but they must never smile too much, nor appear more enthusiastic than the sovereign.

When the queen is entertaining, talking to guests, seating people and chatting to visitors, a lady-in-waiting is always present to hold bouquets and presents given to the queen; to take any messages; to provide an arm or a hand if necessary; to relay phone calls; to check what Elizabeth is being given to eat and drink; to be on hand with Elizabeth's favourite Malvern mineral water, headache pills, handkerchief or, on rare occasions, with any money she may require. They also deal with Elizabeth's personal correspondence while one or two ladies also do some of Elizabeth's personal shopping.

In fact, these women are considered so important that the senior ones are given titles. The most senior is mistress of the robes who, by tradition, is a Duchess; then there are two ladies of the bedchamber, always peeresses, and two women of the bedchamber, daughters of aristocrats. The rest are described as extra ladies. Most duties in fact are carried out by the four women of the bedchamber, who are younger, more agile and more capable of sustaining the sometimes arduous travel and long hours involved.

Finally, there are those important but faceless people who care for all the queen's inherited wealth: the paintings, drawings, engravings and etchings, the furniture and the exquisite *objets d'art* which number about one million different items and are part of the royal collection.

Management consultants, hired in 1986 to reduce the royal retinue, recommended that all the paintings, the library and the works of art should be put under the direction of one man, Sir Oliver Millar. Sir Geoffrey de Bellaigue now holds that post. From this great collection Elizabeth insists a handsome profit must be made, because there is no other revenue for the royal collection except the queen's own purse. For example, whenever a photograph of one of the queen's pictures, paintings or works of art is used anywhere in the world, in any form, a reproduction fee is paid. In this way, not only are the running costs kept to a minimum but the salaries of those employed in the department are covered.

There are craftsmen constantly engaged in restoring furniture, preserving the *objets d'art*, cleaning the paintings, keeping the superb collection in perfect condition. Three people, working full time, look after the three hundred clocks in the queen's four residences. Elizabeth decreed, again following advice, that every single one of the one million pieces in the royal collection should be categorised and stored on a computer. That enormous task is still going on, and some eight years later a small team of photographers is still engaged in photographing, printing and developing pictures of every single item so that a precise and detailed record can be obtained.

This is the way Elizabeth likes assignments carried out, to her wishes, unhurriedly and diligently with care and attention to detail. Ever since she was a little girl Elizabeth has been like that, careful and sure-footed, but always with a quiet determination, and a confidence that her wishes will always be carried out. For the greater part of her reign that systematic way of doing things has worked without fail. But today the world is moving much faster, and the great institutions on which she has built her monarchy are no longer so steady. It is unclear whether the old approach will continue to suffice, or if a new one is necessary to keep the influence and authority of the monarchy from slipping away.

14. ELIZABETH AND HER PRIME MINISTERS

When Margaret Thatcher became Prime Minister at the age of 54 in May 1979, Elizabeth was 53 and had been on the throne nearly thirty years. There had never before been a woman prime minister. For most of her life Elizabeth had known the politicians who became Prime Ministers for some years as they climbed the political ladder, but Margaret Thatcher was different. She was unknown to the queen. She had held a cabinet position under Edward Heath's premiership in the early 1970s and had been leader of the Opposition since 1975 and yet Elizabeth had rarely had a long conversation with her – she had certainly never had an intimate head-to-head chat in private over political or any other matters.

Elizabeth, of course, followed every general election with great interest. Now from her private sitting room Elizabeth watched on television as Mrs Thatcher entered No. 10 Downing Street for the first time as premier and recited a magnanimous exhortation from St Francis of Assisi:

'Where there is discord, may we bring harmony,
Where there is error, may we bring truth,
Where there is doubt, may we bring faith,
Where there is despair, may we bring hope.'

When Elizabeth met Mrs Thatcher at the first weekly audience she asked whether St Francis's words were the basis of her political creed. 'Absolutely,' Mrs Thatcher replied, 'Absolutely.'

Later, as Mrs Thatcher confronted the trade unions and seemed to attack the very fabric of Britain's welfare state, Elizabeth commented to a friend about her own sadness that Mrs Thatcher seemed to have forgotten the words of St Francis.

In retrospect, Margaret Thatcher, still finding her way as premier during those early months, did not know how to treat Elizabeth, a woman whom she had been brought up by her royalist parents to respect and admire, if not revere. While Mrs Thatcher never appeared nervous in confronting her politcial opponents or her cabinet colleagues, she did find her weekly audiences with Elizabeth somewhat difficult.

She would arrive every Tuesday evening between fifteen minutes and half an hour early for her private chat, whereas other Prime Ministers would usually arrive, as requested, the required five minutes before the appointed hour. Mrs Thatcher would read through her notes and chat with one of Elizabeth's senior advisers, while waiting for the summons from the queen.

After a few weeks, a palace adviser suggested to Mrs Thatcher that she might like to save time and leave No. 10 a little later. Mrs Thatcher replied that the reason she left so early was to give herself sufficient leeway in case of heavy traffic. It was an interesting reply for her to make because Buckingham Palace is only half a mile from Downing Street and the Prime Minister's car is always flanked by police outriders who ensure that the traffic gives way to the Prime Minister.

Her reply suggested her nervousness at having to talk for 30 minutes with the queen from a subservient position. The daughter of an alderman from middle England, Mrs Thatcher had achieved a remarkable rise to the pinnacle of power through her dogged determination and political good fortune. She also knew that her power could be swept away within hours either by her Conservative party colleagues or by the voters in a general election, while the queen would remain in power till the day she died or chose to step aside.

Elizabeth could have seen Mrs Thatcher as soon as she arrived at the palace so that her Prime Minister did not have to wait, patiently, for the appointed time. But that was not Elizabeth's nature. She has always demanded punctuality which she believes shows respect, not for her, but for the monarchy. And that was the lesson she continued to give Mrs Thatcher – respect for the monarchy was paramount; prime ministers had to wait. Of course, being forced to wait riled the already uncomfortable Mrs Thatcher.

Those who saw Mrs Thatcher in company with the queen noted that her behaviour was contrary to her usual rather bossy nature. Margaret Thatcher would curtsy far more deeply and bow her head far lower than most women when meeting the queen in public as though trying to exaggerate her respect. As one South American ambassador noted, 'Watching Mrs Thatcher curtsy was like watching a magnificent crimson sun sink beneath the horizon.'

The Prime Minister held a deeply royalist view of the monarchy. In an interview, Mrs Thatcher paid tribute not only to the constitution, based on a hereditary monarchy – like Britain's – but also to the work of the monarch. In so doing, of course, she paid unsolicited praise to Elizabeth herself.

'A monarchy, a hereditary monarchy,' Mrs Thatcher said, 'is wonderfully trained, in duty and in leadership. It understands example, which is always there, which is above politics, for which the whole nation has an affection and which is a symbol of patriotism . . . It gives a nation stability and assurance . . . It is not only a symbol of unity, but you respect and admire the monarch as well.'

Margaret Thatcher began her relationship in awe of Elizabeth but that was to change as Mrs Thatcher became more and more confident, more in control of her party, her cabinet colleagues, the House of Commons and the country. Friction between the two women developed which never disappeared.

Margaret Thatcher's long period in office – from May 1979 to November 1990 – was remarkable in post-war Britain, but for many she had become too authoritarian and over-confident. Indeed, many voters considered that Mrs Thatcher had became more royal than the monarchy itself. And Elizabeth was one of the first to note her regal ways.

At the close of the Conservative Party Conference in October 1990 – when Mrs Thatcher was still leader – the entire assembly rose and in customary style stood respectfully as the National Anthem was played. As they stood singing, the BBC television cameras panned slowly along the government ministers standing on the platform, and closed in on the face of Mrs Thatcher just as the last line 'Long to reign over us, God save the queen', was sung. Even the hundreds gathered in the hall witnessed the scene on huge screens on either side of the platform.

Mrs Thatcher, standing erect as a guardsman and dressed in her royal blue suit, even looked suitably regal. She was at the height of her power, treating the electors, some foreign ministers and all her own cabinet ministers as mere subjects to heed her words of wisdom and obey her commands.

One apocryphal story illustrates the degree of her power and dominance at that time and how people felt about her. The head waiter serving dinner to Mrs Thatcher and the entire cabinet asks what she would like to eat. She replies, 'A small steak please.'

The head waiter then asks, 'And the vegetables, Ma'am?'

'Oh, they'll have the same.'

It was obviously only a House of Commons joke, but the story touched a raw nerve in the country and particularly among government ministers. For that was the way the nation perceived Mrs Thatcher had come to treat even her cabinet members.

There were no such jokes, however, between Elizabeth and Mrs Thatcher during their eleven years of weekly meetings. This was unusual for Elizabeth who had got on remarkably well with most of her prime ministers, often sharing light-hearted comments, beginning with the father–daughter relationship with Winston Churchill back in the 1950s.

It had been expected that the two women would reach an early understanding for they had much in common. Both were mature women with families, holding the most responsible positions, sacrificing their lives for the nation and devoted to duty. Neither of them was particularly interested in fashion, music or the arts either. And yet this is where the similarities end.

The product of small-town life in Grantham, Lincolnshire, Mrs Thatcher grew up above a grocer's store where her father, the grocer, was enmeshed in local politics. Her quick brain and determination helped her to university and she carved out a major political life for herself. Elizabeth, born into a royal household and destined to be queen, was a country woman at heart. They had no common interests. The irreverent British TV puppet show *Spitting Image* portrayed Elizabeth and Mrs Thatcher as having nothing in common except that they both clung, leech-like, to their handbags.

The first hint of trouble between the two women came in 1982 when the political journalist Anthony Sampson wrote that 'the weekly meetings between the queen and Mrs Thatcher are dreaded by at least one of them'. Mrs Thatcher may have been nervous to start with, but from early on, Elizabeth had perceived a woman who seemed to think she should lecture and pontificate rather than hold a discussion and inform her sovereign about what was going on. 'Dreaded' may have been an overstatement, but it is most likely that neither looked forward to the meetings with any enthusiasm.

As we have already seen, Walter Bagshot's *English Constitution*, published in 1867, stated that 'the sovereign has three rights – the right to be consulted, the right to encourage, the right to warn.' From the moment Elizabeth became queen, this short, pithy, most accurate sentence became her creed. She has lived by it ever since in all her relations with successive Prime Ministers.

Mrs Thatcher's regal approach to her own position was a source of some amusement for Elizabeth. It is not known exactly when Mrs Thatcher began using the royal 'we' when referring to herself alone. She used the famous royal expression many times and yet it is an expression which Elizabeth has never used in public except, of course, when she is outlining the government's programme at the start of a new parliamentary session. One of Mrs Thatcher's more famous examples came *en route* to Moscow when she said, 'We are in the fortunate position in Britain of being, as it were, the senior position in power.'

Another instance which caused much amusement and scoffing throughout the country occurred before a television interviewer, when she rejoiced at the news that her daughter-in-law had just given birth, saying 'We are a grandmother'!

Her regal attitude also had its serious side. Many people, both inside and outside parliament, believed Mrs Thatcher deliberately used the royal 'we' to suggest her own near-regal, permanent position in the nation's political life, just like that of the monarch.

Like the queen, Mrs Thatcher did not surround herself with women, preferring to seek men to advise and work with her. Even today, save for ladies-in-waiting, maids and dressers, there are virtually no women employed by Elizabeth who work closely with her. All senior advisers, courtiers and those in charge of various departments throughout the palace are men. And that is Elizabeth's choice. During her 11 years as Premier, Mrs Thatcher was even more dismissive of the possibility of employing women in senior government positions. She did have women in her cabinet, but not for very long. Whenever a cabinet vacancy came up it was frequently suggested that perhaps she would want a female replacement. Every time, Mrs Thatcher replied firmly in the negative, but gave no explanation.

And Mrs Thatcher wasn't only dismissive of women. Elizabeth was informed, unofficially, by one of her mandarins that Mrs Thatcher was having problems with her senior civil servants: relations were described as 'dreadful'. Mrs Thatcher had made little attempt to conceal her contempt and mistrust of their ineffectual and detached attitude to her priorities. Elizabeth was told in 1980 that her Prime Minister had held a dinner for permanent secretaries – very senior civil servants – which had been a disaster. She berated them all evening. In the end she insulted them all by saying, 'If only I had officials like the man [herself] they had come to see, things would be a lot better.'

At one of her subsequent weekly meetings, Elizabeth let Mrs

Thatcher know that she had been informed of the problems she was having with her civil servants. Mrs Thatcher told her, 'There is no problem. You know what servants are. I just wanted to put the fear of God into them.'

Problems continually arose between Buckingham Palace and No. 10 Downing Street. Through the 1980s there was a spate of air disasters. It has always been the tradition of the royal family that in such circumstances a member of The Firm would be selected by the queen to travel to the scene of the tragedy to show the nation that the royals cared. However, Elizabeth has always told the respective authorities that she would not attend immediately after a disaster for fear of getting in the way or being a nuisance when the emergency services needed all their energies to care for the dead and injured. Thus members of the royal family would usually arrive a few days after a disaster.

Before Mrs Thatcher became Prime Minister, no issues arose over such matters between the palace and No. 10. Discussions would take place and a decision taken by the queen or a member of the immediate family was always granted so that the royals would not be seen to be upstaged by a politician. Mrs Thatcher put an end to that cosy relationship. She wanted the nation to see *her* caring side.

Despite Mrs Thatcher's insistence that her instinct was to rush to the scene of a disaster to offer comfort and help, some people believed she was not unaware of the political gain. Since she would rush off to any tragedy without consulting or advising the palace, her behaviour did not help the relationship between the queen's advisers and Mrs Thatcher's senior aides.

So angry did Elizabeth become with Mrs Thatcher's behaviour on such occasions that she ordered her advisers to collate evidence of people's reaction to the absence of a member of the royal family at the scene of a disaster. The report came back that such an absence was seen as negligence on the part of the royal family. 'If Mrs Thatcher can arrive within hours, why can't a royal?' was the usual complaint.

Elizabeth discussed the problem with Mrs Thatcher and gave her the evidence of the palace research. Mrs Thatcher not only ignored it but even issued orders to her aides that they must never permit the royals to arrive before she did at the scene of any disaster. Such behaviour explains the occasional icy coolness that existed when the two women met each Tuesday evening.

Hugo Young in *One of Us*, his fine biography of Mrs Thatcher, states that when the cross-channel ferry, *The Herald of Free Enterprise*, sank off Zeebrugge, Belgium, in March 1987, with the loss of 200

British lives, Mrs Thatcher 'firmly instructed her staff to see to it that the palace presence, in the persons of the Duke and Duchess of York, did not upstage her own'. Knowing how sensitive the queen felt on such occasions, the Prime Minister's actions indicate to what depths their relationship must have sunk to treat Elizabeth with such disdain and disrespect.

Some have suggested the formal relationship between the two women was 'frigid', others that it was 'cool', still more in the palace and government circles preferred the word 'professional'. But their answers may have been diplomatic. One senior palace adviser commented, 'Mrs Thatcher was punctilious in all modes of address and courtesies. She acknowledged, of course, the queen's right to be kept informed and to be consulted. On the queen's side, she acknowledged, as she must, a Prime Minister's right finally to take the decisions. Her Majesty is very capable of offering her own opinions about things, when she holds them, and would certainly express them if they were contrary to those of her Prime Minister. However, once she had done that she would feel that she had exercised her constitutional rights and prerogatives, and it was the Prime Minister who had to take the decisions.'

In reality, Mrs Thatcher treated the queen in the same way as she treated her husband, Denis. 'Of course I consult Denis,' she once said. 'Then I make the decision.'

Another major area of conflict between the two matriarchs concerned the Commonwealth, that great conglomerate of emerging nations, mostly from the third world, many former members of the old British Empire, on which the British Government once boasted 'the sun never set'.

At the end of the Second World War some said Britain lost an Empire without finding a role. Elizabeth was determined to do all she could to promote the Commonwealth of Nations into a force for good throughout the world. She took the concept of a former Conservative minister Rab Butler, the same man who had tutored Charles during his three years at Cambridge. Butler's vision consisted of 'a Commonwealth of independent nations, emerging out of an Empire purged from superiority of race and the false pride of dominion'.

When Elizabeth succeeded to the throne in 1952 there were only a handful of Commonwealth nations, and many people felt that with the emergence of a European common market the Commonwealth of Nations would wither and die. Far from it. She insists on attending every single two-yearly Commonwealth conference where she has private meetings with every Head of State. On occasion, Elizabeth has acted as a diplomatic go-between, for many heads of Commonwealth countries remain in power for decades and they happily discuss their nation's problems with the queen. They not only trust her but realise that she has no political axe to grind.

Mrs Thatcher had little time for the Commonwealth. Sir Shridath Ramphal, former Commonwealth Secretary-General, once stated: 'Mrs Thatcher came to the Commonwealth not knowing and not caring very much about it. Then she came to like the style of the heads-of-government meetings, but grew more and more irritable with the critics of her South Africa policy. Mrs Thatcher argued that imposing sanctions against South Africa only hurt the black majority. She had a schizophrenic attitude where the Commonwealth was concerned, and I must say I never felt that there was a wholly relaxed attitude between herself and the queen. No warmth on either side.'

Throughout the 1980s Elizabeth became less and less impressed with her Prime Minister as well as her attitude and policies regarding the unemployed and the underprivileged. Mrs Thatcher's great battle was fought against the National Union of Mineworkers who feared their jobs were at risk under a Thatcher government. As the strike ran into weeks and months, and miners' families found life extremely difficult, Elizabeth repeatedly raised the question of miners' wives and their families with Mrs Thatcher during their weekly meetings. The atmosphere became increasingly frosty as the queen asked pointed questions which Mrs Thatcher found irritating.

But her second general election victory gave her a fresh mandate and further confidence to continue her 'Thatcherite' policies. Elizabeth could only note that her Prime Minister had the continued confidence of the electorate and, as a result, their weekly chats became less confrontational and more amenable. The two women seemed to come to an understanding: they had to work together so they should make as good a fist of it as possible.

But the whiff of confrontation between the two women emerged again from the palace and No. 10, and the media sniffed a good story. The problems between the two women exploded into the open in 1986 when an article in the *Sunday Times* entitled 'The African Queen', suggested the queen was disturbed at what she sensed was a lack of compassion in some of Mrs Thatcher's policies towards the underprivileged in Britain and her attitude towards sanctions on South Africa. During Mrs Thatcher's 11 years of premiership, the poorest among the electorate became financially worse off. And Elizabeth believed that trade sanctions against South Africa should *not* be lifted. At the time, they were two of the most divisive domestic and foreign issues facing parliament.

The palace was horrified. Never had any suggestion been made at any time during her reign that the queen wanted to interfere with government policies, whether Labour or Tory. Senior courtiers were most concerned because, constitutionally, the British monarch must not interfere in any way with the policies of the government. In any matters concerning politics, both domestic and foreign, the monarch is not permitted to become involved or even utter an opinion in public. If the monarch did so it is possible the great mass of the people might prefer the policies of the monarch to those of the elected government and that could lead to political turmoil and all sorts of constitutional problems.

But the *Sunday Times* accurately summed up the Queen's views. Elizabeth has always held the vision of a 'One-World', working towards the unification of black and white nations. She believed fervently that South Africa should be punished for its apartheid policies, its suppression of free thought and imprisonment of government critics.

The crisis over South Africa threatened the break-up of Elizabeth's beloved Commonwealth and, as its head, she was determined to use her influence to prevent that. By doing so she set herself against Mrs Thatcher. She let the Commonwealth Secretary-General know that if there was anything she could do to save the situation then she would happily use her influence. The row over sanctions ended with sixteen Commonwealth nations boycotting the Commonwealth Games of 1986; but the Commonwealth remained intact. No other matter of policy throughout Mrs Thatcher's office proved so divisive to her relationship with Elizabeth.

There were other differences. One involved the Church of England of which the queen is also head. Margaret Thatcher, a devout churchgoer, had numerous run-ins with the Palace of Lambeth, the church's London headquarters. She demanded a greater say in the appointment of bishops but they, understandably, did not want Mrs Thatcher poking her nose into affairs of which she knew little and had no experience.

As Prime Minister, however, Mrs Thatcher had the right to 'advise' the queen on her choice of senior bishops. A commission produced two names and handed them to the Prime Minister who selected one and sent it to the queen for approval. Elizabeth was given no choice; she was obliged to sign the recommendation. The fact that Mrs Thatcher acted in that arbitrary way, in effect negating the queen's accepted participation in the appointment of a senior bishop, incensed Elizabeth. No other Prime Minister had acted in such a manner over the appointment of senior bishops, preferring instead to discuss the rival candidates with the queen and then offering her a choice.

Towards the end of her premiership the time came for the appointment of a new Archbishop of Canterbury, the highest office in the church. Two names were put forward: Dr John Habgood, the Archbishop of York and the favoured choice; and Dr George Carey, Bishop of Bath and Wells, a 25 to 1 outsider and the Prime Minister's choice. Once again, Elizabeth had to honour Mrs Thatcher's recommendation but she was not at all happy.

George Carey was the personification of Thatcher's self-made man: the son of a cockney hospital porter, he had left school at 15 and worked his way to the top of an intensely political clerical establishment. Today, eight years after his appointment, critics from within now openly attack his leadership which has led the church from one crisis to another; his promised decade of evangelism has degenerated into a series of crises and a vacuum of leadership, with the very legitimacy of the Anglican communion as the established church of the land now in question. Thatcher would also have known that Elizabeth much preferred Dr Habgood, a highly intelligent man, a leading liberal and a friend of Elizabeth's.

Cynics muttered that the decision to go for a relatively inexperienced figure was Margaret Thatcher's final revenge on the church which, under Lord Runcie, had frequently challenged her policies.

Margaret Thatcher was the first woman Prime Minister of Britain and the first Elizabeth had to deal with. It was perhaps natural there should be some settling-in difficulties but those who suggest that the two women were on friendly terms are somewhat fanciful. Their meetings frequently proved difficult. Any questions Elizabeth asked were often taken by Mrs Thatcher as a criticism of her and her government, which riled a woman of Mrs Thatcher's character, particularly as she grew in confidence and authority.

Mrs Thatcher was never happy with her relationship with Buckingham Palace. In an angry aside, she once commented after a row with senior palace aides, 'Politics is meant to be a dirty game but we politicians could never teach those at the palace anything.'

Elizabeth knew from past experience that one day Mrs Thatcher would go the way of all prime ministers – removed from office. But no one had any idea that the departure of Margaret Thatcher in

November 1990 would be so dramatic. She was still Prime Minister with a large majority in the House of Commons and, so she believed, in absolute control of her party and cabinet. But the Tories knew from their grassroots supporters in the constituencies that Mrs Thatcher was becoming a liability and that under her, the Tories were likely to lose the next general election. Tory leaders gathered and plotted her downfall and Mrs Thatcher realised too late that her support inside the party had vanished. She quit six weeks after standing queen-like at the Conservative Party Conference. The strong woman premier who had appeared so tough and invulnerable for so long left No. 10 in the back of her official Jaguar, with tears streaming down her face.

In her memoirs, *The Downing Street Years*, published in October 1993, Mrs Thatcher barely mentioned the queen in her 900-page tome. Only in chapter one does Mrs Thatcher write of her relationship with Elizabeth: 'The audience at which one receives the queen's authority to form a government comes to most prime ministers only once in a lifetime. The authority is unbroken when a sitting prime minister wins an election, and so it never had to be renewed throughout the years I was in office.

'All audiences with the queen take place in strict confidence – a confidentiality which is vital to the working of both government and constitution. I was to have such audiences with Her Majesty once a week, usually on a Tuesday, when she was in London and sometimes elsewhere when the royal family were at Windsor or Balmoral . . .

'Perhaps it is permissible to make just two points. Anyone who imagines that they are a mere formality or confined to social niceties is quite wrong; they are quietly business-like and Her Majesty brings to bear a formidable grasp of current issues and breadth of ex-perience. And although the press could not resist the temptation to suggest disputes between the Palace and Downing Street, especially on Commonwealth affairs, I always found the queen's attitude towards the work of government absolutely correct.

'Of course, under the circumstances, stories of clashes between "two powerful women" were just too good not to make up. In general, more nonsense was written about the so-called "feminine factor" during my time in office than about almost anything else. I was always asked how it felt to be a woman prime minister. I would reply: "I don't know: I've never experienced the alternative."'

All other references to the queen in Mrs Thatcher's memoirs are only mentions that she was in attendance.

Throughout her forty-year reign, Elizabeth has found friendship, even affection, with a number of her former Prime Ministers which now number nine men and one woman. Framed photographs up the stairway at No. 10 start with Winston Churchill and continue through Anthony Eden, Harold Macmillan, Alec Douglas-Home, Harold Wilson, Edward Heath, James Callaghan, Margaret Thatcher, John Major and Tony Blair.

James Callaghan (1976–79), with whom Elizabeth got on remarkably well, commented after leaving office about his relationship with her, 'What one gets is friendliness but not friendship. Indeed, one gets a great deal of friendliness. And Prime Ministers also get a great deal of understanding of their problems – without the queen sharing them, since she is outside politics . . . Of course she may have hinted at things, but only on the rarest occasions do I remember her saying, "Why don't you do this, that or the other?" . . . She is pretty detatched on all that. But she's very interested in the political side – who's going up the ladder and who's going down.'

Lord Charteris, who was Elizabeth's first Private Secretary and saw six premiers come and go, commented, 'The universal response is one of admiration, respect and a warm regard for the queen. They all come out of the audience on the balls of their feet, having gone in on their heels. She obviously has the same tonic effect on them as she does on others.'

It seems that the two Labour leaders, Harold Wilson and James Callaghan, were Elizabeth's favourite premiers; she found them more friendly than some of the Tories, particularly Edward Heath, whom she found to be 'very hard work'. As yet, there is no information concerning Elizabeth's relationship with Tony Blair except that he appears somewhat nervous whenever they meet.

Her relationship with Churchill was difficult because she had relied so much on him when she became queen in 1952. Churchill was almost certainly the greatest Englishman of the century: statesman, politician, writer and painter. He had led his country to victory in a war that it had been close to losing. In 1953 he was venerated almost like a god. He had not only been Elizabeth's hero but her father's too, and, most importantly, he was the man who had put such faith and power in the hands of Lord Mountbatten. Their relationship was also difficult for Churchill. In their own way, each was nervous of the other but for very different reasons.

Elizabeth used to worry that anything she said to Churchill might sound stupid; he was nervous, as many old men are, at the prospect of having to chat with a pretty young woman who understandably made him feel positively ancient. The old man, who was 80 years of age when Elizabeth became queen, told his Secretary Jock Colville at the time, 'How can I adapt to her after serving her father for seven years? I don't know her. She's a mere child. I knew the king so well and had a deep affection for him.' And that was the trouble. Churchill, who was then becoming senile, did treat Elizabeth as a child and explained everything to her. It was difficult for Elizabeth, too, because she realised she had so much to learn. It was during these years that she clung tenaciously to her Uncle Dickie for advice, a relationship which was to continue until his murder in 1979.

Fortunately, the nervousness on both sides disappeared and when Churchill finally left office in April 1955, a special relationship had developed between the old man and the young queen. Elizabeth has always said there was a special feeling for Winston Churchill that she never had with any other prime minister. When someone asked her, 'With which of your prime ministers did you enjoy your audiences most?' she replied immediately, 'Winston of course, because it was always such fun.' And she has never changed that view.

According to Churchill the 'fun' he had with Elizabeth consisted mainly of racing talk. It was true that his Tuesday audiences got longer and longer, sometimes lasting nearly two hours instead of the usual 30 minutes. After most meetings with the queen, Churchill told his Private Secretary rather mischievously, 'Nothing to report; we talked about racing.'

Undeniably Elizabeth's three years with Churchill helped the young sovereign gain confidence and experience in her new role that stood her in good stead in the years to come. When Elizabeth became more confident she took the advice of Lord Charteris and Dickie Mountbatten and began to show her mettle, deliberately putting the premier of the day under pressure. She would read her state papers with great care and then ask questions relating to them, often of obscure matters, which sometimes caught out the Prime Minister, making him feel unprepared. It was a wonderful way of making Prime Ministers realise that she not only read the state papers but understood them. It also ensured that no Prime Minister ever treated her as someone who did not know precisely what was going on, gaining their lasting respect. It is a neat trick which Elizabeth has often used, sometimes to the annoyance and embarrassment of certain premiers.

As Harold Wilson confessed sometime after he left office, 'Whenever the queen quoted from a state paper that I hadn't read I felt rather like an unprepared schoolboy.'

Following in the footsteps of Churchill came Anthony Eden

(1955–57), who had been deputy to the grand old man for some years and who was eventually broken by the failure of the ill-judged Suez campaign of 1956. Apparently Elizabeth found Eden tense, a little twitchy and awkward to talk to.

But Elizabeth did get on well with Harold Macmillan (1957–63), an astute man who handled the young queen with gentleness and consideration. She had faith in his ability and experience and felt he was 'one of us', with his background of Eton and the Guards, and his pretence of being an amateur when it came to politics. In fact he was a professional to his finger tips.

The Scottish aristocrat, Sir Alec Douglas-Home (1963–4), who renounced his title in order to enter the House of Commons and take over the premiership, seemed 'at home' with the queen and her Scottish family: he shared their love of Scotland and the wild country north of the border. But he was not around long enough to build a real relationship with Elizabeth.

Harold Wilson (1964–70 and 1974–6) began his relationship with Elizabeth rather warily but ended up adoring her. As Richard Crossman, who served in Wilson's cabinet, related in his diaries, 'The nearer the queen they get the more the working-class members of the cabinet love her and she loves them.'

As Prime Minister John Major arrived at Buckingham Palace in November 1990 to accept the office of Prime Minister, a senior member of the royal household recalled, 'Her Majesty seemed very happy to welcome him. She was smiling broadly.'

At Tony Blair's first meeting with Elizabeth in May 1997, the incoming Prime Minister, a little nervous but with a smile on his face, checked first of all with household officials what was expected of this first audience. Elizabeth has taken to the youthful premier and apparently their weekly meetings have, thus far, been remarkably friendly affairs. She nevertheless finds it very difficult to refrain from intervening and advising a young man thirty years her junior who has no experience of high office – so different from the elderly Churchill with whom she began her reign.

Tony Blair won his spurs, however, in the aftermath of Diana's death. Through constant dialogue with senior members of the royal household, he urged Elizabeth and the family to fly from Balmoral to London to be seen by the public to be mourning the loss of Diana rather than staying aloof from the tragic scenes that gripped the capital, something which brought criticism from a grieving British public. In retrospect, Elizabeth saw the wisdom in this advice and now there is a greater sense of equality in their working relationship.

15. PRINCESS MICHAEL OF KENT

A chauffeur-driven car with an armed detective at the wheel arrives at the front door of a London house in a wealthy residential area of the capital. A young lady, immaculately and expensively dressed, sits discreetly in the back seat, her head slightly bowed, trying to look invisible. The chauffeur jumps smartly out of the car, opens the rear door and the young lady slides decoratively out and hurries across the pavement to the house. As she climbs the steps the door opens and she disappears inside. Outside, the chauffeur returns to his car to wait patiently.

After an hour or two the young woman, still immaculately dressed, re-appears. She does not look back as she hurries to the car and slides into the back seat. Within a second the car speeds away without the woman glancing or waving towards the house.

For most of that time, the young woman, a married lady of the royal House of Windsor, was making love to a man who was not her husband.

This was the secret life of three members of Britain's royal family in the '80s and '90s, all of them young women who led adulterous lives.

The first young woman, one of the most famous faces in the world, was Diana, Princess of Wales, married to Prince Charles, heir to the throne; the second Sarah, Duchess of York who married Prince Andrew, third in line of succession; the third, Princess Michael of Kent who married Prince Michael, the queen's first cousin. All three took lovers during those years: they indulged their passions in what they mistakenly believed were safe houses around London.

The houses of course were not safe – and the identities, backgrounds, jobs, personal lives – even the sexual preferences – of each and every man they took to bed was known not only to Britain's security services, but also to Sir Robert Fellowes, the queen's principal Private Secretary and to the royal police protection squad. More importantly, Elizabeth was fully informed about the adulterous behaviour of all three women. She knew the names and backgrounds of their lovers.

And yet Diana, Fergie and Marie-Christine threw caution to the wind as they recklessly indulged their lustful adventures in and around London during those years. Among senior officials at Buckingham Palace the three women became known as 'The Three Witches of Windsor'.

Princess Michael was the first to stray. Born Baroness Marie-Christine von Reibnitz in Czechoslovakia in January 1945, she was the daughter of Baron von Reibnitz, an SS Officer during the Second World War. Marie-Christine's mother and father separated after the war and Marie-Christine, her mother and brother emigrated to Australia in 1949 while her father went to live in Africa.

In Australia her mother remarried, this time to a Czechoslovakian Count, but once again there was no money in the family. They all lived in a charmless little house on the outskirts of Sydney. By the age of 18, Marie-Christine had decided she wanted to be rich. She was tall, with a good, strong figure, dark hair, a strikingly beautiful face and a charming, bubbly personality. She soon became part of the élite set of Australia's thrusting young rich men and women.

She felt she needed money to give herself the life she wanted so she joined J.Walter Thompson, the advertising agency, as a secretary and was popular with her fellow workers, particularly the young men. But they weren't wealthy enough, nor were they socially important.

She decided that with her background and title she could make more money as a dressmaker to the rich and famous and quit J.Walter Thompson to set up her own business. At 20 she met Ted Albert, the son of a wealthy Australian family of high social standing which had made its fortune by selling sheet music. Ted Albert's father, Alexis, had known Prince Philip during the war and he was also an honorary aide-de-camp to Sir John Northcott, then Governor of the State of New South Wales. Ted Albert was exactly the young man Marie-Christine wanted for a husband.

Despite Marie-Christine's titles however, and Ted Albert's passion for her, his mother took exception to Marie-Christine's background, dismissing her as a war-time immigrant, a new-Australian, not worthy of her son. She went so far as to ban her son from continuing the relationship, threatening to cut off his inheritance. Angry and humiliated, and realising she would never be allowed to marry young Ted, Marie-Christine quit Sydney and took a boat to London.

In Australia, Marie-Christine had discovered a useful gimmick, a way of making sure she was always noticed. Before going to the races or attending a charity bash she would telephone society editors of the Sydney newspapers and inform them that Baroness Marie-Christine von Reibnitz would be present, wearing whatever and partnered by so-and-so. As a result she appeared regularly in the social columns. In Britain she was determined to make a good marriage and decided to use the same technique to promote her ambitions, but it didn't work so well. Like other young starlets with obscure European titles in London at that time she discovered she was only one among many.

To make herself more socially acceptable, Marie-Christine took drastic action: she dropped her Australian twang, adopted a more sophisticated mid-European accent, changed from brunette to blonde and studied interior design at the Victoria and Albert Museum. But she needed to work to survive and joined Charles Baker, another up-market advertising agency. She was 22 and caught the eye of a number of wealthy, attractive men. She began to date in earnest, living life in the fast lane.

While flying to Austria for a wild boar hunt, Marie-Christine met her first husband Tom Trowbridge, a handsome banker. They both spoke German and amazingly Marie-Christine fell instantly in love. They were married just one year later. It was on her wedding day that Marie-Christine met her first member of the royal family, the bachelor Prince William of Gloucester, then 29, who was an old friend of Tom Trowbridge. Captivated by his friend's wife, Prince William became a regular visitor to their Chelsea home.

One day Prince William invited them for a weekend house party at his family home, Barnwell Manor, in Northamptonshire. Another guest was Prince Michael of Kent, then 28 and also a bachelor. A woman who attended the house party recalled later, 'By the end of that weekend, Marie-Christine had both princes eating out of her hand; she flirted outrageously with them and they did with her. She adored it.'

Back in London they virtually became a foursome with Marie-Christine the only woman among them. They attended parties together, went to dinners, social events and weekend house parties. Marie-Christine was in her element and those around her noted that she spent most of the time flirting with Prince William. A year later tragedy struck, and Prince William died in an air crash while piloting a light aircraft in the Goodyear Air Race.

Tom Trowbridge took a job in Bahrain and Marie-Christine joined him there for a while but Bahrain society wasn't big enough for Marie-Christine; she wanted to be back in London, enjoying the high society life, getting to know the royal family and, more importantly, being near the handsome Prince Michael.

Prince Michael was a charming, likeable bachelor who had spent most of his adult years out of the royal limelight in one of Britain's senior regiments, The Royal Scots Greys. There he enjoyed such a quiet life that no one realised he was the queen's first cousin. Not being the first-born he wasn't required to carry out any official royal duties and didn't want to either. He much preferred the seclusion of the Officers' Mess, where he was most popular. Bob-sleigh racing, for which he showed great talent and considerable courage, became his great hobby. He was somewhat shy of women and although he was often seen with different attractive young ladies on his arm he rarely became romantically involved with them. Marie-Christine would change all that.

For the next three years Tom Trowbridge worked in Bahrain, while in London, Marie-Christine spent as much time as possible mixing in the circles where she would constantly meet Prince Michael. And whenever she met him she would take the initiative, inviting him to various events, organising parties for them to attend together and making it obvious she wanted him.

According to Marie-Christine, their relationship began in a quiet, introspective way. 'For a long time Michael and I cried on each other's shoulders. For a year I saw him simply as a friend. Then, by 1975, I knew I was in love with him. Now I'm glad we had that time, because friendship is something you never lose – and when you are in a rocking chair, friendship is what counts.'

It became known that Michael and Marie-Christine were lovers. Whenever they were out together, at parties and dinners, Marie-Christine would spend the whole time on his arm, holding his hand, nuzzling his neck. On occasion he would appear rather embarrassed by her attentions, but he liked the fact that Marie-Christine was a striking, sexy young woman. When Marie-Christine and Tom Trowbridge were divorced in 1977 Tom Trowbridge's family and friends gave a great party for him to celebrate his freedom from her.

I came to know Marie-Christine around that time for she stabled her Arab horse at the same stables at Ham, near Richmond Park, where I kept my polo ponies. Marie-Christine, who rode out most days, was to say later, 'As luck and Cupid would have it, my beautiful dancing Arab steed fell madly in love with this rather churlish animal, ridden by Prince Michael, and from miles away would whinny and gallop up to him. Then it was "Oh, hello, what a surprise. How nice to see you."' She made it all sound like some cheap novelette.

There was, however, a problem: Marie-Christine was Catholic and she was divorced. Under the Royal Marriages Act of 1772, Prince Michael needed the queen's permission which, being over twenty-five, should have provided no obstacle. Elizabeth did not like the idea of Prince Michael marrying Marie-Christine, primarily because she was a divorced woman. She also knew about the young woman's background. She asked Sir Philip Moore, then Private Secretary, to organise a detailed briefing on her life, including her rather dubious ancestry and details of her earlier years in Australia. She was not impressed with what she read when the briefing was handed to her some weeks later. The palace was inadvertently helped by the press which had investigated Marie-Christine when it became public knowledge that she and Prince Michael seemed about to become engaged.

Elizabeth still believed that divorce was not only a taboo at court but she was deeply disturbed that a member of the royal family, particularly someone as close as her first cousin, could even countenance marrying a divorced person. Even if he was only sixteenth in line to succession, she still believed the royal family had to set an example and Prince Michael's plan to marry Marie-Christine set a very poor example indeed.

In early 1978, senior courtiers suggested to Prince Michael that he might be better advised to find a more suitable bride, primarily because of the queen's attitude to divorce and the effect it might have on the royal family. After all, it was only 40 years earlier that Britain's king had been stripped of his crown and exiled for the remainder of his days because he wanted to marry a divorced woman. Worse still from the queen's view, as Head of the Church of England and Defender of the Faith, this divorced woman was a Roman Catholic as well.

To circumvent the growing opposition to the marriage, Marie-Christine came up with a new idea which she believed would succeed; she would have her marriage to Tom Trowbridge annulled.

She immediately approached the Catholic Church and argued that her husband Tom Trowbridge had never wanted children, a claim considered good enough for the marriage to be annulled. However, in cases of annulment, the Catholic Church requires the spouse to give supporting evidence. Tom Trowbridge seemed somewhat taken aback by his ex-wife's allegation and even more so when he was not invited to give evidence to the Vatican in support. Nevertheless the Vatican granted an annulment to the marriage in 1978, and Marie-Christine immediately reverted to her maiden name, Baroness von Reibnitz. She was now free to marry whomsoever she wanted.

Elizabeth spoke to Princess Margaret about the whole matter, one reason being that 25 years earlier Margaret had been forbidden to marry a divorced man, Group-Captain Peter Townsend. Margaret was appalled that Marie-Christine, then 33, should be permitted to marry Prince Michael, primarily because she believed, from all the gossip, that Marie-Christine was an opportunist whose only reason for marrying Michael was to reach the ultimate social rung and become a member of the House of Windsor. She questioned Marie-Christine's love for Michael; hadn't she first fallen for Prince William and only changed tack on his untimely death?

Princess Margaret argued against Elizabeth giving her permission for yet another reason: Marie-Christine had happily married Tom Trowbridge in a Church of England ceremony, yet had claimed a sudden burst of Catholic religious fervour when she needed an annulment. The princess described Marie-Christine as 'an upstart'.

Before she married Prince Michael, Margaret wrote to Marie-Christine informing her that if she did not 'do the decent thing' and convert to the Church of England – the religion of the House of Windsor – she would never speak to her again. Marie-Christine did not convert and the enmity between the two women has continued to this day.

In desperation, Prince Michael turned to Uncle Dickie Mountbatten – Mountbatten was also his uncle – and appealed to him for help. Michael said that he was in love with Marie-Christine and wanted to marry her but he did not want to upset or anger the queen, nor did he want to do anything that might bring the royal family into disrepute.

Mountbatten asked him outright, 'What do you think would do more harm to the royal family, for you two to live in sin together or get married?' Michael shrugged his shoulders and replied with little conviction, 'Live in sin.'

'Right,' Mountbatten replied. 'Then if you are determined to live with this young woman we had better find a way for you to marry her. After all, she is not a shop girl. She comes from a good family. She's a natural.'

He invited Prince Michael and Marie-Christine to dinner and was rather taken by the flamboyant young woman. However, though he found her highly attractive and initially rather engaging, he did see another side to her. During the meal, he wrote a note and slipped it to his Private Secretary, John Barratt. It read, 'If that woman doesn't stop talking, I shall scream.'

Once again Mountbatten was in his element. Pitched into the centre of a family fracas, he found he could manipulate royal events yet again. After much lobbying from Mountbatten and direct pleas from Prince Michael, Elizabeth finally gave permission for the marriage to go ahead but only if Michael renounced his claim to the throne because he could not become the English sovereign while married to a Catholic. He was only too happy to do so.

Marie-Christine now determined to have a full-blown white wedding in Westminster Cathedral as though she had never been married before. For once, however, this determined young upwardly mobile socialite on the verge of becoming 'a royal' was to be thwarted. As a member of the royal family, Michael was not permitted to be married in a Catholic church or a register office, so it would have to be abroad.

As the daughter of an Austrian nobleman, and having reverted to her Austrian maiden name, Marie-Christine decided to get married in Vienna. She booked the world-famous Vienna Boys' Choir, arranged for the marriage ceremony to take place in the Schotten-kirche, a church in the aristocratic quarter of Vienna, and spent days agonising over the guest list. Then the Vatican stepped in and forbade a church wedding because Marie-Christine had agreed that any children of the marriage would be brought up in the Anglican faith. In the end a chastened Marie-Christine married her royal prince in the Vienna town hall.

On her wedding day a beaming Marie-Christine, resplendent in the Kent jewels, walked towards the town hall where, waiting to greet her, were Mountbatten, Princess Anne, Prince Charles as well as some other members of the family. In a bitchy swipe at the grand Marie-Christine, Anne queried with a smile, 'Do we curtsy to the new queen of Czechoslovakia, or is it a republic now?'

Marie-Christine would, however, win in the end. After five years of constant badgering by Princess Michael, the Pope announced his recognition of the marriage in July 1983 which permitted Michael and Marie-Christine to renew their vows in church. The Vatican changed its mind because Prince Michael had permitted children of the marriage to be brought up as Catholics.

Before marrying the irrepressible Marie-Christine, Prince Michael was a delightful, quiet, amiable sort of fellow who went about his everyday business in the army and kept very much to himself. Marie-

Christine changed all that. She was to prove herself one of the most outrageous royals in the close-knit House of Windsor.

Once she had actually married into royalty, stories surrounding Marie-Christine's behaviour became legion. On one occasion, two girls were standing at the top of ladders fixing curtains when she ordered them to descend after she had entered the room so they could curtsy to her. She insisted that all her staff bow and curtsy to her whenever she passed them in the house or walked into a room; she insisted on everyone, even many old friends, calling her 'Your Royal Highness' whenever they met.

Even the queen, in a tone of irony, commented that Marie-Christine sounded 'far too grand for us'.

Still, she continued to play her royal card to the hilt. She first persuaded Michael that he must immediately quit the army, which he did; then she persuaded him to grow a beard to look more dashing and authoritative; then she set about organising parties to which she would invite high-profile, well-connected names from London's financial district, people who might be interested, for a considerable sum of money, in having the 'Prince Michael of Kent' as one of their company directors. It worked, to a small degree, because Michael was thought of as a 'most decent type' but Marie-Christine's ambitions knew no bounds.

She wanted a country mansion, fit for a princess, and went in search of one. Because Princess Anne lived in Gloucestershire she decided she would reside there. She first checked out Highgrove, the Gloucestershire home Charles eventually bought before marrying Diana, but that wasn't large or grand enough. In the end she chose Nether Lypiatt Manor in Gloucestershire which, unfortunately, needed £100,000-worth of repairs to bring the house up to her exacting standards. The only way Prince Michael could afford to grant his wife her wish was to sell all his private investments.

The enmity Charles felt towards Marie-Christine, which continues today, bubbled over when she announced her decision to buy Nether Lypiatt which was just 15 miles from Highgrove. Charles had by then decided to purchase Highgrove. He first tried to prevent the sale of Nether Lypiatt and then told his secretary, 'Let that woman know that she will never be invited to Highgrove at any time or for any reason. Let her know that I don't ever want to be invited to her place, either. Nor do I want to speak to her.' To this day, neither has visited the other's house. By the early '80s, then, Prince and Princess Michael had their wonderful country home, its interior designed by the princess, but very little money.

To help the situation financially, Marie-Christine decided to turn her talent to writing books, something she had never tried before. She decided that royal subjects could make best sellers. Her first book, about European royal princesses, sold rather well despite the fact that two authors accused her of using some of their ideas.

In another money-raising project, Princess Michael decided she and Prince Michael should hire themselves out for functions since they were not included on the Civil List. She argued that other royals earned money indirectly for attending royal occasions so she didn't see why they shouldn't be paid directly; it amounted to the same thing. In her opinion, the queen's first cousin and his wife *should* be on the Civil List because she felt they were popular with the general public and would be an asset compared to 'some of the stuffier' royals. She argued that if Princess Alexandra, her husband's elder sister, was on the Civil List then Prince Michael should certainly be.

Royals hiring themselves out like entertainers is, of course, anathema to the monarchy because of the fear of bringing the Crown into disrepute. Undeterred, Marie-Christine went ahead and charged between £500 and £5,000 a time for attending social events.

Still, their income proved insufficient to match their outgoings for Princess Michael was determined to lead the life of a high-profile royal. At Nether Lypiatt she employed a staff of five for the Manor, as well as four gardeners, a groom for her three horses and a chauffeur for her Rolls-Royce. They also had to pay towards the upkeep of their London apartment in Kensington Palace.

Elizabeth, who learned about the couple's way of life from her Private Secretary, made it plain she did not wish nor require Prince Michael to undergo any royal duties. Elizabeth could not have dismissed Princess Michael's appeal more insultingly for she did not even bother to address herself to Marie-Christine, who was furious at being ignored.

But Marie-Christine gave as good as she got. Having been advised on one occasion to wear black to a funeral, Marie-Christine turned up in black but carrying a black handbag with gold clasps. The following day she received a note from Elizabeth which read, 'When I say black I mean black. Not a black handbag with gold clasps.' It was Elizabeth's way of trying to keep the irrepressible Marie-Christine in check.

She became more recalcitrant. During a television interview she committed what many would describe as the 'ultimate sin' in the eyes of the royal family, suggesting that the queen's corgis 'should be shot'.

As Prince Michael's wife she had been invited to the family's traditional Christmas dinner at Windsor in 1986. However, she felt ignored by the rest of the family and stayed away from the dinner table, a serious insult after accepting the invitation from the queen. Her absence was noted by Elizabeth.

Hours later Marie-Christine received a type-written memo from one of the queen's senior staff. It read, 'It is understood that in the future you will join the rest of the family for dinner.' Furious at the note, Marie-Christine ordered her bags to be packed and left immediately for London. She had gone too far. Elizabeth refused to speak to her for some years, either by phone or personally. If she needed to give the princess any information she would write her a note.

Determined to force the queen's hand, Marie-Christine tried another tack. She would make herself so popular that by public demand the queen would have to re-think whether she could afford not to involve the Kents in royal duties. Marie-Christine knew that if she and her husband carried out royal duties they would automatically be entitled to receive money from the Civil List, which covers all travel, a substantial clothes allowance and help towards administrative costs.

Marie-Christine believed she would only be truly royal and a full member of the House of Windsor if and when she was included in the Civil List, and that had always been her goal. Despite her considerable intelligence, Marie-Christine's rise to fame and massive ambitions were due for a fall. She had grossly underestimated the Palace and Elizabeth.

She continued offering her services, and those of Prince Michael, to anyone who would accept them as royals, opening garden fêtes, clubs, shows. If asked, they would travel anywhere. At first they carried out all these functions for no money, but their bank account soon dwindled which led Princess Michael to comment rashly that she would 'go anywhere for a free meal'.

Her Secretary, John Barratt, who had been a good servant and close confidant to Earl Mountbatten for 20 years, had been taken on by Prince Michael following Mountbatten's assassination in August 1979. He organised their schedules, their charity work and their growing number of public engagements.

He recalled some of Princess Michael's antics, 'I remember on one occasion she opened a store for a well-known electrical firm and a few days later a van arrived at the house with ten television sets which she had asked as a gift from the firm. They were for the servants' rooms. She was shameless.'

She received gifts including horses, cars, holidays, airline tickets, jewellery, perfume and cash, cheques and any items offered by whatever firm or person she met. But that wasn't enough for Marie-Christine. She was determined to obtain the money she needed to pursue the life she wanted.

She became friendly with a wealthy Arab prince who was heavily involved in arranging deals on behalf of the Saudi royal family; Senator John Warner of Liz Taylor fame; and Ward Hunt, cousin of the Texas billionaire Bunker Hunt. They had met in Texas in 1983 at a fundraising dinner for the United States Friends of the English National Opera. Hunt and Princess Michael became lovers a year later.

A wealthy, 44-year-old millionaire, Ward Hunt had been divorced by his wife Laura in 1984. He lived in a luxurious Dallas apartment where Marie-Christine used to visit. On occasion he travelled to London, once accompanied by his mother when they stayed at Kensington Palace. Ward Hunt lavished Marie-Christine with gifts and money and Marie-Christine would take extraordinary risks to be with him. One time she and Prince Michael were visiting Dallas, staying at the Turtle Crook Hotel, when Marie-Christine let it be known she wanted her secretary to arrange for Prince Michael to be flown to New York ahead of her because she wanted to see Ward Hunt. The two men in fact passed each other in the lobby; Prince Michael was being escorted to his car as Ward Hunt was sitting in the lobby waiting for him to leave. That night Ward Hunt and Marie-Christine stayed in Dallas and she joined her husband the following day.

She enjoyed her lover's company and even more so his presents. Recklessly, she invited Ward Hunt to London for a week's holiday, but those closest to her decided that her behaviour was becoming too scandalous. Royal servants, at every level, know that the private and intimate lives of those they serve are none of their business and that on most occasions their duty is to look the other way. But Marie-Christine's behaviour had gone beyond the bounds of recognised adultery. It wasn't that she had taken a lover; she was risking scandal for her husband Prince Michael and the Crown.

Details of her numerous indiscretions had already been passed to Elizabeth, through the usual channels of Private Secretary to Private Secretary. Appalled, Elizabeth decided the time had come to put an end to Marie-Christine's activities.

Stuart Kuttner, an assistant editor with the *News of the World*, who had excellent contacts in royal circles, takes up the story: 'One day I was invited to lunch and as we walked by the Thames that afternoon I was asked whether we had noticed how often Princess Michael of Kent visited America. It was suggested to me that my paper should investigate the record of her trips. By the end of the conversation I had the name "Ward Hunt" and the rest was left to us to investigate. I thought it would take time.'

Within a matter of weeks, the same royal contact phoned to say that Ward Hunt was arriving in London on 24 June 1985, and would stay at the Carlton Tower in Cadogan Square, near Harrods. Before he arrived Kuttner received another call from his source informing him that Hunt would indeed come to London but would stay at a luxury private apartment which belonged to the brother of Princess Esra of Hyderabad, a mutual friend of Hunt and Marie-Christine who lived in California. Kuttner continued: 'We were informed that Ward Hunt and Princess Michael would spend a couple of days at the apartment and then move to the country to Rosie Northampton's country home in Gloucestershire. On the appointed day Princess Michael arrived at the apartment with groceries and an ill-fitting red wig. Later Ward Hunt arrived and there they stayed together. All the time they were watched by *News of the World* reporters, and whenever they left the apartment, photographers hiding nearby caught them on film.'

Having quit London to spend a few days together in the country, Princess Michael received a mystery phone call informing her that the *News of the World* had photographs and details of her liaison with Ward Hunt, and that the story would hit the headlines the next day. Distraught at being caught *in flagrante delicto*, Princess Michael organised a helicopter to pick up Ward Hunt from the country house where they were staying, and fly him to Manchester 150 miles north, to catch a plane to New York. Once he had left, Princess Michael announced she was suffering from exhaustion and went straight into hospital where she remained until the fuss had died down.

A few days later, she was photographed with her husband Prince Michael at the Wimbledon tennis championships, holding his hand, leaning on his arm and acting as an attentive, charming, smiling wife. Elizabeth however had not been fooled, even if Prince Michael did accept whatever excuse was proffered by his money-obsessed wife.

When Elizabeth saw the photographs of Prince Michael and his wife together at Wimbledon she was amazed at Marie-Christine's effrontery for she had expected that the scandalous newspaper headlines would finish their marriage and that Marie-Christine would be sent packing, certainly out of the Royal House of Windsor and perhaps out of the country. Phone tapping had revealed that Ward Hunt was in love with Marie-Christine and wanted to marry her. He hoped that she was fully prepared to leave Prince Michael, obtain a divorce, and make a new life for herself with him in Dallas.

Elizabeth's handling of this incident illustrates the lengths to which she, supported by her senior advisers, will go to uphold the dignity of the Crown and remove someone likely to bring disgrace to the monarchy. Elizabeth never forgets that her principal task in life is to uphold and if possible strengthen the Crown. One way of upholding that dignity is to keep scandal at arm's length. Only a few years later, Elizabeth was to show her ruthlessness yet again when she had to deal with the sexual adventures of the Duchess of York.

There were reasons why Princess Michael did not end her marriage and return to Dallas with the likeable, wealthy Ward Hunt: the first concerned her two royal children; the second the fact that she loved being a royal princess; and it also emerged that following his expensive divorce settlement, Ward Hunt was not as wealthy as she had at first thought.

Marie-Christine's first child, Lord Frederick Windsor, was born in April 1979, just nine months and five days after her wedding to Michael, and her second, Lady Gabriella, arrived exactly two years later in April 1981. Princess Michael said after her daughter was born, 'April is the ideal time to have a baby. You can have the pram outside and the fresh air on that child for the whole spring, the whole summer and the whole autumn. That was why my second child was also born in April. I organised it like that so that both my children could have this benefit.'

Princess Michael is known to believe in discipline for both her children and it is indisputable they are both well behaved; it is also obvious to those that see her with her children that she cares for them. It was not always so.

Her son Frederick was a beautiful baby and child. Some described him as having 'chocolate box looks'. However, poor Gabriella did not come up to the exacting standards her mother had set. Indeed, Gabriella was such a disappointment to her mother that Princess Michael began to comment upon her own daughter. She confessed to her Private Secretary, 'She is so plump and unattractive. Why can't she be like Frederick who is so beautiful?'

Princess Michael knew that she would not have been permitted to take her son and daughter to America with her if she had gone ahead, divorced Prince Michael and set up home with Ward Hunt. Elizabeth would have issued instructions to Prince Michael that his children would have to be brought up and educated in Britain and not be allowed to live with their mother.

With the evidence of Princess Michael's sexual adventures to hand, Elizabeth had planned to instruct Prince Michael to make them wards of court, if necessary, and so obtain care and custody of the children legally. All this was explained to Princess Michael through the private secretaries and she was left in no doubt that if she left Michael and quit Britain she would lose her children.

Elizabeth made sure she never had to see or speak to her on any occasion. Princess Michael was cast into outer darkness to repent and atone for her sin, namely that she had been found guilty of bringing the monarchy into disrepute by being discovered cheating on her husband.

Elizabeth banned Marie-Christine from attending any public functions where she would be present, and vowed never to permit her to become part of the Civil List. Through palace officials Elizabeth let it be known that she was most displeased with Princess Michael of Kent and that invitations sent to Princess Michael should not associate her in any way with the royal family.

The princess vented her fury on her hapless husband, accusing him of being weak and pathetic, of not standing up to the queen and of not defending her own good name.

Princess Michael has been known to harangue him, criticising him in front of guests. It is so very, very different from those days before they married when she referred to him as 'my beloved Michael'.

To top it all, Marie-Christine has a most fearsome temper and will change in a second from a pleasant, smiling woman to what has been described as a 'true virago': shouting at everyone until the moment of fury has passed and she calms down again. And Prince Michael has been on the receiving end of much of her venom.

It is Marie-Christine, now 55, who threatens Prince Michael whenever they have an argument. On numerous occasions she has told him that if he dares seek a separation or a divorce she will make sure he will never see his children again. For whatever reason, he worships her. Above all else, Prince Michael dearly loves his children. His temperament and personality mean that he is not only prepared to put up with all the trouble he receives from his wife but is happy to do so.

She has a rule which she demands is strictly adhered to and which both Prince Michael and the children obey. Each evening between six and seven Marie-Christine retires to her bedroom and insists on not being disturbed, not even by her husband. It is during that hour that she makes her telephone calls and receives them on a private phone specially installed in her room. That's also when she plans her lunches, dinners, parties and weekends.

Since those torrid days and nights with Ward Hunt however, Princess Michael has not been quite so forward in her adulterous relationships. Nevertheless, she still flirts with various men and somehow makes ends meet, financially. To this day, neither Prince nor Princess Michael of Kent has ever received money from the Civil List but they still attend functions and events, open exhibitions and make sure they are paid handsomely for their appearances. It is their only source of income and Princess Michael still works hard at bringing in the money and making herself as popular as possible, hoping to widen her net and attract more people, organisations and companies prepared to pay for their presence. And they do.

After eight years in the wilderness, the queen permitted Prince Michael to attend royal functions, but the effervescent Marie-Christine is still, more often than not, excluded from royal gatherings, much to her annoyance and chagrin.

16. SARAH, DUCHESS OF YORK

In Elizabeth's eyes both Diana and Princess Michael had behaved deplorably, reneging on their duty and responsibilities to their husbands as well as to the House of Windsor. Elizabeth considered the behaviour of both women to be unforgivable errors of judgement, major aberrations which would not be tolerated or forgotten. The second Windsor witch, whom Elizabeth warmed to and whom she liked far more than either Diana or Princess Michael, was to behave like a loose cannon, leading a truly amoral life and apparently not giving a damn what anyone thought.

Sarah Ferguson was known all her life by her schoolgirl name of 'Fergie' except to her family and close friends who all called her Sarah. To everyone, Sarah was a surprise choice for Prince Andrew to marry. With her titian hair and well-built figure she was not the usual type of girl Andrew liked to bed.

In his early twenties, Andrew was regarded as arrogant, proud, high-handed and a show-off. Those in the Palace who knew him well believed that he seemed to have inherited these genes from his father, which did not make him very popular either at school or in the Royal Navy. And as regards Fergie, he believed like his father did, that he was irresistible to women. He certainly gave that impression to many of the young women he dated before he met Fergie.

Andrew had known virtually nothing of sex until he was in the Caribbean serving as a junior officer on a few days' leave from his Royal Navy ship. There he met Vicki Hodge, a beautiful, mature, fashion model. He was just 21. They spent the best part of a week together. A colleague of Prince Andrew said later, 'When Andrew left that island he was dead on his feet; he had been well and truly decanted.'

A strong sexual chemistry which they both enjoyed existed

between Andrew and Fergie. For the first few months together Andrew and Fergie could not keep their hands off each other. Great sex and a sense of fun kept them together. They enjoyed each other's company. Neither Andrew nor Fergie is particularly bright, but they enjoyed active sports as well as the same television shows, films and music. Both loved kidding around, throwing bread rolls in restaurants or indulging in cream-bun fights, enjoying the attention and the limelight.

Elizabeth and Philip had welcomed Fergie's arrival. They felt she would be a far greater asset to the House of Windsor than the attractive American actress Koo Stark appeared in a soft-porn movie. In fact, Koo Stark was typical of the women that Prince Philip found so attractive throughout his life. And not just Prince Philip. Many royals have had affairs with actresses through the ages, not least Edward VII at the turn of the century who had a long-lasting affair with the British sex symbol and leading actress of that era, the lovely Lillie Langtry.

Both Elizabeth and Philip, of course, had known Fergie all her life. She had an impeccable upper-class English background which included Charles II as an ancestor. Her father, Major Ron Ferguson, had once commanded the sovereign's Escort of the Household Cavalry Regiment. Sarah was often at Windsor as an infant when her father played polo and as a result, she had virtually grown up with Andrew. She was well acquainted with the rules of royal protocol and etiquette and knew how the royal family worked. Furthermore, Elizabeth rather liked Fergie's freshness and vitality: they both wanted their rather boisterous second son to settle down, get married and start a family in the hope that this would make him more responsible. When Andrew announced he wanted to marry Fergie they were both genuinely pleased and relieved. They believed Sarah Ferguson would keep their son in line.

Fergie's bubbly personality brought out the friendly, relaxed side of Elizabeth's nature and she enjoyed her company, especially at weekend parties. They had much in common – both enjoyed country life, riding, stalking, polo and walking the dogs.

Such were her feelings towards Fergie that the queen agreed to give them whatever wedding present they wanted and the couple decided on a brand new ranch-style home near Windsor. Elizabeth provided everything, including the carpets, the furniture and the instant garden. Despite costing £500,000, architectural snobs thought their new home was in poor taste, some describing it as 'cheap and nasty', more like a 'burger restaurant' or 'supermarket' than a home.

But Elizabeth had no idea what a little vixen Fergie really was, nor that Fergie had a remarkable sexual appetite and was wholly unconcerned with conventional morality. It was to be her undoing. When younger, and with little confidence, Fergie had had a number of lovers as a teenager. None had lasted very long. She seemed to need to have a boyfriend on hand at all times for her self-confidence and it was during those years that she realised her sexual needs were prodigious.

During the early 1980s, Fergie had been in love with Paddy McNally, a man 22 years her senior, a wealthy motor-racing manager who lived in Verbier, Switzerland, with his two teenage sons. His wife had died of cancer some years before. For three years Fergie and Paddy had all but lived together during the winter ski months. Fergie was a good skier and a good hostess for Paddy. Throughout the relationship Fergie felt the underdog, pushing for acceptance and McNally's affection and love.

This did little for Fergie's confidence. There were often other good-looking young people in his Verbier home. McNally liked to keep an open house where people, including attractive young women, could always feel at home. Finally, in October 1985, six months after her first date with Prince Andrew, McNally told Fergie that he did not want to marry her and told her that he didn't think he would ever remarry.

The ending of that relationship hit Fergie hard. It wasn't the first time she felt rebuffed by a man she loved, but she had set her heart on staying with McNally. Another of Fergie's earlier loves, Kim Smith-Bingham, a handsome British regular skier, had also lived in Verbier, known affectionately by the Brits as 'Chelsea-on-Ski'. Their affair went well until Fergie went to Argentina to visit her mother Susie Barrantes. On her return to Verbier, he had met another girl, Sarah Worsley, a niece of the Duchess of Kent. Fergie was distraught.

Ever since her mother had fled the family home to go and live with the wealthy Argentine polo player, Hector Barrantes, Sarah had lacked confidence. She was 13 at the time, a vulnerable age. Her father had treated Sarah more like a teenage son than a daughter. As a result Fergie became a first-class horsewoman and a good skier but she lacked confidence with young men and would fall in love instantly if a man showed interest. Despite good advice from many girlfriends no one could help Fergie as she stumbled from one disastrous love affair to another.

Paddy McNally would be the last straw. She had given her all to him, running his house for him as well as sharing his bed. One of

Fergie's girlfriends with whom she had spent the following summer on the Mediterranean island of Ibiza, recalled, 'During those weeks together Fergie poured out her heart. Her life had been shattered; her relationship with McNally had eroded her confidence. And Fergie believed her fling with Andrew was just that, a fling. She was not a happy lady.'

She believed she would never find anyone to love her when she met Prince Andrew at a dinner party in London. They had known each other since childhood. Fergie was bowled over. One of the reasons she loved her relationship with Andrew in those early months was the fact that he wanted her, wanted to spoil her, and be with her.

Naturally, Fergie loved it all and Andrew's attention gave her the confidence she needed. They enjoyed each other's company immensely. To Fergie and Andrew a good sex life was of paramount importance in a relationship. The 26-year-old Andrew proposed to a deliriously happy Fergie, then 27, and a magnificent royal wedding at Westminster Abbey followed in July 1986.

Despite growing up around royals, Fergie seemed not to have the faintest idea how to behave when she married Andrew and became the Duchess of York. Marrying into the royal family seemed to go to her head, and she believed she could now do anything and everything she wanted and yet accept no responsibility. She helped to spend Andrew's 1987 allowance of £90,000 a year from the Civil List as if it was hers to do as she wished. She accepted every free opportunity that came her way – every flight, every holiday, every weekend away.

She steadfastly refused to accept advice given her by senior palace officials, her ladies-in-waiting or friends she had known for years. She read the newspapers that roundly criticised her for the life she was leading and though these attacks hurt, she made no effort to change her lifestyle. She believed she was perfectly within her rights because she had joined the royal family. Andrew might have reined in her excesses, but unfortunately he was not only away at sea most of the time but he did not possess the strength of character to control his wayward wife.

During those first few years, Fergie came in for the most appalling roasting from the tabloid press which, with inverted snobbery, had decided from the very beginning that Fergie wasn't royal enough for the House of Windsor. It was ironic that in the last decades of the twentieth century the republican-biased British press devoted so many of their critical attacks to Fergie for being too ordinary and not sufficiently royal for their tastes. At every opportunity they criticised her figure, make-up, hair style, clothes, wardrobe, holidays, sense of fun and lack of commitment. According to the popular press, Fergie could do nothing right.

Unfortunately, Fergie didn't do much to ameliorate the situation. Throughout 1990 she only carried out 108 royal engagements, just ten more than the Queen Mother who was 90 that year. And she played into her critics' hands, indulging in a never-ending round of dinners, balls, society events and parties. She seemed to take overseas holidays every other month at fashionable beach and ski resorts. She was dubbed 'Freebie Fergie' and later 'Doolittle Duchess' for two reasons: one, that she wasn't doing much for the £250,000-a-year pay cheque from the Civil List and secondly, that her pedigree was on a par with the famous uneducated Cockney, Eliza Doolittle.

Much of the criticism was unfair but she believed the underlying factor was the ever-present comparison with the perfect princess, Diana. Seduced by the beautiful Diana, the people of Britain believed in the 1980s that to be a 'real princess' one had to be a Diana look-alike: super slim, super cool, super sophisticated. Fergie was none of these.

The incessant onslaught from Fleet Street finally got to Fergie and she decided to change everything about herself: her image, her looks, her wardrobe. Firstly, Fergie needed to slim down. From her teenage years she had always been a bit heavy but had lived with it and had accepted the teasing and the jokes. So she went on a crash diet and lost nearly 30 pounds. She bought a new wardrobe to suit her new svelte body, changed her hair and experts revamped her make-up, but still the press critics continued their attacks.

Fergie therefore turned to an astrologer, a medium and a palmist in an effort to become a 'new woman'. Perhaps the most famous was Madame Vasso, a Greek mystic healer who practised New Age philosophies such as the healing power of the pyramid. Fergie would go to Madame Vasso's very ordinary basement apartment in an unfashionable part of London and sit on a stool under a blue glass pyramid while the astrologer tried to drain away all her tensions. It didn't seem to work.

Like Diana, Fergie also sought the help of the astrologer Penny Thornton. Indeed, she was prepared to try anything and anyone to help her. She experimented with facial massages, hypnotherapy, aromatherapy and acupuncture, all in an effort to become a new, slim-line, more beautiful woman. As she seemed to be winning the battle of the bulge, Beatrice arrived in 1988 and then Eugenie in 1990.

Both Andrew and Fergie were perceived as the living epitome of bad taste. They even allowed themselves to be photographed in their new home, which they had helped design, and which the press christened 'Southyork' because it resembled a ranch house from the television series *Dallas*.

Elizabeth saw the mistakes the couple were making and decided to try and help the situation by offering Fergie advice. She knew how wounding bitchy journalists could be, particularly to someone like Fergie, whose figure wasn't like that of a catwalk model and whose natural personality was bubbly and excitable. Elizabeth wanted to help Fergie because she believed she would be good for Andrew and therefore beneficial to the House of Windsor.

Shortly after her marriage, Fergie discovered that being a member of the royal family certainly encouraged the men to come forward, to show interest, to flirt. She had never experienced such attention before and she revelled in it. Even when pregnant, Fergie sought the attentions of young men.

In November 1989, when five months pregnant with Eugenie, Fergie went on an official royal visit to Houston, Texas, to represent the queen at the British Festival at the Houston Grand Opera. There she met Steve Wyatt and fell in love. To start with, Fergie fell for his good looks: Wyatt, then 35, was a serious, athletic, young-looking man with a mahogany suntan who did not smoke, drink or take any form of drugs. Fergie became smitten by his talk of karma, astrology, divinity and other New Age subjects, interests dear to her heart and a million miles from the conversations she had with Andrew. She spent much of that evening dancing with Steve. It was a real-life fatal attraction.

The die was cast. Fergie invited him over to London, invited him to Buckingham Palace, and arranged invitations for him to lunch at the palace and take dinner at Windsor Castle. She introduced her 'new friend' to Prince Andrew and apparently they all got on famously, having supper and barbecues together. In 1990 Fergie took Bea and Eugenie on holiday to Morocco and Wyatt went along too. Unknown to Andrew, Fergie had fallen in love with Wyatt and they were having a passionate fling. Back in London, Wyatt took an apartment close to the palace and the two spent afternoons and evenings making love there. Fergie seemed unable to say 'no' to Wyatt and thereby risked her marriage, her future and the lives of her two daughters whom she professed to adore.

Andrew, the cuckold husband, was blind to what was going on, but the royal protection squad was not. Every date, every clandestine meeting would be noted and reported back to the squad's senior officers who, duty bound, gave the information to their seniors in the palace. Eventually, the reports landed on the desk of Sir Robert Fellowes. It is not known at what stage Sir Robert passed on the information to the queen but at some stage she was informed of the affair.

Alarm bells rang in 1991 when Wyatt escorted Fergie to a private London dinner party to which he had not been invited. He sat down next to her with the immortal words, 'Mah woman and I sit together' – words that were to reverberate around Buckingham Palace and the corridors of MI5 within the next 24 hours. The guests and the hosts were flabbergasted at Wyatt's remark and the fact that the Duchess of York didn't seem to mind.

During the summer and autumn of 1991 Fergie continued to stray and Elizabeth decided the time had come to act. The fling appeared to have become an intense love affair. She asked Sir Robert Fellowes to have a word with her errant daughter-in-law. At their meeting, Fellowes tried to make Fergie understand that rumours suggested she was becoming too friendly with Wyatt and that people might jump to the wrong conclusion. Worse still, if the press discovered Wyatt's existence they would have a field day.

The police continued their surveillance and Fergie was called to see Sir Robert again. This time she was left in no doubt that the palace knew what had been going on. She was told the queen had been informed and she was advised most strongly to end the affair immediately.

Yet Fergie continued to see Wyatt. After further advice from the queen, Fellowes was urged to have yet another talk with the stubborn Sarah. He realised he had to put a halt to the affair once and for all. He knew that she was not only putting her marriage at risk but if her affair became public knowledge she would be involving the House of Windsor and the monarchy in a scandal they could ill afford. One of the principal duties of the queen's Private Secretary is to defend the reputation of the monarchy at all times. He was angry that Fergie should take no notice of his earlier warnings and seemed equally oblivious to potential scandal.

Throughout her marriage Fergie had frequently been called to see Sir Robert about a variety of incidents and stories that appeared in the press. At first he had tried to be friendly, to guide her, educate her on how to behave, what to wear, the hundred and one idiosyncrasies of royal life and traditions. Finally, in one single interview he read Fergie the riot act. He not only warned her to stop seeing Wyatt but he also ordered her to stop demanding money for newspaper and magazine articles, stop accepting 'freebie' trips and holidays, and stop accepting any invitations that didn't come through the palace.

For her part, Fergie felt the palace wanted to control every aspect of her life and she rebelled.

In one memorable shouting match with Sir Robert, she said, 'If I can't lead my own life without you telling me what to do then I'll go my own way. I'm fed up being told what I can and cannot do – by you.'

Fergie pleaded with Andrew to come to the rescue, appealed to him to see Sir Robert and demand that he leave her alone to lead her own life, because she was at the end of her tether. She told Andrew, 'I can't take any more of him preaching and shouting at me. You must make him stop.' Andrew's response, however, was one of non-intervention – it was a matter for her and Sir Robert.

But Fergie's resentment grew at Sir Robert's continued involvement in her life and their relationship gradually deteriorated. Whenever Fergie spoke about him she would refer to him as 'Bellowes', rather than 'Fellowes', because of their frequent bawling matches.

Then, for no apparent reason Wyatt suddenly announced to Fergie that he had decided to return to America. There had been no hint of plan to return home and Fergie became unhappy and perplexed. He said his father wanted him to return to help run the family business. But Fergie knew in her heart that the Establishment had been at work. Someone had spoken to Wyatt. In that most discreet British fashion, Wyatt had been quietly advised to leave London and not wanting to land himself in trouble, he agreed. Fergie was left behind and once again she felt rejected by a man whom she had loved.

Wyatt's decision to take the advice 'and get the hell out of the Duchess of York's life' angered and upset Fergie. Alone, she became nervous. She believed she was being followed everywhere she went, that her phones were tapped, her mail checked, her life subject to scrutiny, and all orchestrated from the palace. Fergie couldn't take the pressure – towards the end of 1991 she began to go to pieces.

In a remarkably candid interview in the summer of 1991, Fergie described how she felt 'owned and controlled' by the royal family. She agreed to be interviewed by *Tatler* magazine in the Yorks' office in Buckingham Palace, a chaotic room, part nursery, part gymnasium, part workplace. Fergie wore no make-up and her hair was still damp from a recent workout on her exercise bike. Little Princess Beatrice, then three, ran in and out throughout the interview half-naked and, at one point, Prince Andrew walked in, did a double-take and tiptoed out, a pantomime expression of comic horror on his face. This was no normal royal interview where the agenda is agreed beforehand, where a palace press officer is present and where the royal is seen perfectly dressed, perfectly turned out and in command. Fergie was none of these.

Fergie was reacting against being 'on show' 24 hours a day, unable to escape the intense heat of the limelight. She said, 'Real life isn't like this, living in a palace. I don't even feel happy at Sunninghill, what the tabloids call Fergie's Dallas Palace. I love to get away, to have my own privacy. I don't even feel any privacy at Sunninghill. Some nights I ask every member of staff to leave so that we can be a family, on our own, like a normal family.'

She went on, 'I just have to get away from The System and people saying to me all the time "no you can't, no you can't". That's what The System is like. I can't stick to all the guidelines, to all the rules because they're not real. It's not a real life living in a palace. And so I feel inhibited.'

Fergie revealed that she liked to relax by escaping to the mountains to ski. She said, 'If I lived in Europe no one would be any the wiser if I went to the mountains. I could go skiing for the weekend and no one would bat an eyelid. But here, everyone thinks skiing is an élitist sport. The mountains are my security. I love them. The mountains talk to me and they give me strength. And I'm not allowed to go because of being seen, because of what people might say or write, and all because I'm owned. Therefore I don't go and I feel trapped. And it's The System that is trapping me.'

She confided that she was hurt by the constant criticism, much of which, she claimed, was totally incorrect. For example, after Eugenie was born Fergie's hair began to fall out and, on advice from her hairdresser, she had much of it chopped off. One newspaper proclaimed that she did it purely to spite Prince Andrew because he liked her hair long.

After saying that she tried to keep herself as independent as possible, she concluded, 'At the end of the day you die alone. As long as you're kind and you get up in the morning and you're happy to look at yourself, and you're straightforward and thank God for everything you do because He knows, then they can write what they want to write ...' She did not finish the sentence because tears were forming in her eyes.

Andrew, fed up with the accusations in the press of Fergie's love affair with Steve Wyatt, a man he had invited into his home and trusted, began to shun his wife and spend much more time on the golf course. Fergie couldn't cope. With Wyatt no longer there,

Fergie had no one to whom she could turn. She tried to talk things through with her father but he urged her to make it up with Andrew.

Fergie found solace and companionship with another American, Wyatt's friend Johnny Bryan. He was a tall, balding, well-built bachelor in his late thirties who described himself as a financial adviser. As troubles brewed between Andrew and Fergie he offered to act as peacemaker. He went along to Sunninghill and talked to both of them, ostensibly in an effort to help sort out their marriage problems. However, the more time Fergie spent with Bryan, the more she became attracted to him. And Andrew witnessed that attraction. He didn't want to know about patching up the marriage and Fergie realised that she was being edged out of the family.

In some ways Bryan, as a financial adviser, was able to help Fergie in his professional capacity. During the first years of married life Fergie had not been idle in feathering her nest. She had known how her father had struggled throughout most of his life, always being short of real money and often living a hand-to-mouth existence, sometimes needing to borrow from friends and family. She wanted to ensure that never happened to her. She had given interviews to newspapers for money, one to the *Daily Express* which had paid her £100,000; another to *Hello!* which had paid her £200,000 for a set of photographs showing Andrew, herself and the children inside Sunninghill. She had also written highly successful children's books entitled *Budgie the Helicopter* which had earned her some £300,000.

Within a short time, Johnny Bryan had taken over where his friend Wyatt had left off – he became Fergie's new lover. Within days of their sleeping together in 1992, Buckingham Palace was made fully aware that Fergie had gone off the rails again, indulging in yet another love affair.

Sir Robert Fellowes ordered an immediate report on Fergie which was undertaken by the Special Branch. It revealed Fergie's past sexual trysts. The report described Fergie's sexual appetite in critical terms.

In February 1992, photographs were discovered in Wyatt's old London flat showing Wyatt on holiday in Mexico with Fergie, Bea and Eugenie. The pictures, which had never been seen before, were splashed all over the tabloid press. Prince Andrew was furious. One in particular infuriated and upset him for it showed Wyatt holding Bea in a most paternal pose.

During the previous few months Andrew had frequently confronted Fergie about her relationship with Wyatt. But Andrew, who is not a strong character, was no match for Fergie's fire. She would round on Andrew for daring to suggest for one minute that she would be unfaithful.

Allegedly the pictures were found accidentally on top of a wardrobe by a cleaner working there some months after Wyatt had quit the apartment. But the hand of Britain's security services was suspected. Conspiracy theories have mushroomed in Britain ever since the 1970s, when Peter Wright, a former MI5 agent, retired from the service and moved to Australia intending to write a book about MI5's senior officers. He was angry and appalled at the licence taken by MI5's senior officers whom he claimed had taken it upon themselves to interfere in the politics of the nation. In the book, called *Spycatcher*, Wright revealed that officers of MI5 had spent the 1970s burgling and robbing their way across London in the most brazen fashion with utter disregard for the law. The British government had tried to prevent the book being published, but after a series of famous court cases in the 1980s, it failed to do so. *Spycatcher* finally appeared, causing considerable political damage and enormous embarrassment to MI5.

The pictures had shocked Prince Andrew who now knew for sure that his wife had been having an affair with Wyatt for some time. The pictures also outraged the press and the public, convincing the nation that Fergie was beyond the pale, indulging in open and blatant adultery. It meant that both the press and the public would understand – and would not condemn Prince Andrew – if the Yorks did separate and eventually divorce. It also meant that Fergie had no chance of remaining a member of the royal family.

Fergie, Elizabeth and the entire royal family then discovered they had to contend with the scandalous behaviour of Fergie's father, Major Ronald Ferguson. While expecting her first baby, her father had returned to his old antics, frequenting so-called massage parlours. He had become a member of the Wigmore Club, a high-class brothel, which employed attractive young women who specialised in massages. Ferguson had not only enrolled at the club under his own name but had openly bragged to the girls who worked there that he was the Duchess of York's father and a close friend of Charles and Diana.

In May 1988, *The People* ran a front-page story about Fergie's father. The headline read, 'FERGIE'S DAD AND THE VICE GIRLS'. The story ran:

> To the outside world Major Ron is a friend to the queen, polo manager to Prince Charles, confidant of Princess Diana, and one of the royal circle's most colourful characters.

> But attractive young prostitutes working at a high-class London brothel, called the Wigmore Club, know another Major Ferguson. He is one of their most valued regular customers. The galloping major pays blondes, brunettes and redheads for sexual services – and even rewards his favourite girls with gifts of perfume.

Elizabeth and senior aides at Buckingham Palace were outraged while Fergie was desperately embarrassed and ashamed. Six months earlier Major Ferguson had been warned by a senior palace official that his involvement with vice girls could lead to exposure and deep embarrassment to the queen. He was strongly advised to stay away from such clubs.

Ferguson took no notice of the warning believing that since his daughter was now a member of The Firm he was free to behave however he wished. He was wrong. The palace had no intention of permitting Major Ron to continue his scandalous life.

There was another matter causing concern in the palace: Fergie's father was using his daughter's position and title to secretly make money for himself. Fergie had no idea, but it was a fact.

Days after Sarah's engagement in 1985, Major Ron threw a dinner party inviting a number of people to an expensive restaurant in fashionable Pont Street to celebrate. One invited guest commented, 'I remember it well because Ron never threw dinner parties. This was an exception.'

Someone sitting at the next table, however, heard much of the conversation. Major Ron boasted, 'Until this moment I have been a nobody, but now I am a personality everyone knows and I am beginning to like it.'

Major Ron enjoyed his new-found fame for a different reason. Unknown to Fergie, her father would arrange dinner parties, polo events, cocktail parties and other occasions at which he would promise people that – for a suitable sum of money – he would arrange for his daughter, and sometimes Prince Andrew, to attend. The people he invited never imagined they would be privileged enough to rub shoulders with royalty, let alone meet, chat and dine with them and they would jump at his offer. Major Ferguson would then demand a fee, payable to him, and usually in cash.

The Major had a copy of his daughter's diary and would fix his 'private' events so they would not clash with others in his daughter's life. Many people were happy to pay between £1,000 and £5,000 for the privilege of meeting the Duchess. And, because Fergie believed she was helping her father, she happily agreed to attend the odd dinner, polo match or other social occasion.

Senior courtiers at the palace learned of the Major's new fundraising activities and told the queen. She asked to be kept informed. It was during this series of events that Elizabeth herself came to the conclusion that perhaps it would be best if Andrew and Fergie were divorced because she feared for the good name of the House of Windsor.

John Barratt, private secretary to Prince and Princess Michael of Kent, knew most members of the royal family extremely well and many of the family secrets. He also knew all that was going on behind the scenes. He commented, 'There was no doubt that the Duchess of York was pushed. She didn't just walk away. The Establishment realised that the Duchess would become a danger to the family and they persuaded the queen that it was necessary for her to be ousted so she could bring no further discredit on the family. So out she went.'

Diana and Fergie had been close pals, indeed best friends, (BFs in Sloane Ranger slang) for some time during the '80s and Fergie had helped Diana come to terms with her role as a princess, encouraging her to take a more positive attitude to life. Fergie had encouraged Diana to lead a more active, independent 'royal' life, to branch out on her own and involve herself in charity work. She felt Diana had cut herself off, leading such a cloistered existence in Kensington Palace.

In late 1991, when she knew that Diana wanted to separate from Charles, Fergie confided to Diana that she couldn't cope with a life married to Prince Andrew. Diana knew precisely how Fergie felt. She had often broken down in tears with Fergie when telling of her life and the breakdown of her marriage. Both knew that Diana would have a far greater problem 'ditching' Charles, heir to the throne, than Fergie would in leaving Andrew who, after the births of William and Harry, had slipped to fourth in the line of succession.

The fact that Diana had broached the subject with Elizabeth gave Fergie confidence to do the same. Fergie was fed up with the constrictions of royal life, fed up that she never saw Andrew because of the time he spent at sea with the Royal Navy. She also felt the spark had gone out of their marriage and their sex life. Buckling under the strain of the constant stream of criticism from palace advisers and the tabloid press Fergie knew she could no longer take the pressure.

Five years, and two children after her marriage to Andrew in 1986, Fergie had come to the conclusion that she and Andrew had never really known each other before rushing into marriage. She now realised their relationship had been based on sex as much as anything else and, worse still, she had married Andrew on the rebound.

Fergie decided she wanted out, and in February 1992, went to tell the one person she believed would help: Elizabeth, her mother-in-law. As she sat down, Fergie said, 'I've got something awful to tell you. I cannot take it any more. Everyone at the palace is against me and it has ruined our marriage.'

Elizabeth reassured Sarah that it was quite wrong for her to think for one minute that there were people in the palace who wanted her out of the royal family. She said that everyone took their orders and instructions from her and the last thing she wanted was a broken marriage in the family.

Elizabeth tried to persuade Fergie to change her mind. She called Andrew home from the Royal Navy and discussed the situation with him. She wondered if a home-based posting would help heal the rift between them, so she arranged for the Admiralty to organise a course near home for Andrew, a man-management course at the college near their new Windsor home, where he could live with his wife and young family. In the previous 12 months Andrew had spent only 43 days at home, the rest at sea or at his naval base. Privately, Elizabeth was not a little angry that Andrew and Fergie, who in many ways had seemed ideally suited, should be unable to make a go of their marriage.

In a heart-to-heart with his mother, Andrew told her that Fergie was in control of the home and the children and seemed to behave exactly as she pleased, no matter what he said. Andrew told her that during the last few months when he had been at home they had rowed constantly. He claimed that Fergie had acted independently and selfishly and confirmed to his mother that Fergie believed senior palace officials wanted to be rid of her.

In fact, Fergie was right. A number of senior palace advisers *did* want to be rid of her, convinced her behaviour would bring discredit to the family.

It was Prince Andrew who finally convinced his mother that his marriage to Fergie could not survive. He now knew of Fergie's adultery with Steve Wyatt and he had witnessed at first hand Fergie's attraction to Johnny Bryan as she had flirted in front of him at their Windsor home. Andrew believed that the love that once existed between them had disappeared and that Fergie had no further interest in him. He told his mother he believed the marriage to be a lost cause. Eventually, Elizabeth reluctantly agreed. Later, Elizabeth told one of her ladies-in-waiting, 'One day I just had enough. I went to my bed and lay down and wept. I didn't even know whom the tears were for – myself, my children, or the awful, frightful situation. Those months were the worst of my life. Sometimes as I thought how dreadfully everything had turned out for my children, tears would fill my eyes and I would have to retire. It was awful.'

Fergie now accepts that she did behave stupidly, believing that once she had become a fully-fledged member of the royal family she could behave exactly how she wished and not be reprimanded. She failed to realise that before she could do as she pleased she first had to earn the respect of the nation, the media, members of the household and the rest of the royal family. She had won over none of those vital interests and paid the price.

If Fergie had taken a leaf out of Diana's book, however, all would have been fine, for Diana had made sure that she was firmly established in the hearts and minds of the nation and the media before she decided to cut loose and make her own dash for freedom. It was a move that would put considerable pressure on Elizabeth and throw down a challenge that was to cause serious concern to the queen's advisers.

More than anyone, Elizabeth knew how precarious Charles's marriage had become and she had done all in her power to ensure Charles remained married to Diana. To be faced with another marriage failure was too much.

To a stunned British nation, news of the Yorks' split came in March 1992. For months the tabloid press had been speculating on the marriage of Charles and Diana, not bothering much about the Yorks' marriage because most believed everything was basically fine between them.

And yet it would be unfair to point the finger solely at the wayward Fergie. Prince Andrew was always thought of as the good-looking Windsor, the macho one, with the flashing smile and dare-devil image whom some girls saw as the British equivalent of a Hollywood hunk. To some that may have been true, but they didn't know what the real Andrew was like or how he behaved in mixed company when he could be arrogant. Even at his private school, Gordonstoun, which was predominantly male, Andrew was called 'The Great I Am' because of his demeanour.

His attitude to young women in particular had been graceless. As a Prince of the Realm, Andrew believed that all young women would happily fall into his arms; they would feel privileged to be chatted up. As one girl who spent some time in Andrew's group explained, 'Andrew became truly embarrassing in a party. He thought he had the right to every girl in the group, to flirt with them and, if he fancied them, kiss them. And if he thought they were willing, he would openly suggest bedding any girl that took his fancy. At first it was very difficult for girls to know how to react but after a while they learned how to say 'no' to him without bruising the royal ego too much. But he was pretty awful.' Andrew hadn't earned his title 'Randy Andy' for nothing.

Most of the girls Andrew met were usually too shy to deal with the bumptious prince as they should have done. But Fergie wasn't. At one dinner party, when Andrew tried to force Fergie to eat three chocolate profiteroles, knowing she was on a diet, she turned and slapped him hard across the face in front of everyone. A moment's stunned silence, then everyone cheered. Andrew blushed, not only from the firm slap, but because he realised, in that instant, what all his friends thought of his behaviour. Some contend that at that moment Andrew fell in love. He had met a girl who would put him in his place, and that was really what he wanted.

From the outset of their five-year marriage, Fergie had taken command. Macho Andrew, the young Royal Navy helicopter pilot who had won his spurs in the heat of battle during the Falklands war of 1982, was no match for Fergie's forceful personality. The arrogant prince was reduced, overnight, to accepting the lead provided by his wife. Andrew may have appeared tough and rugged but underneath he had the genetic trait of most of the Windsor men, an inherent weakness in the company of powerful women and a willingness to follow their lead.

Throughout their marriage Fergie called the shots: she had chosen the setting for their 'dream' home, Sunninghill, on the edge of Windsor Park; she approved the architectural design, chose the interior colour schemes of their home and the furniture, curtains and carpets, the dinner services and the cutlery. She decided on their cars, holidays, dinner and weekend guests, the food they ate, the staff they employed, even the television shows they watched.

Fergie's mother, Mrs Susan Barrantes, saw the danger in such a one-sided marriage. After the separation she said, 'Prince Andrew's weakness was the reason the marriage failed. I am afraid he is spineless and lacking in character. Andrew is a good-looking boy who has a heart of gold to the point of being without money himself just to help someone. But he has not got any character, absolutely none. If he had, maybe this marriage would not have broken up.'
Susan Barrantes was not trying to excuse her strong-willed daughter or apportion blame for the marriage failure, but simply described

what she saw in the relationship; the forceful Fergie dominating the rather weak Andrew.

Elizabeth and Susan Barrantes, then living in Argentina, spoke extensively on the telephone about the break-up. They had, of course, chatted at the wedding in London in 1986 but had not spoken since. The two women knew each other from years watching polo together at Windsor.

The queen's official announcement of the separation of the Duke and Duchess of York was made from Buckingham Palace on 20 March 1992. The announcement was worded to indicate that the Duchess had instituted the proceedings, not Prince Andrew, so that the blame for the separation would be put on Fergie's shoulders and the public would see Andrew as the innocent party.

However, while briefing the BBC's court correspondent, Charles Anson attacked Fergie. Never before had royal reporters heard such venom in a briefing from a palace spokesman about a member of the House of Windsor. He told the BBC that the Duchess had deliberately ordered media leaks, that she had personally employed a high-powered public relations firm, and that her behaviour showed she was not fit to be a member of the royal family.

The specific behaviour Anson criticised occurred when Fergie had flown back to London from the United States with her father earlier that year. On that commercial flight she had put a paper bag over her head, stuck her tongue through a hole in the bag, and then pelted her father with bread rolls and sugar lumps. All this in full view of a number of British journalists who had never witnessed royals behaving so crassly.

Elizabeth, furious that Anson should have taken it upon himself to openly criticise a member of the family in such a way, ordered that he make a humiliating public apology. But Elizabeth knew where the blame also lay, for she knew better than anyone how the palace hierarchy worked and whose job it was to brief the wretched Anson on all matters, great and small. She knew Sir Robert Fellowes must take a share of the blame.

Some sections of the press revelled in the royal embarrassment and pontificated on the reasons for the marital failure. Unusually, Elizabeth herself was not spared criticism.

'BLAME THE WAY YOU BROUGHT 'EM UP MA'AM', proclaimed *The Sun*. 'Kids starved of affection', suggested the tabloid under the headline 'DEATH OF THE ROYAL MARRIAGE'. The comment column read, 'The queen must take some of the blame for the breakdown of the royal marriages . . . Her distant relationship with her children starved them of affection and left them unable to form loving partnerships . . . such youngsters often end up divorcing . . . '

The Sun maintained through interviews that the kids had to learn to suppress their emotions, that duty to the nation came first.

Further evidence of the palace attitude towards Fergie and their treatment of her was revealed by a woman who had no axe to grind and whose views could be seen as being thoroughly objective. Lesley Abdela, who stood for Parliament and founded the all-party 300 Group for women in public life, remembers the problems facing the Duchess of York when she spoke at the Woman of the Year lunch at the Savoy in October 1991. And she remembers the extraordinary behaviour of palace officials.

Fergie had been given a prepared speech which read so badly she had to discard it and speak off the cuff, and Ms Abdela wrote to the palace mildly criticising officials for not preparing the duchess sufficiently. She recalled: 'Afterwards I got a phone call from a guy at the palace who said they take these things extremely seriously and asked me to help them by saying what had gone wrong at the lunch. He told me he had shown the letter to the duchess. I was devastated. I really felt for her. I didn't want to hurt her. I wanted to have a go at the professionals so they could do a better job. Suddenly he said words to the effect that if you haven't got a good product to work with in the first place, you can't do much about it. I was amazed. There was definite contempt for her and it was obvious that it was not just him who felt this. He kept saying "we" so I knew it was more than one. I got the impression there was this rather old-fashioned male group at the palace who didn't approve of her.'

A week later Ms Abdela received a phone call from the palace. Fergie was on the line and told her, 'I was deeply hurt by your letter. You have no idea how it hurt me. I really like to get things right and that's why I'm phoning you.'

Then Fergie continued, 'There are people at the palace who are really quite happy to see me fall on my face . . . some are quite happy to see me fail . . . I even believe some are deliberately trying to drop me in it and enjoy it happening.'

Ms. Abdela went on, 'Fergie indicated that she was actually being frozen out or even sometimes virtually set up; that "they" at the palace were working against her, not *with* her. She was calm, factual and sad, not in the least hysterical or neurotic – just a tone of resignation.'

Fergie herself said later, 'I frequently feel as if I'm trapped in a nightmare by the brothers Grimm, alone at one end of a lonely castle, the corridors long and echoing; and at the other end a light burns where around the light a group of Cyclopses are plotting my downfall.'

Elizabeth decided Fergie would not last the course and decided to use the break-up of Fergie's marriage as a sign to Diana of what fate would befall her if she pursued her intention of seeking a separation. It seemed Elizabeth was sacrificing a pawn to retain a queen.

The queen's personal lawyer, Sir Matthew Farrer of Farrer & Co arranged the financial side of the settlement in which a trust was set up for Bea and Eugenie which would cover their every need, including clothing, private education and a substantial dowry for when they married. A house would be purchased for Sarah and the children near Windsor. Fergie would be given a generous annual allowance out of which she would have to pay staff, bring up the children and feed and clothe herself. Throughout her short marriage Fergie had been most judicious with her own money, not spending a cent of it while happily running up a substantial overdraft of more than £1 million on Andrew's account – despite the fact they had been receiving an allowance of £250,000 a year. Much of Fergie's expenditure had been on dresses, ball gowns and overseas travel.

Sir Matthew Farrer personally informed Fergie after Elizabeth had briefed him. He told her that she would be permitted to keep her title, Duchess of York, on separation, but would have to quit the family home immediately. He also told her the queen had decreed she would never be included in any future royal family gatherings and would be excluded from representing the royal family at any event or function. The queen had not yet decided of which charities she would be permitted to continue as patron but she would be informed later, after palace officials had talked to the charities involved.

To strip Fergie of her charity patronages would, in effect, put an end to all Fergie's royal status. By giving her a breathing space, Elizabeth put Fergie on parole, hoping she would now realise that she had to behave and take great care of her two daughters. Elizabeth's concern was twofold: to tame Fergie's wild behaviour and to make sure Bea and Eugenie were brought up properly.

Weeks later, the nation witnessed the effect of the separation during Ascot Week, the height of the flat racing season, when the queen, other members of the royal family and members of the aristocracy spend four days at Royal Ascot. In 1991 Fergie had ridden in an open carriage down the centre of the course in the celebrated royal parade. In 1992, television viewers saw Fergie with her two daughters, standing and watching from a distance, three lone figures half-hidden by trees, as the queen and her retinue swept past.

In one of the carriages rode Diana who smiled and waved at Fergie and her children. That sight must have brought home to Diana what fate awaited her if she, too, decided to fly the royal nest.

Within months of that separation Sarah Ferguson found herself at the centre of the sex scandal with the man she had led the nation to understand was her friend and financial adviser, Johnny Bryan.

Bryan, Fergie and her two children were pictured frolicking in the sun by the side of the pool. The photographs showed the bald-headed Bryan leaning over Fergie and kissing her full on the mouth as she lay on a sun bed. He was also pictured sexily sucking Fergie's big toe – this display from a man who had denied, repeatedly, any romantic involvement with Fergie.

The photographs were taken by a *paparazzi* Daniel Angeli who made, photo-journalists judged, more than £1 million from the pictures. The pictures appeared to have been taken from inside the villa grounds and one or two showed the children's bodyguards sunbathing in nothing but swim trunks when they were allegedly on duty. Newspapers pointed out that if a photographer could take snaps twenty to thirty yards from the children, then a gunman could just as easily have lain in wait in the villa grounds. In royal protection circles officers said it was 'beyond credibility' that a photographer would have been able to infiltrate a private villa, remain in the grounds for some time and emerge undetected without someone having knowledge that the photographer was there.

Angeli refused to say how he knew where and when Fergie, Bryan and the children would be at the private villa. He simply stated he had been informed. He did not claim that he had accidentally stumbled across them on holiday. They were staying at a private and secret hideout which could not be seen from any public road or path. Once again, the question raised speculation: Who had revealed Fergie's whereabouts? And why?

Many believed the pictures were again the work of MI5 and that it was the British secret service that had tipped off the photographer. The argument ran that MI5 had decided to reveal the Duchess of York as a person unfit to remain as a member of the House of Windsor because of her sexual proclivities. They informed Angeli of the time and dates Fergie and Bryan would be in residence at the holiday villa. Others were adamant that ultimate permission for the pictures had to come from inside Buckingham Palace. It would not have been the first time senior courtiers at the palace had arranged for a newsman to be on hand to deliberately embarrass a member of the royal family. They had done so a few years before in 1985 when

Princess Michael of Kent had become involved in extra-marital affairs.

Neither Elizabeth nor senior palace aides approved of Johnny Bryan. Following the announcement of her separation, Bryan had appointed himself her public relations man to put across her side of the story. He talked to journalists, off the record, blaming Fergie's problems 'on those bastards at the palace'. He described the royal household as 'a sick bunch' and once shouted at the editor of a glossy magazine that the duchess was not some 'dead common fucking trashy little model'.

No one could understand why Fergie had allowed someone like Bryan, with no knowledge of the royal household or the Establishment, to take command of her life and, in the process, orchestrate the destruction of what little remained of her reputation.

It is understandable that Fergie, having been cast out from the family, should need sound financial advice. But Johnny Bryan began escorting her around the world, visiting such exotic locations as Phuket in Thailand, Buenos Aires, New York and Paris. When in London she would spend evenings at fashionable Annabel's nightclub in Mayfair drinking bottles of champagne, always in the company of her financial adviser.

The press began questioning Bryan's real relationship with Fergie. He repeatedly denied any romance between them and claimed their relationship to be that of client and financial adviser. 'My job is to negotiate a fair and equitable settlement for the Duchess of York,' he would reply with a confident smile, 'There is absolutely no question of any romance between the Duchess of York and myself, nor will there ever be.'

August 1992 brought the St Tropez photographs which were to unmask Bryan and reveal him as Fergie's lover. As the French papers put it with Gallic amusement, 'Fergie's breasts shake the royal palace.' There was little amusement at Balmoral that day where Elizabeth had just started her summer holidays.

From Elizabeth's standpoint, Fergie's decision to take Johnny Bryan as her lover, or even as her financial adviser, ranked as one of her more crass ideas. Anthony John Adrian Bryan was born in Wilmington, Delaware in June 1955, the son of Tony Bryan, an Englishman who had grown up in England but had flown Spitfires for the Royal Canadian Air Force during the Second World War and won the DFC, a gallantry award. His mother, Lida Redmond, was from St Louis, Missouri. Bryan's father graduated from Harvard Business School and was a shrewd businessman, who was eventually appointed to the boards of both Chrysler and Federal Express. He too was something of a ladies' man. In 1964 he divorced Lida and married a wealthy Houston heiress, Josephine Abercrombie. That marriage ended in scandal when he began an affair with the wife of Houston Stores magnate Robert Sakowitz and after a much publicised divorce action, he subsequently married Pamela Sakowitz in 1978.

Johnny Bryan decided to follow in his father's footsteps and studied for a master's degree at Katz Graduate School of Business at the University of Pittsburgh. He became renowned as an all-round sportsman, playing tennis, golf, ice hockey, squash, skiing as well as flying aircraft. And he had a reputation with the girls. He loved to be thought of as a macho American male with a rippling 'six-pack' and a good body.

Little is known of his early business career but in 1985 he put together a consortium of investors which raised £750,000 to take over Encom Telecommunications and Technology in Atlanta, Georgia. He became vice-president of business development negotiating rental deals for spare satellite channels but it was a disaster: the company crashed in four years and the investors lost their money.

Among the investors was Taki Theodoracopulos, the Greek millionaire and columnist who had invested £30,000. He said, 'I was obviously disappointed when the deal went sour but not angry. Bryan is not a bad fellow. He is a sweet guy really, a typical, loud American full of shit, but basically decent.'

Bryan and his father came to London in 1987 and took over Oceanics, an ailing marine electronics company. Within two years they had recouped their investment and made a healthy profit. But Oceanics ran into trouble and losses mounted. The Bryans did the decent thing and resigned. But Bryan kept his stake in the German off-shoot, Oceanics Deutschland, which has an office in Frankfurt and in 1993, the company was believed to be worth around £15 million.

Johnny Bryan fell for the social side of life in London and became something of a Don Juan. Prematurely bald, Bryan acquired the nickname 'Osram' because his head looked like a light bulb, but it hardly stopped him. He squired the most fashionable and sophisticated society girls, most of them heiresses with fathers worth fortunes. But his reputation began to sink fast.

Girls talked openly about the sort of man Bryan had become. A Houston photographer, Pam Francis, who had dated Bryan at university branded him 'a little rat'; another former girlfriend described him as 'the greatest chateau-bottled shit of the 1990s'. An English girl, Catherine Loewe, from a wealthy family, seduced by Bryan's charisma and persistence described him later as 'sneaky, devious and a King Rat'. However, Catherine also said, 'Johnny was very much into fitness. He was action man between the sheets, a very aggressive, very active lover who could keep going for a long time. I felt at one point he could go on for ever and ever. That's probably one of the reasons Sarah became so attached to him. She's a very sexy lady.'

One of his father's ex-wives, Pamela, commented, 'It is perhaps no coincidence that his father seemed to single out wealthy, influential and sometimes married women for conquests, me included. I think John has the same approach.'

Once Bryan's true role became known he decided to launch the Duchess of York on the open market, offering her to newspapers and magazines for photographs and interviews, at a price. Along with James Hughes, an American lawyer, he set up ASB Publishing in 1990, two years before the Duchess decided to leave Andrew. Bryan hawked his own story 'Fergie and Me' around Fleet Street and one tabloid agreed to pay £250,000 but the deal fell through.

Bryan even offered to sell a story to *The People*, naming a girl with whom he claimed Prince Andrew was having an affair. He said he wanted £25,000 but when *The People* discovered the story was bogus, Bryan claimed the whole thing had been a joke. *The People* reported, however, that there was no joking whatsoever in the discussions, or the manner in which they were conducted by Bryan, before they had discovered the story was without foundation.

Another story is told by Lesley Player, then 34, a beautiful divorcée and successful businesswoman, who fell in love with the game of polo and found herself at the centre of a sensational scandal that revealed her affairs with both Major Ron Ferguson and Fergie's lover, Steve Wyatt. It became a scandal that would embarrass both Elizabeth and Fergie.

Lesley Player revealed that when she first met Bryan he had claimed to be in the film business, part-owner of a nightclub in New York and in the process of building a hospital in Germany. Later that evening, after she had seen him snort cocaine through a rolled £10 note, he had invited her and another girl to join him in a 'three-in-a-bed' sex romp.

Later Miss Player wrote a book, *My Story: The Duchess of York, Her Father and Me* detailing her affair with Major Ronald Ferguson. She claimed Fergie had connived at the affair, providing a bedroom at her new home, Sunninghill, so that Player and Fergie's father could sleep together. At the time her two daughters Bea and Eugenie were also there.

Lesley Player did not flatter Major Ron. She wrote, 'I couldn't help noticing how thin his legs were. I had expected iron-man thighs from someone who rode as often and as brilliantly as he did.'

To Fergie's greater embarrassment and humiliation, Lesley Player also revealed that Fergie had given her the position of 'acting' lady-in-waiting so that she could travel free with Fergie as a 'cover', enabling her to continue her affair with Major Ferguson around the world; all at the expense of their hosts who had footed the bill.

Of her affair with Steve Wyatt, whom she had met in the spring of 1991, Lesley commented, 'With his permanent tan and easy charm he reminded me of the actor George Segal and radiated a similar boyish charm. Within three days the handsome Texan had romanced me into bed.'

Lesley claimed she had no idea that Steve Wyatt was having an affair with Fergie at the time. She claimed to be amazed when Major Ron confessed that at the same time that Wyatt was enjoying an affair with her, he was also having an on-going affair with Fergie.

There were still more embarrassing claims. Lesley said Major Ron had informed her of his daughter's love affair with Steve Wyatt claiming that, as a result, she no longer wanted to stay married to Prince Andrew, so involved had she become with Wyatt. She also told of a dinner Wyatt had had with Major Ron at Claridge's, while Fergie was still married to Andrew, in which he had all but asked for Fergie's hand in marriage.

Lesley Player claimed she had offered Fergie the loan of her basement apartment in London as a safe house where she could meet Wyatt in secret but Fergie had declined, believing it to be too dangerous. Player's relationship with Fergie and her father came to an abrupt end, however, when Wyatt confessed to Fergie he had been having an affair with Lesley. The latter wrote, 'We were all in Florida together when she took a phone call from Wyatt. Within seconds her attitude to me had changed. She turned her back on me, refused to answer my letters or take my phone calls. She began to chill me out the way she in turn would be chilled out by the royal family a few months later.'

To Elizabeth's advisers and those connected with the royal family, Bryan was seen as a sleazy opportunist, a deeply insidious influence on the Duchess of York who had brought nothing but shame and dishonour to her and further embarrassment to the beleaguered House of Windsor. The embarrassment caused by Bryan's activities on behalf of Fergie also demonstrated to Elizabeth the risks taken by exiling Fergie from the royal family and making her feel unwanted and cut off from the family. It seemed no one had thought of the possible damage to be caused if Fergie should fall in with someone, or a set of people, ruthless enough to manipulate her and her two daughters for gain and profit.

As a result of the Bryan factor however, Elizabeth, with Philip's advice, became determined not to make the same mistake if and when Diana should go through with her threat to separate from Charles. Of course Diana, as Princess of Wales, was constitutionally far more important than Fergie, and consequently at a far greater risk of possible manipulation by adventurers and opportunists. Diana had already demonstrated her naïvety by permitting her doctor friend to tell her 'true story' for a book. That had caused untold embarrassment for her, Prince Charles, her children and the entire family. Elizabeth realised that she would need to treat Diana's separation with great diplomacy and not permit her to quit the family and become a loose cannon capable of causing even greater damage.

As Bryan's affair with Fergie continued through 1992 and 1993, Bryan became the favourite uncle to Bea and Eugenie, growing in confidence as he took greater control of Fergie's business affairs. They were seen everywhere together. But one of Bryan's former lovers, Catherine Loewe, who had known him for two months, warned, 'Johnny Bryan is into all the things that men like him want in life: power, money and status. And he acted like an American on the make, telling me all the time he was determined to crash the royal inner circle – it was blatantly obvious that both he and Steve Wyatt set out deliberately to do just that.'

She added a rider, saying, 'But I honestly cannot believe for one minute that Johnny Bryan is in love with Sarah.'

And then came the photographs.

Elizabeth immediately instructed her Press Office to issue a statement in the name of her son Prince Andrew and herself, which said, 'We strongly disapprove of the publication of photographs taken in such circumstances.' Once again Elizabeth and Philip were trying to lay the blame on the press but they knew all the blame lay with the wretched Fergie.

Reaction from politicians was divided. Some MPs felt the controversy demonstrated, once again, a need for privacy legislation, at least to guard members of the royal family. Others argued that public figures, including the royals, had to recognise that their behaviour was of public interest and should act accordingly.

Elizabeth, of course, knew full well that the problem for both Diana and Fergie was that they weren't born royal. And yet, on marrying, both had accepted they would not be permitted to separate or divorce but had now chosen to ignore that promise they had openly and plainly agreed to. Both young women had taken all the privileges, the glamour, the money and the titles but had refused to accept the sacrifices and the responsibility that came with royal marriage. She knew that neither duty nor self-sacrifice came easily to non-royals who enter the unreality of the royal family, and she understood the strains of marriage between prince and commoner. Yet, throughout her entire life, she had accepted that duty came above all else, and it riled her that both young women could walk out on their obligations, and their husbands, without thinking of the effects their decisions might have on others.

That summer Elizabeth felt at her most vulnerable since she had ascended the throne in 1952. She felt a Damoclese sword hung over the monarchy and the threads were becoming dangerously thin. Increasing numbers in the media, the Establishment and both Houses of Parliament – the Commons and the Lords – feared such revelations would undermine the monarchy itself.

17. DIANA, PRINCESS OF WALES

The third witch of Windsor is perhaps the last person to be considered a witch: the lovely, beautiful, megastar Princess Diana, who became the Princess of Wales in a breathtaking fairytale wedding which captured the hearts of nations when she married Prince Charles in July 1981.

The innocent, shy, sweet, gauche Diana Spencer, just 20, would change dramatically within a few years into someone barely recognisable to those who had known her well and had worked with her during her late teens.

Diana had a rotten childhood. Born in July 1961 on an estate next to the royal family's country home at Sandringham in Norfolk – when Prince Charles was nearly thirteen years old – her mother quit the family home when Diana was only five. Looking back, it is ironic that Diana's love life and her married life should so closely mirror that of her mother Frances.

Frances was only 16 when she met her husband-to-be Johnny, then an officer in the Brigade of Guards, an equerry to the queen and a handsome man-about-town. She fell hopelessly in love with him, obsessed with this good-looking, wealthy aristocrat, in the same way that Diana would do with Prince Charles.

The similarity of their lives continued. Married at 18, Frances recalled an idyllic honeymoon, just like Diana, and then the rot set in. She became bored with her handsome husband who had taken to the country life of a gentleman farmer and enjoyed his quiet existence in the backwoods of Norfolk. Surrounded by his four children and happy with his beautiful, still young wife Frances, he loved his life.

Frances produced five children: Sarah, born in 1955, with whom Prince Charles was to have an ongoing love affair lasting several months; Jane, born in 1957; their third child, John, born in 1960, survived only ten hours; then came Diana in 1961. Finally, Charles, a son and heir, was born three years later.

After the birth of Charles, Frances began visiting London more frequently, attending parties, dinners and the theatre while visiting friends. Then in 1966 she took an apartment in fashionable Cadogan Square.

Before long, Frances had fallen in love. Peter Shand Kydd was a wallpaper millionaire: a graduate of Edinburgh University and a former Royal Navy officer, he was married to a talented artist when he began an affair with the attractive Frances. He had taken his wife and three young children to Australia and bought a 500-acre sheep farm, but that venture had failed. He returned with his family to England and met Frances.

In a sensationally frank statement to the press in 1967, Frances announced, 'I am living apart from my husband now. It is very unfortunate. I don't know if there will be a reconciliation.'

To her husband Johnny, at their estate in Norfolk, the statement came as a thunderbolt. He later said, 'How many of those 14 years were happy? I thought all of them, until the moment we parted. I was wrong. We hadn't fallen apart. We'd drifted apart.'

Diana was just six, her brother Charles only three. After her parents divorced the young Diana told one of her nannies, 'When I marry it will be for ever. I will never, never get divorced.' Twenty-five years later, when Diana forced Queen Elizabeth and the British Prime Minister to agree to a formal separation from Prince Charles, her sons were a little older; William was ten, Harry just six.

Her parents' divorce had a devastating effect on the young Diana. She changed from a happy, smiling, confident and sociable little girl to a rather unhappy, often miserable child who became increasingly insecure and shy.

Diana put much of that down to the fact that her mother had quit the family home and moved to London's bright lights in search of excitement. In the bitter divorce action that followed, Frances lost custody of her four children and they went to live with their father. Diana spent the greater part of her young life with her sisters and baby Charles in Norfolk away from their mother, except, of course, for occasional visits to the home Frances set up when she married Peter Shand Kydd in 1969.

Diana's childhood experience of loneliness and misery are the principal reasons for her vowing she would never relinquish care and custody of Wills and Harry. Everyone who saw Diana with her two sons agreed that a strong bond existed between them. Yet like her mother, Diana yearned for the bright lights and the good times; like her mother, she was fed up with her married life and her dull, boring husband. Johnny Spencer enjoyed the peace and quiet of the country and loved farming; Charles loves life in the country, tending his private walled garden, taking long country walks and shooting, hunting and fishing. Neither Frances nor Diana wanted that kind of life. They both preferred life in the fast lane, partying, meeting people, dancing and gossiping over long social lunches. In the same way that Frances could not bear a life of isolation in Norfolk, nor the restrictions, discipline and commitment of marriage to Johnny Spencer, so Diana could not stand living in Kensington Palace with the same restrictions, discipline and commitment of marriage to the Prince of Wales.

In her divorce action, Frances accused Johnny Spencer of mental cruelty and more, and Princess Diana complained to friends of exactly the same while married to Charles. Diana also accused Charles of turning his back on her, spurning her love and leaving the marital home to live with his lover Camilla Parker Bowles at Highgrove, his country home in Gloucestershire.

There was a further extraordinary coincidence: both Frances and Diana made their dramatic separations from their husbands at exactly the same age, shortly after their thirtieth birthdays. But both would later be seen as women who bore some responsibility for the hostile environments of their marriages, pleading that they were the unfortunate parties caught up in unhappy marriages.

In her desire to escape from her boring, restrictive marriage to Prince Charles, Diana's view of him changed dramatically from her obsession with her 'wonderful prince' who could do no wrong, to seeing him as a rather strange, ordinary man with opinions, hobbies and interests completely different from her own.

Education became one of the major problems that divided Charles and Diana. Prince Charles had attended a good preparatory school and Gordonstoun in Scotland – a tough but good public school – which he left with six 'O' levels and two 'A' levels. He spent three years at Cambridge and graduated with a BA honours degree. He achieved a 2.2, in university parlance, a rather ordinary degree, but his tutors were convinced that if he had not been subjected to royal disruptions (for example taking a three-month break to learn Welsh at Aberystwyth University) he would have earned a much higher degree, possibly a first.

By contrast, Diana's academic achievements were abysmal. She took six 'O' level exams and failed them all and resat four subjects only to fail them too. Indeed, she has the unenviable and remarkable achievement of having attended good schools from the ages of six to seventeen and achieved not a single exam pass in any subject. That fact was to embarrass her greatly. She not only tried to hide her failure, but frequently lied about it. Once the world discovered the truth, however, Diana changed tack, frequently joking about her lack of brain power.

But the jokes did not last forever. In their early days together, Charles would tease Diana about her education – she would laugh at his comments and Charles would comfort her by telling her it didn't matter she had no exam passes because he loved her anyway. But when problems began to emerge in the marriage Diana took exception to being teased – and she was, frequently – not only by Charles but also by other members of the royal family like Prince Philip, Andrew and Edward. It embarrassed her but sometimes the teasing would go too far and she would end up in tears.

Many jokes were made at her expense when she began making public speeches. Mortified at speaking in public, it took four years for her to sum up the courage to make her first speech. Her delivery was poor, her voice strained and it seemed as if she had received no instruction whatsoever. She blushed as she spoke and fluffed her lines even as she read them. Charles and Andrew, meantime, found it hilarious which only added to her humiliation.

As she told Sarah Ferguson, then her close friend, 'It just makes me want to curl up and die. I hate making speeches because I know what they will all say afterwards. Even the queen looks at me oddly and unnerves me after I've made a speech.'

Diana was an anomaly not only for the royal family but for the British public. On the one hand she appeared to be semi-regal and, strictly speaking, she had more English blood than Prince Charles. (Charles's blood line is mainly German and Danish.) She was always known as 'Lady Di' from the very beginning and never simply 'Diana'. Nevertheless, she hated being called 'Lady Di' and no one addressed her by that name within the walls of Buckingham Palace.

When she appeared on the royal scene in 1979 she was so different from most of the girls the world had seen with Charles. She appeared to be an ordinary, well-educated young woman with no pretentions, shy and reserved. She had none of the brash sophistication of a typical Sloane Ranger, those upper-crust young women who live around Chelsea's Sloane Square. Most have no particular ambition but swan around looking beautiful, waiting to snare some young man from a wealthy background and his own handsome income. She wore little make-up, spoke without the strangulated accents of her class and dressed in a manner more akin to her mother's generation.

Her poor educational standards endeared her to many ordinary people, as well as the fact that she had worked as a mother's help – for some months even as a char woman – to earn some money for herself. And she lived happily with several young women in a London apartment, surviving on spaghetti and other inexpensive meals, just like the great majority of other young single people. Even Barbara Cartland, whose daughter Raine would marry Diana's father Lord Spencer, described Diana as 'a perfect Barbara Cartland heroine' which, of course, she was. A true-life Cinderella, Diana was noble yet humble; she lived an ordinary life and yet had been known to royalty from birth, waiting like the quintessential virgin for a prince to find her, and love her, so that they would live together happily ever after.

From the moment of her engagement to Prince Charles in February 1981, the media propelled Diana into the ranks of a worldwide cover girl even before her wedding in July of that year. In those six months leading up to her wedding, Diana was given a quite magnificent makeover by the fashion team at *Vogue*. Diana responded with enthusiasm and delight and the nation immediately took her to their heart. Yet something was going on that the nation knew nothing about: during those six months Diana was, allegedly, living with the Queen Mother at Clarence House, a stone's throw from Buckingham Palace. In reality, however, she spent those months living in an apartment at Buckingham Palace next to Prince Charles and throughout that time they would spend each and every night together. It was obvious to all who knew them well that they were both in love, regardless of what has been said subsequently. Diana was in love, infatuated by the prince she adored.

Even the austere Archbishop of Canterbury began his nuptial address in St Paul's Cathedral with the words, 'Here is the stuff of which fairytales are made.' And due to the arrival of satellite television, the whole world was able to take part in the ceremony and the spectacular royal occasion. Many who had never seen Diana in the flesh admitted to crying that day.

This single event propelled the British monarchy into a false state of security. Elizabeth read the reports that flowed into Buckingham Palace during the ensuing days and weeks from every corner of the globe reinforcing the belief that a constitutional monarchy makes a modern nation strong. Diana's wedding also helped dispel the idea of republicanism in Britain though, ironically, the ending of her marriage to Charles 11 years later stirred the entire nation to debate whether the British monarchy might wither and die at the end of Elizabeth's reign.

The wedding created a star, and although Charles and Diana kept out of the public limelight as much as possible, the tabloid press were determined to keep their readers titillated with every morsel of gossip and innuendo. The fact that much of what they wrote was untrue did not trouble the media in the slightest.

Foreign tabloids and magazines followed the British press coverage but some European media wanted more sensational stories. The Italians, allegedly from interviews with unnamed housemaids at Buckingham Palace, described Diana as a 'sexual volcano' who studied Japanese erotic manuals. Apparently she was so determined to exhaust Prince Charles day and night that 'Il Principe Don Giovanni' would have no surplus energy for other women. The Germans quoted Diana as saying that her main aim in life was to be a 'good housewife' while the French concentrated on 'the fortunes' she spent on clothes.

Magazines around the world began providing readers with as much detail of Diana's habits as possible – her clothes, shoes, make-up, hair, diet and her life-style – so that readers could emulate the fairy princess's life. In Britain, whenever Diana altered her hair-style, thousands of young women would copy it within days. Manufacturers would take their cue from whatever little fashion accessory she decided upon, like when she wore a small bow on the heel of her stockings, for example. The demand was insatiable.

The world expected Diana to play their vision of a dream role and the less she did the more she captivated everyone's attention. In those first few years, Diana rarely appeared in public, preferring to retain her privacy inside Kensington Palace. She continued to look shy, to smile engagingly and chat to little children. As a result, the media pounced on what they could – her appearance, her clothes and rumours. And she went along with this transformation, from a round-faced, overweight, rather awkward kindergarden teacher into a sophisticated, elegant, beautiful model the world wanted to be and the fashion designers to dress.

No one seemed to bother much about the effect all this adoration might have on the young, impressionable Diana. Never before had there been an instant creation of a global megastar, whose girlish looks and shy simplicity were being dramatically catapulted into every corner of the world, all enhanced by the dream-like overtones of royalty. Most certainly Elizabeth, and her senior advisers, should at least have investigated how this notoriety might affect the new member of the royal family who had arrived like a shooting star to outshine them all.

Within a couple of years Diana would become a *femme fatale*, an enchantress who began to believe in her own powers. Every day she would order all the newspapers and magazines and would sit and read everything written about her, examine the pictures of herself and talk to her ladies-in-waiting about the outfits she should order to keep up appearances for the avaricious press. Worse still, Diana showed signs of actually believing the hype about herself. She spent more time selecting her clothes, choosing her designers and examining herself in front of the mirror before leaving Kensington Palace to attend royal engagements.

Diana had been told by her mother, Frances Shand Kydd, that she should make sure she appointed her own advisers when she moved into Kensington Palace so that she did not have to rely on Charles's old cronies, many of whom had been with him for years and who owed their allegiance solely to her husband.

Diana needed help to settle into a life that would be so different from anything she had experienced before. Until her engagement to Charles, Diana had been a free spirit, moving around London unnoticed, unattached and happy. All of that had changed overnight and she could not cope. The first signs of what the future might hold occurred within days of Charles and Diana ending their honeymoon on *Britannia* and arriving at Balmoral to join the royal family.

One week after the honeymoon Diana broke down in tears. Charles was out shooting and Diana had decided she didn't want to join the royal party for the traditional picnic lunch. Charles was unaware of what was going on at Balmoral as Diana poured out her heart to aides as she wept openly. Through her tears, Diana complained of the 'impossible, disciplined life of Balmoral . . . how she hated living in the country . . . how she hated the fact Charles enjoyed shooting birds and deer . . . and how she wanted to be free to live her own life.'

Within hours, both Charles and Elizabeth had been informed of Diana's day of tears and all hoped that these were simply the frustrations of a young bride projected into a new and totally different life. They prayed she would start to enjoy her new life as a married woman.

But she didn't. Back in London she felt trapped in the palace and, of course, she was confined to the palace for days and weeks at a time. Even her pregnancies didn't seem to bring her any happiness. Diana herself did not wish to be seen in public or photographed looking big and, in her eyes, hugely unattractive, so she hardly ever appeared in public when her pregnancies were apparent.

Diana began to take out her frustrations on Prince Charles. She sought from Charles the love she had not received as a young child; she wanted and needed reassurance and comfort; to have her confidence boosted on a daily basis. Diana believed Charles to be the one person who could do all these things for her. She had worshipped him. Before their marriage she would look at him making speeches with pride and love in her eyes, some thought adoration. No man could have provided Diana with all she needed and, unfortunately, Charles least of all.

Shortly after their marriage the image began to crack and Diana realised her prince was mortal, not unlike her father who had also been unable to give her the love, the confidence and the reassurance she craved to tackle the world.

In Kensington Palace, the staff would often hear Diana plead with Charles, 'Please don't leave me. Please, please darling don't leave me. I can't cope without you.' And then the pleading would often end with Diana screaming at Charles, sometimes swearing at the top of her voice. The encounter would result in Charles leaving, looking shaken and sheepish and Diana in tears in her room.

Diana became jealous of the time officials spent with Charles, hating the fact that they seemed to have a greater claim on his time than herself or young William. She seemed unable to understand that Charles, as Prince of Wales, had a varied and very busy life; that he had a vast estate, the Duchy of Cornwall, to preside over; he had a hundred and one official duties and functions, visits and speeches every year, many of which had to be written and checked. He also had the daily chore of reading his 'red' boxes – a duty of the heir to the throne as well as the queen.

Diana believed that all would change for the better if she dismissed all Charles's former secretaries, advisers and officials who had always had access to him. That was one of the prime reasons his old cronies – some of whom were personal friends – began leaving his staff in those early years of the marriage. Diana would pick battles and make life awkward for them until, in the end, they had no recourse but to resign. Diana, on the other hand, became no happier.

Perhaps the best example of Diana's wayward nature was over the appointment of Oliver Everett, as we saw earlier. After a catalogue of incidents, Everett appealed to Charles reluctantly to let him go because he felt his presence harmed Diana and indeed strained the royal marriage. The day Everett left, Diana was in an ecstatic mood and danced around the palace. To many who knew the parties involved, Everett's was believed to be the most catastrophic out of the 40-odd that occurred in those first few years of the marriage. There were other good men that Diana managed to fire or, more accurately, persuade to resign, including one of the best legal and constitutional brains working in the palace, Edward Adeane, Prince Charles's private secretary and principal adviser. Diana was jealous of the access Charles permitted Adeane and she was determined to be rid of him. Repeatedly Diana appealed to Charles to fire his private secretary but Charles refused.

Edward Adeane had been no palace flunky. His great-grandfather, Lord Stamfordham, had been private secretary first to Queen Victoria and later to the Prince of Wales in the early years of the century. Lord Michael Adeane had been first equerry and then principal private secretary to Elizabeth. Edward himself was noted as a brilliant barrister. Nine years older than Charles and with an impeccable background of Eton and Camridge, he was the perfect royal courtier. Confronted by what Charles believed had turned into an impossible situation, he went to see his mother to discuss what he should do. Elizabeth, however, gave him no advice at all. She simply told her son, 'You will have to make the decision. It is your problem.'

Charles tried to placate Diana and Adeane but without success. As a result, some months later, Charles could no longer put up with his wife's demands and Adeane's subdued anger. The man who had guided him so skilfully over a number of years resigned. Adeane was furious; Diana overjoyed. Within days of leaving, Adeane predicted trouble in the marriage, so disturbed was he that Charles had permitted Diana to wield such influence and power.

Charles asked Michael Colborne, his friend from the Royal Navy, who had been working in his private office since 1976, to step in to help and advise Diana. Charles knew that Diana liked and trusted Colborne. But within two years Colborne had reluctantly asked Charles for permission to quit. Despite her victories within the palace and the forced resignations of more than forty royal servants, Diana became more depressed and unhappy following the birth of Prince William in June 1982. Most now describe her state as the result of post-natal depression coupled with her inability to accept the restrictive atmosphere of the palace.

It was of Colborne that Diana asked, during one of their frequent *tête-à-têtes* shortly after her marriage, 'Michael, tell me, do you think I will change?'

Colborne replied, 'Yes, I do. From when you married the Prince of

Wales your life changed. You only have to order a meal or a snack and it will be presented to you perfectly prepared and at the exact time you requested. You only have to order a car and within minutes it will be waiting for you outside, a chauffeur at the wheel.'

'And will that have any effect on me?' she enquired. 'Will it change me?'

'Yes it will,' replied Colborne, 'you will become a bitch.'

Diana didn't bat an eyelid but she made no response.

Diana would confide in Colborne, telling him of her unhappiness and feelings of desperation which she could not control. Colborne, Charles and Elizabeth were concerned for this was no simple case of post-natal depression. If anything, Diana seemed to be fading away, eating less and becoming less communicative with everyone. She looked pale and listless, the spark that had ignited the world on her wedding day gone. Elizabeth decided the time for taking action had arrived and took advice from Mr George Pinker, the royal family's gynaecologist who had brought Diana's two sons into the world. During the following months and years Diana was seen by doctors, psychiatrists, psychologists, consultants, a dietitian and a fitness instructor, though later she would claim that the royal family had done nothing to help her during the traumatic years when she suffered from anorexia nervosa and bulimia. In fact, Elizabeth took a far greater interest in her daughter-in-law's well-being than she did when her own children were growing up.

The nation, however, remained unaware of life behind the high walls of the palace. All they saw were pretty pictures of the royal family smiling at the camera in idyllic surroundings, their children well dressed and spotlessly clean next to their loving parents with fixed smiles on their faces. Virtually every photograph Buckingham Palace released to the media in those first years portrayed the perfect family, the image Elizabeth wanted to project to the nation.

After official royal photographs had been taken by the favoured appointed photographer and the film processed, every frame was sent to the palace and Elizabeth would insist on seeing every one, not just a selection. In consultation with several senior advisers, Elizabeth would decide which photographs should be given to the media to ensure the correct image was received and understood by the people.

Diana's attitude towards rearing both William and Harry was entirely different from royal tradition. She breast-fed her babies, and cuddled them, fed and bathed them, changed their nappies and dressed them, and generally gave them all the love and attention that a mother naturally gives her children. Diana positively smothered them with motherly love. One of the reasons for smothering baby William with love and affection was that Diana believed she was receiving little love and affection from Charles because of the time and energy he spent on his royal duties.

One year after the birth of Prince William a new man appeared in Diana's life: a young, affable, friendly officer of the Household Cavalry named James Hewitt, then a Lieutenant in the Life Guards. They met at a cocktail party during the summer of 1983 and after chatting and laughing together for thirty minutes or so, Hewitt offered to teach Diana to ride. Diana had found herself instantly attracted to the young cavalry officer who was obviously flirting with her as they chatted together. Before they parted, Diana said she would telephone him at his Knightsbridge Barracks office overlooking Hyde Park and fix a riding lesson.

In *Princess in Love*, the book Hewitt secretly co-authored with Anna Pasternak, he claimed that he had only met Diana in the summer of 1986. But this goes against the evidence of those people who worked at Kensington Palace in the early 1980s who saw James Hewitt quite regularly at the palace from 1983 onwards.

Days after their first meeting, Diana phoned Hewitt and asked him, 'Are you serious about giving me riding lessons?' Hewitt replied, 'Of course, any time.'

A couple of days later, Diana arrived at the barracks with her lady-in-waiting, Hazel West, a tall, blonde woman and an experienced horse woman. After slowly walking around the indoor school on a dependable grey for an hour or so, under the experienced eye of Hewitt and West, Diana began to relax. Diana had never recovered her confidence since falling from a pony at the age of eight and breaking her leg. Somehow Hewitt instilled confidence in her and slowly she began to relax and enjoy her early morning lessons. Within a couple of weeks they had ventured out together in Hyde Park, accompanied by her lady-in-waiting, police and plainclothes detectives. After riding for an hour or so, with Diana and James riding side-by-side, they would return to the barracks and call in to the Officers' Mess for a cup of coffee.

According to *Princess in Love*, Diana and Hewitt became lovers four months after they had first met. The affair is reputed to have taken place after a roast-beef dinner at Kensington Palace. Hewitt would write of their moments of stolen love, of their weekends of passion together at his parents' house in Devon, taking long walks along Exmouth beach or driving across Dartmoor. The affair would last on-and-off until after the Gulf War in which James Hewitt fought as a squadron commander with the Life Guards. During Desert Storm, Hewitt would receive letters which, he claimed, Diana sent him each and every day, protesting her love and fearing for his life. On occasions, Hewitt would phone her from the battlefield, sometimes borrowing a mobile phone from a tabloid newspaper's war correspondent.

But the relationship would end shortly after Hewitt returned to England at the end of the Gulf War. In the book, Hewitt claimed that the relationship had foundered because Diana had no further need for him; that through him she had regained the strength to enjoy life once again. Diana had a different interpretation. She confessed that she had wanted to separate from Charles and live with Hewitt but that he could not find the courage to go through with the drama and the trauma their relationship would create. Diana contended that in the final analysis Hewitt had shown weakness when Diana needed a man of strength to stand by her side and share her life.

But despite her passionate love affair with Hewitt, Diana's life became a turmoil of emotions as she struggled to continue living a normal life with Charles, hating the discipline and restrictions of palace life and desperately wanting freedom to live her own life. It was these conflicts of interest that caused Diana extraordinary mood swings and deep psychological traumas which led to her anorexia and bulimia.

Elizabeth had hoped that Diana would begin to relax and enjoy her life after the birth of her sons. Unfortunately, Diana's post-natal depression muted her joy as she fought to sort out her emotions and her life. Sometimes she would turn to Charles for comfort and affection but she didn't feel the love for him that she had experienced during their heady days of passionate love before their wedding. So she found herself turning to Hewitt more and more not only for support and solace but also for the excitement of an illicit love affair.

Incapable of understanding his wife's needs, Charles continued trying everything to please Diana and make her feel happier. For four years Charles did all in his power to inspire, cheer up and humour Diana, giving in to most of her demands. From the outset, Charles was determined to make a success of his marriage. But whatever Charles did he found Diana's moods becoming more intense, more unyielding, and prone to dramatic change without reason. She would demand all Charles's time and his constant attention at one time and then at another she would rant and rage at the hapless Charles, telling him to get out of her life. Unable to cope, not knowing what more he could do to help his tearful wife, whom he believed was suffering from stress and depression, Charles began to spend more time away from Kensington Palace.

Diana's mother Frances Shand-Kydd talked frequently to her daughter during those problem years but found herself unable to get close to her. The two had never been close, in fact, because Diana had never known her mother and resented the fact. Furthermore, Diana never forgave her mother for walking out of the marriage leaving four young children. Frances always felt a certain antagonism, even hostility, from Diana and though she tried to overcome the problem and get closer to her youngest daughter she never succeeded. She always felt the relationship with her daughter was on a knife edge and, as a result, felt she had little or no influence over her. In any case, Frances was never sure that she should become more involved in Diana's marital problems, not wanting to interfere too much in a royal marriage.

Six months after Harry's birth, Diana was struggling to cope, not knowing whether to turn to Charles or James Hewitt for support and comfort; often she just wanted to be with her children. During that time she did, occasionally, take a handful of laxatives in her determination to return to her sylph-like appearance as well as deliberately make herself sick by drinking salt water. She would even go further and stick her fingers down her throat to make herself vomit.

She talked to former girlfriends about her condition but never gave the full details of how badly she suffered. Diana found it impossible to control her tantrums and bad moods, screaming and shouting at Charles, picking arguments each and every day and even refusing to attend royal functions or some of the engagements at which she had agreed to appear. In Charles's eyes, brought up to put duty above all else, Diana's attitude amounted to gross dereliction of her responsibilities. Charles could not forgive that behaviour and nothing infuriated him more than when Diana would refuse to carry out royal functions.

Following the birth of Harry, doctors, psychiatrists and consultants specialising in post-natal depression came to see Diana as Charles and Elizabeth worried over her deteriorating health. They could see that she was depressed, losing weight, sometimes looking painfully thin, but Diana wanted nothing of the attention and flatly denied she was suffering from anorexia or post-natal depression. Sometimes she would even refuse to see the specialists who had been called in to examine her. There was little Charles could do but hope that she would accept help, take the advice of the experts and, eventually, pull out of her depression.

But Diana believed that the royal family had turned against her. She wanted nothing whatsoever to do with Charles and told him that their marriage was over in all but name. In desperation, she refused the advice of the professionals and sought help from others instead. In early 1986 she sought the advice of Penny Thornton, an astrologer who was well known in aristocratic circles. Penny Thornton believed that no emotional problem was insoluble if you placed your faith in the stars. She told Sarah Ferguson, the Duchess of York, that she had used astrology to help save a number of marriages.

Penny did give Diana hope for the future and raised her spirits. 'Penny was a revelation to me,' she said. 'She made me totally re-think my life. She taught me things about myself I never knew. She has been a godsend.'

Charles, meantime, would escape from Kensington Palace as often as possible. He would go to Scotland to fish, shoot or stalk deer; he would escape to Highgrove to tend his beloved garden and relax in peace as he tried to fathom a way out of his awful predicament. He still wanted the marriage to work but he had not the faintest idea how to succeed. In the end he turned to Camilla, the one woman who had always understood him, the woman who had urged him to marry Diana. He would invite her to Highgrove from her house which was just 15 minutes away. They would talk of his marriage, of the problems, of Diana's behaviour and her depression. At that time there was no question of rekindling the affair Charles and Camilla had enjoyed back in 1979.

When he first realised that his marriage was in deep trouble Charles had first only sought the advice of one or two close and trusted friends. He said nothing to his mother. Most of his friends suggested that Charles just let the matter ride, permit Diana as much freedom as possible in the hope that she would rationalise her life and her position and accept the constrictions which her marriage had placed on her life.

On occasion, during the first two years of his marriage, Charles had turned to Camilla, chatting to her on the phone and seeking her advice. Following the birth of Harry, however, when Diana had all but turned her back on him, preferring the company of James Hewitt and her other young friends, Charles had fled to the security and peace of Highgrove away from the maelstrom of Kensington Palace. Camilla talked sense to Charles and he quickly discovered that in Camilla he had found someone to whom he could confide his innermost thoughts with trust and confidence. She became a regular visitor to Highgrove, believing she had a duty and a responsibility to help this man she had always cherished and often loved.

Once again, love blossomed between the two as it had done twice before. The first time occurred in 1973 when Charles first met Camilla. At that time Camilla was also dating the dashing cavalry officer Andrew Parker Bowles, then ten years older than Charles and Camilla. She would date Andrew and spend time with Charles at Broadlands, Mountbatten's country home. But Charles was about to go to sea for five years with the Royal Navy and marriage was far from his mind. Within six months of Charles's departure, Camilla had married Andrew.

Their second love affair began in September 1979 following Earl Mountbatten's murder by the IRA while he was fishing in Ireland. Charles was angry, frustrated, depressed and traumatised by the murder of his Uncle Dickie, the man who had been more of a father to him than Prince Philip. Camilla came to the rescue: they spent six months together, seeing each other most days, while she nursed Charles back to the man he had been before the tragedy struck.

During those months, they spent days and nights together indulging in the most passionate sexual relationship Charles had ever experienced. Fortunately for both Charles and Camilla, Andrew Parker Bowles was spending those six months in Rhodesia serving with Lord Soames as Rhodesia introduced black majority rule and the country became Zimbabwe. Elizabeth was consulted prior to Parker Bowles's posting and she agreed to the plan, as long as Camilla's husband raised no objection.

But Charles, who barely knew Diana at this stage, had realised that he could never marry Camilla and remain heir to the throne. He knew that neither Elizabeth, nor the Queen Mother, the Establishment, the church or the government would permit that. Together, Charles and Camilla discussed what might have been. Both knew the drama caused by the marriage of King Edward VIII and Charles knew his mother's strict view of divorce. He and Camilla realised that if indeed they did marry then Charles would have no option but to withdraw from the line of succession. While Charles wanted to marry Camilla and turn his back on the throne, his upbringing meant he had to put duty first, his own wishes a distant second.

Indeed, it was the sensible, down-to-earth Camilla who finally persuaded Charles to even contemplate settling down and marrying Diana because of the catastrophic effect it might have on the monarchy. Despite their intense affair that had brought them so close, Camilla pushed Charles away, telling him to follow the advice Uncle Dickie had given him some years earlier. 'A young man in your position should go out, sow his wild oats and then find a young virgin; marry her, and train her to be the next Queen of England.' Within a matter of weeks he had met the lovely Lady Diana Spencer, only 19, a virgin and a girl who had been in love with him from afar for years. And Charles was captivated that such a nubile, lovely young woman should be so desperately in love with him that she could not bear to be separated from him for more than a day.

Diana certainly knew that Charles had had many girlfriends before she began dating him. She had known the intimate details of the on-off love affair between her sister Sarah and Charles which had lasted nearly a year. By simply reading the newspapers Diana had become aware of the girls Charles had known. Most, though not all, had been catalogued, noted, checked and probed by the insatiable tabloid press. And, quite early in her relationship with Charles, she had learned of Camilla Parker Bowles.

At first Diana believed that Camilla and Charles were 'just friends' who had known each other since they were teenagers. She believed that out of friendship Camilla had given Charles a shoulder to cry on following the murder of Mountbatten. She had not known of the deep love they had for each other nor of their heavy sexual and emotional relationship. And she had no idea that Charles had seriously considered giving up the throne to marry her. But when she discovered all this in late 1986 everything fell into place. She knew instinctively that Charles was again seeing Camilla during his sojourns at Highgrove. Diana confronted Charles with the accusation that he was sleeping with Camilla but for several months Charles denied this.

One day in January 1987 Diana decided to put her theory to the test and drove down to Highgrove unannounced. Later, she told a girlfriend what happened: 'As I drove up to Highgrove early one morning, around 8.30 a.m., with my detective in the car, I saw a car driving away through another exit. It was Camilla. I went straight in and Charles was having breakfast. I asked him if Camilla had been there and he looked away and asked me why I wanted to know.

'That made me see red and I raced upstairs to the bedroom, my bedroom, and the bed was unmade. It was obvious that two people had slept the night there. I went down again and asked him again whether Camilla had been there. He didn't answer.

'I then knew for sure that he was having an affair. I kept challenging him but he wouldn't answer me and I lost my temper. I just had a go at him, telling him what a shit he had been, having an affair with an old girlfriend, treating me like shit, leaving me in London with the children while he bonked away at Highgrove.

'In the end I just broke down in tears. I didn't know what to do. All my worst fears had been proved. I knew he didn't love me any more. I knew he loved someone else. It was awful, awful.'

Diana would tell her friends that that was the defining moment in her relationship with Charles. That revelation changed her view of Charles, their marriage and, more importantly for Elizabeth, her duty as Princess of Wales. Overnight, it would appear, she became a mature woman. The Princess of Wales, mother of two children and the next Queen of England was 25 years old and had her whole life ahead of her, a life with a husband who didn't love her any more and for whom she had lost all respect.

By relating these stories to close friends, Diana was, of course, making sure that her friends heard her side of the story. She said nothing of her adultery; nothing of her love affairs, not only with James Hewitt but also her relationships with a succession of men. Nor did she relate how she would scream and rage at Charles, ordering him out of the palace, telling him to get out of her life.

It was some time in 1987 that the new Diana emerged. And what a change had come over the bashful Di everyone loved: in contrast to the woman of before Diana would go out of her way to attend every party, when and with whom she wanted, determined to enjoy herself and flirt madly with the men who took her fancy. Old friends like Kate Menzies and Anne Beckwith-Smith were recruited to get invites for Diana to dinners and parties.

Sir John Riddell, her private secretary at that time, could barely cope with her succession of instant parties, dinners, cocktails, nights on the town, theatre and cinema outings. He asked Prince Charles if he would speak to Diana about her casual outings. Diana's schedule, planned six months in advance – as all royal diaries have to be – would be changed at a whim as she freely accepted casual appointments and made Sir John's life almost impossible. Charles did speak to Diana but to no avail and so Sir John was left with little option. He resigned.

Meanwhile Diana had a ball. She flirted outrageously. She dined and danced and partied with whomever she wished. She had affairs with various men, and remained apparently unconcerned as to what Charles knew or did not know. But Diana did try to hide her behaviour from the press. She did not want her mother-in-law to know what she was doing for she was always frightened of the queen.

One example reveals Diana's relationship with Elizabeth. Like many other members of the royal family, Diana became rather a good mimic. Indeed, it is one of the royal family's traditional games that they happily make innocent fun of some individual or other by mimicking them outrageously. In The Firm it is bound to earn a good laugh and not a little ribaldry and Diana found that she was quite good at it. On one occasion she proved too good.

At Balmoral one evening while waiting for the queen to come down to dinner, the family were all standing round, as they always do, for the arrival of the monarch. Elizabeth is most strict that this protocol should be rigorously adhered to, even when the family are all on holiday together. While they waited, Diana began to mimic the queen, adopting the same high, rather shrill, pathetic voice which the irreverent *Spitting Image* television show always uses when making fun of the queen. However, it has forever been a golden rule within The Firm that no one ridicules the queen. Indeed, even in the privacy of the royal kitchens at Buckingham Palace no servant would dare to mimic the queen because it would probably end in instant dismissal. On this occasion, however, Diana, who had been practising the queen's *Spitting Image* voice, was giving her impression when Elizabeth walked in.

Diana didn't see her mother-in-law until silence descended like a blanket. And then Diana saw Elizabeth, her eyes blazing as she pierced her with a withering look. Diana fell instantly silent in mid-sentence and blushed a bright red. 'I was only joking,' she stammered nervously as Elizabeth continued to look at her. Elizabeth not only did not reply, but never spoke a single word to Diana that entire evening.

That was typical Diana, not thinking before launching into something she thought wickedly amusing. It was also typical of Elizabeth, who never forgets that she is the monarch and always insists that every single one of her subjects, including her own family, give her the respect due to the sovereign.

Diana knew that the power of The Firm lay with the queen and, if you crossed her, your life would become a misery. Her mother-in-law had the whip hand and would use it whenever she thought necessary if she believed the reputation of the monarchy was being threatened.

Gradually Diana's popular support waned as the media projected her as a spoiled brat, causing trouble within the palace, firing Charles's loyal staff and spending thousands of pounds of taxpayers' money on clothes for herself.

Until Harry was about twelve months old, Diana had become patron of only a few charities and organisations, always taking advice from the palace and from Charles. As a result she was hardly ever seen in public except when attending royal functions, usually accompanying Charles, where she would be photographed in a sensational full-length ball gown topped with a tiara. She would look stunning, but that wasn't the real Diana.

She had always shown considerable warmth when dealing with people, particularly on a one-to-one basis. Whenever she toured hospitals, old people's homes or child care centres the effect was instant and remarkable: everyone she met commented on her warmth and sincerity. It was a characteristic that neither Elizabeth, Prince Philip, Charles nor any of their own children possess. Indeed some describe Elizabeth and members of her immediate family as 'cold fish'.

So Diana decided to involve herself with more deserving charities. A week never went by without at least two or three letters arriving at Kensington Palace asking her to be patron of their particular charity or deserving organisation. She began to select the ones she wanted to support. It was due to this that from 1986 onwards she came into contact with far greater numbers of ordinary British men and women and particularly children. She set up an immediate rapport with them. People turned out in their hundreds to catch a glimpse of her, waiting patiently in all weather to cheer her and, if possible, talk to her. The press suddenly changed tack, giving her their support as she took on more charities and showed she had what every other member of the royal family, including Elizabeth, lacks – the common touch. Suddenly people believed that Diana cared, really cared, not just for herself but for everyone, especially those in need.

Diana volunteered to become patron of those charities that other members of the royal family fought shy of. Heart-searching discussions took place within Buckingham Palace when Diana announced she wished to become patron of an AIDS-related charity. Some royal courtiers advised Elizabeth that it would be a bad image for the monarchy if Diana was seen associating with charities concerning homosexuals who had contracted the disease.

Elizabeth had a word with Diana and asked whether she thought it was a good idea. The latter played her part brilliantly, showing unusual courage before her mother-in-law for she realised that this apparently innocent question from Elizabeth was her way of showing disapproval. Diana told her that she thought it vital that someone from the royal family should be seen to be openly supporting AIDS patients and she would be happy to do so. Her decision to become the patron won much praise and public acclaim.

Diana would be seen and photographed touching lepers and hugging AIDS patients, talking enthusiastically to drug abusers, the terminally ill, the handicapped and the homeless. She befriended them just as naturally as she did small children. Some cynics called her a publicity-seeking disaster-junkie, a 'Mother Teresa in a tiara'. But charity workers knew better.

By the end of the 1980s Diana had become patron to more than one hundred and ten charities and organisations. And she worked hard, winning praise on all sides. Those who ran the charities talked of her 'wonderful commitment' and testified to the fact that her involvement did not cease when the spotlights were turned off.

Diana's own self-confidence rose as she realised people were responding to her, wanting her for herself, not just because she was the wife of the Prince of Wales. From her point of view her marriage was over in all but name. And she determined to lead her own life in her own way, carrying out royal duties only when obliged to do so. The more media attention she received, the more confident Diana became. The more her photograph appeared in the press, attending her own charities, the more she determined to outshine her 'boring' husband and the entire royal family whom she believed had turned against her. She adored being in the limelight, the centre of attention. She overcame her shyness and her eating disorders; she swam every day, played tennis two or three times a week and attended a gymnasium; and she indulged in all the new health crazes, from aromatherapy to colonic irrigation. As a result, Diana felt like a new person and her new confidence spilled over into her personal life. She became a woman bewitched, using all her seductive powers, from fluttering her eyelashes to running her hand through the hair of the man to whom she was attracted. She danced with whoever she wished at parties; she loved the way men looked at her, raising the eyebrows of other women in the party as she brazenly flirted on the dance floor. She was seen with eligible bachelors dancing so closely during smoochy numbers that she appeared to be all but making love as they moved slowly around the dance floor.

Even when Charles did accompany his wife to parties, Diana would continue her new flirtatious role. She seemed to revel in being outrageous with a number of the men whenever Charles was present. Some believed she wanted to interest her husband, others that she wanted to make him jealous, but most believed she was trying to discredit Charles, seeking revenge. And it was revenge that Diana wanted. She had convinced herself that she was the 'wronged woman', that Charles was to blame for the breakdown of their marriage. The fact that she had been having a passionate affair with James Hewitt on-and-off since 1983 never entered the equation.

Despite the occasional newspaper story, the general public had no idea what Diana was up to – they knew nothing of her outrageous behaviour and the fact that she was acting like a bachelor girl rather than the wife of the Prince of Wales and the next Queen of England. And the public did not want to believe those few stories that did emerge for they felt Diana could do no wrong. Neither the media nor the public had any idea that Diana was living a double life, sharing her loneliness and unhappiness with the world while secretly enjoying various love affairs.

But Elizabeth knew. She was constantly fed reports of Diana's behaviour and knew of her various lovers. Elizabeth feared that sooner or later the truth would emerge in some tabloid newspaper and that would spell disaster for the royal family. But Elizabeth had no idea that Diana would go to such lengths to persuade the British people – her devoted fans – that she had been treated appallingly by Charles, the queen and the Establishment.

In the autumn of 1990 Charles phoned his mother and asked if he could visit her. It was most unusual for Charles to want to drop by 'for a chat'. Mostly they talked on the phone about formal matters and hardly ever indulged in idle gossip. Elizabeth feared the worst.

Twenty-four hours later Charles walked into the lovely airy drawing room overlooking the gardens at Buckingham Palace. It was time for afternoon tea. Throughout those hours waiting to see her son, Elizabeth had hardly been able to eat or sleep, instinctively fearing that the reason for Charles's visit was Diana.

Elizabeth had prayed that Charles's marriage would not end in utter disaster, that it would be possible to salvage. Every Sunday for the previous few years Elizabeth had knelt and prayed for their marriage. Elizabeth had told the Queen Mother of her fears and she, in turn, had told her daughter to relax and pray everything would work out. Elizabeth had known that Charles and Diana had been living separate lives for some years. Stubbornly she had hoped that one day they would understand an accommodation had to be reached for the sake of the children and above all else, for the monarchy. Elizabeth also knew that many aristocratic marriages were shams: that after a wedding and a couple of children, the husband and wife went their own ways, almost living separate lives, but still contented to live under the same roof. Such arrangements had been a fact of life for generations.

The separations and divorces of both Elizabeth's sister Margaret and her only daughter Anne could not compare to the trauma that the rocky marriage of Charles and Diana caused her. For this would be far more serious than any adulterous affair that either Charles or Diana had contemplated. Elizabeth knew that if Charles and Diana separated, or worse, divorced, this would be damaging, if not destructive, to the crown.

Elizabeth knew she could rely on Charles – she had always done so and he had never let her down. He had been brought up since childhood with the understanding that duty had to come above all else.

Elizabeth had never interfered in Charles's love life, even when Charles produced a string of girlfriends, many of whom Elizabeth would not have deemed suitable to become the next Queen of England. She had not advised Charles about his intended marriage to Diana. Indeed they had hardly spoken about it. Elizabeth saw Diana as a lovely young girl from a good aristocratic family and perfectly suited to be his bride and the future queen. Philip hardly said a word to his son but commented to a former polo friend, 'I am very happy that the girl he has found to marry is a long-legged, good-looking blonde. I had feared he might decide on someone awful.'

Charles would have continued his bachelor life but for Mountbatten's murder which made him realise how thin was the dividing line between life and death. He realised it was his duty to produce an heir to the throne, a view his father had repeatedly pointed out to him.

Since his marriage in 1981 Charles had become lonely. Those he had relied on for advice and friendship had been forced to quit by the demands and outrageous behaviour of Diana, and his father had never been a friend to him. The relationship with his mother was one of respect, not friendship. And Charles missed desperately the advice, the warmth and the friendship of Uncle Dickie. The only person Charles could wholly rely on was Camilla.

Diana herself was lonely. The relationship between her and Elizabeth had always been problematic. Elizabeth, so used to informal chit-chat, found talking to Diana hard work. Elizabeth was only being honest when she said, without rancour, 'It seems that the only topics of conversation one can have with Diana are about clothes or the weather.

On another occasion Elizabeth said, 'It's not as though she hasn't a brain in her beautiful head but she certainly acts as though she doesn't. I try everything to talk to her, to bring her out of her shell but I simply cannot get her to relax and chat to me in the same way as I can Anne or Sarah.'

It had not taken Elizabeth long to see selfishness and determination behind Diana's apparent bashfulness and nervous disposition. Elizabeth considered Diana strong willed, even wilful. She had watched Diana change from a nervous teenager into a young woman who would appear to stop at nothing to get her own way. Elizabeth had been unhappy at the way Diana talked to Charles, becoming moody until he did as she had requested. Yet Elizabeth felt she should not intervene as she witnessed Diana manipulate and control her eldest son. Elizabeth had quickly come to realise when Charles was an immature young man that he suffered from the one character trait which seemed to run through the male line of the Windsors – a weakness, a lack of willpower and a lack of confidence with women. She would often wish that, in that respect at least, Charles had taken after his forceful father.

Only once had she talked to both Diana and Charles together, some months after Harry was born when she sensed things were going badly wrong. Elizabeth knew that Diana was the root cause of the problem but she believed the only way the marriage could succeed would be for Charles to be more firm. To Charles's surprise and Diana's delight, Elizabeth had spent most of the time castigating Charles for not taking control of his marriage. She had told him quietly but forcefully that his marriage was his business but that if it was going to be successful he had to be more authoritative. She reminded him that one day he would be king, and that would mean taking command of everything, including the entire royal family.

Elizabeth had hoped the arrival of William and Harry would not only help bring Charles and Diana closer but would channel Diana's energies towards her children and away from constant confrontation with Charles. Elizabeth also hoped that with more maturity and the responsibility of a family, Diana's violent mood swings and tantrums would come to an end. She hoped it might help to break down the barrier between Diana and herself, a barrier which Elizabeth knew often disappeared when young married women become mothers themselves.

Elizabeth was sitting on the sofa in the drawing room when Charles walked in for his chat. She had three of her pet corgis around her, talking to them as though they were children. They were hoping for a tidbit from the royal hand, but Elizabeth's mind was elsewhere.

Charles rang for the maid to bring tea and sat down at the other end of the sofa. Dressed in a double-breasted grey suit, blue shirt and tie, Charles coughed and, between sips of tea and a biscuit, delivered the bombshell his mother had feared. To all intents and purposes their marriage was over and he had little or no hope that the marriage could be saved.

Elizabeth didn't know how to respond. Charles knew that his mother's marriage had not been a success. She had endured years of Philip and much unhappiness. Elizabeth knew from her own experience how the wronged person felt trying to put a brave face on a difficult marriage. But Elizabeth also knew that Diana had lovers, numerous ones, which she presumed Charles knew nothing about. All she could do was hope that Charles and Diana would come to some sort of accommodation, and stay together, for the sake of the Crown and for the children. Elizabeth knew how involved Diana was with Wills and Harry and hoped that that alone would encourage her to stay married and remain a part of the royal family.

Elizabeth had also been informed of Charles's close involvement with Camilla and she understood that the two had so much more in common than ever Diana and Charles could have hoped for. She also feared that after the catastrophe of his own marriage Charles would decide that Camilla was the woman with whom he wanted to share his life. But that only made Elizabeth think of her uncle Edward who had risked the existence of the monarchy itself for the love of a woman. Only too well aware that her uncle's selfishness had created a constitutional crisis and nearly brought down the House of Windsor, she feared that another marriage to a divorced woman might be the last straw.

For once Elizabeth did not know what to do so she decided to follow the advice given her as a young woman being trained to succeed her father – seek advice. Uppermost in her mind that afternoon, however, was the conviction that Charles and Diana must be dissuaded from the idea that they could simply separate like any other couple living a miserable existence together.

As a matter of urgency Elizabeth decided she had to have far-reaching discussions and opinions on the subject before she could take the matter further. She would need to discuss all the implications with her advisers, constitutional lawyers, church leaders and the Prime Minister, the Attorney-General and other political figures. She would need to brief her own lawyers to check the constitutional position.

In her childhood, Elizabeth had barely been aware of the crisis at the time of Edward VIII's abdication but in a short time she had learned how near that crisis had come to threatening the Crown.

Now, only 55 years later, she was the monarch faced with another royal divorce and the same threat to the monarchy. And she knew this could be the greatest test of her entire reign. It needed to be handled with skill and diplomacy and, if necessary, with firmness and Machiavellian cunning.

Of course, Charles had been under no illusion that divorce was out of the question no matter what marital problems he faced. And Diana knew that too. She was happy for the *status quo* to continue. She was riding the crest of a wave; the nation adored her and thought she could do no wrong; she was enjoying life partying and flirting, taking lovers whenever the mood took her but enjoying all the privileges and prestige of her status, Her Royal Highness, The Princess of Wales.

One of the men Diana turned to for a shoulder to cry on was James Gilbey, six foot three inches tall, well educated and a man-about-town. They had met in the late 1970s shortly after leaving school and had kept in contact. But the more Diana became estranged from Prince Charles the more she found solace and comfort from James Gilbey. Though Hewitt was her lover, he was also a Guards officer with duties that meant he was often away, sometimes serving with his regiment in Germany. Gilbey had lived a champagne lifestyle but the severe British recession had taken its toll on his second-hand car business which went into liquidation in 1991, leaving debts of £600,000. Deeply in debt, he joined the British specialist car manufacturer, Lotus, as its marketing director.

Gilbey was so gentle by nature and easy to talk to that Diana found him an ideal man to confide in. She believed he knew and understood her and her predicament of having to live in a hostile environment surrounded by royal courtiers who treated her as an upstart. More importantly, Diana knew that ever since the birth of Harry, she and Charles had lived separate lives and she had no wish to share his bed.

Throughout the years Diana would keep up the pretence of being the injured party complaining to a number of her girlfriends, 'No one seems to care about my feelings now. They don't seem to care whether I'm miserable or happy. They think I'm dispensable now; I've finished my life's work; I've produced two male heirs.'

Gilbey revelled in his new-found role for he had worshipped Diana for more than ten years though the relationship had been one-sided. Diana had never been particularly attracted to Gilbey whom she likened to an affectionate spaniel. In 1992, when the world believed Diana was having an affair with Gilbey, she told one of her friends, 'Oh no, never. James asked me out when I was a teenager and

I didn't want to know then. He has been very, very kind to me but there was never anything between us, never; though he *was* rather keen.'

Diana's relationship with Gilbey was close. But from everything Diana has said it is highly unlikely they ever became lovers though they behaved like lovers and called each other 'darling'. Diana liked the fact Gilbey was 'in love' with her. It boosted her confidence and made her feel good. They would hold hands, kiss frequently, but never passionately. Sometimes, Gilbey would smother her hand with kisses and profess his love for her. Their phone conversations were smoochy. But their relationship was, of course, brought to the notice of Sir Robert Fellowes and he kept Elizabeth informed of their relationship.

Diana had no idea she was being watched for she believed her own personal police bodyguard was answerable only to her and treated everything she did or said with total confidence. It was part of her naïvety not to understand the extent to which those in command at Buckingham Palace have the most extraordinary powers, their tentacles capable of reaching into every nook and cranny of British society, whether political, legal, the church, the civil service, the armed services or the City.

Protecting Diana and keeping her confidences formed only part of her bodyguard's job. As Princess of Wales, Diana would be vulnerable, not only to physical attack or kidnap or some deranged maniac, but perhaps to a more subtle approach. Society smooth-talkers or more perverse people might try to blackmail her or simply try to use her position for their own unscrupulous advantage. Every eventuality had to be guarded against by those whose duty it was to protect her. And a most important part of her bodyguard's responsibility included reporting back to his superiors any visits or friends Diana made that could be questionable or a possible embarrassment to her, to Charles, the royal family or the monarchy.

Eyebrows were raised, and senior courtiers became anxious when Diana's friendship with James Gilbey seemed to be taking on a more serious vein. Gilbey's name had always been on Diana's 'Approved List', those few privileged people whose phone calls would be put through immediately to her apartment. All members of the royal family have such a list but it usually includes the names of remarkably few people. The royals like to do the phoning and not be hassled by people they don't want to talk to.

Since Diana's visit to Gilbey's apartment in 1989, a tap had been put on the phone calls he made to her. Not a constant one, but from time to time a tape would be taken of his calls so that senior palace advisers could ascertain the state of their relationship. Ostensibly, it was done for 'security reasons'.

The greater Diana's need for emotional security the more she poured out her heart to Gilbey. He came to know the secrets of her marriage. He listened with concern and sympathy as she told of her problems, her unhappiness and her misery. He heard the bitterness in her voice. She told him of her anorexia and bulimia in the same way as she had told two or three of her girlfriends. But to Gilbey she over emphasised and dramatised everything. The more she poured out her heart the more concerned he became. She had his full attention and Gilbey enjoyed the privilege of being privy to the innermost secrets of the royal marriage. Diana also told him that her feelings of misery and unhappiness had sometimes been so agonising she had even considered suicide.

In her meeting with Diana, Elizabeth told her that she understood that things were not going very well between her and Charles but she made no mention of separation or divorce. Instead, Elizabeth talked of Diana's responsibilities as the wife of the Prince of Wales and as mother of the two young princes and heirs to the throne. The queen called upon her to consider her duty to the monarchy both in the present and when she would become Queen of England. To all Elizabeth's words of wisdom, Diana nodded. However, Elizabeth did not ask her if there was anyone else in her life and Diana would have realised that Elizabeth already knew of her alleged affairs and Major James Hewitt.

The chat with the queen had unnerved Diana for she felt that Elizabeth knew a great deal more than she cared to admit. Whenever Diana went out alone – to lunch, to the cinema or to a friend's house – she felt guilty though the occasions were, more often than not, perfectly innocent. In any case, the tabloid press would pre-empt her every move and the *paparazzi* would be there to capture the moment on film. Diana felt a conspiracy against her and she became paranoid. She reached the conclusion that the only way the paparazzi could know such precise details of her private life was by information given to them by someone in the palace. Diana did not believe for one moment that any of her staff at Kensington Palace would stoop to such skulduggery to earn a few extra pounds from tipping off the press. She came to believe that the palace were secretly trying to reveal to the nation – through the press – her secret dates and assignations and turn public opinion against her.

The nation did take note of Diana's nights on the town but

decided that she was simply trying to escape the strict confines of life in Kensington Palace, trapped in a loveless marriage because her cheating husband had returned to the arms of his old mistress, leaving the angelic Diana alone in the palace. Sometimes she would even take off in her car in the late hours to go cruising around the West End of London, wanting to be near the action and buzz of night life, but never actually venturing outside her car. Charles was believed to be the culprit; his actions were the sole reason for her unhappiness and her eating disorders, and nothing would change the mind of the public.

Diana took great confidence from the fact that she had become the darling of the nation, that no other royal, including Charles or the queen, attracted the same interest and enthusiasm as she did. Every poll conducted from 1987 showed Diana becoming increasingly popular at the expense of all the other members of the royal family. A 1991 Gallup poll revealed Diana to be the favourite royal with 22 per cent of the votes, almost twice as many as a survey taken only three years before. Prince Charles, first in the earlier poll, had been pushed into joint second place with his sister Princess Anne, both with 15 per cent. The Queen Mother, then ninety, was next with 14 per cent and Elizabeth had only 12 per cent. The remaining 22 per cent included the rest of the royal family.

Elizabeth resented the fact that an outsider, who was causing problems by her secret *risqué* behaviour, should become the most popular royal. Elizabeth hoped Charles and Diana would continue to behave in a friendly, courteous manner towards each other in public but she worried about Charles's relationship with the married Camilla and reports of Diana's indiscretions as she seemed to be flaunting her sexuality and her lovers to an ever-growing circle of people.

Throughout her life Elizabeth has gone along with the simple principle which has guided the royal family for a century or more: it doesn't matter what sins members of the family commit, the only sin is in being found out. That is the overriding principle which decides what course of action will be taken when reacting to any incident. Elizabeth did not really care about Diana's feelings, her unhappiness or her awkward predicament, because she felt she had brought it all on herself. All that mattered to her was the good name of the House of Windsor and protecting the monarchy which, from the moment she became queen, had been her life's work.

In 1990 Diana decided that the time had come for action, to let the nation know the hellish life she had been forced to live, 'imprisoned' in Kensington Palace and cut off from the outside world. Diana had convinced herself that her unhappiness, her need to take lovers, her entrapment by the royal family had been caused not by any of her own actions, but by Charles.

She consulted one of her oldest and dearest friends, Dr James Colthurst, a doctor she had known since her bachelor days and who had tried to help Diana through her eating disorders. By chance, Dr Colthurst played squash quite frequently with the author Andrew Morton who had been the royal correspondent of the *News of the World*. A suggestion was put to Diana that Morton would write a book of her life with the help and assistance of Dr Colthurst. A deal was struck with his publisher Michael O'Mara and Colthurst would be the go-between. Morton never talked directly to Diana and never interviewed her. Most of the information was supplied by Colthurst, the rest coming from one or two selected girlfriends. O'Mara made a deal with Diana's late father Earl Spencer, who died in 1992, that he could illustrate the book with unpublished photographs of Diana from her childhood years. In return, O'Mara apparently agreed to pay £100,000 to Diana's favourite charities.

When the book was published in 1992, however, even some of Diana's closest friends were surprised to learn that she had attempted, allegedly, to commit suicide on seven separate occasions. None of her friends referred to in the book had ever heard Diana talk of suicide. But the world believed that Morton's book revealed the truth of Diana's ghastly life, trapped in a loveless marriage and surrounded by a cold, unloving, dysfunctional family.

Occasionally, Diana would visit Highgrove at weekends when the boys were there. But those weekends were hardly ever joyful family affairs. Charles spent much of the day in his walled garden where Diana and the children were forbidden. Indeed, Diana didn't even have a key to the walled garden. That infuriated her. Charles did sometimes take the boys into his garden to explain things to them and show them around. But they preferred to go swimming or riding or play around the grounds with their mother. Their lack of interest in gardening was hardly surprising at their young age. Most weekends a violent shouting match would ensue, and Diana would end up driving back to London angry, frustrated and miserable.

As one of the kitchen staff revealed, 'Diana would get so angry with him. She would shout and scream at him telling him she had no intention of letting their marriage continue; and warning that unless some action occurred soon then she would go her own way and get a divorce.'

On one occasion during a violent argument, Diana threw a heavy glass paperweight at Charles hitting him on the base of the neck and knocking him unconscious for a few seconds. He slumped to the floor but sat up seconds later unsure as to what had happened. Diana confessed to turning pale at the thought of having done Charles some serious damage. But nearly everyone who heard the arguments claimed that the only raised voice was that of Diana's while Charles stayed calm, trying to placate and quieten her.

The separation of Fergie and Andrew had given Diana new hope that she would be able to continue her separate life with Charles, leading her own life and carrying out her own agenda of charitable activities. She wanted to continue being the Princess of Wales; for she loved the title and the privileges and trappings the title brought to her life.

Worried that Charles would seek a separation, Elizabeth had taken advice from all the responsible quarters and all had greeted the suggestion of a separation with horror, certain that nothing but harm would ensue. They were all concerned that such a separation would markedly weaken the authority and the prestige of the monarchy. And the very thought that Charles might then contemplate marrying a divorced woman sent some senior members of the royal household into fits of hysteria. Elizabeth felt precisely the same though she didn't let on when taking her soundings. Elizabeth told a lady-in-waiting during the summer of 1992, 'I have had nightmares and so many sleepless nights worrying about Charles and Diana, knowing that a break-up in their marriage could cause so much harm. I kept remembering the effect the abdication had on the family and especially on my father who had to step into the breach. People don't realise the strain everyone was under at that time. We can't let it happen again.'

Only weeks after the press and public had learned of Charles's romantic relationship with Camilla, she and her husband, Brigadier Andrew Parker Bowles, were invited by the upmarket Dunhill company to their sponsored day at The Guards polo ground at Windsor Great Park. As usual, Dunhill sent through a list of the guests they intended to invite to Buckingham Palace to see whom the queen would like to invite into the royal enclosure.

Those privileged to attend the match, as well as the media, were astonished to find that sitting in the royal enclosure that day was Camilla Parker Bowles, the woman the nation knew to be Prince Charles's mistress and who had been figured in every newspaper as Princess Diana's sworn enemy. Sitting beside her was Brigadier

Andrew Parker Bowles, whom the world knew to be the unfortunate cuckold.

As newspaper photographers clicked away at such an unexpected scene, Elizabeth went further. In full view of the nation's photographers and television crews, she politely waved to Camilla. And, during the tea interval, Elizabeth sought out Camilla for a chat while everyone stood watching, fully realising the remarkable statement Elizabeth was making – she knew precisely what she was doing, giving tacit approval to Charles's relationship with Camilla. But there was more to her actions. Elizabeth knew her acceptance of Camilla that day would be seen as a deliberate snub to Diana, and a warning of possible future treatment if she didn't toe the line.

From that day in August 1992, Camilla Parker Bowles, the countrywoman who some believed responsible for the breakdown of the Prince of Wales's marriage, had been accepted, awarded the highest respect by the sovereign herself and officially made welcome at Elizabeth's court. By her action, Elizabeth showed everyone – including Diana – that Camilla, far from being shunned, would now be treated as a close friend of the royal family and given the respect that entailed. The spectacle of Camilla chatting happily to the queen enraged Diana.

The queen knew that Diana had taken Hewitt as a lover in 1983 and she was also fully aware that Diana had since taken several lovers. But what angered Elizabeth, and worried her, was the fact that Diana was behaving like a loose cannon, behaving publicly at parties and dances as if she were a single woman, dancing, cavorting, smooching and flirting. Sooner or later, her behaviour would reach the media and Charles would be seen as the cuckold, an image she did not want for her son.

Hardly a week had passed since the sensational photographs of a near-naked Fergie had been flashed around the world than rumours of *risqué* tapes involving Diana and a mystery lover began to circulate through the media. Back in January 1990, *The Sun* had been handed a tape which they had decided not to reveal. It had been kept in their safe at Wapping, Murdoch's London headquarters. However, when *The National Enquirer*, the sensational US tabloid, published a transcript of the same tape, *The Sun* decided to release their 'Dianagate' tape.

In the tape, the woman's voice, which was later verified as Diana's, spoke of her life as 'being a torture . . . of her uncaring, selfish husband'. There was also much romantic talk, the couple calling each other 'darling' and talking of 'love'. The man persistently called Diana

'Squidgy'. *The Sun's* 12 million readers were invited to telephone a special number and listen to the 23-minute tape so they could hear the full conversation. It was a most revealing and highly personal recording. It was confirmed later that the man on the other end of the tape was James Gilbey.

A highly respectable retired bank manager, Cyril Reenan, who loved listening to telephone conversations on his ham radio, told how he had picked up the 'royal' phone call on New Year's Eve, 1989, and had handed the tape to *The Sun*. However, the tape was handed to Sony experts to examine and one of their experts, Martin Colloms, concluded the tape had been made from 'a direct wire tap on to a telephone line' and that this 'had been processed afterwards so that superficially it sounded like a cellnet broadcast'. In short, Diana's phone had been tapped by a person or persons unknown and somehow this conversation had ended up being broadcast to be monitored by people such as Reenan.

Some British newspapers delved deeper asking, 'How could the princess's telephone at Sandringham have been bugged? Who had the technical expertise to do this? Why would those responsible waste time by broadcasting the tape? How could they be sure anyone would pick it up and sell it to a newspaper?'

As a result, some responsible and distinguished members of society, such as Lord Rees-Mogg, Chairman of the Broadcasting Standards Council and a former editor of *The Times*, maintained the whole Dianagate scandal was a conspiracy perpetrated by the security services; and that this tape had been deliberately leaked. But once again the questions were asked, 'Why? And by whom?'

Later, further extracts of the Dianagate tape were revealed in which Diana talked of the fear of becoming pregnant and referred to an episode in *Eastenders*, one of Diana's favourite soaps, in which a character had had a baby by a man who was not her husband. Many people believe this particular tape confirmed that Diana was having an affair with Gilbey. But that was not the case. Diana did not have an affair with him. In fact the reference to pregnancy showed Diana was discreetly trying to put off Gilbey, as though she didn't want to have a sexual relationship with him for fear of becoming pregnant. And, others suggested, if their relationship was so physical it seems strange that there was no reference to any past or planned sexual relations between them.

The revelation that Diana had been having some sort of love affair with a mystery man helped to balance the allegation that Charles had been having an affair with Camilla. Here was conclusive proof that the blame for the marriage breakdown could not be laid solely at Charles's door, and that perhaps Diana had not been the innocent, blameless wife after all. Throughout the entire marriage break-up this was one of the most damning pieces of evidence made against Diana – but the revelations made little difference to the nation's view that Diana was the innocent, injured party and Charles the wicked adulterer who had left the lovely Diana to pine alone while spending his nights in the arms of an old flame.

Throughout the autumn of 1992 Elizabeth stepped up her interviews with all those with whom she wanted to discuss the possibilities of a real rift in the marriage, and the way to proceed if a legal separation became necessary. During her weekly meetings with Prime Minister John Major, Elizabeth spoke at length of the probability that a legal separation and eventual divorce might take place. She felt she could no longer trust Diana and, after much consideration, decided that separation would be for the best.

A separation was the last thing Diana wanted. She was now thoroughly enjoying her life, carrying out her own agenda and free to see the men she wanted because the world now knew that she and Charles were separated in all but name. She no longer had to stay at Balmoral, the castle and atmosphere she hated or take part in royal functions, visits and official tours which she had always loathed.

Previously, Diana would complain to her senior staff before a day of official visits around Britain, 'I don't mind attending one or two visits but I can't take six or seven different events. It drives me mad having to keep smiling and shaking hands all day. And the conversations I have to endure bore me stiff. You know how I dread a whole day of royal visits. I feel I'm there on show.'

But when Diana organised her own visits she became a different person, thoroughly enjoying herself and making others happy simply by her presence and her natural *joie de vivre*. Diana had a wonderful magnetic personality, a charisma that made her almost unique and which showed up the queen and Charles as boring, ordinary people who lacked warmth and sparkle. Some have suggested that Elizabeth pushed for the separation because Diana had become such a favourite of the entire nation that no one was much interested when the queen and Philip undertook royal visits around the country.

She spoke to constitutional lawyers and to the Archbishop of Canterbury of the problems such a separation might have on the monarchy and the succession and, of course, the possibility of a divorced man, Charles, as Head of the Church of England, being crowned monarch. Problems of the succession caused Elizabeth far more concern and heartache than the wishes of Diana, wishes which were nothing compared to the future of the House of Windsor.

Everybody Elizabeth confided in was sworn to secrecy and all kept their word. She took Charles into her confidence, so that at all stages, prior to the announcement in the House of Commons on 9 December 1992, Charles would be fully aware of the constitutional position.

To a hushed House of Commons Prime Minister John Major read out the statement that the Prince and Princess of Wales were to separate after eleven years of marriage. The only surprise, which brought gasps of disbelief from the crowded Commons, was when Major announced that there would be no constitutional implications and that Diana could still be crowned queen. The statement made clear that the couple's decision to lead separate lives had been reached amicably, that both would continue to carry out public duties and that both would participate fully in the upbringing of their two children.

Buckingham Palace announced that the queen and the Duke of Edinburgh, although saddened, understood and sympathised with the decision and hoped that intrusions into the couple's privacy would cease. Elizabeth watched the Commons announcement live on television, alone in her sitting room. It was the darkest day of Elizabeth's long reign.

She thought nothing more could possibly go wrong: after years of pretence, the marriage of Charles and Diana had been revealed as a sham. Elizabeth and her palace advisers knew Diana to be the person who had to shoulder most of the responsibility even while the nation believed Charles to be totally responsible.

Within weeks, however, Elizabeth and Charles were faced with further embarrassment. *New Idea*, an Australian Murdoch magazine, published intimate details of an alleged conversation of a remarkable, frank and sexual nature between Charles and Camilla Parker Bowles. The magazine claimed the conversation, which was dubbed 'Camillagate', had allegedly been taped on 18 December 1989, about the same time as Diana's conversation with James Gilbey had been taped. There is no doubt that the voices on the tape were those of Charles and Camilla. *New Idea* commented:

> For the first time, amazingly intimate details of a bedtime phone call between Prince Charles and Camilla Parker Bowles have shown why Princess Diana pulled the plug on her sham of a marriage. In the touching late-night conversation, the depth of

the star-crossed couple's love for each other, and their desire to be together, comes across with shocking frankness. And it finally confirms Camilla's long-standing, passionately familiar relationship with the man who would be king. The sexy secrets of the conversation will shock those convinced Charles is a 'cold fish' because he hasn't had a physical relationship with Di for years. He shows that with the woman he loves, he can be warm and unashamedly physical.

The source of the Camillagate tape stirred controversy in Britain, in the same way as the earlier speculation over those responsible for taping and leaking the Dianagate conversation. The fact that phone calls from both Charles and Diana had been taped, allegedly accidentally, by amateur radio hams, did not hold water. Most commentators believed it would be stretching coincidence to breaking point to suggest that highly embarrassing phone calls made by both the Prince and Princess of Wales to their respective lovers had been picked up by accident.

Further fuel was added to the flames when a third tape suddenly came to light, this one a recorded telephone call between Prince Andrew and Fergie, again recorded in 1989, and again with one of the callers speaking on a mobile phone. Like the other two taped calls, this one included a sexy conversation.

The quality of the Camillagate tape was superb and most media commentators came to the conclusion that the bugging had to be the work of professionals. In all three cases one party had been on a mobile phone and the other on a fixed line. Those arguing that the bugging was purely accidental claimed the use of mobile telephones was responsible for the calls being picked up by third parties, because radio hams with inexpensive scanners could tune to the signals from mobile phones with ease. However, experts ruled picking up and recording both sides of such telephone calls to be extremely difficult, requiring highly sophisticated equipment. And more than that. To record both sides to such a high standard, as these royal tapes were, would mean scanning across thousands of channels to find the other half of the conversation, a virtual impossibility.

The quality of all three conversations, along with their detail and content, pointed to the recording being achieved at the fixed-link end. That meant a bug had been used, sending out a signal to a recorder. As the arguments raged, nearly every expert consulted came to the same conclusion: the phone calls must have been bugged by professionals.

As speculation intensified over who had the resources and the motive to make the tapes, senior MI5 officers tried to shrug off accusations that their agency was responsible. Security sources indicated that the allegations were not of sufficient substance to even warrant a response. But that was their trite attempt to quash the accusation. Most people – in government, politics, the judiciary and the media – believed MI5 was the prime suspect.

Elizabeth demanded of Prime Minister John Major, the ultimate boss of the security services, what information he had been given about the source of the taped messages. It is not known what action the Prime Minister demanded, or indeed whether he had been informed by the head of MI5, then Mrs Stella Rimington, whether any agents had been involved, with or without direction or supervision. Nor is it known what Major told the queen.

But the separation proved a magnificent bonus for Diana. She decided that as she had been dismissed from the House of Windsor, she would show Elizabeth and Charles and everyone connected with the palace the power she had become in the land. She determined to outshine the royal family, to take centre stage and become the world's most loved, and lovable, royal.

Elizabeth and her advisers became seriously worried as the nation showed its love and support for Diana and disdain towards the Windsors. Public opinion polls throughout the 1990s showed Diana to be way ahead of the rest of the royal family, though the great majority still believed that Elizabeth was a good queen who carried out her duties with dignity and responsibility.

Cleverly, Diana decided to try and persuade the media, and particularly the tabloid press, to give her their support. She would invite editors and media executives to informal lunches at Kensington Palace taking them into her confidence. Diana would woo these men, flatter them, make them feel there was a special relationship, a one-to-one contract. She would look them straight in the eye, flirt ever so slightly and make a fuss of them, making them feel important, massaging their inflated egos. They became Diana's private lobby. The *quid pro quo* with Diana was that in return for access to her, the editors would be broadly sympathetic to her charity work and, more importantly, her private life. The system worked wonderfully well and continued until her death.

Diana needed the media on her side not only to protect her against the power and prestige of the palace whom she knew had turned against her, but also because she had a plan for which she needed their support. Diana determined to become someone in her own right, not simply famous for being the wife of the Prince of Wales, but recognised for the work she carried out on her own. Somewhat naïvely, Diana hoped she would be permitted to take on more worldwide charity work and that was one of the reasons she dropped more than a hundred patronages after her separation. There was also another reason: Diana had become fed up with supporting charities which, she believed, had sometimes been thrust on her simply because she was the Princess of Wales. She wanted to concentrate on issues that interested her not just in Britain but throughout the world, broadening her popularity and, at some stage, becoming a worldwide royal ambassador.

Diana suggested the roving royal role to Prime Minister Major, seeking his support. In turn, he raised the matter with Elizabeth and senior members of the household. The very idea horrified them for they believed this was a calculated attempt by Diana to usurp the role of the sovereign herself, let alone her husband. Diana was speedily informed that the Prime Minister could not support her in such a role and was strongly urged to drop the idea. But Diana would not be so easily put off.

Diana had begun to believe the praise and the public worship heaped upon her. And she made her greatest mistake. She decided to appeal to the nation over the heads of the Prime Minister and the queen believing that by explaining her side of the story she would win the hearts and minds of everyone. Then, she believed, no one would be able to stop her ambition to become a royal ambassador.

In secret, Diana arranged for her famous *Panorama* interview of November 1995 which many pundits believed to be the most extraordinary and damaging royal statement since the abdication of Edward VIII in 1936. She spoke of her eating disorders, of her bulimia and of her self-mutilation as well as her affair with James Hewitt. But Diana reserved her most deadly remarks to injure Charles. Her answers to questions about him revealed a bitterness within her, a malice bordering on hatred. With great subtlety, Diana managed to impress on the 23 million viewers who watched the programme that Charles was not fit to be king.

Diana took an even greater risk, bringing herself in open conflict with Elizabeth and her 'enemies' within the palace by criticising both the queen and the monarchy. She said, 'I would like a monarchy that has more contact with its people – and I don't mean riding around on bicycles and things like that, but just having a more in-depth understanding . . . '

As they watched the interview, senior aides at the palace were outraged that Diana had had the audacity to insult the queen by telling the nation how the monarchy should operate. As one 60-year-old palace veteran said, 'Some advisers were apoplectic at what they saw as an upstart's decision to go on TV and tell the queen what to do. Some thought she must have lost her marbles. Others were resigned to Diana's determination to destroy her husband and organise the future of the monarchy around her son William, guided, of course, by his mother.'

Elizabeth, too, was outraged by the interview. The mood of the Establishment, including the royal household, was summed up by *The Daily Telegraph* which commented in the autumn of 1995:

> It is true that Diana has suffered a great deal, and that her situation, though privileged, is not enviable. But it is also true that what she is doing is not good for the country. The princess melodramatically 'retired from public life' in 1994 but now she seems to have returned to it, with equal melodrama. She remains royal, in title, in prestige, in her residence and paid for by royal money. Yet she is royal only when she chooses, not allowing her engagements to be run by Buckingham Palace and avoiding the full, irksome round of duties. She remains married, but to a man she is known to dislike, and with a rather too obvious interest in attracting his successor.
>
> Even her undoubted brilliance as a public performer has more of a filmic quality about it than that of restrained, formal, self-effacing altruism which best suits the British monarchy. Her style is more Monaco than monarchy. She is damaging herself, and the public interest. Since she cannot be reconciled with her husband, she should divorce, and learn to hide her dazzling light under the bushel of motherhood.

Diana's bravura performance in the *Panorama* interview convinced Elizabeth that Diana had to be removed from the royal family. She was now not only acting like a loose cannon but had become too powerful and too arrogant, a real danger to the House of Windsor. Diana had won the hearts of the nation, as Elizabeth had always hoped, but not to the extent that she should dominate all sections of the media to the exclusion of every other royal. Now she seemed determined to usurp the sovereign's role. Until that moment, Elizabeth had permitted her offspring to lead their own lives and hoped that they would abide by the rules, the traditions and the protocol in doing so. Now she knew she had to take firm action for the sake of the monarchy for she was convinced Charles would never take any action that might have an ill effect on his sons. So Elizabeth took matters into her own hands, determined to be rid of the young woman who had become a viper in the bosom of the royal family. She wrote to Diana all but ordering her to divorce as soon as possible.

And there was evidence of how successful Diana had become. In the past, whenever Elizabeth, usually accompanied by Prince Philip, made official visits and tours, either in Britain or overseas, reports and pictures would appear in the media. No longer. It seemed the only person the media and the people wanted to see and learn more about was Diana. Her determination to steal the limelight from the Windsors had proved brilliantly successful. But it would be her undoing.

Elizabeth now believed that Diana's ambition knew no bounds. One of the reasons Diana had enthusiastically taken up the issue of banning landmines was her desire to become a world figure. She also saw it as a golden opportunity to snub her nose at the royal family for she had convinced herself they were responsible for clipping her wings, refusing her permission to become a royal overseas ambassador. Becoming closely associated in the controversial and burning issue of banning landmines propelled Diana from being a mere patron of good causes to being on the leading edge of world affairs, at the heart of international politics. Whenever she was pictured with victims of landmines those photographs and film clips would be shown across the world bringing her instant acclaim and gaining her megastar recognition. At the moment of her death Diana had succeeded in moving away from the image of the glamorous princess with the beautiful face to becoming a political force who had succeeded where others before had failed.

A number of Charles's close friends were angered and appalled at what they saw as a totally unfair and unwarranted attack by Diana. Not once throughout the horrendous and embarrassing saga of the marriage break-up did Charles ever say a single word against Diana and he would not permit his friends to do so either. He knew that Diana had taken a lover in 1983 and yet he had tried his damnedest to try and heal the marriage. From the moment of their marriage in July 1981 until late 1985, Charles had done all in his power to keep the marriage going. Often against his own common sense, Charles had agreed to every one of Diana's whims and now Diana had repaid him by undermining his lifelong responsibility to succeed his mother. The world never realised that far from walking away from his marriage, Charles had behaved in an exemplary fashion towards

Diana, knowing that she was involved with another man, but refraining from doing anything in the hope she would return to him. Only after three years did Charles realise that all was lost and turned to Camilla.

But three women, Lady Susan Hussey, Elizabeth's most trusted lady-in-waiting, Camilla Parker Bowles and Patti Palmer Tomkinson, an old skiing friend, were determined to speak up for Charles if he refused to defend himself. They knew the truth of Diana's behaviour and treatment towards Charles and they believed the nation should be made aware of the true facts of the marriage. They appealed to Charles to permit them to use their contacts in the media to put across his side of the argument, to show that he was no mean, miserable man leaving Diana to suffer alone because he had wanted to return to Camilla. But Charles would hear nothing of their plan.

So the three women took their plan of action to Elizabeth, seeking her permission to right the wrong they believed had been perpetrated for years on the hapless Charles. Elizabeth responded with a promise that she would think about the proposition, but after talking to Charles she told the three that she was opposed to the idea and urged them not to go ahead. In deference to Charles's wishes, they dropped the idea.

Diana was furious at her mother-in-law's demand for divorce. And so she determined that if she was to be 'kicked out' of the family, then she would make the Windsors pay, and heavily. She was determined above all else to fight tooth and nail to keep her title, Princess of Wales. After considerable legal wrangling, not only was Diana permitted to keep her cherished title, she also won a remarkable settlement which some senior household staff believed was far too generous.

And then there was Dodi. It was in the summer of 1997 that Diana became involved with Dodi Fayed, the 42-year-old playboy, erstwhile film producer and eldest son of Mohamed Al Fayed, the billionaire owner of Harrods, a man with a dubious background who had never been accepted by the Establishment. Mohamed had offered Diana his St Tropez villa as a holiday home for her sons and Dodi had gone down there to see that Diana and the two princes wanted for nothing. Quiet, polite and unobtrusive, Dodi was every inch the perfect gentleman throughout that holiday, dancing attendance on Diana when requested and playing rough-and-tumble games with the boys in the swimming pool. Diana returned from that holiday with a spring in her step, believing she had found in Dodi a man with whom she could enjoy a liaison. Three weeks later, Diana and Dodi flew from Stansted together on a Harrods Gulfstream jet for a cruise around Corsica and Sardinia aboard Fayed's yacht, the Jonikal.

Diana was enjoying her summer fling with Dodi. Back at Buckingham Palace, however, Elizabeth was at her wits' end wondering what on earth Diana was playing at, flaunting herself with such a well-known cocaine-sniffing playboy. As the summer wore on the fear that Diana was becoming seriously involved with Dodi caused alarm bells to ring. Senior courtiers feared that Diana and Dodi might set up home together in California and Paris, and that William and Harry might be exposed to the pitfalls of life when spending time with their mother during school holidays. They imagined the two princes on holiday in Los Angeles, their young minds exposed to the temptations and dangers of California. Such a thought horrified them.

Then fate took a hand. The death of Diana in a motor accident in a Paris underpass stunned the world. The shock waves numbed the nation and the emotional outpouring was overwhelming; the tears, the anguish and the weeping were visible for all to witness. Tens of thousands flocked to London to lay flowers, to pay their respects and say farewell to a young woman whom few had known but all had loved.

At Balmoral Castle, where Elizabeth and the royal family were enjoying their summer break, as well as in the hushed corridors of power in Buckingham Palace, the death of Diana was greeted with mixed emotions. To many, including Elizabeth, there was a deep sense of shock at the appalling car crash. But there was also relief that the thorn in the side of the royal family had been removed. Some went so far as to liken Diana's death to the removal of a cancer, so dangerous had she become.

To many, stunned by Diana's sudden death, their immediate reaction was that, in some way or another, she had been murdered. The reasoning behind their argument was sound but there was no hard evidence whatsoever to support the accusation. There were only two pieces of evidence which could in any way have lent credence: the first was the report of a a bright, dazzling light – much brighter than a camera flashlight – which the chasing *paparazzi* photographers believed they saw seconds before the crash. Such lights are used by the security services to 'blind' people for twenty seconds or so; and then there was the mysterious white Fiat Uno which French police are convinced was in collision with Diana's Mercedes immediately prior to the crash. At first it seemed extraordinary that the driver of the Fiat Uno would not have stopped after such an incident and then, more strangely, that the French police have been unable to trace either the Uno or the car's driver.

Elizabeth did, however, seriously misjudge the mood of the nation in the immediate aftermath of Diana's death. She and Philip remained at Balmoral where they were taking their customary ten week summer break and barely showed their faces as though the death of Diana was of no great importance to them. Prince Philip, backed by the Queen Mother, who had become appalled at Diana's antics, wanted to play down her death and her funeral but his opinion was cast aside by Charles, Prime Minister Tony Blair and advisers who believed Diana should be treated with all the majesty normally allied with the death of the Princess of Wales.

The mood on the streets of London, particularly around Buckingham Palace where the mourners gathered to grieve, turned from open criticism of the queen to a more ugly, defiant attitude towards the monarchy which had never been witnessed throughout her long reign. The newspapers took up the sentiment of the mourners and the front pages of the tabloids left Elizabeth in no doubt that her policy of private, family grief was one which the nation did not appreciate.

Since his arrival back in Britain with Diana's body, Charles had been urging his mother to show that the family cared for Diana. The week of official mourning declared by the queen was in danger of becoming a week of severe embarrassment for the monarchy. In death, Charles argued time and again, Diana appeared to be exposing the royal family's detachment which she had always complained about in her life. Charles's arguments won the day and protocol, so hated by Diana, was turned on its head. She would be given a 'unique' funeral service, one befitting a princess. For once, the ordinary people had made their voices felt and they had changed the status of protocol for the young woman they had adored.

For Elizabeth, who went so far as to stand at the gates of Buckingham Palace and bow as Diana's cortège passed in front of her, the lesson of Diana's life and death had been a painful one. Now she had to face the future and restore the credibility and respect which the monarchy had so very nearly lost.

18. ANNUS HORRIBILIS

On a grey, overcast Tuesday in November 1992, Elizabeth, accompanied by Prince Philip, drove in one of her long wheelbase Rolls-Royce cars from Buckingham Palace to London's Guildhall virtually unnoticed by the office workers and shoppers as they hurried about their business.

This lunch was the City of London's principal celebration marking the queen's glorious jubilee. Guests included dignitaries of the City of London, leading politicians, members of the Establishment, Lords and Ladies of society, the legal profession as well as the pillars of the nation's financial empire, the City. There were aldermen and councillors of the City of London all in their exotic robes and finery, just as their forebears had worn two and three hundred years before. The lunch, given by the City of London, had been planned for more than two years to celebrate the fortieth anniversary of the queen's accession to the throne.

It was far from being a magnificent celebration: Elizabeth made the most remarkable personal speech of her life, which amounted in effect to an extraordinary public confession.

Never before had the public seen the queen so downcast, so open and apparently so vulnerable. Her speech was broadcast on television and radio for the nation to see how their queen had survived the most traumatic year of her reign.

That November day she was suffering from a cold which made her voice croaky. She barely spoke above a whisper, which added to the poignancy.

There were those at Buckingham Palace who had advised Elizabeth against such an open speech to her people. She asked that two speeches be prepared for the jubilee lunch. One more upbeat, challenging, looking to the future, ignoring the travails, upsets, embarrassments, sadness and traumas of 1992 which had wreaked such havoc and disappointment for her and her entire family. But Elizabeth also demanded that another speech, the one she finally delivered, be written as well. She wanted to open her heart to her people and win their moral support.

As she rose to polite applause at the middle of the top table in the huge Guildhall to address the 500 people present, Elizabeth seemed a slight, vulnerable, inconspicuous figure in her dark green, short-sleeved dress and matching hat. It added to her sense of vulnerability.

The queen's accession to the throne at the age of 25, coming so soon after the end of a war that had sapped the lifeblood of the nation, provided cause for hope that her reign could be as glorious for Britain as that of her namesake Queen Elizabeth I who had reigned for 40 years in the sixteenth century.

But the Britain of the 1950s was still struggling to recover from six years of devastating war. It was the first time that war had visited the entire nation, and it brought with it restrictions, food rationing, clothing coupons and every imaginable shortage.

The queen's speech that November day broke with tradition, tearing away the mystery of the divine right of kings in which the queen had for many years believed. The mystery of the monarchy, which many considered to be its strength for so many generations, was being exposed, and at the queen's insistence. She told the privileged assembled listeners: 'There can be no doubt, of course, that criticism is good for people and institutions that are part of public life. No institution, City, monarchy, whatever, should expect to be free from the scrutiny of those who give it their loyalty and support, not to mention those that don't. But we are all part of the same fabric of our national society and that scrutiny, by one part of another, can be just as effective if it is made with a touch of gentleness, good humour and understanding.'

Elizabeth was hoping not only to rein in the more violent attacks on her and her family, which had reached crisis proportions during the previous two years, but also to win the moral high ground, appealing over the heads of the critics and the press directly to the people. She believed the bulk of the nation was behind her and her family, and she was prepared to take the risk of appealing to them directly. She pushed home the point still further: 'I sometimes wonder how future generations will judge the events of this tumultuous year. I dare say that history will take a slightly more moderate view than that of some contemporary commentators. Distance is well known to lend enchantment even to the less attractive views.

'After all, it has the inestimable advantage of hindsight. But it can also lend an extra dimension to judgement, giving it a leavening of moderation and compassion – even of wisdom – that is sometimes lacking in the reactions of those whose task it is in life to offer instant opinions on all things great and small. No sections of the community have all the virtues, neither do any have all the vices. I am quite sure that most people try to do their jobs as best they can, even if the result is not always entirely successful.'

She had begun her speech ruefully, commenting, 'This is not a year I shall look back on with undiluted pleasure. In the words of one of my more sympathetic correspondents, it has turned out to be an *Annus Horribilis*.

'I suspect I am not alone in thinking it so. Indeed, I suspect that there are very few people or institutions unaffected by these last months of worldwide turmoil and uncertainty.'

This was a reference to the devastation wrought on the country by three years of severe recession with three million unemployed in Britain, a record number of people whose homes had been repossessed, a record number of personal bankruptcies and thousands of firms and companies going bust. Elizabeth knew she would win support from many in linking her misfortunes with those of her subjects.

She ended her speech by reminding her critics of the wide range of support she still attracts, saying: 'Your hospitality today is an outward symbol of one other unchanging factor which I value above all – the loyalty given to me and my family by so many people in this country, and the Commonwealth, throughout my reign.'

Elizabeth's speech had broken the golden rule of monarchy articulated by the most famous of British constitutional advisers, Walter Bagehot. He wrote that for the Crown to retain its dignity, honour and glory, 'Magic should not be exposed to the light of day.' On this occasion Elizabeth had revealed a great deal about herself – her fears, and her regrets.

Little did the public or the press realise when she made that historic Guildhall speech, however, that 48 hours later her Prime Minister, John Major, would announce to a shocked House of Commons that the queen had decided the time had come when she should pay income tax on her private income. Furthermore, she had agreed to meet the working expenses of most members of the royal family.

John Major told the Commons: 'The queen had approached me in July 1992 to ask for a change in the current arrangements to be considered. She asked me then to consider the basis on which she might voluntarily pay tax and further suggested that she might take responsibility for certain payments under the current Civil List arrangements.'

The queen's decision to pay tax and meet the working expenses of most of the royal family removed at a stroke the two principal sources of annoyance and unease which a growing number of her subjects had come to question during the past decade. Whenever one or other of the junior royals, or lesser far-flung members of the royal family, did anything outrageous, ridiculous or scandalous, or appeared to be taking advantage of their privileged position, the tabloid press in particular attacked them virulently, always asking the same question: 'Why should the nation pay people who lead such privileged lives vast sums of money when they behave so badly and without apparent due reverence?'

It was a question which the Press Office at Buckingham Palace, and those courtiers and advisers close to the queen, had been finding more and more difficult to answer as revelations of the intimate lives of Prince Charles, Princess Diana and Sarah, Duchess of York, flooded into the public domain.

Twenty years earlier, Earl Mountbatten had strongly advised Elizabeth to clarify the royal finances for the British people. Even then he was concerned about the escalating cost of the monarchy, particularly because the nation, fed inaccurate stories by the press, believed Elizabeth to be enormously wealthy. Mountbatten, always a close reader of public opinion, had written to Elizabeth, 'The image of the monarchy will be gravely damaged unless the nation realises the truth of that fortune.'

Mountbatten ended his note saying, 'Will you please ensure all this gets into the public domain, perhaps in an authoritative article in *The Times*, and both please believe a loving old uncle and *not* your constitutional advisers, and do it.' It took Elizabeth nearly twenty years, and a never-ending spate of scandals, to heed Mountbatten's advice.

The growing public enthusiasm to see the queen pay tax represented less a taxpayers' revolt about money than a growl from an increasing number of loyal subjects who sensed that the royal image had become tarnished and thought lesser royals were having too easy a life. In this they were encouraged by the press who seemed gleefully mean-spirited and irresponsible towards the royal family throughout the late 1980s and 1990s.

Elizabeth's decision to pay tax had been the subject of intense debate inside the palace during most of 1992. No legal requirement existed for the queen to pay income tax: all revenues collected in her name are by right exempt. Some household advisers believed that acquiescing to such demands was caving in to critics, especially the republican sections of the press, an argument the advisers had used against Mountbatten's proposal years before. In the debate that raged for months, some advisers argued that becoming more like ordinary citizens and adopting the social regime of every other member of society, created the possibility of the monarchy's extinction.

But Elizabeth was worried. She believed that the royal family had sustained so much damage throughout 1992 that, as Head of State, she had to do something to appease the critics. For some months during that year, Elizabeth had had difficulty in sleeping through the night as she agonised over how she could stem what seemed to be a rising tide of resentment towards the royal family.

Outwardly, and at all the official functions she attended, Elizabeth displayed not the slightest sign of anxiety. Back at Buckingham Palace, however, she ordered her staff to keep her informed of any changes they perceived in the mood of the nation and people's attitude towards the throne. She approached many friends and advisers, as well as politicians, including Prime Minister John Major, seeking their advice as to what would be best for the monarchy, the royal family and the people. She wanted to know, above all else, about the mood of the people.

Throughout 1992 she paid close attention to opinion polls that were frequently published about the royal family, analysing them for any signs that the public mood was changing towards her and her family – and the job they were doing.

As late as November 1992, Elizabeth still hadn't made up her mind about whether or not to begin paying taxes. Chancellor of the Exchequer Norman Lamont went so far as to tell the House of Commons that the queen had no plans to pay income tax. That answer caused some anger on the Labour benches in parliament and some MPs called for a review of the royal finances. The queen could see that criticism and resentment were mounting.

The last straw came when Elizabeth came to the conclusion that it would be best for the House of Windsor if Charles and Diana separated. The appalling embarrassment to the queen personally, hearing the love tapes between Diana and her confidant James Gilbey and the taped telephone conversation between Charles and Camilla, had shaken the nation's respect for the royal family.

The queen recognised that something had to be done to appease the public's attitude of resentment and derision. Elizabeth had talked to Charles on several occasions seeking his opinion on the paying of tax and he had encouraged his mother to make the changes voluntarily, rather than being seen to be simply reacting to events and demands from the nation. She called Charles to her rooms one day in November and told him of her decision. Charles had always believed that the royal family should never be seen as a burden on the taxpayer, and he was in absolute agreement with his mother and told her that he would enthusiastically follow her lead and agree to pay income tax on all his personal income.

Elizabeth also asked Philip for his views. But, as Elizabeth would explain later, Philip seemed more of a hindrance in her hour of need, occasionally exploding in anger that the turmoil in the family was symptomatic of the lack of discipline throughout society and the fact that young people seemed to have lost all sense of responsibility and duty.

Elizabeth chose this moment to announce her historic decision to pay tax in order to divert the public attention away from the problems of marriage facing the heir to the throne. She was fully aware that paying income tax would be seen as a major climbdown for the monarchy and worried that her decision to pay tax would be seen as the result of press criticism. Elizabeth most certainly did not want to be seen to be bowing to pressure from the press, especially as she, the rest of her family and her senior advisers despised most of the tabloid newspapers. Agreeing to pay income tax would be one single but important step to show Elizabeth was in touch with the life and concerns of ordinary people as well as a gesture of penance acknowledging that many members of her extended family had not been earning their keep.

Elizabeth and Charles's decision to pay tax on their private incomes had nothing to do, however, with the Civil List. This latter dates from 1760 when George III agreed to surrender certain hereditary revenues in return for a set sum agreed by Parliament. At the time the List was set at £800,000 – a vast amount in 1760.

Through the last two centuries the principle has never changed, though there have been frequent wrangles between monarchs and Parliament. Only in this century, however, has the sovereign been relieved of paying income tax. Queen Victoria and her son Edward VII both paid income tax. In 1910, however, when George V came to the throne, Parliament agreed to abolish tax for the sovereign when the Chancellor of the Exchequer, David Lloyd George convinced Parliament that it was pointless to hand over money to the sovereign with one hand and take it away with the other. George V did pay some form of income tax, but Elizabeth's father George VI paid none.

The shape of the current List was set in 1952 when an agreement was reached for the sovereign to surrender the Crown estates – 250,000 acres of prime agricultural land and substantial property in London – in exchange for a fixed income. In 1972, annual rises in the Civil List were introduced when it became apparent that the queen's private income was being used to supplement official expenses. Roughly speaking, 70 per cent of the Civil List goes on salaries for staff and 30 per cent on official travel, entertaining and administrative costs.

In 1990, Prime Minister Margaret Thatcher announced a fixed ten-year settlement of the Civil List hoping to put paid to the annual unseemly wrangle over the queen's finances when some tabloid papers would splash the headline 'BIG PAY RISE FOR THE QUEEN', which ignored the fact that inflation had made the rise a necessity. That agreement ensured the royal household could plan ahead on the basis of a known budget. From 1991 till the year 2000 it was proposed that about £10 million would be shared out each year among eleven members of the royal family.

Neither Prince Charles nor Diana ever received anything from the Civil List. As Prince of Wales, Charles inherited the Duchy of Cornwall which owns substantial agricultural land as well as property in London. By agreement with Parliament, Charles took 75 per cent of the revenue from the Duchy tax free, handing the remaining 25 per cent to the Exchequer. Now Charles pays income tax, like everyone else, handing 40 per cent of his income to the Exchequer after deducting all legitimate costs including staff salaries and administrative expenses. In 1998, the Duchy of Cornwall made a profit of £6 million, an increase of about 9 per cent on the previous year. The money is used, as it has been since the Duchy was created by Edward III in 1337, to provide an income for the heir to the throne to cover the costs of both his public and private life. Charles, Wills and Harry receive nothing from the Civil List. After tax, Charles is estimated to have received about £4 million.

No one knows the precise annual income of the queen nor the amount of money she pays in tax – she is entitled to keep those secrets like every other taxpayer in Britain. Estimates of her annual income and her personal fortune vary, however. Arguments as to how much the queen is worth have raged for decades but, as previously stated, Elizabeth's private income is judged to be about £7.5 million a year, based on her portfolio of stocks and shares of about £150 million and income from the Duchy of Lancaster. Sources close to the Palace suggest the queen pays between £1 million and £1.5 million a year income tax after all salaries, expenses and allowances have been deducted. The queen also receives money awarded by Parliament under the Civil List, amounting to £8 million a year.

The only other royals who still receive money from the Civil List are Prince Philip on £360,000 a year and the Queen Mother on £640,000, which pays salaries and administrative costs. The queen now meets the cost of all the other royals, paying Prince Andrew £250,000, Prince Edward £100,000, Princess Anne £230,000 and Princess Margaret £220,000. The queen has also been paying the Duke of Gloucester, the Duke of Kent and Princess Alexandra a combined total of about £630,000 to enable them to carry out various duties on her behalf.

The state, however, also pays £56 million a year towards the upkeep of the royal palaces including Buckingham Palace, Windsor Castle, Sandringham and Balmoral, as well as Kensington Palace where a number of royals live. Much of that money, of course, goes on staff as well as maintenance and repairs.

In February 1993, Prime Minister John Major gave details in the House of Commons about the tax that the queen and Prince Charles had agreed to pay; and revealed the tax they would still escape.

Later that day, Lord Airlie, Lord Chamberlain, head of the queen's household and one of her principal advisers, called the media to St James's Palace and talked for the first time ever about the queen's finances. In a remarkably revealing statement Lord Airlie made a confession that would have been unimaginable only a few years earlier. He told the assembled journalists, 'Paying tax and meeting the costs of other members of the royal family will place a considerable burden on the queen's finances. Her Majesty has taken this decision to ensure the monarchy develops with the times, particularly during a recession. The recent emphasis on royal wealth had tended to obscure the queen's contribution to national life, and this – not the embarrassing publicity surrounding her children – had prompted the change.

'Estimates of the queen's private funds range from £100 million to billions of pounds. But Her Majesty has authorised me to say that even the lowest of these estimates is grossly overstated.

'The wilder estimates frequently include the Crown Jewels, Buckingham Palace and Windsor Castle, and the royal collection of art treasures which belonged to the Crown, and were not the queen's personal property.'

And he explained that all those items would be exempt from tax as they are regarded as part of the national heritage.

The queen also owns stud farms and stables at Sandringham, West Ilsley and Sunninghill Park. These are also taxable but it is unlikely they will generate any profit whatsoever; it is expected, indeed, that they will be included in her tax return as a substantial loss each year. So, just like other citizens, she will have the odd credit but they will amount to very little compared to the tax she will pay.

Elizabeth also agreed to pay tax on private income from the Privy Purse, principally income from the Duchy of Lancaster which is mainly agricultural land and property, dating back to the thirteenth century. It comprises 11,800 acres in Staffordshire, Cheshire and Shropshire; 10,700 acres in the Fylde and Forest of Bowland in Lancashire; 8,000 acres in Yorkshire and 3,000 acres in Northamptonshire and Lincolnshire. In 1992 the entire holdings yielded a net surplus of £3 million. Most of that money, however, goes to meeting official expenditure not covered by the Civil List.

For Prince Charles, who announced that he, too, would pay tax and would continue to pay tax when he becomes king, there is one important difference from the liability of the ordinary taxpayer: Charles will not have to pay the 40 per cent inheritance tax which everyone else in Britain does. John Major announced that the queen would be able to pass on to her successor, tax free, assets such as her private homes, Balmoral and Sandringham. But bequests and gifts to others are subject to inheritance tax. Mr Major explained to the Commons why the decision had been taken: 'Special arrangements have been made for the queen's inheritance tax because it is necessary to protect the independence of the monarchy. Any other arrangements would have posed the danger of assets of the monarchy being salami-sliced away by capital taxation through generations, thus changing the nature of the institution in a way few people in this country would welcome.'

Neither John Major nor Lord Airlie gave any hint of the extraordinary behind-the-scenes arguments that had gone on before that decision had been reached.

Elizabeth did not want to pay income tax at all but felt she had no choice, given the nation's attitude towards the royals. She refused point blank, however, to pay inheritance tax as well. She was unhappy enough at being forced into a corner and having to agree to pay any tax whatsoever. There were those in Buckingham Palace who believed she should have agreed to pay some inheritance tax, perhaps at a lower rate, but she was adamant. On one occasion she angrily told one of the secretaries, 'Do you really think for one minute that I would ever agree to the slow death of the monarchy by a thousand cuts? I am here to uphold the monarchy; don't people realise that my duty in life is to preserve the monarchy? I have not the slightest intention of entertaining any thoughts of abandoning that duty, not for anyone.'

So a way had to be found, a way which would be politically and diplomatically acceptable to the closest scrutiny. Royal trustees, a body set up to watch over the monarch's finances, drew up a report, claiming that 'the monarchy as an institution needs sufficient private resources to enable it to continue to perform its traditional role in national life, and to have a degree of financial independence from the government of the day.' They argued that there had to be a distinct separation between the queen's private and official lives.

Two areas proved tricky: the queen's personal art collection and the Crown Jewels. The art treasures, one of the single most important and finest family art collections in the entire world contains 7,000 oil paintings, 30,000 drawings and watercolours and 1,000 minatures. Most of the great names among the Old Masters are included in the collection which was begun by Charles I in 1625 when he purchased the Gonzaga pictures from Mantua. King George III (1760–1820) purchased the fabulous Consul Joseph Smith collection from Venice in 1762, King George IV (1820–1837) and Queen Victoria (1837–1901) also bought wonderful Dutch and Italian collections. Though never officially revealed, its value is estimated to run into billions of dollars. The Crown Jewels are simply priceless.

The trustees finally came up with the idea of putting the jewels and all the works of art into a special trust set up to conserve the treasures and, as a trust, no tax will ever have to be paid. Elizabeth readily agreed, approving of the plan and of the trust's title, The Royal Collection.

Although part of the art collection is always on view at the Queen's Gallery at Buckingham Palace, it is likely that under the terms of the new trust, more of the pictures will be on display or will be loaned out to exhibitions around the country. All income from the art exhibitions will in future go to funding the trust. Since the setting up of the trust, the art collection has generated about £2.5 million a year from admission charges.

Most Members of Parliament appeared relieved and satisfied that the queen had finally agreed to pay income tax, but there were a number, especially those on the Labour benches, who believed she should also have agreed to pay some inheritance tax.

The tabloid press smelt blood. The following day the *Daily Mirror* splashed the front page with 'H.M. THE TAX DODgER' with a vicious cartoon showing the queen smirking as she worked out her tax with the aid of a calculator. Inside, under the headline 'SAVE AS YOU REIGN' the paper argued that the queen's offer was nothing more than a tax dodge, an insult to the ordinary punter.

But the general view was that the queen had made the right decision. *The Daily Telegraph* wrote:

> Among those who applaud the queen's consent to pay tax, there are two factions. The first, and by far the larger, merely wishes to see the royal family contribute some proportion of its private income to the public weal, as do the queen's subjects. A much smaller faction regards this as a first step towards the dismantling of royal wealth, and a reduction of the royal family to the economic status of ordinary mortals.
>
> Those who espouse the latter view should be honest about its logical destination, and admit their republican ambitions. The balance that most of us would wish to see struck is that the queen should not be so distanced from the circumstances of her subjects that her isolation puts their sympathy at risk. As never before, perhaps, she needs that sympathy. To be a citizen is to be a taxpayer, and one of the roles of a contemporary monarch is to be seen to be chief citizen . . . a focus of the aspirations and ideals of Everyman, rather than a unique, non-citizen quite unlike everybody else.

The *Sunday Times* commented:

> By joining the ranks of sovereigns who pay income tax, the queen has seized the opportunity to sweep away some of the cobwebs that have surrounded the royal finances for centuries. In doing so, she has taken a historic step towards putting the monarchy on a new, more modern footing, which is to be welcomed.

That Elizabeth's agreement to pay any tax at all was grudging was confirmed by one of her ladies-in-waiting two weeks after the official announcement by the Prime Minister. During a visit to East London, her lady-in-waiting was asked by an old woman, 'Does the queen mind having to pay tax now?' The answer was emphatic: 'She is not at all happy about it.' The queen herself had said to one of her political advisers: 'I believe that if the monarch agreed to pay tax, then there would be no difference between the monarch and the people. And that cannot be good for the Crown. There has to be a difference and the people should see there is a difference.'

But the big question remained. Had she done enough to end the growing criticism of the royal family and the monarchy? The days of fawning deference had been finally laid to rest but there were those who wondered whether the monarchy still commanded the respect that mattered or whether the events of 'annus horribilis 1992' had so eroded that respect that the royals had become at best a charade, at worst an affront people would no longer tolerate.

The new arrangements meant that the principle of the state's funding the royal family's public duties remained intact even though this meant the queen now receives money from the government only to repay much of it to the exchequer. The queen and her advisers were adamant that her gesture was a voluntary one and that her decision to pay income tax on her personal income did not mean that Prince Charles or any other succeeding monarch would have to do the same when they ascend the throne.

Elizabeth believed her decision would result in a loss of respect and esteem with which the great majority of her subjects had regarded her for 40 years, but that this loss would be less severe than the consequences of doing nothing. Intensely annoyed by the decision she felt forced to make, Elizabeth blamed her plight on the weakness of Charles for not being able to control his wife and what she saw as Diana's selfish, wayward and headstrong attitude.

As a result, the gulf between Diana and the queen became greater. Diana had told Charles and other friends that she felt 'very awkward' whenever she was in the presence of her mother-in-law and had never been able to relax whenever they were together. As Diana told her close friends, 'Whenever we are together, at tea or lunch or whatever, everything is so formal. I cannot relax for a minute and I feel so embarrassed all the time not knowing what to talk to her about. We all know that most young women don't get on very well with their mothers-in-law; well, think what it's like having the queen as your mother-in-law.'

Elizabeth was well aware that her daughter-in-law found conversation difficult with her and had tried over the years to find a way through to Diana so they could enjoy friendly, convivial conversations, but as Diana explained, 'The only thing we seem to have in common are children. She asks me questions about Wills and Harry but I just get the feeling that she's only asking the questions because she feels she should, not because she really wants to know.

As far as I have learned from Charles, his mother expects respect from her children; there never seemed to be much motherly love at all. And it seems she wants the same respect from her grandchildren as well. Whenever she meets Wills and Harry, which is very rarely, she tries to be sweet to them but it all seems rather forced.'

Diana was aware of what her mother-in-law thought of her because she had read it often enough in the newspapers. 'Life is more difficult now that we've got this tiresome girl,' Elizabeth is alleged to have said of Diana. Elizabeth had read the same report and told Diana to pay no attention to newspaper accounts; the stories were just made up. Diana wasn't so sure. Elizabeth's 'Annus Horribilis' was remarkable in that not a month passed without some problem, trauma or disaster.

The final tragedy was the fire that erupted at Windsor Castle on 20 November. It began when a strong halogen lamp ignited inflammable liquid which was being used for restoring paintings in the queen's private chapel within the castle's Chester Tower. Inflammable materials are part of the restorer's essential equipment, for example as solvents for the removal of old varnish. Halogen lamps generate extreme heat, so they are never allowed near the surface of a picture, but the bright light from halogen lamps is needed to enable restorers to cleanse and patch the surfaces of paintings. The resultant fireball set light to tapestries and drapes that had been coated with protective fluid; within seconds the wooden panelled walls were ablaze.

Minutes later the fire had spread along the ceiling to neighbouring St George's Hall, the magnificent scene of state banquets, where many world leaders had been entertained in true royal style during the past decades. The alarm was raised immediately and the restorers and workers frantically began removing paintings, pictures and any other works of art and furniture they could carry.

Prince Andrew, on leave from the Royal Navy, was in the castle when the fire alarm rang out. He took charge, galvanising as many staff as possible to help in the dramatic rescue work as the flames moved with terrifying speed through the castle. His military training, at least as regards coping under pressure, helped that day and much that would otherwise have been destroyed was rescued, particularly priceless paintings hanging in St George's Hall.

That night, television viewers saw the flames leaping hundreds of feet into the air as fire crews fought to bring the blaze under control in an effort to preserve one of Europe's most magnificent castles. But the shock to the nation came after the fire had been extinguished and TV cameras revealed the full horror of the destruction.

Many were moved as they saw Elizabeth, a diminutive figure beside the well built, uniformed firemen who had battled the blaze, walking through the gutted apartments. Their hearts went out to her as they watched their monarch, dressed in a long, waxed, hooded coat looking sad, and some thought rather pathetic, as she surveyed the damage. She squelched through the debris-strewn quagmire of water and burned embers in her green 'wellies'. Of all her residences, Windsor Castle was the one she always thought of as her home: Buckingham Palace she considers her office; Sandringham and Balmoral her holiday homes. The fire was personally devastating for her.

The horrible stench of burning hung over the castle and the town of Windsor; one tattered, discoloured Union flag flew sadly from the ramparts. Aircraft flew overhead *en route* to Heathrow giving passengers an overall view of the gutted, roofless ruins. And the rain was incessant. For centuries the castle had seemed impregnable, especially to the townspeople of Windsor, but suddenly they realised it was indeed as vulnerable as anyone else's home. More poignantly, perhaps, the fire appeared as a sign from heaven, graphically illustrating to the nation as well as to Elizabeth that she was a human being as susceptible to life's problems and ill-fortune as any other citizen.

After spending an hour surveying the damage a dejected Elizabeth emerged into the pouring rain and went over to her youngest son Edward. At one point she laid her head on his chest, as though in despair and resignation and he, in turn, put a comforting arm around his mother's shoulder. It was the most moving and natural scene the nation had ever witnessed throughout Elizabeth's public life and some felt as though they were impinging on personal grief. The fire lent an air of unease to the nation; the photographs and television shots of the queen amid the scene of carnage epitomised the mood of desolation and disaster that had befallen her and her family.

St George's Hall lost its famous, centuries-old roof; its immense carvings were gone completely. Along the length of the great room a visitor saw only a huge pile of black rubble. The adjacent Waterloo Chamber, said to be the most beautiful room in the world, was just an empty, stinking shell.

Historian Sir Roy Strong, former director of London's famous Victoria and Albert Museum, had often spent days inspecting and surveying all the pictures and other works of art at Windsor Castle. 'Windsor Castle is home to the queen's private collection of art works – perhaps the greatest and most important in the world,' he said. 'In reality, the treasures there are priceless. Windsor is a lump of England, a huge chunk of our heritage and history. The castle is like an A–Z of the history of Great Britain, from the portraits of all our kings and queens, to the maps and books.'

The collection at Windsor included paintings by Michelangelo, Raphael, Gainsborough, Rembrandt, Van Dyck, Rubens and Canaletto; the Garter Throne Room was lined with portraits of the nation's sovereigns from George I to the present queen; finest examples of furniture from the reigns of French kings including Louis XIV, XV and XVI; statues of kings, queens and noblemen; magnificent carvings and centuries-old pieces of armour. Throughout the castle were priceless carpets, tapestries and drapes as well as drawings and sketches by Leonardo da Vinci and Holbein and a magnificent royal library housing books and maps dating back hundreds of years.

The nation was fortunate that the staff and restorers were able to save many of the works of art and that the fire crews could contain the blaze. But the mood of the nation, fanned by some of the tabloids, was so resentful towards the royal family at that time, that gratitude for the preservation of a treasure trove of historical artworks was overcome by spite and meanness.

Believing he was speaking with the support and sympathy of the great majority of the British public, Heritage Secretary Peter Brooke, in his upper-crust, rather plummy, aristocratic voice, stood before the ruins and proclaimed that the government – that is, the taxpayer – would pay the full cost of the repairs to the castle which would come to at least £50 million since Windsor was not insured. He was stating what had been accepted practice for decades, that the British taxpayer was responsible for keeping and sustaining their monarch in luxury and splendour. Little did Peter Brooke realise that day how hostile would be the reaction.

Hours later, ITV's *This Morning* programme asked callers to phone in with their answer to the question, 'Who should pay for the repairs to Windsor Castle?' An amazing 95 per cent out of a total of 30,282 callers said the taxpayer should not have to foot the entire bill and urged the queen to contribute.

The tabloid press took up the cry. 'GIVE AND TAKE', screamed a Murdoch tabloid *Today*, 'We're giving, the royals are taking'. The right-wing *Daily Mail* asked the question: 'Why should a populace, many of whom have had to make huge sacrifices during the most bitter recession, have to pay the total bill for Windsor Castle, when the queen, who pays no taxes, contributes next to nothing?'

The left-leaning *Daily Mirror* accused the House of Windsor of 'sowing the seeds of its own destruction – meanness, greed and blinkered disregard for the feelings of the people are the mark of a dying, not a lasting dynasty.'

The Sun organized a phone-in and revealed that 48,876 readers said the queen should pick up the tab to repair her own castle; only 2,877 reckoned the taxpayer should pay.

The Times commented that the announcement that the taxpayer was to pay for the repairs 'had struck a jarring note. The fire has brought to a head questions that can no longer be fudged . . . the crunch comes with the decision over who is to pay.'

The *Guardian* put the accusation most succinctly, commenting, 'All the warm words of sadness for the queen in the House of Commons can't hide the growing wash of public cynicism; not yet republicanism, but carping disaffection.'

It was powerful stuff. There were calls from Labour members of parliament that the taxpayer should not be called on to pay for the entire cost of repairs but the MPs' criticism was more muted than that of the press.

The Windsor fire became one of the most traumatic events in Elizabeth's long reign – for it brought about the realisation that the British people's attitude to the monarchy and the royal family had undergone a sea change. The recognition came as a surprise despite the fact that the writing had appeared to be on the wall for some months, if not years. With the fire still smouldering, Elizabeth, the Establishment and Parliament were forced to face the unpleasant fact that the myth that the British people were totally supportive of the monarch and the royal family – at any cost – had, almost overnight, been swept away.

During the days that followed Elizabeth read with growing sadness and dejection all the papers – broadsheets as well as the tabloids – and she could hardly find a crumb of comfort. Elizabeth became listless and took to her bed for a few days, finding it difficult to shake off the cold she had been suffering. A close friend commented, 'Her Majesty had realised, of course, that the mood of the nation was becoming less sympathetic to the royals but she had not realised there appeared to be such a serious deterioration in their respect and loyalty. That realisation seemed to lay her low.

'It is, after all, a devastating realisation for someone who has spent all her adult life loyally and honourably serving her people to the best of her ability, to discover at the age of 66 that the nation has become disenchanted with her and her family.'

Distinguished royal author, Robert Lacey, wrote in November

1992: 'This has been the year in which the fairytale ended. If the late 1970s and 1980s were *anni mirabilis* for the House of Windsor, it is hardly surprising that the current and painful unravelling of all those promises of happiness should be producing an *annus horribilis* – with the queen's first tax demand as the price of her children's marital incompetence. They screw up and she pays the price.'

As the criticism thundered over Elizabeth's head, there were some loyal monarchists, not only MPs or Members of the House of Lords, but ordinary citizens, who tried to set the debate on a more even keel in letters to the newspapers. Typical was one to the right-wing *Sunday Telegraph*: 'Before the queen-bashing reaches any new harsh pitch of sanctimonious wrath, perhaps we might all bear in mind that this unique and truly noble lady has fulfilled her personal pledge which, so solemnly, she expressed as a young girl . . . to dedicate her life to her country and its people.' Another letter writer commented: 'The queen must be particularly dismayed by the stupid, spiteful and small-minded attitudes displayed by so many of those to whom she has pledged her devoted service – the abominable and fickle British public: abominable, because they are prepared to believe any suggestion of royal impropriety, however absurd; fickle, because they feed like voracious vultures on the salacious, regurgitated offerings of the loathsome tabloids. In this respect it seems a pity that we no longer employ an axeman: the thought of serried rows of tabloid editors' heads stuck atop Traitors' Gate is an alluring one, and has much to commend it.'

The mood throughout the country, however, seemed to be swinging inexorably against the monarchy and the royal family despite some strong royal defenders. The telephone switchboards of radio stations up and down the country lit up in unprecedented numbers as ordinary people vented their disenchantment with the royals. Many spoke on radio or wrote to newspapers, along the lines: 'Years ago I was an ardent royalist but, over the past few years, my opinion has changed and I now say the royal family is a luxury that will have to go.'

The Sunday Times devoted a three-page special focus on the monarchy under the banner headline 'THE PEASANTS' REVOLT'. It detailed the 'seven days that shook the Crown' and one article by Godfrey Smith was headlined 'TIME TO LAY DOWN THE CROWN.' Tongue in cheek, he wrote a spoof speech for the queen suggesting that it should be her Christmas message to her people.

It read: 'I propose to retire on 1 January. Forty years is a good innings and I am already past the age when most of my subjects retire.

I do not say abdicate, because that would mean I was giving up the throne for a new occupant.' Godfrey Smith then outlined what the queen's plan should be, which entailed Charles not becoming king but remaining Prince of Wales because Britain, now a member of the European Community, was more a principality than a kingdom. He suggested Charles should hold the post until he was 60 and then hand over to his elder son William. The speech also proposed that the queen renounce her role as Head of the Church of England and that the royal palaces and her other residences should be bequeathed to the people.

During that last weekend of November 1992, Elizabeth turned to one of her most senior courtiers and spoke her mind. He revealed later: 'Her Majesty spoke quietly and slowly, thinking very carefully the words she was using. She said: "I wonder sometimes whether I have failed the nation, or the monarchy, or the family. It seems that whatever way we turn there is nothing but disaster surrounding us all. It is all most unfortunate and most disturbing."'

Elizabeth and her advisers were left with the problem of funding the huge cost of repairing Windsor Castle which experts believed would cost perhaps £50 million. One of her advisers came up with the idea of opening up parts of Buckingham Palace to visitors and using the admission charges to pay for the repairs to Windsor. Elizabeth abhorred the idea despite the fact she only thought of Buckingham Palace as an office, not a home. When she became queen, Elizabeth had no intention of living in Buckingham Palace, where she had never felt at home. It had been Winston Churchill who persuaded her to spend her weekdays at the palace and her weekends at Windsor. Nevertheless, the notion of millions of strangers tramping through 'her' home, gawking at everything, prying into private areas, examining the royal furniture, royal carpets, royal ornaments and royal family portraits, was repellent to her. As she commented, 'The thought sends a shudder down my spine.'

But there was no other way. Eventually Elizabeth capitulated but only on the strict understanding that the hordes of visitors be kept far away from the living quarters as well as the offices and working areas of the palace. Elizabeth personally walked through those areas which her advisers suggested should be opened, and she made the final decision as to which rooms would be available to the public gaze. Finally it was agreed that certain rooms at the palace would be opened for two months each year – from July to September – the months Elizabeth always stays at Balmoral.

'If only I had acted earlier,' Elizabeth said to one of her advisers, almost chastising herself. 'If I had spoken out earlier when I first decided that paying taxes and curtailing the Civil List was on my mind, I do believe that this awful fire would have helped to heal the rift that seems to have developed between myself and the nation. If only we had acted sooner.'

Even as Head of the Anglican Church did Elizabeth consider herself a failure. Elizabeth had watched helplessly as the nation gradually turned its back on the Church from the end of the Second World War – indeed by the mid-'90s, less than 2 per cent of the population attended Sunday services. In vain had she hoped that by her example, as head of the most important family in the land, she could persuade others to follow her lead and attend religious services. As a young girl and a teenager, Elizabeth had seen whole families crowding into church every Sunday, praying together. Not only had the mass of the population stopped attending church, they had also turned their back on religion.

Facing the realisation that great swathes of the nation were turning their backs on the royal family as they had on the Church, Elizabeth and her advisers came to the conclusion that she and the royals should adopt a lower profile. From 1993 onwards the nation witnessed the royals fading into the background as Elizabeth ordered gatherings of the clan to be severely cut back for royal occasions. She hoped that by removing from public view those royals whom she believed had caused all the problems, the long process of winning back the nation's affection and respect might begin.

Until then, Elizabeth had made it an imperative that the family show they were a family unit on every occasion possible. Whenever state or private occasions came about the queen ordered her immediate family to attend, standing together on the balcony at Buckingham Palace, attending royal birthdays or going to church. It had been customary for royal pageants such as the Trooping the Colour, celebrating the queen's official birthday, to end with all members of her extended family standing on the balcony of Buckingham Palace waving to the cheering crowds below and watching the Royal Air Force fly past overhead. No excuses were permitted. Every royal turned out, the men usually in full military No. 1 dress, the women in their best finery and always wearing hats. Palace balcony scenes were often used as the first opportunity for royal children to make their public début, to introduce them to life as a royal and let the people see how the little royals were coming along.

Only the older royals were on parade in 1993. None of Elizabeth's grandchildren were at her side and many of the younger generation were missing, including Prince Andrew, Prince Edward, Princess Diana, Princess Anne and her new husband Commander Timothy Lawrence. Elizabeth was flanked only by Prince Philip, Prince Charles, the Queen Mother, Princess Margaret and the Duke and Duchess of Kent.

Elizabeth's official birthday celebration on Saturday, 12 June 1993, one week after the fortieth anniversary of her Coronation, should have been one of the most glorious occasions of her reign. Television, newspapers and magazines had been running special features commemorating Coronation Day in 1953 with pages of old pictures showing jubilant scenes. To many, the official birthday in 1993 represented a watershed for the royal family. And as Elizabeth and the older generation of royals came out on to the balcony that day to wave to their loyal subjects, they noted that far fewer people than usual had turned out for the celebrations.

Polls produced made for gloomy reading. The nation wanted a dramatic change from the type of distant, aloof, old-fashioned monarchy Elizabeth had epitomised throughout her reign. They wanted a slim-line, Scandanavian-style monarchy with fewer royals involved. They also wanted all the lesser royals to take proper jobs, rather than just open the occasional hospital wing or summer fête, presiding over a charity meeting or representing the queen at the odd function. Polls showed that 50 per cent of the nation wanted a cut in the cost of the royals and their upkeep, and 14 per cent thought the royals 'should not receive any public money at all'. People under 34 years of age were especially keen to see a slim-line monarchy. Figures published by the Heritage Department in 1994 showed that 268 members of the royal family, relatives and staff were living at the taxpayers' expense. The figures were far greater than MPs or the public had ever suspected.

It showed that aunts, uncles and cousins of every member of Elizabeth's 'royal' family lived rent free in grace and favour apartments in royal palaces, all attended by lavish staff, even though they are not included in the Civil List. At Kensington Palace, where Diana, Wills and Harry used to live, there are homes for Prince and Princess Michael of Kent, who have four bedrooms and six reception rooms; the Duke and Duchess of Gloucester, four bedrooms and seven reception rooms; and Princess Margaret, three bedrooms and four reception rooms.

St James's Palace, which Princes Charles and his sons now use as their London residence, also houses the London homes of Princess Alexandra and her husband Angus Ogilvy who have five bedrooms and four reception rooms, and the Duke and Duchess of Kent, four bedrooms and six reception rooms.

To service the royals, free homes are provided for 13 chauffeurs, 55 private secretaries, 47 domestic servants, 41 stable and farm staff, and 6 gardeners, along with 42 additional craftsmen, porters and other staff. Living free at Windsor Castle are 13 military knights, all pensioners, and 27 other pensioners who had previously worked for members of the family.

As Labour MP Alan Williams, who served on the Public Accounts Committee, commented, 'It is outrageous. In no other western democracy is the wider royal family and ancillary people supported by the taxpayer. I do not think it should be allowed to go on.'

These polls hardly encouraged Elizabeth either. The great majority – 81 per cent – believed Elizabeth had done a 'good job' as queen. But now there was a feeling of sympathy, even pity for her. Elizabeth wanted the nation's respect and admiration, not pity. Of those polled, 65 per cent believed 'she had been a good mother to her children, but they had let her down'. But only 61 per cent of women thought she had been a good mother.

Despite Elizabeth's conscious effort to smile more and look happier in public, 64 per cent said she still looked too glum and urged her to be more cheerful in public. Yet those who know her well understand, and she knows herself, that she is simply not an innately joyful, happy, smiling person.

Throughout the 1990s, however, the focus of the nation's attention moved inexorably away from Elizabeth to Princess Diana, and it was widely held that Diana's mistreatment at the hands of Elizabeth and the royal family was on account of straightforward jealousy because Diana had stolen the limelight, leaving all the other royals in the shade licking their wounded pride.

Diana's star continued to burn brighter whatever she did. And it seemed Elizabeth could do nothing to counter the extraordinary power she seemed to hold over the great mass of the people. The longer Diana remained a single mother, cut off from the royal family, the more the nation took her to their heart.

One year after her divorce, Diana had virtually swept away the nation's interest in any other members of the royal family, usurping their place in the affections and respect of the great majority of the British people. To many, Diana became an angel of hope, visiting the sick in hospitals throughout London and the south-east of England on a weekly basis, as well as hospitals further afield. The great majority were private visits, never open to the press and always gauged so that

Diana could spend time chatting to some of the seriously ill patients. Diana brought warmth, compassion and hope even to the terminally ill for she had that unique quality of instantly winning the hearts of those she met, particularly the more vulnerable members of our society.

Elizabeth could never match this and knew it. And no matter what she did, no matter how much effort she put into her heavy schedule, the crowds who turned out to see her became smaller as the numbers who flocked to cheer and get a glimpse of Diana mushroomed. The greater Diana's popularity became the less respect and admiration was offered to the queen and Prince Charles. And Camilla Parker Bowles was treated with even more contempt, the general opinion being that she was directly responsible for the break-up of Diana's marriage, her anorexia and bulimia and even her separation and divorce.

By 1997, Diana had all but eclipsed the royal family. On one occasion, Prince Charles was undertaking a full-blown, four-day royal visit to Germany and only one reporter and photographer from the British media went along. Days later Diana went on a flying visit to Asia and 400 reporters, photographers and television personnel accompanied her. Elizabeth realised that Diana was undermining the prestige and primacy of the royal family and yet there was nothing whatsoever she could do to counter the situation.

Fate intervened, however, and Elizabeth once again found herself centre stage. But Diana had already changed the nation's perception of the royal family, revealing them as cold and uncaring and consequently, the respect which had always been due to Elizabeth as sovereign had become dissipated. A decision had been taken years before Diana appeared on the scene to bring Elizabeth and some senior royals closer to the people. It was Elizabeth who introduced the walkabout, removing once and for all the *cordon sanitaire* of formal etiquette that had always surrounded the monarch, and it was Prince Philip who had advocated the 1968 television programme in which the royal family was seen barbecuing sausages, just like any other family.

It was all part of a campaign to make the royal family modern and accessible and yet the whole point of the monarchy is that it is different and should be seen to be different from the rest of the nation. Elizabeth tried to let a little light into the mystery of monarchy but that experiment failed miserably. In the end, Diana's revelations caused irreparable damage to the royals' image: their subjects now see them as a highly dysfunctional family with an abnormally high divorce rate who show little love or affection to those who marry into the family, especially those who are not of royal blood, or 'commoners'.

Diana, Sarah Ferguson, Captain Mark Phillips, Princess Michael of Kent, Tony Armstrong-Jones (Lord Snowdon), to name the principal people who married into the royal family, can all testify to how they were treated by 'The Firm'. Not many enjoyed the experience for they never felt part of the family, never felt they had been wholly accepted or made welcome. And that must be a criticism of both Elizabeth and Philip.

For now, Elizabeth is determined to continue in her efforts to draw a blind over the personal disasters of the past two decades, but not for too many years, according to those she has taken into her confidence. Nevertheless she is only too happy – and much relieved – that the rehabilitation of Prince Charles in the eyes of the nation has become so evident less than two years after Diana's death. The man who had been despised by many, for leaving his wife and running off with a married woman, has now reclaimed some respect as the nation witnesses the strong relationship between Charles and his sons. Not many years ago he had been treated as a crank who talked to flowers and burbled on about architecture and organic farming. Now he has become the hero of the hour, praised for his foresight and vision, the prophet crying in the wilderness against genetically modified foods.

And slowly but surely the nation is accepting that Charles has a right to happiness as long as he puts young William and Harry first and foremost. Less than two years after Diana's death, Camilla has attended dinners, parties and charity balls as Charles's companion though everyone knows she has been his mistress for twelve years or so. For his part, Charles is rather enjoying his life again as he did in those far-off days when still a bachelor, leading an action-man life-style and enjoying being surrounded by his trusted friends and advisors.

For Charles, his marriage to Diana was truly horrendous. Their life together before their wedding had been a wonderful, idyllic honeymoon full of love and passion. But within days of returning from their *real* honeymoon the rot had set in. He hoped that time and a family would solve their problems. It never did. Charles tried his damnedest to make the marriage work but his hopes were dashed when Diana took her first lover in the autumn of 1983, only fifteen months after the birth of their son William.

Charles's experience of marriage has made him wonder if he should remain single and simply enjoy the intimacy and love of his affair with Camilla without the need to commit himself once more to matrimony. And yet, the longer he knows Camilla, the more relaxed he is becoming and the more he enjoys her presence around Highgrove. Charles is in no hurry to settle down again and marry Camilla but that does not mean that in a few years, as he approaches 60, he may not decide that he should honour the woman he truly loves by making her his wife. The signs are that the nation is happy to accept Charles as a stand-alone king with no queen by his side, but public opinion might one day even come to accept a Queen Camilla.

Elizabeth recognises all this, and is prepared to wait and see whether the nation at large will one day come to approve of the sensible down-to-earth Camilla. Elizabeth also realises that at the end of this century there are more closet republicans and monarchist critics than at any time for more than a hundred years. She realises that the monarchy may not survive far into the next century as today's Government gradually undermines the palace's privileges, blurring the differences between the sovereign and her subjects. Members of Parliament, even Members of the House of Lords as well as sections of the press are questioning the very role of the monarchy while at the same time criticising the institution.

At present, Elizabeth knows the monarchy is safe. She still achieves a remarkable 73 per cent approval rating for the task she has carried out for the past five decades and no one dares to raise a finger in protest against the role of the monarchy while she remains on the throne. She does fear, however, that if she steps aside a real debate over Britain's constitutional monarchy might open up and, in the present climate, she believes such a debate might lead to the birth of a totally new constitution with no role for a sovereign. Elizabeth has proved herself a notable monarch, maintaining standards of duty and diligence in difficult times as the nation has declined from a world power to an average-sized European country. It is true that there have been few major achievements during her reign but that criticism cannot be laid at her door.

Her prodigious workload continues, her sense of duty is unfailing; but the strain is beginning to show.

EPILOGUE

One of the most important results to have come from a recent poll relates to Charles and his succession to the throne, a subject I have only briefly touched upon thus far. Much to the queen's relief, the majority of her subjects are content for him to become king, despite his divorce. For months after Diana and Charles's separation, constitutional lawyers had argued over the problems facing the monarchy and Prince Charles in particular. Finally, the lawyers decided that no constitutional implications corresponded to either separation or divorce for the heir to succeed to the throne – the reason being that the rules governing royal marriages, which go back 200 years, merely require that the monarch should not marry a Roman Catholic. Those acts of parliament said nothing whatsover about separation or divorce. Within the British constitution, precedence is all-important. And a precedence was found: when George I succeeded to the throne in 1714, he had not only divorced his wife, Sophia Dorothea, but kept her imprisoned for life in a dark, damp and gloomy castle. Edward VIII's abdication in 1936 was a crisis over convention not the constitution. He was challenging the rules of morality that pertained at that time, and the church, politicians, media and public opinion were not prepared to accept a twice-divorced American lady as queen consort.

Despite the collapse of royal marriages, there is no reason to believe a majority of the British people want to be rid of either the House of Windsor or the monarchy. No poll has suggested it despite the numbers of books and magazine and newspaper articles on the subject that have led to an open public debate.

Nevertheless, despite the popularity of the British royal family across the world, Australia decided to hold a referendum to see whether its people wanted to drop Elizabeth as Head of State and appoint their own. Australia had been one of the most loyal countries. In fact polls taken until the 1990s showed Australians to be more passionate about the British Crown than British people themselves. The capital city, Canberra, has a motto, 'For the queen, the law and the people'. It is full of memorials to emotional, flag-waving royal visits, and yet all that warm attachment to Britain and the Crown changed dramatically, and rapidly.

Monarchists in Britain fear that if Australians had cast aside the monarchy like a worn-out coat, the day would not have been far away when the British might do the same. The latest poll has revealed that 85 per cent of the population believe the monarchy will still exist in Britain in 2002 but less than half the nation believes it will be around in 50 years' time.

Australia's apparent keenness to become a republic made Elizabeth realise that other Commonwealth countries might take the same action. A month after Paul Keating had personally told Elizabeth of his government's wish to drop the monarchy, Elizabeth addressed Commonwealth leaders at their biennial conference in Cyprus.

Elizabeth told the Commonwealth leaders at that 1993 conference, 'I have enough experience, not least in racing, to restrain me from laying any money down on how many countries will be in the Commonwealth in 40 years' time, or who they will be. I will certainly not be betting on how many of you will have the Head of the Commonwealth as your Head of State.' The speech revealed that Elizabeth is prepared to move with the times, accepting that nations will want their countries to become republics at some future date. Her wisdom in first broaching the subject openly with friendliness and good grace was greeted with applause.

Surprisingly, Australia voted to keep the crown in a close-fought referendum, much to the pleasure of Elizabeth who had steeled herself to accept the country would turn its back on the monarchy. But though the monarchists of Australia won the day it appeared that the decision had gone against a republic primarily because Elizabeth would have been replaced not by an elected president but a person (probably a politician) appointed by the Australian prime minister. She fears that if another referendum is held within the next five years the decision might go against keeping the ties with the old county.

Elizabeth fears that increasing irrelevance, rather than outright opposition to the crown, will be the undoing of the British monarchy. Some politicians argued after the announcement of the breakdown of Charles and Diana's marriage that it was preposterous at the end of the twentieth century that Princess Diana's possible coronation should be treated as an issue of national importance and announced in Parliament by the Prime Minister.

There is still so much admiration for Elizabeth and, of course, the Queen Mother, however, that not many would think of rocking the throne while they are still alive. Discussion about replacing the hereditary sovereign with an elected president is rare. And yet there is a gut feeling that the monarchy, and that means Elizabeth and her iconoclastic advisers, must accept a new, and less regal, status.

At the start of a new millennium the consensus seems to be that the British monarchy must change. Elizabeth's decision to pay tax and meet the expenses of lesser royals has been a start but politicians wonder whether a monarch who has lived her entire life in an ivory tower can be relied upon to make the right decisions. Many politicians believe that those who advise her daily are simply not up to the job, unaware as they are of the realities outside the close confines of royal palaces. The fact is that the political blows now being rained on the monarchy by the nation's closer involvement with Europe and politicians at Westminster, along with the divisions in the Church of England are undermining its very fabric.

For centuries Britain has been governed by those who have lived, worked and exercised power in three of London's palaces: the Palace of Lambeth, the epicentre of the nation's established church for 500 years; the Palace of Westminster, where the mother of parliaments has held sway for 300 years; and the Palace of Buckingham, where the nation's monarchs have lived a privileged existence for 150 years. In the new millennium all three centres of power are in crisis.

While several senior politicians believe tampering with the present monarchical institutions would put Britain at the top of a slippery slope leading to turmoil (like John Major, for example, who considers the monarchy to be an essential part of the English landscape and should be left alone), there are calls from other politicians and sections of society to modernise the monarchy. Paddy Ashdown, who stepped down as leader of the Liberal Democrats in the summer of 1999, believes the monarchy should be dragged from the nineteenth century to the twenty-first century. He has called for 'fundamental modernisation'. Prime Minister Tony Blair, on the other hand, is working his way towards a gradual modernisation of the monarchy. He has so far found the queen a useful figurehead, seeking to involve her as a Labour partisan in political controversies. Within two years of his premiership, Tony Blair has invoked the queen's alleged support concerning the Succession to the Crown Bill, which treats sons and daughters of the sovereign on an equal footing, and has called on the queen to publicly support the advice her Foreign Secretary had submitted to her when she visited Pakistan and India. On a more personal note, Tony Blair muscled in on the funeral of Princess Diana and glad-handed the crowds waiting to cheer the queen on her golden wedding anniversary.

Public opinion polls taken in the 1990s reveal that the great majority of Britain's middle-classes is generally in favour of change, believing Britain's monarchy should follow the north European example and become less aloof and austere, more open and exposed.

A survey among 100 Labour MPs, following the marriage breakdowns of both Charles and Andrew, has shown republicanism gaining ground. A remarkable 24 per cent said Britain should become a republic while another 32 per cent said the monarchy should be reformed along Swedish and Dutch models, stripped of pomp and pageantry. Only 14 per cent wanted no change. Within a couple of years of that survey, Labour had swept to power in a landslide victory.

Elizabeth realises that her long reign, originally dubbed the New Elizabethan Age, has exposed her in recent years to a succession of rebuffs and reforms and displays of ingratitude and envy, from ministers, the press and citizens alike. It appears that in the twentieth century the survival of a constitutional monarchy has rested not in the sovereign's exercise of political skills but in their relinquishment. Now that the sovereign has relinquished the right to appoint a new prime minister there are very few *real* rights of any substance remaining except, of course, the three enunciated by Walter Bagehot: to be consulted, to encourage and to warn.

During Elizabeth's reign there have been some constitutional changes, though minor: life peerages were introduced in 1958 making the House of Lords more representative; and people wishing to reject hereditary peerages were granted permission from 1963. But in 1999 the Labour Government put forward their plans to take away the right of hereditary peers to sit in the House of Lords altogether. With such a large majority in the Commons it is taken for granted that this fundamental constitutional change will be passed within the lifetime of the present parliament. To Elizabeth, however, the removal of that right is yet another nail in the monarchy's coffin, for the sovereign will become more exposed than ever before. With a strong hereditary second chamber the British monarch had a first line of defence against all calls for a republican constitution; with no hereditary second chamber, that defence will have gone forever.

The House of Lords does, of course, have a most important function, operating as a corrective, delaying and advisory body, subordinate to the House of Commons. One of its great attributes is straightening out poorly studied legislation which would remain in any second chamber. The problem that still remains is deciding the constitution of a reformed House of Lords and whether it should be an elected body, a nominated one, or a mixture of the two. It is expected that after much debate there will be a mixture but with the inclusion of a few hereditary, working peers.

But no hereditary changes have touched the fundamental issue of privilege in Britain throughout Elizabeth's entire reign. In 1999, 90 per cent of the nation's wealth is still owned by only 5 per cent of the people. And those demanding change see Elizabeth as the figurehead of this state of affairs and blame her for the principle of hereditary privilege which some describe as 'obscene'.

Prince Charles, unlike his mother, believes there is an even more fundamental issue which the sovereign should face – the divorce of the Crown from the mitre, the removal of the sovereign as Head of the Church of England. Elizabeth and Charles have discussed the matter but whereas Elizabeth would prefer a long and open debate on the matter, Charles believes that disentangling church and monarchy should be considered a priority. He also believes divorcing the two would be in the interests of both.

As Paddy Ashdown commented, 'I don't think having the monarch as head of the established church does the church any good. I don't think it does the nation any good, nor the system of Government, to have a linkage between something which is primarily about ethics of religion and the power of the state.'

One suggestion Charles has mooted would be the setting up of a bipartisan commission of Privy Councillors by the Prime Minister to consider the matter. Elizabeth, the church's 'Supreme Governor', is in favour of reforming the doctrine but is not convinced ultimately that the church should sever all links with the state. If such a divorce should take place it would mean the sovereign was no long Supreme Governor of the Church of England, a situation many churchgoers believe would make for a more healthy, transparent Church, unencumbered by the traditions of having a monarch at its head.

At the same time, Prince Charles believes an urgent repeal of the Royal Marriage Act of 1772 is called for. Under this act, parliament has authority over royal marriages by vetting the intended bride or groom. No one believes parliament would now intervene to stop a proposed marriage of William or Harry, for example, and certainly Elizabeth's children have been permitted to marry whoever they wished and there is no one, in or outside parliament, who thinks otherwise despite the scandals and disasters of the recent past.

The relevance of the monarchy to Britain in the twenty-first century was last debated in London in May 1993 when *The Times* and Charter 88, a human-rights group, organised the most comprehensive forum on the subject since the seventeenth century. Indeed, if such a debate had taken place 25 years ago, it might have been deemed treasonable, revealing how far public opinion has moved in such a short time. No consensus emerged from the 90 speakers and 500 guests but the conference did capture a mood of national anxiety about the constitutional arrangements that shape the way the British live. More doubt than decision was provoked. Some monarchists were persuaded that the Crown might gain from scrutiny; some republicans were reminded how unpredictable the upheavals might be following their success. Needless to say, Elizabeth followed the conference closely and read the daily reports in the newspapers.

She noted the conference's revelation that the prospect of European union would be an important momentum for possible change, not just in the monarchy but also the church, parliament and the courts. Many expressed concern that an unwritten constitution and a hereditary monarchy, like Britain's, would have no place in the new Europe.

The conference also threw light on Elizabeth's other role as Head of the Church and 'Defender of the Faith'. Few in Britain see Elizabeth in that role though the letters 'FD' for '*Fidei Defensor*' are on every single British coin.

Senior clergymen in the Church of England are now urging the disestablishment of the church, an idea that would have been greeted with horror a generation ago. Elizabeth realises the church is in deep crisis. Since 1945, Anglican church attendances have collapsed and today only 2 per cent of the population attend church each week. As a result the authority of the church and its teachings have diminished accordingly.

The church's latest turmoil was caused by its decision to permit the ordination of women priests, which split the clergy. More than a thousand traditionalist vicars threatened to leave the church when the first woman was ordained. Three thousand clergy opposed women priests out of a total of ten thousand. Many threatened to join the Church of Rome which has more weekly churchgoers than the Anglican church, and when the ordination of women became a reality, that is exactly what many of them did.

But Britain, like the rest of Europe, is slowly integrating. In the

Treaty of Rome, the legal bedrock of the European Union, direct elections to the European Parliament were introduced and today it has 410 members. As Europe becomes more closely integrated, more power will be passed to the European Parliament which will, in turn, undermine the power of parliaments in every European nation, including Britain. Consequently, that would affect the power of the British monarchy, rendering it virtually obsolete in its present form. The monarch could still sit on the throne, wear a crown, live in Buckingham Palace and occasionally ride down the Mall in a glass coach. But the sovereign would have less of a role to play in the constitutional life of the nation.

The changes that Elizabeth has initiated in the role of the monarchy in general are a start to necessary radical change but need to be taken much further so that a modern outlook emerges, free from superstition, the divine right of kings and those divisions in society that perpetuate the tradition of monarchy. Everything that the crown stands for – inherited wealth, inherent virtues, inequality – are the aspects of the monarchy the nation will no longer tolerate.

As the British slowly edge towards a more equable society there is a belief that the nation's ancient class divisions – upheld by the traditions of monarchy – have caused so much discord and unfairness that it must come to an end, and soon. Many, including scores of Labour MPs, believe the institution of monarchy in its present form encourages deference, glorifies the past, entrenches class divisions and manifests a divisive feeling of 'them and us'.

Beyond the major inequalities that exist among the people of Britain, there are other divisions in society which many believe must be eradicated if the Crown is to survive, let alone prosper. No division of British society is more damaging than the separation of the races. And in Britain race and religion often go hand-in-hand. It seems extraordinary that Britain has a Head of State that is head of only one brand of religion – in fact, Elizabeth is also the sovereign of Catholics, Nonconformists, Jews, Hindus, Moslems, Sikhs and Buddhists, and many hold it to be grossly unfair that the monarch is head of an established church when there are six or seven other faiths for her to defend. Prince Charles caused a furore when he commented that when he becomes king he might well become 'Defender of Faith' – meaning all religions – not 'Defender of the Faith'.

Now in her seventies, Elizabeth has no one in whom she can trust or turn to for advice. She had realised long ago that the advice offered by Philip was suspect and often subjective. She had lost Mountbatten, Patrick Plunkett, Lord Rupert Nevill and her beloved 'Bobo', the gardener's daughter who had become one of the most influential people in Elizabeth's life. No longer does Elizabeth like to burden her mother with problems. Today she puts little faith in her senior household courtiers and none whatsoever in the new 'career' members of the household who have no grasp, as far as she is concerned, of the issues at stake.

As a result, Elizabeth herself must decide how the monarchy should change; how much her court and family should change their ways, live their lives, educate their children, share their wealth. Only now, after a lifetime of dedication to her people that has earned their respect, does she have the esteem to push through these changes. She now faces the most fundamental decisions of her entire reign, and only time will tell whether she has the foresight and the courage to decide wisely.

And then there is the future. Elizabeth wants Prince Charles, now 50, to succeed to the throne before he becomes an old age pensioner. Elizabeth is already feeling the weariness of her long reign and believes the nation will understand her motives when she finally decides to abdicate and enjoy her well-earned retirement. She would hardly consider it an abdication, in fact, but rather a stepping down from the treadmill of monarchy, handing on the sceptre and crown to the next generation. After such an abdication, Elizabeth would be only too happy to act as an adviser whenever called upon by Charles.

And yet Elizabeth is not certain that Charles really wants the job *for any length of time*. His close friends believe Charles would only want to reign for a year or so, depending on his age and the ability and maturity of young Prince William. Charles has discussed the benefits Britain would gain by having as its sovereign a young, dynamic monarch to lead and represent the nation in the new millennium. Some believe Charles would probably step down in favour of William when his son reached the age of 30 or settled down with a wife and family. If that came about, Britain could well see the day – in the not too distant future – when there would be a King William on the throne, a retired King Charles at Highgrove and a dowager queen at Balmoral.

BIBLIOGRAPHY

All published in London unless otherwise stated.
Alexandra of Yugoslavia. *Prince Philip: A Family Portrait*, 1949.
Bagehot, Walter. *The English Constitution*, 1898.
Barratt, John. *With the Greatest Respect*, 1991.
Barry, Stephen. *Royal Secrets*, 1985.
Birkenhead, Lord. *Walter Monckton*, 1969.
Boothroyd, Basil. *Philip: An Informal Biography*, 1971.
Bradford, Sarah. *Elizabeth*, 1996.
Cathcart, Helen. *Her Majesty*, 1962.
Colville, John. *Footprints in Time*, 1976.
Davies, Nicholas. *Diana: A Princess and Her Troubled Marriage*, New York, 1992.
Dempster, Nigel. *HRH The Princess Margaret: A Life Unfulfilled*, 1981.
Grigg, John. Title TK *National and English Review*, 1957.
Hall, Unity. *The Private Lives of Britain's Royal Women*, Chicago, 1991.
Hall, Unity. *Philip: The Man Behind the Monarchy*, 1987.
Heald, Tim. *The Duke: A Portrait of Prince Philip*, 1991.
Higham, Charles, and Roy Moseley. *Elizabeth and Philip: The Untold Story*, 1991.
Hoey, Brian. *HRH The Princess Anne*, 1984.
Hoey, Brian. *All the Queen's Men*, 1992.
Holden, Anthony. *Charles, Prince of Wales*, 1982.
Junor, Penny. *Diana, Princess of Wales*, 1982.
Lacey, Robert. *Majesty: Elizabeth II and the House of Windsor*, 1977.
Longford, Elizabeth. *Elizabeth R*, 1983.
Morrow, Ann. *The Queen*, 1983.
Morton, Andrew. *Diana: Her True Story*, 1992.
Nicolson, Harold. *Monarchy*, 1962.
Oaksey, John. 'The Queen's Horses', *The Queen*, 1977.

Pearson, John. *The Ultimate Family*, 1986.

Philip, HRH Prince. *Selected Speeches*, 1957.

Pimlott, Ben. *The Queen*, 1996.

Player, Lesley. *My Story: The Duchess of York, Her Father and Me*, 1993.

Sampson, Anthony. *The Changing Anatomy of Britain*, 1982.

Thatcher, Margaret. *The Downing Street Years*, 1993.

Townsend, Peter. *Time and Chance: An Autobiography*, 1978.

Wapshott, Nicholas, and Brock, George. *Thatcher*, 1983.

Wheeler-Bennett, Sir John. *King George VI: His Life and Reign*, 1968.

Windsor, HRH The Duke of. *A King's Story: The Memoirs of HRH The Duke of Windsor*, 1951.

Young, Hugo. *One of Us*, 1989.

Zeigler, Philip, *Mountbatten*, 1985.

INDEX

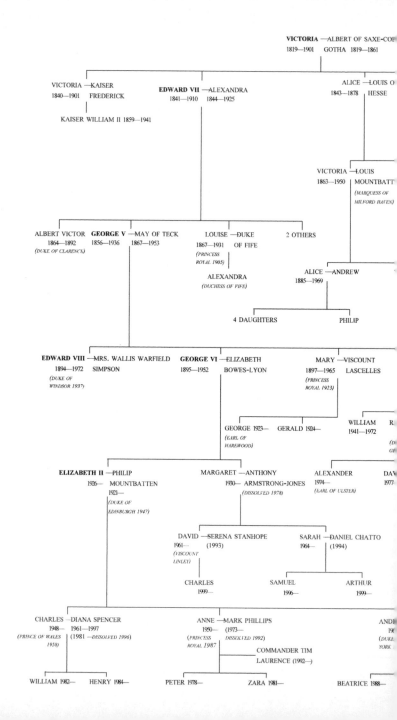

VICTORIA —ALBERT OF SAXE-COB
1819—1901   GOTHA 1819—1861

VICTORIA —KAISER   EDWARD VII —ALEXANDRA   ALICE —LOUIS O
1840—1901 FREDERICK   1841—1910 1844—1925   1843—1878 | HESSE

KAISER WILLIAM II 1859—1941

VICTORIA —LOUIS
1863—1950 | MOUNTBATT
(MARQUESS OF
MILFORD HAVEN)

ALBERT VICTOR GEORGE V —MAY OF TECK   LOUISE —DUKE   2 OTHERS
1864—1892   1856—1936 1867—1953   1867—1931 OF FIFE
(DUKE OF CLARENCE)   (PRINCESS
                                          ROYAL 1905)

ALEXANDRA
(DUCHESS OF FIFE)

ALICE —ANDREW
1885—1969

4 DAUGHTERS   PHILIP

EDWARD VIII —MRS. WALLIS WARFIELD   GEORGE VI —ELIZABETH   MARY —VISCOUNT
1894—1972   SIMPSON   1895—1952 BOWES-LYON   1897—1965 LASCELLES
(DUKE OF   (PRINCESS
WINDSOR 1937)   ROYAL 1923)

GEORGE 1923— GERALD 1924—   WILLIAM   R
(EARL OF   1941—1972
HAREWOOD)   (D
                                           GE

ELIZABETH II —PHILIP   MARGARET —ANTHONY   ALEXANDER   DAV
1926— MOUNTBATTEN   1930— ARMSTRONG-JONES   1974—   1977—
       1921—   (DISSOLVED 1978)   (EARL OF ULSTER)
       (DUKE OF
       EDINBURGH 1947)

DAVID —SERENA STANHOPE   SARAH —DANIEL CHATTO
1961— (1993)   1964— (1994)
(VISCOUNT
LINLEY)

CHARLES   SAMUEL   ARTHUR
1999—   1996—   1999—

CHARLES —DIANA SPENCER   ANNE —MARK PHILLIPS   AND
1948— 1961—1997   1950— (1973—   19
(PRINCE OF WALES | (1981 —DISSOLVED 1996) (PRINCESS DISSOLVED 1992)   (DUKE
1958)   ROYAL 1987   YORK
                                          COMMANDER TIM
                                          LAURENCE (1992—)

WILLIAM 1982— HENRY 1984—   PETER 1978—   ZARA 1981—   BEATRICE 1988—

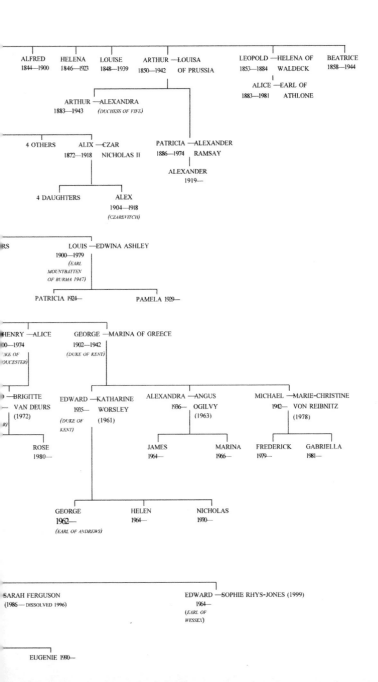